The Kings
of Wrestling

The Kings of Wrestling

*Anecdotes and Stories
of Wrestling from the Distant Past
to Our Times*

EDMOND DESBONNET

Edited and Translated by
DAVID L. CHAPMAN

McFarland & Company, Inc., Publishers
Jefferson, North Carolina

ALSO OF INTEREST
AND FROM MCFARLAND

*The Kings of Strength:
A History of All Strong Men from Ancient Times to Our Own*
(Edmond Desbonnet and Edited and Translated by David L. Chapman, 2022)

This book was originally published in French *as Les Rois de la Lutte: Anecdotes et Récits sur la Lutte depuis les temps les plus reculés jusqu'à nos jours* (Paris: Librairie Berger-Levrault/Librairie Athlétique, 1910). Unless otherwise noted, all images are from the original edition or from the collection of David L. Chapman.

Frontispiece: "Wrestlers at the Valentino Hall and their Audience" by famed artist Gustave Doré from the *Journal Amusant*, 3 May 1856. The artist satirically records the early days of wrestling in the French capital as he contrasts the muscular, nearly nude athletes with the fat, well-clothed, and generally indifferent audience. The distance between statuesque fighters and smug spectators has been erased as everyone sits in the same circle, thus making the comparison of physiques even more apparent and uncomplimentary. Doré presents wrestling as a metaphor for French society with a vacuous gentry at the top and a struggling but noble proletariat at the bottom.

LIBRARY OF CONGRESS CATALOGING-IN-PUBLICATION DATA

Names: Desbonnet, Edmond, author. | Chapman, David L., 1948– editor, translator.
Title: The kings of wrestling : anecdotes and stories of wrestling from the distant past to our times / Edmond Desbonnet ; edited and translated by David L. Chapman.
Other titles: Rois de la lutte. English
Description: Jefferson, North Carolina : McFarland & Company, Inc., Publishers, 2024. | Translation of: Les rois de la lutte. | Includes bibliographical references and index.
Identifiers: LCCN 2024004596 | ISBN 9781476694078 (paperback : acid free paper) ♾
ISBN 9781476652467 (ebook)
Subjects: LCSH: Wrestlers—Biography. | Wrestling—History.
Classification: LCC GV1196.A1 D4713 2024 | DDC 796.81209—dc23/eng/20240215
LC record available at https://lccn.loc.gov/2024004596

BRITISH LIBRARY CATALOGUING DATA ARE AVAILABLE

ISBN (print) 978-1-4766-9407-8
ISBN (ebook) 978-1-4766-5246-7

© 1910 Edmond Desbonnet. Translation and additions.
© 2024 David L. Chapman. All rights reserved

*No part of this book may be reproduced or transmitted in any form
or by any means, electronic or mechanical, including photocopying
or recording, or by any information storage and retrieval system,
without permission in writing from the publisher.*

Front cover image: *Mr. Doublier and His Turkish Wrestlers from the Imperial Palace, Constantinople*, poster by Charles Lévy for the Folies Bergère, 1895 (from the collection of Sam Irvin)

Printed in the United States of America

*McFarland & Company, Inc., Publishers
Box 611, Jefferson, North Carolina 28640
www.mcfarlandpub.com*

To David Berryman

Table of Contents

Preface and Acknowledgments	1
Introduction to The Kings of Wrestling	5

The Kings of Wrestling
by Edmond Desbonnet

Foreword: Wrestling Is the Primordial Sport	23
The Kings of Ancient Wrestling	25
The Kings of Wrestling: The Early Years	28
The Kings of Wrestling: Contemporary Wrestlers	115
Appendix and Metric Conversions	183
Appendix 1: Timothée Trimm, "Truly Strong Men"	186
Appendix 2: Jules Vallès, Excerpts from The Street	191
Appendix 3: X, "Among Men"	197
Appendix 4: Edmond Renoir, "Wrestling and Wrestlers"	200
Appendix 5: Léon Ville, Excerpts from Wrestling and Wrestlers	212
Appendix 6: Bertrand Fauvet, "Fairground Performers"	218
Appendix 7: Rémy Saint-Maurice, "Wrestling and Wrestlers"	225
Appendix 8: Frantz Reichel, "Wrestling: A Music Hall Sport"	233
Appendix 9: Paul Pons, Excerpts from Wrestling	237
Appendix 10: Alberto Cougnet, Excerpts from Greco-Roman Wrestling on the Mat	271
Appendix 11: Adolf von Guretzki, Excerpts from Modern Wrestling	283
Chapter Notes	293
Bibliography	325
Index	327

Preface and Acknowledgments

The first great international sporting craze to captivate Europe was not soccer, cricket, boxing, rugby, or even pedestrianism; it was wrestling. Prior to the mid-nineteenth century, most sports were local and practiced only in a relatively small geographic area with idiosyncratic rules; they were rather like local dialects—similar to others in neighboring areas but still uniquely insular.[1] Wrestling was the earliest and most commercially important sporting activity that attracted fans and competitors from a variety of countries and cultures. Greco-Roman wrestling developed around 1850 out of traditional grappling that was practiced in southern France, and it grew steadily more widespread despite wars, economic disruptions, and cultural differences. The reasons for this rapid diffusion are easy to determine; having a common wrestling style offered more entertainment, sporting competitions, and excuses to wager. There was consequently plenty of money and glory to be earned. Greco-Roman was also much less dangerous than other forms of wrestling since it did not allow any dirty tricks like punching, gouging, or kicking. Fighters from all over Europe soon met in the squared circle, and they were quickly joined by Americans, Australians, Africans, Turks, East Indians, South Americans, Siberians, Japanese and others.[2] The French style was eventually adopted by nearly all the countries of continental Europe (and beyond), so tournaments could be held in St. Petersburg or Buenos Aires because everyone wrestled in the same style.

No matter where it was conducted, the athletes and the audiences of wrestling matches were mainly working-class men who were familiar with the Greco-Roman style. Eventually, it attracted fans from the more prosperous classes, but there was always an element of slumming when bourgeois or aristocratic spectators bought the good seats in the front of the arena while less prosperous onlookers were exiled to the bleachers. The core audience was always drawn from the workers; wrestling was something that the down-and-out could relate to. They could witness the struggle of the weak against the strong acted out on the floor of the arena, and if the outcome was predetermined, well, so was life itself. Wrestling was something that any participant could do no matter whether his purse was full or empty—provided he had the requisite strength, courage, and aggression. Unlike many other sports, wrestling required no special or expensive equipment, and because of this, it was open

1

even to the poorest of the proletariat. However, the French were not the only ones to be seduced by Greco-Roman grappling.

Greater economic stability, intervals of peace, improved transportation and a new love of athletic competition drew non–Europeans from the far corners of the French, Russian, Ottoman, and British empires. Their exploits were celebrated in the new sporting press, and spectators crowded into arenas in unprecedented numbers. By welcoming athletes of all races and nationalities, wrestling served as a model for other international sporting ventures including the modern Olympic Games.

Although interest in professional wrestling began in the 1850s, it has continued in one form or another to the present day. Even though its popularity has proven to be long-lasting, the sport has been remarkably bereft of reliable histories. It is consistently ignored by scholars for a couple of reasons. The first problem is determining if it is even a real sport. From the very start, most wrestling matches have been elaborate charades in which the winner and the loser have been predetermined. Professional wrestling has always been tainted with accusations of fakery and deception. These allegations are largely accurate, but they beg the question of whether wrestling is any less a sport than other "judged" activities like bodybuilding, figure skating, synchronized swimming, or ballroom dancing that require great skill, athleticism, and grace. As many proponents of wrestling have noted, just because the outcome of a match has been predetermined, does not mean that it requires any less exertion, strength, or talent. If it is little more than a display of acrobatics, does that make it less of a sport?

The second issue involves socio-economic class. Pro wrestling has always been a working-class amusement and some scholars are queasy about devoting time and energy to its history because of wrestling's lack of social cachet and its circus-like atmosphere. Participants are often under-educated, inarticulate and, unsophisticated. In addition, professional wrestling has no real international governing body or hall of fame and little social legitimacy.[3] Even amateur and Olympic wrestling are shamefully under-studied. Adding to its indignity, wrestling was nearly eliminated entirely from the Olympics in 2020; it survived, but only just.[4] One can count the number of academic histories of wrestling on the fingers of one hand (and still have a thumb and a few digits left over).

This is not to say that there are not plenty of non-academic books in English on wrestling history, but they tend to be strictly regional in scope (USA, Britain, Canada, etc.) and usually vague about sources. For the most part, these books have a few words to say about the ancient Greeks, and then spring forward to the 1950s when a wave of televised wrestling crashed upon the western world. When these authors jump from Milo of Crotona to Gorgeous George, most of the real history has been overlooked. Those who seek the history of wrestling must dig into primary-source materials like contemporary newspapers and magazines. Now that many of the global archives have opened up their searchable publications, it is much easier to do the research. Gallica, British Newspaper Archive, and Munich Digitization Center have all been invaluable aids. Currently, the best in-depth sources in English for the early or non–Anglo-Saxon history of wrestling can be found on a blog and a Facebook site. WrestlingClassics.com (especially the message board) is chock-full of tidbits of pre–World War II wrestling history, and *Wrestling Historian Salon* is very good on Facebook.

Aside from the sheer pleasure that I gained from learning about the unfamiliar world of wrestling history, another important reason that I decided to translate this book is because, in some ways, it is the prequel to my earlier translation of *The Kings of Strength*. The current work was initially published a year before its more famous partner volume, and it gives a great deal of background information on the characters and milieu of the later volume. As I worked on the text, I began to see that in some cases Desbonnet had little concrete information to go on. His best sources were interviews with the men themselves, and beyond that (like most modern wrestling historians) he had only newspaper articles to go on. I thought that it would help understand both the sport and its background if I included some of the journalistic evidence that was either unavailable to the author or that he might have missed. The appendix of the book consists of articles and excerpts from books which help flesh out the history of wrestling. One of the greatest discoveries was *La Lutte* (Wrestling) first published in 1912 by Paul Pons who, as it turns out, was a talented writer and a careful amateur historian.

In addition to the hitherto hidden history of the sport, I have been very fortunate to find a rich visual record of the wrestlers themselves. Desbonnet was acutely aware of the value of photographs, and the current book is enhanced by many wonderful photographs and illustrations. Thanks to the kindness of several good friends, I have been able to locate many original photographs from the late nineteenth and early twentieth centuries which I have incorporated into the current edition. The first person that I must thank in this regard is Michael Murphy of Westerly, Rhode Island. Examples from his impressive collection of original photographs can be seen throughout the book, and *The Kings of Wrestling* would have been a much poorer work without his help. Another collector who was unstinting in his kindness and generosity was Christian Gaildraud of Limoges, France. His knowledge of French wrestling history and his beautiful collection of photographs and materials have been a great help. Polyglot wrestling historian Phil Lions of Plovdiv, Bulgaria was also a major help to me. Whenever I had a sticky question about Turkish or Eastern European wrestlers, he could almost always point me in the right direction. Everything that Lions writes is research-based and reliable.

I am grateful for the moral and material support from several others. Historian Joe Roark of St. Joseph, Illinois, gave me a copy of *Les Rois de la Lutte* over three decades ago, and I am still grateful for that generous gift. Physical culture and sports historian Conor Heffernan of Ulster University encouraged and helped me from the very start. Art collector and movie mogul Sam Irvin provided the illustration that graces the cover of the book, and I am very grateful for his generosity. K. Mitchell

Snow of Arlington, Virginia, and Krishna Godhania of Warwick, England, gave me frequent encouragement and great advice. Thanks also to Frédéric Desbonnet, the great-grandson of the author of this work, Edmond Desbonnet, and to Léna Schillinger, curator of documents (and her staff) at the Musée national du Sport, Nice, France.

Finally, I must thank my constant collaborator and husband, David Berryman. Without his help with scanning and correcting the many murky, blotchy and blurry images, this book would not look as good as it does.

David L. Chapman, Seattle

Introduction to
The Kings of Wrestling

By almost any metric, Edmond Desbonnet, the indefatigable author of *The Kings of Wrestling*, was an extraordinary man. Over the course of his long life, he owned a string of physical culture salons, was the publisher of several important sporting magazines, was a talented writer and a skilled photographer, and was a tireless advocate for physical culture. He was also the author of two very important works that preserve the memory of hundreds of strongmen, strongwomen, and wrestlers.[1]

Desbonnet was born into a well-to-do family in the northern French city of Lille in 1868. When he was thirteen years old, he was inspired by leafing through an old magazine that pictured the athlete and physical culture teacher Hippolyte Triat (1812–1881) in a muscular pose. In his own account, the boy felt a blinding flash of inspiration and decided on the spot that he, too, would endeavor to build a body as massive as the athlete in the pictures. His career had begun.

Desbonnet opened his first school of physical culture when he was a mere eighteen years old. It was in this school (and those that followed) that he evolved his own particular brand of exercise, which he called *la gymnastique des organes* (organ gymnastics). This was supposed to improve one's internal organs with specific exercises. Perhaps the most revolutionary aspect of his system, however, was its reliance on weights and other muscle-building apparatuses rather than calisthenics, which popular wisdom decreed was the correct way to improve strength. After several failed attempts to make a go of his schools of physical culture in his hometown, he moved his operations to Paris. Once there, he quickly acquired a reputation as a man who could build muscular bodies in a rapid and scientific manner. Eventually he became a respected member of sporting and medical society.

Success did not come quickly, and Desbonnet used much of his inheritance to bankroll his gymnasiums, his education, and his first publications. In 1896 he began a magazine that emphasized sport and exercise; he named it *L'Athlète*, and the response was so positive that in 1902 he decided to create another journal, *Education Physique*. Two years later he founded his best and most famous magazine, *La Culture Physique*. Finally, in 1912 he started *La Santé par les Sports* (Health Through

Sport). While he was running his schools of physical culture and editing his magazines, Desbonnet also found time to write sixteen books.

He was a person of seemingly boundless energy when it came to his favorite subject, physical culture. Among other duties, Desbonnet sat on numerous committees and boards, he invented several pieces of exercise equipment, and he instituted occasional physique contests. In 1900 he was instrumental in creating the prestigious Haltérophile-Club de France (French Weightlifting Club of France), and it was through this organization that he was able to assist many worthy athletes and to sponsor innumerable contests. By the early 1950s Desbonnet had become the grand old man of physical culture. Athletes, politicians, and dignitaries made it a point to pay their respects to the elderly man. Active and energetic to the end, Desbonnet lived until 1953 when he passed away at the age of eighty-five.

Edmond Desbonnet poses as a respectable businessman in 1909. By this time he was the publisher of *La Culture Physique*, proprietor of a growing chain of gymnasiums and an author of several books (photograph by Waléry).

As much as Desbonnet looked to the future (and in many ways helped form it), he did not forget the past. He was always interested in preserving the memories of deserving athletes, and he began a photograph service that sold many pictures to the public. He also wrote one of the best and most complete works on the history of strength and weightlifting, *Les Rois de la Force* (The Kings of Strength), in 1911. It remains to this day one of the finest histories of the early days of the sport, but one year before the publication of his best-known work, Desbonnet published *Les Rois de la Lutte* (The Kings of Wrestling). Like many Frenchmen of his generation, Edmond Desbonnet was fascinated by the rough-and-tumble sport of wrestling, but he was in a position to encourage, publicize and champion grappling in his books and magazines. And he was hardly alone in his love of the sport and spectacle of wrestling.

It is difficult to overstate the popularity of wrestling in nineteenth-century France. Before cycling, before tennis, and even before soccer, wrestling was king of sports in the French republic. The rich could raise and race thoroughbred horses, but for those of modest means, there were few competitive activities that did not call for elaborate uniforms, expensive equipment, or membership in exclusive clubs; all that a wrestler needed was strength, courage and a pair of trunks. Wrestling was born in the working class, but interest in it soon spread up the French social pyramid, and by the second half of the 1800s wrestling was by far the most important sport because it was so accessible. It took little knowledge to appreciate wrestling since it is both instinctual and primitive. As Desbonnet points out in the preface to his book, humans have always practiced some form of body-to-body conflict.

Prior to the nineteenth century, wrestling was practiced all over the world, but an athlete from Japan would have to change his style drastically if he wanted to confront someone in India, the Ottoman Empire, or Africa. An Anglo Saxon would likewise have problems if he chose to grapple with a Russian, German, or Frenchman. The problem was that every country (and in some cases every region), had its own rules and styles. In some the losing opponent had to be pushed out of a designated space, in others he had to have his shoulders pinned to the floor. Fighters wore a variety of distinctive costumes, often dictated by locale—sometimes a brief pair of trunks, or perhaps a pair of leather breeches; in others the athletes sported belts and straps that were grabbed in order to take down a man; in other cases the wrestlers were completely naked. Sometimes a fighter could strike his rival with his fists and indulge in other types of dirty tricks (think eye-gouging, nose biting, finger breaking, and kicks to the groin), and these were all perfectly legal. In other places these brutal maneuvers would get a wrestler instantly disqualified. Sportsmanship and fair play were generally determined by the local referee. But midway through the nineteenth century things changed, and the world of wrestling experienced a tectonic shift.

It has been noted that the sport of grappling might have been born in ancient times, but modern, professional wrestling is the child of two revolutions: the French and the Industrial. In the first, "the individual began to develop as a person equal to others and freer to pursue his own interests. In the Industrial Revolution, the shift from countryside to city and the breakdown of old associations such as guilds created a need for new forms of companionship and socialization."[2] It is no accident that the German Turnverein, the Slavic Sokol societies, and the British sporting movement all happened about the same time because they were all wrapped in the same mantle of physical exercise, social interaction, and a healthy dose of nationalism.

The history of continental European wrestling begins in the aftermath of the Napoleonic Wars. After Waterloo, a returning French soldier named Jean Exbroyat came back to his hometown of Lyon where he opened a fruit and vegetable stall in one of the city's suburbs. Since he was a born wanderer and a veteran of many battles, this peaceful occupation did not keep him happy for long. He occupied his leisure time wrestling in several athletic cabarets in various neighborhoods of his city. These combination tavern-gymnasiums-performance halls were as close to a wrestling school as existed at this time, and when he could no longer stand the sedentary life that he had tried, Exbroyat sold his business and took off on the roads of central and southern France. The vagabond's life was the one that he wanted, and he apparently eked out a living by doing odd jobs and wrestling others for a bit of spare change; but he was also planning a new venture. He had discovered that there was money to be made by wrestling, so around the mid–1840s he assembled a troupe of amateur wrestlers from Lyon and patched together a primitive stage made of canvas and lumber. Thus, equipped with his men and his rudimentary "arena," he started out traveling the roads of southern France.

As he went from town to town, Exbroyat hired the best amateur wrestlers that he could find. Many of these men later became renowned athletes and some of their biographies are in *The Kings of Wrestling*. Thanks to the existence of a thriving wrestling culture in this region, they had little trouble finding an audience for their performances. They were able to try the various styles of wrestling being used, and to establish some rules and order to a welter of differing styles. Exbroyat therefore is usually given credit for codifying the rules of what he called "flat-hand" or French wrestling.[3] A version of this style of combat was already being practiced in the Gironde region around Bordeaux, but the former Napoleonic soldier spread its renown far beyond its original location.[4]

In this style of wrestling the competitors cannot strike their opponents nor can they use holds below the waist. This means that a wrestler cannot trip his adversary's legs in order to bring him down. The emphasis is thus placed on throws since he cannot use his lower limbs. Strength, experience, and agility are the principal weapons in this form of fighting. Here are the basic rules for flat-hand wrestling as they were drawn up in Aix-en-Provence, France, in 1848.

- It is forbidden to take hold of the opponent below the waist
- Contrary to the ancient style practiced by the Greeks, striking an adversary is banned
- The stranglehold and headlock are not allowed
- Optional rest periods can be instituted after ten minutes of wrestling
- Using the legs to trip or entangle an adversary is prohibited
- If lifted off the ground, the wrestler has the right to trip his opponent with his legs
- On the floor, it is authorized to use the legs to entangle with those of the adversary, but it is forbidden to grab the legs with the hands
- Wrestling can be conducted either standing or on the ground, depending on the conditions of the match.[5]

Although these rules usually prevented excessive violence and injury, they did nothing to limit the time that the combatants could engage with one another. It was common for matches to continue for two or three exhausting hours.[6]

One modern historian has dismissed flat-hand or Greco-Roman wrestling as "a French folk style with classical pretentions."[7] It was actually much more refined and widespread than that, and over the years it became even more precise, understood, and respected. French wrestling became virtually the only style for all of Europe from the Atlantic to the Urals (apart from Great Britain), and it is still practiced at universities and at the Olympics.

If flat-hand wrestling took shape in the south of France, it quickly gained acceptance in other regions of the country, and it was especially popular in Paris. When in the 1840s wrestling matches were held sporadically, the sport began to attract many enthusiastic fans. As writer Léon Ville noted, "Parisians did not become passionate about wrestling until 1848, when the arena on the Rue Montesquieu was opened; then the athletes came running from all points in France. The Montesquieu Hall lasted three years. Every year, for several months, there were fights. It was then that we successively saw the best wrestlers."[8] The "hall" where these matches were held was actually an indoor *gallerie* or shopping mall where merchant's stores surrounded an open space; some nights this open place served as a dance hall, and on others as a venue for events like wrestling. A few other commercial wrestling ventures like this one drew both large crowds of spectators and talented athletes, but the Montesquieu Hall was the first. Almost as soon as the matches began to grow in public awareness and popularity, they had to be discontinued. Sport, along with most other pleasures of urban life, was occasionally disrupted by political violence and uncertainty.

This was not an easy time for France because it was convulsed by rapidly changing governments and a succession of rulers. Monarchists battled with Socialists, and Legitimists with Bonapartists. If we take Delacroix's famous painting at its face value, Liberty may have been leading the people, but where was she taking them?[9] It was a turbulent time that was vividly described in *Les Misérables* with riots, disruptions, and barricades in the streets of Paris. Naturally, this did not make the pursuit of wrestling or other sporting events easy. There was another revolution in 1848 that deposed the Bourbon king and established a second republic, but real tranquility did not come until Prince Louis-Napoleon Bonaparte (a distant relation of the Little Colonel) took over the government of France. After a few years as the elected head of a republic, a second empire was declared late in 1852 with Louis-Napoleon at its head. Life in Paris gradually cooled down, and the French had a twenty-year stretch of peace and relative calm so that they could get back to the business of joie de vivre. Paris was certainly not Utopia, but most Frenchmen seemed to realize that a benevolent despot was an acceptable tradeoff for national chaos.

In the midst of the turmoil, the first great star of wrestling arose at the Montesquieu Hall; this was Charles Arpin who hailed from the mountainous region of Alpine Savoy. He was "the victor of victors," and he offered 200 francs to any wrestler who could withstand his terrible onslaughts for a mere three minutes. He was simply, as one writer declared, "the idol of the public that frequented the Montesquieu Hall." The handsome wrestler was "tall, broad, barely thirty years old, and he recalled the wrestlers of antiquity," and his ecstatic fans "raved about his splendid torso."[10] But far to the south, there was a man who had heard of the Savoyard, yet was not intimidated by Arpin's manly torso; in fact, he was determined to knock Arpin off his lofty pedestal.

The man who set off from the south to defeat Arpin was named Henri Marseille (1817?–1897), and he had wrestled briefly in Exbroyat's troupe, so he already knew a thing or two about his chosen sport. Some versions of the story say that the challenger rode all the way to Paris on the back of a mule (a distance of around 740 kilometers) from his home in Lapalud where he was the town's miller. Regardless of how he got there, Marseille was destined to become a celebrity in the sporting world of midcentury Paris. In these early days, wrestling at the Montesquieu Hall was strictly amateur and dedicated to unscripted matches. There were no prearranged fights and the only money that changed hands came from the betting among the wrestlers themselves and that which was wagered in the all-male audiences. The two principals had already made their bets. Arpin had a standing offer of 200 francs to the man who could stay on the mat with him for three minutes without being pinned, but Marseille refused this prize; instead, he made it known to Arpin that he would hand over 500 francs if the more famous wrestler could defeat him. Thanks to all these challenges and the large sums of money that could potentially change hands, the bout raised a great deal of interest in the sporting community and in the newspapers of the day. The match was both a wrestling contest but also a primer on how to raise awareness and garner publicity so that a large crowd would show up.

Despite the posters, reports, and publicity in that pre-photographic era, few people had actually seen Marseille prior to the fight, and it was reported that the audience was astonished when Marseille entered the arena and prepared for the fight. Thanks to the brief trunks that the men wore, everyone could see that the challenger was tall and thin when compared to Arpin, but it quickly became apparent that he could hold his own against the large and muscular Arpin. After forty-five minutes of intense fighting, Arpin, the "Terrible Savoyard," ended up in defeat on the floor while his adversary stood above him in triumph, acknowledging the plaudits of the audience "with a demeanor that was both modest and gracious."[11]

It quickly seemed that wrestling was an activity that could draw support from a wide swath of the sporting public, but shortly after the match between Marseille and Arpin, the Montesquieu Hall shut down and it never again hosted fights. The reason for this was not the sport's lack of appeal but rather its outsized public attraction. France was enduring one of its periods of social and political unrest, and there was a great deal of suspicion among the police when it came to activities that were considered violent or excessively aggressive. Although the constitution of 1791 had recognized "the freedom to assemble peaceably and without weapons," this right had been gradually whittled away and by the time of Napoleon I's regime, it had virtually disappeared. Groups of twenty or more that met without government approval for any purpose whatsoever were judged to be an offense under the penal code. Finally, in 1855, the Paris police banned boxing matches and assemblies of gymnasts and wrestlers; it also made the creation of new organizations or clubs that encouraged such activities subject to police surveillance. All meetings, including those that encouraged physical activities, were considered potential gathering spots for hoodlums, revolutionaries, or political activists.[12] The location of the Marseille/Arpin fight, the Montesquieu Hall, had knuckled under and voluntarily closed in 1852, and for fifteen years thereafter, amateur athletic exercises were denied a place to practice and display their arts.

The principal result of this interdiction was that wrestling collapsed in Paris.[13] It was kept alive in the various smaller gymnasiums around the city, but it was dead as a spectator sport—or perhaps it would be better to say that it was in a deep coma, for there were flickers of life even in those dark times. Most of the wrestlers who worked in Paris were forced to go out to the provinces or even farther afield to Germany, England, or America. For over a decade (1855–1866) the only place to see wrestling in Paris was sporadically at the annual fairs that were typically held in the spring and summer.[14]

By the mid-1860s the political situation had calmed down considerably. Emperor Louis-Napoleon's regime was making sure that Paris ran with reasonable proficiency. Great sporting venues were allowed to reopen, and physical fitness was once again in vogue. An athletic entrepreneur named Eugène Paz established a massive gymnasium in 1865. The newspaper *Le Figaro* welcomed his new enterprise enthusiastically, describing it as 1,100 square meters in size with a large (cavernous, actually) main hall and smaller workout space, fencing room, boxing room, shooting range, hydrotherapeutic rooms, and a reading room. The author concludes by exhorting his fellow citizens to get in shape. "Come on, decadent Parisians. Make yourselves over. Please!"[15]

Late in 1866, the Paz Gymnasium was the location where wrestling was once again conducted after its long hiatus in the French capital. The proprietor wanted a way to increase the renown of his establishment and to make the gymnasium a center of physical activity. His solution was to hold a series of wrestling matches, and to do so he attempted to make them clean, wholesome, and totally above board.[16] Paz clearly knew how to organize and operate a wrestling demonstration, and he engaged men who had mostly come from Bordeaux, Toulouse, and the South of France. The panel of judges were from the respected Jockey Club and were all well-known sportsmen. Paz himself was most often the president of the panel, and since he had an expert knowledge of the sport, he could tell when the fighters were faking it, and he made sure that such behavior was not acceptable. Paz did everything in his power to bring some middle-class values to a hitherto working-class activity. His rules formally forbade the fighters to curse, threaten, or insult each other during the match; they were likewise never allowed to speak to the spectators or question the rulings of the judges.[17]

Paz insured the loyalty of his men by paying them extremely well, in fact everything was done with care, comfort, and class. The wrestlers all wore clean and stylish tights but with bare upper bodies designed to show the men's virile, muscular torsos. These preparations had the desired effect, and the wrestling meets ended up being a roaring success; it is said that they attracted up to three thousand people who packed into the massive gymnasium. Perhaps another reason for the great success of the wrestling matches was that most Frenchmen were unaccustomed to seeing nude or nearly nude men in public, and some of the spectators at the exhibitions seemed less interested in the wrestling and more in the men's bodies. It became a rare opportunity for mid-nineteenth-century men to see what a well-built athlete looked like (aside from viewing statues in the Louvre) in an exciting state of undress. The correspondent for the Paris newspaper *La Vie Parisienne* (who signed his work "X") was clearly amazed by the scene set before him. "You have seen notaries, stockbrokers, seminarians in their suits; it is very pretty I am sure, but go and see what an agile, robust, well-built man is, and just the way the good Lord has made him." The writer is all aflutter with excitement when he describes the actions of the men in the ring. "Personally, I adore these wrestling matches—I quite frankly admit it. In fact, I know of nothing more thrilling and more beautiful than this spectacle." He is especially taken by the black athlete known as James, or "the African Farnese," whom he says is "as handsome as an antique bronze." X has a recommendation for Mr. Paz. He thinks that he should arrange a few private boxes where gentlemen of a certain disposition or ladies could watch the matches in a degree of privacy. He concludes with a sly wink by saying, "I wager these shows would be wildly successful with the opposite sex."[18]

Apparently, the wrestling matches were wildly successful with a great many sectors of the Parisian public. The fact that thousands of men showed up to witness the wrestling matches indicates that there was money to be made. Unfortunately, Paz was not particularly interested in continuing the wrestling matches. He wanted to promote gymnastics as a salubrious activity not a circus or a kind of male burlesque show. As Léon Ville reported, "Mr. Paz had to stop these events, for he feared by continuing them to distort the character of his establishment, which was as we know, above all, an establishment for medical gymnastics. Mr. Paz had wanted to show the public what was happening at his gymnasium; his goal had been achieved."[19] It would be up to others to make wrestling into a broadly popular activity, and after a few other attempts to make the sport into a clean and respectable activity, it returned to its roots with the people.

The cost and overhead were extremely high for a theatrical showing of wrestling, and by banishing wrestling from Paris, it had shown that another good business model was the traveling company which, like the one pioneered by Exbroyat, found that they could take their show to their audience rather than the other way around. This came in the form of the wrestling booth or shed, called in French the *baraque*. A director and/or manager assembled a group of wrestlers; built a flashy "arena" of rough lumber, canvas, and banners; and then all would be piled into horse-drawn wagons that would move from town to town, usually setting up during

A typical *baraque* or carnival booth in Lyon; the speaker is drumming up business, the band is playing, and the athletes are awaiting their turn. "Pépi the Giant," the star of the baraque, is "proud and disdainful" as he observes the weaklings in the audience (*Le Progrès Illustré*, 24 April 1892).

a local fair. The *baraque* itself was more or less uniform no matter where it was erected. Here is a description of a wrestler's "arena" from 1866.

> The wrestler's booth is spacious; it is covered by canvas, and there are wooden steps that lead up to the desk where the tickets are sold. A second set of steps leads into the theater (if you can call the place where the spectators sit a theater) and the arena where the terrible fights take place. There is a banner hanging over the door that was daubed by a "special artist" (who has not forgotten to sign his name and address in a corner), and it displays a Hercules carrying a cannon on his shoulder. On the left is another banner on which the compliant painter has imagined a Hercules lifting a carriage and six cavalrymen which is contrasted by a series of posters pasted up on the right on an enormous board. The posters give all the possible details on the feats of wrestling, and the names of the artists are printed in huge letters.[20]

One of the best and most competent managers of one of these itinerant wrestling booths was a failed law student and former actor named Rossignol-Rollin.[21] He was an odd combination of businessman, athletic promoter, and theatrical Barnum, but he had a gift for showmanship, publicity, and humbuggery that pointed the way for others who would come after him. He was a colorful and unforgettable figure who took the art of *le boniment*, the barker's spiel, to a level never reached before or since. His flights of verbal fantasy both enthralled and fascinated his audiences, and in some cases his introduction was more interesting and entertaining than the actual wrestling match. He delighted in insulting his public by pointing out the obvious difference between the yokels in the audience and his massive athletes. Here is a typical spiel.

> Gather 'round you faint-hearts, you molecules! The terrible men that you see before you will respect your scrawny bodies. The strong should protect the weak. Come closer, we won't eat you. Nature offers exceptional beings for your admiration! Beings who, if they wanted to, could make bronze statues weep under the influence of the pain that they could inflict on them. Approach. Approach imponderable dust. The spectacle that awaits you is well fashioned to stupefy your timorous spirit and make your feeble body tremble like a leaf. Approach and enter. Come and pay homage to the triumph of muscle, flexibility, agility and, I dare say, intelligence that is placed at the service of these physical qualities for the great interest of the unforgettable spectacle that I, Rossignol-Rollin, offer to you fragile individuals at the price of 50, 25 and 10 centimes. And it is a steal at that![22]

In addition to his unique style of oratory, Rossignol-Rollin also had a genius for seeing promotional opportunities that others had missed. According to Desbonnet, it was he who devised the system of giving his wrestlers descriptive names that would "strike the popular imagination much more by attaching high-sounding epithets to his wrestlers." These nicknames were usually based on the athlete's geographic origins, his profession (butcher, sailor, artilleryman), his appearance (beautiful model, elegant, colossus) or his aggressive personality (wild beast, lion, terror). By giving his men memorably ferocious names, Rossignol-Rollin was starting to see into the hidden allegorical heart of wrestling. It was not so much about who won or who lost, but who could best represent the hopes and fears of his audience, and by giving his wrestlers colorful monikers, he was allowing the fans to attach meaning to the roles that the wrestlers played. The wily impresario was promoting superheroes in whom the public could project their deepest aspirations. The fighters were no long merely individuals; instead, they were symbolic of greater, more universal forces. He, more than anyone before, understood the profoundest truth of professional wrestling: it is drama—as stirring as anything Shakespeare ever conceived, but told physically, not verbally or intellectually.

Thanks to his advertising and his eloquence, Rollin enjoyed great fame and popularity. His wrestling company toured all over France between the 1850s and the late 1860s, focusing mainly in the south where the tradition of grappling had never really died. He would sometimes take over large venues and run big shows, but his principal business came from his stays in little towns and villages. The rotund manager traveled around France for almost twenty years, but the good times came to an end in 1870 when France became embroiled in the Franco-Prussian War. This was a disastrous time for Louis-Napoleon and his empire, since the emperor's hubris blinded him to the fact that a war with its powerful neighbor Prussia was a very bad idea indeed. It took only a few weeks for France to be defeated and to cause the useless deaths of many men. Even worse was the subsequent revolt of the Communards in Paris and then their bloody suppression.[23] More civil unrest had returned to France, and while that happened, it meant that wandering companies of wrestlers were halted and the country was plunged into insecurity. War and its aftermath are never conducive to what authorities view as frivolous entertainment.

Rossignol-Rollin died in 1873, but the art and business that he had pioneered into a profitable means of earning a living was certainly not deceased. Both France and wrestling recovered from the troubles in a remarkably short period of time, and soon others were ready to take over. Perhaps the most famous and prosperous of postwar *baraques* was the one that belonged to the family of Henri Marseille, the man who defeated Arpin two decades before. He and his son Jean-Baptiste (1833–1914) had the longest-lasting and most famous group of wrestlers in the country, and it was to his booth that all wrestling fans would eventually come.[24] Eventually, Marseille became one of the wealthiest performers, knowing how to manage and surround himself with the best: "He was the only one at the Neuilly Fair who made money without advances or relying on barbells that were as big as he was."[25]

The golden age of French wrestling was between 1880 and 1910, and that popularity was first engendered in the fairgrounds with operations like those of the Marseille family, but then it gradually crept onto the music-hall and variety stages, and here it reached a new and more prosperous audience. By smoothing down some of the sport's rough edges, by making the wrestlers more performers and less back-alley brawlers, it began to have a broader appeal. Wealthy and worldly audiences had long flocked to the fairground *baraques*, but by removing some of the brutality from the game, it opened it up to a wider audience (and this included women). As French wrestling historian Frédéric Loyer has observed, "This formula of combat without violence was indeed quickly appreciated; it was less disturbing to follow the matches in which the adversaries emerged without trauma."[26] By emphasizing the show-business side of wrestling, it allowed the sport to be presented in fashionable Parisian music halls. With this respect also came a new infusion of money. Soon top-notch wrestlers were lured away from the rather tawdry setting of the fairground and cheap café concerts as they began to appear in posh, theatrical settings.

From the beginning of the twentieth century, wrestling was a very popular show in music halls, especially during the winter season since the matches were held indoors where the surroundings were very comfortable. As an added benefit, they gave those with means something to wager on, and it was these prosperous spectators who most appreciated the show of domesticated violence—of courteous fighting. Just because the opponents had to follow the rules of Greco-Roman wrestling, it did not mean that there was a lack of excitement. The spectators were passionate about this long-awaited moment when one man is dangerously close to being pinned, and even normally reserved middle-class patrons begin to shout like boisterous *Apaches*.[27] A journalist in 1890 described the howls from the audience. "His shoulders touched! They did not touch! I tell you they did! Yes. No. Yes, I swear it!"[28] This enthusiasm did not go unnoticed.

The average physical appearance of wrestlers also made an impact on society. In the early period, wrestlers were thin and muscular, but as the years progressed, their silhouettes became progressively stouter. It would be hard to miss the transformation. Even contemporary sportsmen noticed the effects of massive practitioners of the sport. "If professional training has not endowed all [wrestlers] with an irreproachable elegance of form, it has at least developed in them a means of muscular strength and stamina that gives an excellent idea of this system."[29] Modern French historian Georges Vigarello has noted much the same thing. Wrestling combined strength and thickness of the body, mass, and energy "a power made of flesh more than muscle." The wrestler's body thus "intertwines gravity and vigor, physical volume, and combative value. It is even a unique illustration of fighting that thus promotes the heaviest attacker by attacking the strongest."[30] Some wrestlers relied on sheer avoirdupois rather than skill, strength, or agility, and it was not unusual for many fighters to resemble obese mounds of fat and flesh. Gone were the days of tightly muscled forms and eel-like flexibility. It seemed that in the wrestling ring, pot-bellied Silenus had triumphed over Apollo. Others have theorized that the rise of heavyweights is in part a reaction to the particular style of French wrestling. Since the Greco-Roman style does not allow the use of legs, it is often credited for causing this version to favor larger, heavier wrestlers.[31] The men who did the fighting were generally not from the dominant classes, and they tended to reflect the values of the proletariat. If untoned bodies bespoke proletarian origins, most wrestling fans either did not notice, did not complain, or were happy with the way things were.

Like all fads, the popularity of wrestling rose and fell like the tides, and all it usually took was a charismatic star or some clever ploy to lure the public back to the halls or the carnival booths. This had been a lesson understood since the very beginning. In 1867 there was the mysterious masked wrestler—then another appeared, then three, then wrestlers in different colored masks. The audiences were thrilled and returned to the arenas. By the mid–1890s wrestling had hit another low ebb, but then Joseph Doublier returned from Constantinople with a trio of powerful Turkish wrestlers, and everyone flocked back to the theaters and circuses to see these exotic creatures who made mincemeat of most of the French wrestlers they encountered. Sometimes the answer to flagging interest was to give the event more flash and show-biz slickness.

When French sporting newspapers and magazines teamed up with the major music halls like the Folies Bergère and the Casino, the great era of wrestling tournaments was off and running. The first of these was held at the Casino de Paris in 1898, and it was originally planned by the *Journal des Sports* to be a grand international competition bringing together all the greatest talents from across Europe.[32] It was so successful that it spawned a number of similar events, one just a few weeks after the original—it was called the Grand Prix of Paris, but there were many others as sporting entrepreneurs discovered that there was a great deal of money to be made. The victor of that first competition was Paul Pons who was already a great force in the wrestling world, but his reputation was pushed even higher by this contest. The tournaments began to come quickly one after another, and they soon became more international in scope and more remunerative for the competitors; eventually, there were wrestling championships held in all the major cities of Europe, but none were as important as those held in Paris. There seemed to be a major international world championship every year (sometimes more than one), and the public in Germany, Russia, Belgium, and Austria-Hungary simply could not get enough of wrestling.[33]

At this time, any music hall director who wanted to assure his box-office receipts could not do without a wrestling "act" that was staged over several weeks during the most active part of his winter season. An "act" is the correct word for what went on at these establishments. Indeed, the Parisians who frequented the noisy halls of the time went there to be amused by variety acts produced with care and finesse, and for a while these wrestling tournaments attracted an enormous number of patrons. There was a huge demand, and the sporting magazines and theatrical managers were determined to supply that clamor for wrestling. It was a great time to be a wrestler as long as the candidate looked the part and could master the moves and strike dramatic poses. It had always been a more or less open secret that fairground wrestling was fixed, but when it became known that the tournaments were also largely faked, then much of the enthusiasm for the sport dissipated. The moves and the holds were all predetermined as they generally were in the fairground booths, and the only thing that distinguished these matches were the stature, fame, and reputation of the wrestlers as well as the more luxurious surroundings that could only be supplied by an elaborate Parisian music hall.

Realistically, wrestling in music halls, cabarets, or carnival booths could never be totally honest. It would be virtually

In 1900 the sporting magazine *L'Auto* sponsored a "world championship" to be held at the Casino de Paris. This tournament signaled that wrestling was emerging out of the fairgrounds and onto elegant music-hall stages. Huge prizes attracted both athletes and audiences.

impossible for these men to preserve their physical health without serious injury if they were supposed to perform week-in week-out, sometimes several times a day. The only answer was for them to simulate their fights. As long as they put on a good show that was sufficiently convincing, the audience would be satisfied. On those rare occasions when emotion overcame logic, and one of the wrestlers went off script, there was often an injury—or at the very least, bad blood in the troupe. The predetermined outcome of the matches was something that everyone must have known, but it was never discussed by the actors themselves. That wall of silence was never breached—or almost never.

There was a great scandal that arose in June of 1914 when the illustrated sporting magazine, *La vie au Grand Air* published a letter that had been intercepted by one of their reporters. It was from Maurice Deriaz, a former wrestler who was later the manager of a group of fighters who were performing in Bordeaux while some of his other men were supposed to fight in Brussels in a tournament that was happening at the same time. His letter lays out in specific terms who is to fight, what holds they are to use, how long they are to fight, and who will be the winner.

> Antonitch will fight Essen one time for half an hour. Tell Antonitch to take Essen in a double headlock at ground level like he did in Paris and at the end of thirty minutes, Essen slaps the mat three times and gives up. He has to leave by train as soon after his match as possible. He has to take the 1:22 train to work in Brussels on Sunday evening.[34]

This revealing letter went on for several pages, and it outlined the desired results of every fight. It also settled once and for all the question of whether professional wrestling was a sport or entertainment. It is not known how deeply the letter of Deriaz affected the wrestling fraternity since the account of wrestling's little peccadillos were overshadowed just a month or two later by the start of an even bigger conflict: the Great War.

When war came, wrestling seemed to have lost all its former cachet, and in many ways professional wrestling was yet another casualty of the First World War. By the time the war was over, wrestling was not nearly as popular as it had been before. Now working-class lads were more interested in football; fewer people went to the fairgrounds when it was easier just to take a date to the movies; and upper- and middle-class sportsmen and sportswomen took up cycling, tennis, or boxing. Wrestling was too common and too proletarian for them now. The internationalism of having Turks, Africans, Germans, and Scandinavians wrestling in the same arena seemed to have withered away, and there was less interest in inviting others into the ring.[35]

Fortunately for historians, Edmond Desbonnet was there in the midst of European wrestling's golden age to see, report, and chronicle the great fighters of his day. Even he could not possibly include every great wrestler, and he omits such leading athletes as Eberle, Egeberg, Cazeau, Lundin, Steurs, Tom Jenkins, Fristensky, and many others. This is partly because he was writing at a very early time and some of these men were not yet the stars they would later become. Still, as he did for strongmen in *The Kings of Strength*, Desbonnet saved many of these people from oblivion, and he did so with humor, eloquence, and real respect.[36] As he states modestly and sincerely in the preface of the present book:

> I am not a poet, and I cannot sing the glories of wrestling, but I have loved it all my life. I love and keep up with all its protagonists, and I believe I can serve their cause by bringing together in a book all the memories that I have collected from almost everywhere as well as from my own experience. I can say with pride that these recollections are numerous, and the reader who will do me the honor of reading this modest work, will find here a fraternal reunion of all the kings of wrestling who have amazed France and the French for more than half a century.

Desbonnet is much more of a poet than he gives himself credit for. It has been said that professional wrestling does not have a history; it only has a mythology. If so, it was Edmond Desbonnet's desire to remove some of the fantasy and inject a little factual history into the sport.

The Kings of Wrestling

By Edmond Desbonnet

Foreword:
Wrestling Is the Primordial Sport

If we discuss primitive times when men lived in huts or in caves, it is quite evident that, aside from serious warfare, they could exercise their strength and their skill only by wrestling. Everything leads us to believe that it was freestyle wrestling, because the wrestling that we practice today bears the indisputable imprint of the refinement of an artistic people who were our masters in most of the plastic arts. I refer to the Greeks.

This magnificent people who refined the lines of its architecture and the forms of its statues so superbly, applied the same spirit of aesthetics and the passion for beauty to the sports that they practiced. They prohibited wrestling moves that were too easy and those which unbalanced the man and caused dangerous falls. Similar in this, the English do not knock a man down to the floor if they want to defeat him; an Englishman will only fight his opponent as long as he remains standing. The British also limit the holds to that portion of the body between the head and the waist. Strangulations, twists of the neck, bending back the arm or its joints were recognized as unworthy of a sport which the Greeks made into an art.[1] Yes, wrestling is an art; it allows two fine, honorable men to form an elegant and strong pair whose vibrant musculatures would cause even sculptors of the greatest talent to despair of recreating such physiques. However, the Greeks laughed at pain. Did they not engage in the terrible fight known as the "Pankration"?[2] This form of fighting is almost unknown today, but Professor Dubois, fencing master of the Opéra Comique, has restored such a curious and fierce demonstration in the revival of one of Gluck's masterpieces, *Iphigénie en Aulide*.[3]

Is not wrestling the first game of our young children? While they are too little to walk alone on a path and it would be dangerous for them to approach a river, as soon as they can stand up and are left in a group on the yellow sand of a beach, what do they do? They fight; their holds are clumsy and often (always, even) the two wrestlers roll around on the ground. And the laughter flies up to the blue skies above, because at this age vanity does aggravate their defeats. They roll in the sand, and they expend an ever-increasing and inborn strength. Hearts beat faster, and when babies fall hugging each other, the kiss that should be the eternal thought of humans, joins their innocent lips. Later, when the legs become stronger, when judgment gradually penetrates into brand new brains, wrestling is a school of acuity, courage, and endurance.

I dare not dwell on the wonderful influence that wrestling exerts in the development of muscles. Everyone knows that without exception, the entire muscular system contributes to the demonstrations of this admirable sport.

I am not a poet, and I cannot sing the glories of wrestling, but I have loved it all my life. I love and keep up with all its protagonists, and I believe I can serve their cause by bringing together in a book all the memories that I have collected from almost everywhere as well as from my own experience. I can say with pride that these recollections are numerous, and the reader who will do me the honor of reading this modest work, will find here a fraternal reunion of all the kings of wrestling who have amazed France and the French for more than half a century.

The Kings of Ancient Wrestling

I will not go so far as to tell you, dear reader, that my personal memories of this epoch will be the source of this chapter. No! Although athletes have the reputation for being as boastful as Gascons, even when they are from the North, like yours truly.[1] As I have already declared, the few heroes that I am going to mention had their histories written by others than me. However, I made a choice; I did not balk at repeating the exaggerations that I found recorded, even in serious works. My great experience of strength and my very precise knowledge of the records of world champions have made me overlook many so-called historical accounts. A book like this will be read by many young people. I have too much respect for youth and the efforts it imposes on itself to cite as examples heroes who come from mythology rather than from history.[2]

One of the most extraordinary among Greek athletes was Milo of Crotona. Feats of impossible strength have been cited of him. However, for this man to have given rise to such exaggerations, it is undeniable that he was for many years the most formidable man of ancient Greece. Well, he was beaten. A shepherd named Titormus, whom he met on the banks of the Evenus (today the Fidari), a river in Aetolia [region of Greece near Corinth] was his victor. How? It would be too easy to turn this first known wrestling match into a fanciful tale. I will not do it. So here are the two oldest names that the history of wrestling teaches us.[3]

Polydamas of Thessaly is cited next, who, in a famous combat imposed on him by the king of Persia Darius II, killed the three strongest men of his empire one after the other. Pausanias and Plutarch mention an athlete named Theagenes of Thasos (island in the Aegean Sea near the coast of Macedonia) whose victory crowns attained the number of 1,200 to 1,400. The [Roman] Emperor Maximin (who was Gothic in origin and a former shepherd) possessed an extraordinary strength. It is said that he defeated sixteen athletes in a row without breaking a sweat. This might be a lot to swallow, but perhaps "kayfabe" or prearranged outcomes was certainly not invented at the most recent championships.[4]

It is said that the emperor Commodus could break the leg of a horse with a single blow from his foot. This unworthy son of Marcus Aurelius was murdered; it was indeed justified, because this giant, armed with a club, had the luxury of descending into the arena and fighting against several men—all of them unarmed—and crushing them with his formidable cudgel.

The Greeks had two types of wrestling, the perpendicular and the horizontal [i.e., upright and ground wrestling]. In the first, the holds must be delivered while standing. As soon as one of the wrestlers was on the ground, his adversary had to let him get up so long as he had not suddenly thrown him on both shoulders. Conversely, in the second, wrestling was conducted only on the ground. In modern times the rules have combined the two methods, but it is indisputable that the blows delivered while standing are of a much more noble style. They require a virtuosity that only great champions have acquired.

Horizontal wrestling, that is to say wrestling on the ground, is much less pretty. It is often rather unpleasant for the spectators to watch; the wrestler

Hieronymous Mercurialis published his richly illustrated treatise on ancient exercise, *De Arte Gymnastica*, in the late sixteenth century. This plate shows a group of Greco-Roman *luctatores* or wrestlers.

underneath breathes badly, and although he might offer terrible resistance, it is useless. This sort of a match is interminable; on the other hand, nothing is more beautiful, for example, than a front waistlock delivered with the lightning precision of one like Pietro Dalmasso [1852–1929]. Further on in this book, the reader will find the biography of this marvelous champion whose fiery ardor and style have never been equaled.

I will leave the Greek era and dare to make a tremendous leap across time. However, as I continue, my pen will stumble for a moment to salute a very famous Breton wrestler. He lived in the fourteenth century (1314–1380). He triumphed over the

English and rid France of bands of roving brigands. He is one of the glories of our national history. Do we not all tremble with admiration when we pronounce the name of [Bertrand] Du Guesclin, Constable of France? In his youth, he defeated the strongest champions of Brittany.[5]

The Kings of Wrestling
The Early Years
We now arrive at the year 1845

The Montesquieu Hall

To speak frankly, we know very little about strongmen and wrestlers before the year 1845; it was around this time that there appeared a trio of colossi who astonished Parisians and who quickly earned the success that was as great as it was well deserved. These strongmen were named Meissonnier of Avignon, Quiquine (a veritable wall of flesh and blood), and Mazard of Uzès. We have only scanty information on Quiquine and Mazard, but Meissonnier's end is worth retelling.

For fifteen years, Meissonnier was able to defeat every adversary who stepped forward, and he had acquired a well-deserved reputation. He was especially admired for his physique. He had Herculean strength, had never been sick, and never suffered from pains (or at least, never complained of them). This giant threatened to live a hundred years.[1] But one day in the country near Avignon he met a little girl who was carrying a lunch to her father who was a worker. The child had to pass over a ford in the river, and since she was already late, she ran toward a point in the distance. "Wait, my little one," said Meissonnier, "I will carry you across."

Like a modern Saint Christopher, he carried the little girl across the river in his arms and placed his living burden on the other side of the stream. The happy child then ran off. As he watched her leave, Meissonnier slipped on the gravel and wet his feet. This chill was fatal for him. Thus, Achilles proved himself to be all too mortal since he did not have his heel dipped into the Styx! Meissonnier's final moments approach the sublime. In despair at seeing himself depart this earthly realm—he who was so strong and so young—he clenched his fists, bent his arms, and cried with rage, "Oh, Death! If you were only a man!"[2]

The success that had won over the Parisian public because of matches given by Quiquine, Mazard, and poor Meissonnier led to the creation of the Montesquieu Hall where these men came one after the other: Dumortier; Béranger; Étienne "the Shepherd"; Ambroise "the Savoyard"; Pujol "the Bridge Pier"; the sailor of the *Belle-Poule*; [Félix] Richoux "the Rifleman of Bugey"; Bouyard "the Stone Cutter" of

Remoulins; Anthèlme "Bamboula"; Plantevin "the King of Wrestlers"; Rivoire "Iron Body" of Lyon; Henri "Ocean" of Paris; Bacquet "the Artilleryman"; Lacroix "Good Heart"; Vincent "Iron Man" of Lyon; Odin of the Loire; Louis Vigneron "the Cannon Man" of the Hippodrome of Paris; James the Negro "the Bronze Statue"; Mazard of Uzès; Rabasson of Senas; Creste "the Bull of Provence"; Blas the proud Spaniard with a body of bronze; and Rambaud "Resistance"; all of whom filled the amateurs of the time with a healthy admiration.

It was at the Montesquieu Hall where the fight took place between Arpin "the Terrible Savoyard" and [Henri] Marseille "the Miller of Lapalud" [1817?–1897].[3] Marseille—the name has come down to the present generation, but this was Marseille the elder, the Miller of Lapalud, and [Jean-Baptiste] Marseille the younger [1833–1914] is the brother of the earlier one, and he is called "the Lion of Lapalud." The Miller of Lapalud and the Terrible Savoyard wrestled in 1852 with an unequaled ferocity, and those who were the enthusiastic spectators of this battle of giants still speak of it with exhilaration. Here is an account of the match taken from the newspapers of the time.

Paul Baudry's masterful 1848 portrait of the wrestler Meissonnier emphasizes the man's classical beauty and his effortless grace (property of the Fondation Calvet, Ville d'Avignon, Musée Calvet).

The Defeat of Arpin "the Terrible Savoyard" at the Montesquieu Hall in 1852

For some time now in Paris it has been possible to see wrestling matches between men who are reputed to be the mightiest wrestlers and strongmen from the South of France. And what is more, nearly all these men have acquired a rightful fame. Among them, we have remarked Arpin "the Terrible Savoyard," [1828–1858] justly considered the strongest, the most elegant, the most graceful and the most intelligent of the wrestlers.

In the second line came Blas, the Spaniard nicknamed "Pitiless," a dark-haired man, renowned for his enthusiasm and fearlessness in wrestling; Rabasson "the Little Peasant," an indefatigable fighter; Bouyard "the Stone Cutter" of Remoulins; Creste "the Bull of Provence"; Anthèlme "Bamboula"; Plantevin "the King of Wrestlers"; Rivoire "Iron Body" of Lyon; Henri "Ocean" of Paris; Bacquet "the Artilleryman"; and others.

But by far the most formidable was Arpin. Thanks to his success, he had spread such terror around his name that there was no longer any mortal who dared to measure himself against the man; so he had been proclaimed the king of conquerors. A day came, however, when a reckless young man challenged "the Terrible Savoyard." This young man was none other than Marseille, the hero of his birthplace [Lapalud] which gave him his name and enriched him with its favors.

He had hardly been told that a rival had arrived from Provence, when Arpin hastened to let the presumptuous young man know that if he succeeded in overthrowing him, he would have 200 francs at his disposal if he complied with the ordinary regulations and conditions of wrestling. Under these conditions, the agreement should have been easy. A date for the match was set by mutual agreement, a date too far off for the liking of Arpin's admirers, who were

Arpin, the Terrible Savoyard, and Marseille, the Miller of Lapalud, engage in an Olympian struggle in 1852. The artist has chosen to emphasize the men's physiques and to hide their faces, thus making the match an allegory of human strife.

boiling with impatience; they were so unaccustomed to seeing the Terrible Savoyard challenged.

The big day finally arrived. At ten o'clock precisely Arpin appeared in the arena, his gaze fixed, his head held high. Arpin is a colossus; his bull neck attached to shoulders of enormous breadth and of admirable beauty, his vigorous and solidly attached arms and his Herculean torso made him the living synthesis of strength and vigor. He truly was the Terrible Savoyard.[4]

Marseille appeared in turn; he was a thin and nervous young man who seemed almost spindly next to his gigantic adversary; one might say that he was a gladiator in front of the Farnese Hercules. At the sight of these two men all hearts beat faster; all breasts heaved. The two men shook hands, and the wrestling match began.

Arpin seized Marseille between his powerful arms, but the young athlete escaped him, sliding between his hands like a serpent and in turn rushed at his adversary with unparalleled impetuosity. Arpin seemed startled to see a rival with such determination and breathing with such ease; they twisted, stooped, rose up; every trick, feint, maneuver, and skill that one could imagine were displayed by these two rough jousters. Drops of sweat trickled down Arpin's naked body, while Marseille's body looked like real marble. After forty-five minutes of going at one another, it was still unclear who would be victorious. Who will be the winner—the Terrible Savoyard or the Miller of Lapalud?

Suddenly a hurrah resounded in the enclosure! One of the two opponents had rolled in the dust. It is the victor of victors! It was Arpin!!![5]

It is easy to imagine the amazement of the spectators, they could not believe in the fall of their idol. But the crowd is a fickle woman; its amazement became delirious joy, and the young Marseille was carried off in triumph. Poor Arpin had an untimely end. He sacrificed a little too much to Bacchus, and this was the cause of his defeat and contributed to his death. He died in Cette in 1883.[6]

1852
Great National Arena

Feats of strength, wrestling, and boxing at length had a temple of their own, and Charlemont the elder has furnished us with valuable documents on the Great National Arena.[7] From them, we have taken the details which follow.

In 1852, the director of the Paris Hippodrome built a sort of branch, which he named "The Great National Arena," in the Rue de Lyon near the Place de la Bastille. This immense public arena featured only two shows a week, on Sunday and Monday. Aside from circus work, one could practice feats of strength, French boxing, and flat-hand wrestling.[8] The boxing champions were [Louis] Vigneron, Rambaud (nicknamed Resistance), and Blanc. Wrestling champions included Antoine Dornier and the famous Arpin "the Terrible Savoyard."

One day when Mr. Arnaud, the director of the arena was very upset because "Resistance" was ill and he could not participate that day with Vigneron in a *savate* (French boxing) match. Since there was no one to replace him, Arpin said to him, "If you want, I will take his place. I know what I'm doing. I fear no one when it comes to boxing." The director was satisfied, and he informed Vigneron who accepted with pleasure. If Arpin was at that time the king of wrestling, he was not the king of boxing. He could point to a wrestling hold that was named after him, but in boxing, he could only point to the blows that he had received.[9]

When the bout began, he made a great show of extravagant leaps, senseless attacks, deploying all the resources that he believed himself capable of, but these were all vain efforts. Vigneron remained calm, and replied to him each time with sudden blows, full in the chest and in the face. Several times he attacked him with what he called "the eighteenth" (a crossover kick) and made him jump down from the ring in which they were fighting. The only thing Arpin could do was get back in the ring and then get knocked back down almost immediately, accompanied by great bursts of laughter from the spectators who were very amused by this fierce game. But there was someone who did not laugh, and that was a pretty girl from Marseilles who sold cakes and oranges to the spectators; she was furious about the defeat of her friend, and she was determined to take revenge.

Vigneron was a deadly serious fighter, and he beat Arpin decisively in their match at the Great National Arena, but he was nearly killed by one of his opponent's fierce female fans (collection of Michael Murphy).

While our two athletes circled the arena in a Roman chariot to receive the plaudits of the audience, the beautiful Marseillaise hid behind the dressing room used by Vigneron. She had armed herself with a large gendarme's saber that was used in the pantomime "Robert Macaire and Bertrand."[10] As Vigneron was about to enter his dressing room, she raised her saber in the air to strike him, when a stagehand who had seen everything shouted a warning to Vigneron. At the same moment the attacker slashed the saber down, but it only split the door. A few employees quickly appeared, followed by the director whom they had hastened to alert, and he had the irascible and vindictive Marseillaise thrown out.

Brave Arpin truly possessed phenomenal strength. He first dragged in a 1,300-kilo iron-sided grain wagon, then, after raising the four wheels of the wagon up on blocks, he got beneath and lifted until the wheels were elevated over the supports.

In 1854, boxing professor Leboucher presented fights at the Valentino Hall where he also trained wrestlers, boxers, and strongmen.[11] He had the idea of matching Vigneron with the famous English boxer Dickson who claimed that, using only his fists, he could beat French boxers using their fists and their feet. Many former amateurs still remember Vigneron's magnificent fight, using French boxing against Dickson who did English boxing in the Valentino Hall. Charlemont Sr. was present at that fight, and he remembers that in the dressing room before the fight he saw a man with a superb build and magnificent muscular development who smiled smugly while looking at Vigneron who was fully clothed—it was Dickson. However, Dickson had a change of attitude after he saw his future adversary with his chest bared, but that did not prevent him from saying in English to some of his compatriots who were there that Vigneron would not last three minutes in the ring with him. The remark was repeated to Vigneron, who turned very pale and seemed disturbed for a moment, but almost immediately regained his self-assurance. Dickson had overestimated his own worth. Vigneron not only fought him for more than three minutes, but he beat him masterfully amid the frenzied applause of the audience.[12]

1866
Wrestling Matches at the Paz Gymnasium

In 1866, wrestling moved to the top of the Rue des Martyrs in a gymnasium that Mr. Paz recently established at Number 34.[13] In order to publicize his business, Paz organized wrestling bouts that attracted a considerable crowd. More than 3,000 people attended each showing, and the large Parisian wrestling organizations were all represented there. It is true that things were well organized and that nothing that might have interested the public had been overlooked. Paz was very competent when it came to sporting matters, and he was a great lover of wrestling; consequently, he had engaged the most highly rated fighters from Bordeaux, Toulouse, Montpellier, and Marseille. Certain virtuosos of the wrestling mat were paid up to 150 francs an evening by him. At the time this was an extraordinary remuneration, however paltry it might seem to today's stars.

The bouts were organized with great care and were presented with an imposing

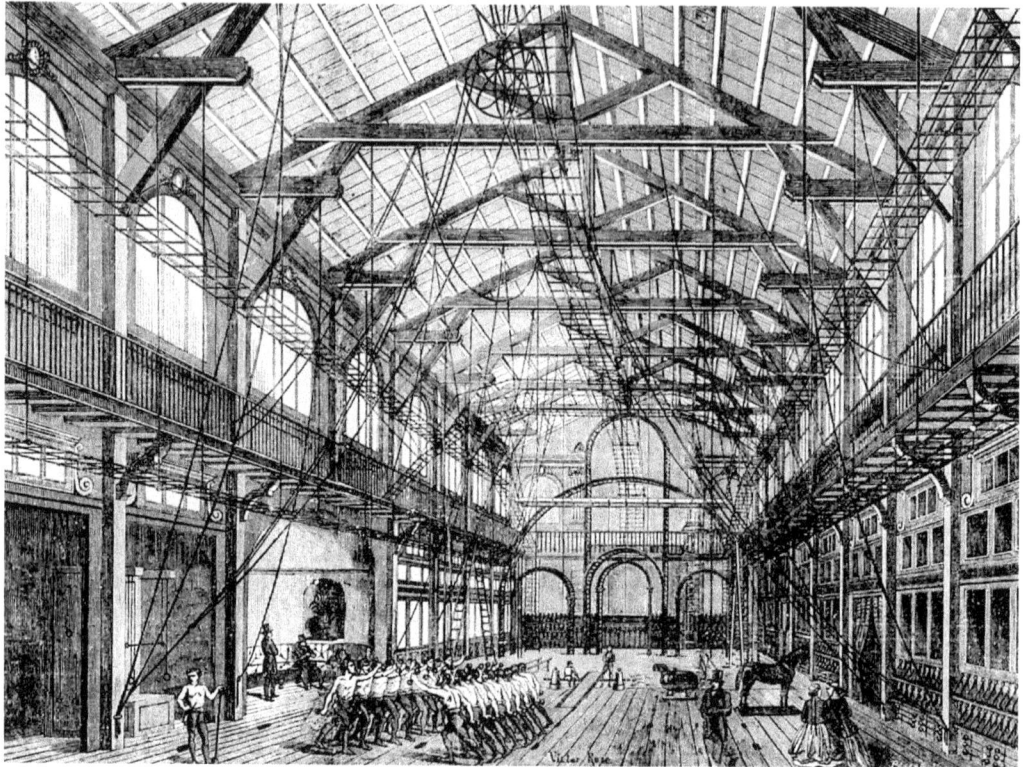

Eugène Paz had a massive gymnasium in Paris, and he lured customers to his establishment by staging wrestling matches. They proved to be so popular that Paz had to stop them because they were more esteemed than his work to improve health and physiques.

style; even more extraordinary for the time was the fact that the men's attire was quite proper. Pairing up the combatants was accomplished as it had been done for the gladiators: the wrestlers were matched by their equal strength. As soon as the three knocks (with which all French theaters signal the start of a performance) had sounded, around thirty of the men entered, marching two-by-two, in their wrestling costumes. These consisted of simple tights, but the leggings were of an irreproachable cleanliness.[14] It is true that Paz kept a close eye on his artists, and when it was necessary, he did not hesitate to send men to the showers before allowing them to enter the arena. After having made their entry, the athletes marched around the arena, saluted the judges, and then returned to the wings where they remained until their names were called.

The judges were most often composed of members of the Jockey Club, and in all cases, they were made up of well-known sportsmen.[15] The chairmanship of this jury nearly always fell to Paz since his expertise forced the wrestlers to fight seriously. In fact, he knew how to fulfill his task with a unique authority, and when necessary, he showed the requisite severity when supervising strapping fellows of this type who were naturally unaccustomed to taking orders.

The rules expressly forbade the fighters to heckle one another during the match, since this was one of their most annoying habits. Wrestlers were never allowed to address the spectators nor to dispute the decisions of the judges. When the referee raised the little tricolored pennant that he held in his hand, the defeated man had to leave the arena without recriminations and without making even the slightest protest.

These bouts were so interesting that Paz had to put on about twenty of them, and they all enjoyed a remarkable success, thanks especially to the orderly and correct way the matches were conducted. In spite of the public's infatuation, Paz soon gave up this type of spectacle. Ironically, he did not want to subvert the original character of his gymnasium, which was above all an establishment for curative gymnastics. By organizing the wrestling matches, he had sought merely to acquaint the man in the street with his gymnasium; once his purpose had been attained, he abandoned the advertising methods which deviated too much from his specialty.

It was at the Paz Gymnasium that the famous Rossignol-Rollin of Lyon got his troupe together.[16] Today, it is curious to read the colorful announcements which he wrote with genuine talent. Rossignol had an additional flair as an orator, and he often entertained spectators by "getting back in the ring" in order to regale them with his very special eloquence.

There were often long lines of superb athletes on view at the Paz Gymnasium: Richoux, the strongest; Béranger, the handsomest and the friendliest of wrestlers; Alfred "the Handsome Parisian Model," looking like a stud bull; "the Shepherd" Étienne, like an ancient marble statue, only a little bigger; "Black James" a statue in bronze; Deligne, Creste, Vigneron, Lacaisse, Grangé, Charpentier, Blondin, and Faouët "the Invincible," nicknamed "the Beast of the Jungle"; Rivoire "the Man of Marble"; Pujol, known as "Bridge Pile" (the famous sailor of the *Belle Poule*), who was also an académie model. All these men were fighters of the first rank, and all were men of exceptional vigor and skill who helped make that time at the arena a golden age.

Everyone knows how muscular and broad shouldered was dear Rabasson, the "Bull of the Gironde," and one knows how solid and marvelous the physique of Rivoire the "Rampart of the South" was. We all know how handsome was young Blas and about what a disaster it was for wrestling when this proud Spaniard with the body of steel died. Arpin the "Terrible Savoyard" was also there, but the old lion had taken to drink, and he had already lost a part of his strength. While his old victor, Marseille the elder, was supple and strong as a panther, in spite of his fifty years and even more wily than an old fox. He was still the despair of all up-and-comers.

All these athletes and several others besides were chosen from among the best or the most famous. They all served to encourage the fans by wrestling so enthusiastically at the matches that were given at the Paz Gymnasium and at the Great National Arena.

1867
Wrestling at the Casino on the Rue Cadet

In 1867 and 1868 the greatest epoch in strength exercise and wrestling began, and the Parisian public became increasingly enthusiastic for these activities. Audiences were growing. The principal meeting place became the vast hall of the Casino on the Rue Cadet (where the Grand-Orient now stands).[17] It was there that the Homeric conflicts all took place between the illustrious [Félix] Richoux; Marseille "the Lion of Lapalud"; Vincent "the Iron Man" (sometimes called "Cannon" or "the Rampart of Isère"); and Faouët "the Baker," otherwise known as "the Wild Beast of the Jungle."

Richoux was one of those of whom the posters of Rossignol-Rollin said that "his glorious shoulders have never known contact with the impure dust of the arena."[18] He was one of the handsomest

Richoux was tall, thin, and thoroughly muscled. It was his costume, however, that must have drawn attention to him.

men that anyone had ever seen. Very tall, thin, thoroughly muscled, and with a flawless physique. He was agile and had a colossal strength, and he demonstrated out of the arena that he was as gentle as could be. Richoux was originally from Ain where he worked as a wood seller, and although he loved wrestling very much, he continued in his first profession and managed to earn quite a nice fortune. Eventually, he even became mayor of his community. He is still alive and, if memory serves, he must still live in Lyon.

One day the management of the Casino announced that they would offer a prize of 300 francs—we have come a long way since then—for whoever could defeat one of the three champions of the house: Richoux; Marseille "the Lion"; or Vincent-Cannon. An adversary appeared; he was Faouët, a Parisian baker. The newcomer was very distrustful, and before wrestling he wanted the money put in the hands of a stakeholder. His first opponent was Vincent.

The two men entered the lists, and after a few passes, Faouët grabbed Vincent in a front waistlock, and hugged him with incredible strength, lifted him off the floor and slammed him to the mat. This was quite a development since Vincent was considered one of the most powerful wrestlers of his time. Soon, everyone was talking about little else but Faouët's unbeatable waistlock. On the next day, the baker went up against Marseille. The two adversaries fought with ferocious energy for five quarter-hour rounds without gaining a single advantage over one another, and the bout remained undecided. But before leaving, Richoux—the great Richoux—threw down the gauntlet to Faouët.

Hardly had the two men come face to face before Richoux raised his arms, offering himself to all attacks. Faouët launched himself forward and wrapped Richoux in his arms of iron. But then the experienced wrestler forced his own arms under the armpits of his adversary. Richoux suddenly broke the man's grip and lifted him up, propelling his tall body into a complete turn, and then pinned him to the mat by his shoulders. After he let him up, he announced, "Your waistlock can take that!"

1868
Wrestling at the Le Peletier Arena
(49 Rue Le Peletier)

We have now arrived at 1868 and are at 49 Rue Le Peltier, across from the old Opera.[19] Parisian wrestling is at its apogee. Under the direction of Charavay, we find there Richoux; the two Marseilles; Dumortier of Nantes; Black James, nicknamed "the African Farnese"; Dubois of Saint Denis; Milhomme of Bordeaux, called "Pitiless," who one day pinned Richoux by surprise;, Bonnet "The Ox," Laroche, Ancelin, the Masson brothers, Stockmann "The Rampart of Belgium," Faouët, Paul the Negro known as "the Senegalese Eel"; Creste the "Bull of Provence"[20]; Périer, known as "the Parisian Eel"; Alfred "the Handsome Parisian Model"; then the masked wrestlers: the "Black Mask" and the "Red Mask"; and finally, Peter "the Coachman."

We reproduce below a specimen of these truly curious posters that announced the program of great days of wrestling to the admirers of the sport in those heroic times.

LE PELETIER ARENA
49 Rue Le Peletier
GREAT ROMAN WRESTLING
Program for ___ 1868

Friends and admirers of wrestling,

In antiquity, those who were greatest in rank as well as by birth, did not disdain to descend into the arena to dispute the palm of strength.

The modern era has nothing to envy from ancient times.

Tomorrow at the Arena in the Rue Le Peletier, Mr. Falcet (who was admitted to the Commercial Court, and whose eloquence has often resounded under the arches of the temple of Themis) will fight against the Chevalier de Carrières, a dramatic artist, whose veins carry the noblest and most generous bloods of France.[21] This is beautiful, this is great.

When man knows his strength better, he is less tempted to abuse it.

Peter, "the Coachman"

One evening a stocky, red-faced little man with a whip in this hand was seen arriving at the arena on the Rue Le Peletier. He came to wrestle against whoever wanted to. Faouët won the job. Oh, it was not long. The little coachman put him in a headlock that Faouët could not fend off, and he took his man and laid him on his back. It was Arpin's famous hold.[22] The champions of Rue Le Peletier could not

The masked wrestler at the Le Peltier Arena caused a sensation. Here he lifts Marseille the Younger in a rear waistlock as the astonished crowd looks on.

believe it. But the next day, Marseilles had been delegated to fight against the Coachman and to uphold the honor of his team.

"No!" cried Alfred, "the Pretty Model." "Marseille is too much for him. Let me have the little runt!" And on that evening Peter the Coachman saw his ephemeral glory evaporate.

The wrestling lasted at the Arena for about a year, but since there was a new show three times a week, at length the crowds began to diminish in number. The manager then devised an easy enough solution. He invented a character known as "the Masked Man," and this enigma became legendary.[23]

This mysterious athlete betook himself to the arena in an elegant open carriage. When he entered, accompanied by his servant who followed him a few paces behind, he created a fantastic impression on the audience. He was clothed in a jersey that covered him from neck to toe, and his head was concealed in a sort of sack of black silk with holes for his eyes, finally he was gloved.

In a very short time the public was convinced that they had before them a real man of the world—an aristocrat and they always gave him a warm reception. But one fine day they eventually noticed that the accoutrement of a masked wrestler hardly allowed him to successfully wrestle with men like Richoux or Faouët, and especially to defeat them in just a few seconds. People then were convinced that the wrestling matches were nothing but play acting. The public became so annoyed at this that the Masked Man, who played the role of an aristocrat but was nothing more than a masseur named Charvet, was forced to return to his customers.[24] Understandably, following this disclosure the Arena of the Rue Le Peletier were practically abandoned.

The Le Peletier Arena was closed in 1870 after a stranglehold proved to be fatal. It was the "collar of strength," which caused the death of a wrestler.[25] City officials intervened after that and banned all wrestling in Paris.[26]

1889
International Athletic Arena
(24 Quai Debilly)

On the occasion of the Exposition of 1889, an athletic arena was opened at 24 Quai Debilly.[27] The following men were engaged and appeared in Greco-Roman wrestling matches, and they earned the public's enthusiastic admiration: Apollon, Crest, Félix Bernard, Eugène of Paris, Pytlazinski [1863–1933]; Alix the Negro (a lightweight but a good teacher who died of tuberculosis); Robin, nicknamed *Badingué* [Silly Billy or Halfwit]; Pietro Dalmasso, Robinet, Boyer of Nîmes, and Boyer of Marseille; Émile Bruyère [1860–1910], called "the Limousin," Conver of Lyon named "Fafon" (died at Grenoble; killed by a revolver shot), and Évillard who was known as "the Tonkinese."

Here are two extracts from articles that were published at this time and which relate to the above information. The first one describes the opening of the Arena, and the other gives a report on its inaugural matches.

> Swiss wrestlers have arrived at 24 Quai Debilly.[28] Incomparable specimens of strength and agility, they challenge all comers. This Thursday evening—premium day—is the first show with the contest of French champions: Bernard, Crest, etc., and Apollon "the King of Human Strength."
>
> Yesterday marked the inauguration of the International Athletic Arena, 24 Quai Debilly, with a benefit performance for the widows and orphans of the press.
>
> We remember how the spectacle of the Roman wrestlers enthralled Paris several years ago. Twelve of the strongest French champions have been engaged by the management of the Athletic Arena and defend the reputation of the French school against foreign champions. Flat-hand wrestling is to be made a part of the physical education curriculum in all secondary schools for the year 1889–1890.
>
> English boxing will be represented this evening by two of the best boxers; Miss Nelly and Miss Mary will also appear.[29]
>
> Finally, feats of strength will be represented in the person of the celebrated Apollon [1862–1928], who, not yet having met his equal, is justified in calling himself the King of Human Strength.[30] Apollon will lift his famous 80-kilo weight and will stretch his expander. Apollon is truly the strongest man we have seen in quite a while. He lifts to arm's length an 80-kilo weight by pinching it between two fingers only. He is the handsomest example of strongman who exists in the world. His perfect physique and his "Justinian" face calls to mind the gladiators of ancient Rome. Apollon is French; he was born at Marsillargues (Hérault).

The wrestling matches had to conclude at the end of a fortnight for lack of electric lighting. Unfortunately, despite the beautiful promises of introducing wrestling in schools, this was soon completely abandoned, and wrestlers again performed exclusively at fairground stalls. It was only in 1897 that a championship was mounted to honor this very interesting sport. Battaglia, a former strongman became an impresario, and he organized a double championship of wrestling and strength in Brussels. This was soon followed by another similar championship which was held at the Roubaix Velodrome under the direction of Theodore Vienne, then manager of this establishment.[31] It was in Roubaix that Constant le Boucher was the victor over Félix Bernard who was then in decline, and this victory was the starting point of Constant's glorious career.[32]

Finally, a bit later Mr. [Alexandre] de Lucenski, director of the now defunct *Journal des Sports*, organized in his turn the first world championship at the Casino de Paris.[33] It was here that Paul Pons was the glorious victor. Then the magazine *Vélo* organized another championship in 1899 that was under the direction of Lacaisse, the former wrestler, and which brought together a troop of colossi that caused a sensation.[34]

Rossignol-Rollin
The King of Wrestling Impresarios

Rossignol-Rollin was an extraordinary man.[35] It was he who gave to wrestling its "naturalization papers," and it is due to this astonishing impresario that we can say that wrestling was popularized. His actions not only affected France, but also abroad. This rogue of a man was versed in classical literature and knew how to revive the ancient soul. No one understood as well as he did the art of firing up enthusiasm and driving away the indifference of his audiences. His implausible advertisements attracted big crowds to his arena.

Wrestling was in a slump when in 1854 Rossignol-Rollin appeared. Rossignol-Rollin! That magic name that fascinated our fathers. Rossignol was a showman who traveled from town to town with a troupe of hired men. At this time the French police tolerated the exhibition of wrestlers who wore trunks, but entrance in the arena was forbidden to women.[36]

Rossignol-Rollin (Claude-Eugène) was born in Paris in 1821, and he truly had sawdust in his veins; he was (even before Barnum) the most incomparable Barnum who ever appeared under the sun.

He was gifted with a stentorian voice, and this king of the barkers excelled at introductory patter. What he said and did was truly epic, from beginning to end, from the announcement of the show to the wrestlers' final engagement! In linguistic flights of fancy that were unique only to him, Rossignol-Rollin summoned the crowds every Sunday by means of huge posters. "Friends, I love you…. A banner to the victor…. On roses, gentlemen…. I appeal to the people…. Wrestling is life…. Get thee behind me, you decadent Romans! … There are muscles in the air!" These fantastic and preposterous appeals that enthused the public were actually written down by Rossignol-Rollin in a café while sipping a glass or two of absinthe. This [Gen. Charles] Mangin (1866–1925) of biceps and wrestling enjoyed impressing the regulars whom he stunned with his volubility and his skill at patter.[37]

It should be noted that in the list of members who first comprised Rossignol-Rollin's troupe were designated purely and simply by their names and the city where they were born, but later the men on the list were endowed with bizarre qualifiers made to attract attention. The reason for this is as follows: toward the end of his career, Rossignol-Rollin was joined by competitors. Ex-broyat, who in addition to the men he hired, poached some wrestlers from his colleague. By the same token, several members of Ex-broyat's troupe might go at any given moment to work with Rossignol-Rollin.[38]

The great impresario and king of the barkers Rosignol-Rollin had a stentorian voice excelled at introductory patter. He did much to make wrestling popular in the days before the Franco-Prussian War of 1870.

But one fine day, Rossignol-Rollin who, even though he had never been a wrestler, had an inspiration which, although not brilliant, has nonetheless withstood the test of time. He told himself that introducing athletes to the public purely and simply under their real names was a process that lacked sonorousness and that it would strike the popular imagination much more by attaching high-sounding epithets to his wrestlers. He gathered his staff together and in a heartfelt speech, made them understand that to pass on to posterity or at least to stand out in the attention of the masses, it was not enough to be called Oliver, James, or Jaberjon. "From today on," he said, "each of you will have a new identity of my creation, and then you can let me know what you think of it." From then on, as soon as a wrestler entered his troop, he gave him a fancy nickname, almost always terrible or at least grand sounding. For instance, there was Auguste the Sailor "the Terror of the Fleet"; Faouët "the Wild Beast of the Jungle," and so on.[39]

When he hired Christol, he found himself a little embarrassed to attach a sufficiently turbulent epithet to his name. "What profession did you pursue before you were a wrestler?" he asked. Christol replied, "A cobbler!"

"Blast it," he replied, "We can't put on the posters 'Christol, the terrible shoe maker.'" And then suddenly he had an inspiration. "I have it! You'll be called Christol 'the Coral Fisher.'"

It was at this time that the "terrors," the "ramparts," the "lions," and the "wild beasts" delighted our grandfathers and made a small fortune of their promoters. Aside from the athletes who figured in the troupe of Exbroyat, Rossignol-Rollin had under his direction the following: Mayard of Nimes; Lacroix "Good Heart" of Vertrieu; Étienne "the Shepherd from Bourg-Saint-Andéol"; Paul the "Hole Puncher of Bordeaux" (who today lives in Paris and is around eighty years old); Le Fram of Cavaillon; Milhomme of Bordeaux; Lacaisse of Paris; Bérenger "the Elegant Parisian"; Christol the Coral Fisher; Alfred "the Parisian Model"; Rambaud "Resistance"; Tamiot of Gard; Auguste the Sailor "the Terror of the Fleet"; Michel "the Rock of Ariège"; Lagneau of Paris; Rivollon "the Serpent of the Loire"; Rousset of Creusot; Marseille the younger; Old Bernard from Bordeaux; Fruchinet "the Scarlet Uprooter," from Nimes; Ambroise "the Colossus of Savoy"; Pujol "the Colossus of the Gironde"; Louis of Tarare "the Lion of the Desert"; Raulin "Toothless"; Charles "the Arab"; Vimard "the Soap Maker of Rouen"; Baraud "the Sand Seller of the Rhone"; Richoux "the Wrestler with Virginal Shoulders"; Creste, "the Bull of Provence" (whose enthusiastic compatriots say of him, "Here we recognize only one God, one sun and one man, and that man is Creste."); Deligne from Norway; Alliot from Morières; Brémont of Marseilles; Sabin of Marseilles; Mordunt of the North; Bainaize from Perigord; Dumas of Bordeaux; Montal of Lyon; Pernet "the Model of the Fine Arts"; Treuvé "Bibus, the Butcher of Lyon"; Vignon of Chateauroux; Jacques Dumortier "the Agile Lyonnais"; Vincent "the Iron Man"; Amédé of Remoulins; Dubois of Paris; Faouët "the Wild Beast of the Jungle"; Rémond of Grenoble; and others.

Sometimes Rossignol-Rollin's "pupils"—that is what he called his wrestlers, even though he himself had never wrestled in his entire life—sometimes revolted against the orders of their boss, and some who had promised before entering the arena to take a fall, but did not want to anymore as soon as he was in front of the audience since he did not want to give himself up to defeat. At that remote time, there were prearranged and fake matches, even though they had not always been completely accepted. Rossignol-Rollin then intervened, and in legal language that the public could not understand, he forced those who were stubborn to keep their commitments.

This scene was repeated often and always to the benefit of Rossignol-Rollin, who had quite legitimately concluded that he could demand anything from the "artists" that he directed. One evening, however, it seemed that he would be thwarted. Faouët, the famous Faouët, Faouët the wild beast wrestler, had to be taken down by some "Rampart" or other who had been hired for this purpose, and whose obscure name has not reached us. Unfortunately, whatever effort the latter made, Faouët proved to be invincible. The fight had already lasted twenty minutes and the audience was beginning to show its displeasure, when Rossignol-Rollin appeared in the arena and made it clear to Faouët that the moment had come to take his fall. But Faouët did not see it that way, and he seized the Rampart by his armpits, intending to pin him to the floor, when Rossignol-Rollin approached the headstrong man. "Monsieur Faouët," he said to him in a stern voice, "your feet smell bad; please retire from the arena." Then he addressed the audience. "Gentlemen," added Rossignol, "in the future no wrestler will ever enter my arena without first convincing me of his personal cleanliness." Faouët withdrew furiously, but the Rampart had not been defeated, and that was the only thing that mattered to Rossignol-Rollin.

Another day Faouët appeared in the arena followed by a young wrestler who was excited and happy as a lark. "Gentlemen," said Rollin, "this young fellow of twenty years, is from Marseilles and knows only the Canebière, but he has fine qualities.[40] What a future! Forgive him, though, he is a little nervous, and he has happy muscles."

"Calm down, calm down, gentlemen," he said another time to two wrestlers. "Control yourselves. Composure is the foremost of the muscles."

After the war of 1870 and the fall of the Empire, Rossignol-Rollin's success plummeted. His final shows took place in Lyon in early 1872, and then he retired to an inn in Villeurbanne accompanied by James, a negro wrestler who had been his personal servant.[41] It was there that he died suddenly and in virtual poverty on 25 January 1873.

Posters of Rossignol-Rollin

The wording of Rossignol-Rollin's posters was admired by the onlookers. Here is a specimen:

Bordeaux, Rossignol-Rollin greets you!

PEOPLE OF BORDEAUX

Plato wrote in his *Republic*, "It is not to cultivate the soul and the body but to cultivate only the soul and to perfect courage and philosophical leanings in it that the gods have given man music and gymnastics."[42]

Well, then, to Plato, the broad-shouldered philosopher, I will yield music for the soul, but I retain gymnastics for the body.

Ah, Divine philosopher! If you could see my specimens—my men—they would amaze you and I am sure I would catch you in the act of applauding my wrestlers.

What success! What men! What wrestling!

Rossignol-Rollin

Faouët "the Wild Beast of the Jungle"

"Step aside, you reeds! Make way for an oak."

Faouët comes to issue a challenge to Ambroise, the "Colossus of Savoy." People of Bordeaux, they wanted to come to your city so that you could be witnesses to this match which will go down in the annals of your lives.

Ambroise the "Colossus of Savoy"

From the mountains of Savoy, the lion has roared! Ambroise has accepted Faouët's challenge! This fight will be excessive and merciless! Strangleholds and hammer locks will be allowed for this match only.

Bronzina

The man of bronze is unmovable even by a boulder, and he will be forced to restrain himself unless he hears your cheers and applause.

The program (a reproduction of which I give below) offers a typical example of the famous impresario's rhetoric. This document, which is as precious as it is authentic, deserves to be saved from oblivion. It could serve as a model for more than one politician seeking to be elected. Here it is in all its splendor.

ALCAZAR PALACE
(Brotteaux District[43])

Doors open   Sunday 22 November 1963   We will finish at 4 o'clock
at 1 o'clock precisely   from 2 o'clock in the afternoon   or later

---

Fight to the Finish

People of Lyon!
Children of Lyon!

Life is wrestling! Wrestling is life!!
Fight to the finish! Win or die!
Not empty words! But actions and facts!
When one is named Rossignol, *noblesse oblige*!!
Behold my athletes! Models of Creation!
All are as beautiful as ancient statues! And strong ... as we no longer are!
Their equals have never been seen before
And even their first attacks are master strokes!
We have often spoken of Hercules and gladiators of antiquity!

They are all miserable and worthless!
You Greeks and Romans of the Decadence! Get back!!!
You are no more than atoms next to my men!

Dear People of Lyon,

I have chosen the most formidable strongmen from all over the world to present to you.

I am inspired by this famous verse:

"To conquer without danger is to triumph without glory."[44]

And now, do not forget that from the heights of Saint-Just and from Croix-Rousse 100,000 Lyonnais will come to contemplate you!!!
    No mercy!
The fight will end when we run out of fighters!

                          Your devoted and grateful
                          ROSSIGNOL-ROLLIN

Seat prices: First rows 2 francs   Perimeter 1 franc
Ladies will not be admitted to these shows.
The Alcazar will be perfectly heated

A Drama

That refined writer Charles Monselet [1825–1888] thought that one day he might become the historiographer of Rossignol-Rollin. On one certain evening a terrible drama bloodied the arena in the Rue des Martyrs, and we borrow the account of this frightful wrestling match from the famous writer.[45] In it a butcher who was called Edouard—but whom Rossignol-Rollin had pompously renamed "the Bear of the Jura"—met his death.

Charles Monselet, who was an eyewitness to the scene, wrote the story of a drama that took place in the wrestling hall in the Rue des Martyrs, this room which in the full splendor of its success Rossignol-Rollin had baptized "the Temple of Muscles." The city was plastered on all its walls with bellicose posters, announcing in letters a foot high of the challenges brought by Faouët to Ambroise or the revenge granted to Bonnet "the Ox," by Milhomme "Pitiless."

In the meantime, Rossignol-Rollin received a visit one day from a kind of a colossus who was ugly, stocky, bearded, and whom I will designate under the name of Lubin "Monselet."[46] Having exhausted all other career possibilities, Lubin wondered why he could not become a wrestler. Rossignol was charmed by Lubin. He raved about the strength of his biceps and the masterful development of his stomach. He had him make a few moves and found him to be a dish fit for a gourmand. "The legs may lack tone," muttered Rossignol. "They will have to be exercised. But you have the makings of a fine athlete, and I want to do something with you. Your physique is felicitous."

Ironic! Rossignol found Lubin's physique "felicitous." His plump features, his charcoal eyebrows, and his thick lips became the three Graces in the eyes of

Rossignol. "For your debut would you like to wrestle with Faouët or with Mr. Creste?" he asked.

"It doesn't matter to me," replied Lubin modestly.

"All right then! I'll have you give a try with Étienne, 'the Shepherd of Bourg-Saint-Andéol.' He'll be easy on you. By the way, you will need a name. That's indispensable!"

"But I already have one."

"Oh," said Rossignol, "I meant a name that's noble sounding, aggressive, scintillating."

"My name is Lubin."

"Yes, well, Lubin is not bad. We can keep Lubin. There is bucolic beauty in that name. But it's important to add a surname. Lubin all by itself would be like a kite without a tail. I will consult this dictionary, but I will need several days of serious meditation for this job. Come back and see me on Sunday."

Lubin returned on the day indicated. Rossignol-Rollin had found the kite's tail, and the poster for his arena announced, "the upcoming debut of Mr. Lubin, 'the Gallant Mastodon.'" During the week, the newspapers spoke of no one but the Galant Mastodon. Poor Lubin must have thought that he had finally found the right path. He could use his strength legally and could justify his exceptional stature in socially acceptable ways.

Étienne "the Shepherd of Bourg-Saint-Andéol," did not need to be easy on him. From the second match of flat-hand wrestling, the Galant Mastodon heroically forced him down on both shoulders. He forced down lots of others too. Lacroix, Étienne—and Creste "the Bull of Provence"—himself. He was a little too good at forcing others down; so much so that Rossignol-Rollin begged him to stop. Lubin had a very serious fault in such a perilous profession; he became passionate too quickly and got carried away immediately. So his comrades threatened to beat him up if he did not start treating them with a spirit of good camaraderie. Lubin promised to do everything that they wanted, and for several shows they could see that he was keeping a careful check on his abilities. Hercules had surrendered his club.

But then a fatal and irresistible occasion presented itself. He was confronted face to face with someone named Edouard "the Bear of the Jura." This was a mistake on the part of Rossignol-Rollin, but he needed the receipts. I will not say why. The Bear of the Jura was himself also a new recruit. He was a presumptuous young man; he had recently been employed in a butcher's shop. He was intoxicated by romantic triumphs, and he had been encouraged by his friends to earn other triumphs in the wrestling arena. That evening he had invited his father and his fiancée to dine with him at a nearby restaurant.

The first time he saw him, Lubin treated the Bear of the Jura as he had recently been accustomed to treating his colleagues, that is to say with indifferent friendliness. But Lubin noted a serious aggression and a certain bearing that went beyond the conventions of the wrestling mat, and he started to look forward to the engagement. The Bear of the Jura would make a good victim and good money; the Gallant Mastodon did not want to give away his game. He smelled fresh meat.

The Mastodon made the first move by grabbing his opponent, and he began to shake him as a hurricane shakes an oak tree. But the butcher was young, and he resisted. The butcher could feel the anxious eyes of his father and his fiancée upon him. It was a fine spectacle. The sweat left clusters of pearls at their temples. Here and there, on their bodies one could see broad blotches and crimson-colored marks. You could hear the cracking of their bones and the panting of their chests; we heard it all the better because the audience had become silent.

Rossignol-Rollin was amazed and could not restrain his enthusiasm; he clapped his hands exclaiming, "Bravo! Bravo! Are you not worthy sons of the Romans and the Spartans?" And addressing the audience that was used to his original announcements, "Pardon me," he told them with great emotion, "These are two of my creations."

In the end, Lubin began to be impatient. He was indignant at seeing himself fighting for victory for so long and he tried to end it all at once. Rossignol-Rollin's applause excited him. He forgot the recommendations, he forgot his promise, he forgot everything. He became terrible once more. Here is what happened.

Lubin suddenly opened his long arms bulging with muscles; he stretched them open as if to restore their suppleness and elasticity, but suddenly he closed them on the Bear of the Jura, but so forcefully that he remained almost motionless and his face turned blue. This embrace lasted so long that several spectators were alarmed and cried, "Enough! Enough!" But the Galant Mastodon heard nothing. He continued to overpower his victim who clearly began to slump forward. At this moment, a hoarse roar came from Lubin's entrails, something indescribable, frightening, and which betrayed a violent pain. Then, immediately, the circle of his arms tightened with rage for his opponent. The vise crushed the man's flesh. The whole room rose up. Startled, Rossignol-Rollin ran towards the two fighters to separate them.

"Hey, hey! What's going on? Oh! The madman!" he said grabbing onto Lubin, "He will never learn." Then, only vaguely restored to himself, Lubin released the Bear of the Jura, who fell and rolled heavily on the sand of the arena like an inert mass, like an insensitive thing, like a corpse.

In fact, he was dead—crushed just like [the mythical giant] Antaeus in the fable.[47] At the same time, the spectators, frozen with terror, saw a long stream of blood flowing from Lubin's neck. In his last convulsions, the Bear of the Jura had bitten him furiously, in desperation, with all his teeth. It was this that had caused Lubin's cry, and it was also undoubtedly this which had caused the death of the butcher. This horrible bite, this deep gash in part absolved the Galant Mastodon who remained stunned, panting, bloody, ignorant, and unaware of the murder that he had just committed.

The Arena was closed for several days.

What Rossignol-Rollin's Wrestlers Earned

Everyone knows about the huge fees that certain wrestlers receive these days, and we have often complained about the demands of the kings of wrestling who are perhaps, not very wrong to seek to benefit largely from the vogue of a sport of which they are its stars. What a difference between the takings of the great wrestlers of old and the princely salaries of today's athletes.

If we consult Rossignol-Rollin's accounts, we find that in 1863 and 1864 at the time when the great impresario organized his marvelous competitions in Lyon, Saint-Étienne, and Clermont, he paid for every wrestling day the following.[48]

Bérenger	50 francs
Étienne "the Shepherd"	35 francs
Marseille the younger	45 francs
Alfred	24 francs
Creste	13 francs 75 centimes
Vincent	19 francs
Dumortier	16 francs 75 centimes
Milhomme	15 francs

These figures are curious when we compare what the great wrestlers of yesteryear earned with what the big names of contemporary wrestling earn; men like Hackenschmidt, Poddubny, Petersen, Zbyszko, Pons, and others.[49]

What Wrestling Shows Earned

It is equally interesting to compare the receipts of old-time wrestling shows with those of contemporary shows. While gross receipts at the Folies Bergère or at the Casino de Paris today sometimes rise to 15,000 or 20,000 francs, in Germany and Belgium to 10,000 and 15,000 francs, a gross receipt of 1,000 francs was once a huge success that could not be expected to happen twice in the same year.

In 1863 and 1864, Rossignol-Rollin gave twenty wrestling shows in Lyon, Saint-Étienne, and Clermont; these were on twenty Sundays and they were spaced far apart. The gross receipts for these twenty shows were 16,260.50 francs; the costs amounted to 14,235.75 francs so that during these two years Rossignol-Rollin's total profits amounted to 2,024.75 francs. It is good, moreover, to remark that Rossignol-Rollin never knew abundance. He was irrefutably honest, and he always paid all his people, but remained poor and died miserably in the arms of the brave Faouët who was the confidant and witness of his final suffering and sorrows.

Allow me to end this account with the story of Rossignol-Rollin's funeral

Rossignol-Rollin's Funeral

Rossignol-Rollin died on the twenty-fifth day of the month of January 1873 at Villeurbanne (a suburb of Lyon) as a result of incurable dropsy. A number of curious incidents happened on the day of his interment. When it came time to take up the body, Faouët "the Beast of the Jungle," Lagneau "the Terrible Left-hander," and Treuvé called "Bibus, the Butcher of Lyon," began arguing over who would have the supreme honor of carrying the much-loved director's coffin. A fight nearly ensued, and seeing this, the pallbearers from the funeral home were about to grab the casket. Then Lagneau the Terrible Left-hander, pushed them all aside with an imperious gesture, lifted the precious remains upon his own powerful shoulders and in this way very carefully descended the building's two floors. As he was doing so, his masculine and energetic face displayed to everyone the poignant sadness which gripped all of Rossignol's friends.

When the corpse was deposited on the bier, a new altercation developed; all the wrestlers present wanted to carry the remains of their venerated director at the same time. As they jostled, they almost caused the coffin to fall onto the sidewalk. Such sincerity is a touching demonstration of the attachment that united these brave men to their old impresario!

It took the energetic intervention of the funeral director to set things right. He himself designated the four biggest men to carry the body. These were Faouët the Beast of the Jungle; Auguste the Sailor (known as "the Terror of the Fleet"); Ambroise "the Savoyard"; and Treuvé called Bibus, the Butcher of Lyon.

Just when it came time to lower the body of this friend of giants and strongmen into the freshly dug grave, Auguste the Sailor wanted to say a few words of farewell to Rossignol-Rollin in the name of all the wrestlers who had loved him so much. Unfortunately, his voice was so racked by sobs that he could barely articulate a few incoherent syllables over the open grave of the man who was the most beloved and the most honest of carnival managers.

Exbroyat

We possess very little information on [Jean] Exbroyat [1798–1872] who died in Villeurbanne, near Lyon around 1868.[50] Yet many old folks in Lyon still speak of "Broyasse," as they had nicknamed him following his famous encounter in America with a Negro whose head he crushed with his hands.

Here is this anecdote as it is told by the old wrestlers of Lyon who are survivors of the troupe. Let us remark that Lyon is on the Marseille circuit.

One day a Negro whose name no one remembers issued a challenge to Exbroyat, and he accepted the challenge. The match took place in a circus in New York. The combat was most eventful; the Negro showed a vigor and a resistance that Broyasse did not expect. Suddenly, the Negro embraced the body of his adversary with his gnarled arms in a front waistlock and in this terrible embrace cracked three ribs. Broyasse was in a lamentable state when he was carried out of the arena. We must believe that this fracture was not serious, because he recovered soon. In turn, he launched a challenge to the Negro that he posted on all the walls of New York. The

Negro accepted the gauntlet. The match took place in the same establishment in front of an even larger crowd.

As soon as they were in the ring, Exbroyat, handed an apple to the Negro, and said to him, "Eat this apple; it's the last you will taste in your life!" Believing it to be a joke, the Negro took the apple with good grace and proceeded to eat it. But Broyasse did not give him the time. He immediately sprang at him, seized his head between his hands, crossed his fingers to give himself more strength, and with a terrible pressure crushed the Negro's head between his powerful hands. The brains squirted all the way up to the circus tent. Broyasse was in no way worried. At this time a Negro's life was not worth much—if Broyasse actually killed the Negro at all.[51]

Exbroyat's chest was studded with medals. He was a member of the Rhone Lifeguards Society.[52]

Jean Exbroyat is given credit for codifying the rules of flat-hand wrestling and for inventing the "baraque" system of fairground wrestling.

The following wrestlers comprised his troupe. Rivoire of Villefontaine; Pichat "the Amiable of Lyon"; Arpin "the Terrible Savoyard"; Meissonnier of Nimes; Charles de Ronville of Paris; Belarbre of Beaucaire; Blasse of Toulon; Raphael of Porte Neuve; Marseille the elder of Lapalud; Cartere of Saint-Étienne; Jean of Vaise; Joux of Givors; Tonio of Vernaison; Rosier of Lyon; Deschamps, "the forequarters Porter"; Cadet-Lange of Rive de Gier; Rabasson of the South; Vincent "the Iron Man"; Bonnet "the Ox of the Alps"; Laroche of the Lower Charente; Masson of Paris; Jacquet of the Ricamarie; Anthèlme Baboula of Lyon; Plantevin of Carpentras; Mathieu of the Loire; Blanchard of Lyon; Duplamut of Brotteaux; Batia of Givors; Olivier of Lyon; Loubet of Nimes; Fafon "the Rampart of the Croix-Rousse"; Maritemp of Vienne; Wolff of Luxembourg; Creste "the Bull of Provence"; Dubois of Paris; Alfred "the Parisian Model"; Quintois "the Stone Cutter"; Jaberjon of Lyon; Quiquine of Avignon; James "the Terrible Negro of Jamaica"; Peillon of Arbresle; J. Dumortier "the Agile Lyon Man"; Tamiot of Avignon; Rousset of Creusot; Lacroix "Good Heart"; Deligne of Dijon; and Milhomme of Bordeaux.

In spite of his courage and prodigious strength, it must be admitted that he possessed only a simple soul. One day the audience was surprised not to see one of their favorite wrestlers. "Gentlemen," announced the improvised stage manager, "Mr. Patte cannot come and participate, on account of his trunks are not clean."

Here is another example of a phrase that is no less authentic. "Gentlemen, Mr. Vulpillat, hurt his ears, but he offers to postpone his revenge until next Sunday."

Another time, speaking to an audience that was a bit irritated by the wait. "Gentlemen, please have patience for just a little longer. Mr. Razzle-Dazzle has gone to get dressed." In wrestling slang, "to get dressed" means to get undressed.

A singular peculiarity can explain the prodigious strength of Exbroyat. There are, it is said, men who have extra muscles. From there comes the popular expression "to have double muscles."[53] Very often these individuals only have a bone insertion, and the other end of the muscle is inserted into a neighboring aponeurosis. But nature, which usually does things right, always attaches to this pretty gift a means of using it. I was told by an old native of Lyon named Chirpaz that the famous Exbroyat had so-called "long back" muscles that were doubled. This same Lyonnais assured me that Broyasse, at a time when he unloaded boats, had carried on his back the extraordinary weight of 500 kilos while walking on the footbridge extending from the barge to the bank and all this despite the inevitable swaying of this narrow track, a track made up of a beam that was only 40 or 45 centimeters in width. He did it on a bet, and he won it. The fact was confirmed to me by another Lyonnais, a former silk worker, Mr. Français.

It is largely thanks to Exbroyat that we owe the renaissance of the sport of wrestling in France.

Béranger "the Parisian Model"

Béranger of Saint-Étienne, the Parisian Model, was a colossus who was more than 1 meter 80 in height. He was a rather handsome fellow; he had a prominent nose, fine teeth, hair on his temples, and looked like he might be an example of a Parisian living in the one of the city's inner neighborhoods. His shoulders were very wide, his legs admirably formed and above all, he had very strong and muscular arms. He was a remarkable weight lifter and was rightly considered one of the best athletes of his time. For example, he jumped over six chairs placed in a row one after another a little more than a meter from each other, each time performing a double arm extension with two 20-kilo weights. It was a unique feat that many of his comrades tried to imitate, but none of them could do it.

For a long time Béranger was part of the Rossignol-Rollin troupe. He was not a technically knowledgeable wrestler, but his weight, his height, and his strength allowed him to compete with any adversary. This is how he withstood superb battles against Garelli, the Genoese colossus, a giant who was 2 meters tall and who weighed 260 pounds! And against Lacroix of Lyon. This Lacroix caused the people of Lyon and the surrounding area to rush to see him every time he appeared in the arena. He had courage and an exceptional constitution; he possessed enormous arms and legs, a wide chest that was extraordinarily developed and a formidable neck. He had a wide, long, fan-shaped beard which made him look fierce. He was also part of the Rossignol troupe for a very long time. He and Béranger were good friends, but one day in Bordeaux during a card game they got angry and almost came to blows. Their director, who knew his business, took advantage of this temporary animosity to have them fight together a few days later. This was a "genuine" fight the likes of which one does not often see. Despite fierce resistance, Béranger had to bow to the knowledge and experience of his opponent and was pressed down on both his shoulders in the second round.

Handsome Béranger prepares to fight with his friend Lacroix of Lyon. Béranger had wide shoulders and "very strong and muscular arms." Even so, he lost to Lacroix.

He was more fortunate in his bout with Garelli, a veritable giant who was taller by a full head than our Béranger.[54] The fight was long and handling such a heavy adversary made it seem toward the end that Béranger might end up succumbing to exhaustion; nevertheless, gathering his last bit of strength, he succeeded in triumphing with a magnificent head over hip move. Béranger had a rather jovial character and took life as it came, and when he suffered a setback, he was not too upset. "Trees fall," he said, "and they do not get up, but me, if I fall, I get back up faster than if I had not even lain down."

One evening in Bordeaux just when he was entering the stage to wrestle with Lacroix, another wrestler named Garaô "the Water Seller," stood before the audience and asked to wrestle with one of his men. Rossignol-Rollin wanted to ignore him, but the public, who knew Garaô well, did not see it that way and they made such a racket that he had to give him satisfaction. Garaô did not choose between Lacroix and Béranger, and it was fate that designated the latter as having to take up the challenge of the "Water Seller." Garaô was no more than 1 meter 54 tall, but he was very heavy set, with huge arms and legs, a broad, hairy chest, and a very strong neck. He was known as the Water Seller or "the King of the Arm Roll." It was Rossignol who, as usual, introduced the two athletes.

"Gentlemen, I ask you to be as you always are, that is to say absolutely impartial and not to cheer more for one than for the other for the reason that they are both professionals. In order to give a greater appeal to their match, I will deposit into the hands of the public 100 francs, which will be given to the Water Seller if he wins over Béranger." Then turning toward the two athletes, he said to them, "Begin."

Pale but resolute, Béranger held out his large hand to Garaô and warily began. The Water Seller, quick as a snake, began his usual game, attacking from right and left, in continual feints, trying to irritate Béranger into making a countermove. But Béranger was aware of this and lost none of his composure, for his part also parrying and waiting for an opportunity. Garaô was the first to make a move and, rushing at Béranger he tried to do an arm roll, but this did not work at all because Béranger had quickly withdrawn his arm; as a consequence, the attacker tumbled headfirst over the edge of the ring. Taking his time, Béranger returned to the on-guard position and waited. Despite being a little dizzy, Garaô quickly got up and rushed at his adversary once again, whom he constantly harassed. Believing him to be a little tired, Béranger attacked more vigorously and finally crashed headlong into Garaô, who grabbed onto his arm to execute his favorite shot [the arm roll]. But Béranger was expecting this, and lifted his adversary to his full height by grabbing him under the armpits, he threw his two legs forward with his knees, and slammed him down violently on both shoulders. Garaô remained stunned by this terrible shock for a few moments, then with a bound, jumped up on his feet and shouted, "Good pin; he got me." And despite his defeat, he left amid loud applause. The amateur wrestlers of Bordeaux even took up a collection for him which brought in 150 francs.

Like many athletes of his era, Béranger did not lead an exemplary life. Excesses of all sorts shortened his career, which would have been long if he had maintained the fine health with which nature had endowed him. He died of tuberculosis at the age of thirty. He was buried temporarily in Saint-Étienne, but five years later when he was exhumed to be transported to a family vault, his remains were found to be intact, to such an extent that one might have thought he had died the day before.

Treuvé "Bibus, the Butcher of Lyon"

Treuvé, or Bibus, the Butcher of Lyon is one of the most famous survivors of the famous Rossignol-Rollin troupe. Treuvé was born in 1841 and he ended up being counted among the celebrities of his era such as Ambroise "the Savoyard"; Dumortier "the Agile Man from Lyon,"; Étienne "the Shepherd"; and Christol "the Coral

Fisher." In 1871 Faouët issued a challenge to all the wrestlers of Lyon. He even promised a prize of five francs per minute to whoever could remain standing in a match with him; it was understood that the timekeeper would deposit a five-franc coin in a hat placed at the edge of the ring for each elapsed minute. Treuvé accepted the challenge, and he remained standing for fifty-five minutes to the great amusement of the public, who noisily showed their satisfaction each time they saw a five-franc piece fall into the hat. Faouët, fuming with rage, had to abandon this game which would certainly have become ruinous for him.

Treuvé was a pupil of the famous Bernard the elder. He was 1 meter 72 in height and weighed 82 kilos when he was at the top of his form.

Treuvé was a strong and excellent wrestler, and many rivals learned to their cost that "Bibus" was not to be trifled with in the wrestling arena.

Dumortier "the Agile Man from Lyon"

[Jacques] Dumortier, nicknamed the Agile Man from Lyon, was born in Lyon as his name indicates. He was rather tall in stature (about 1 meter 75), slender, with curly and very full hair, and quite a handsome face; he was a wrestler endowed with a certain elegance. He was left-handed, and called his left fist "Papa Jacques." He had a very combative character, and he loved fighting, especially when he had a "little shot of syrup" in him. He was part of the Rossignol-Rollin troupe along with Vincent who was his great friend.[55]

He fought nearly all the wrestlers of the time and ended up very often the winner in the arena despite his relatively light weight (he was not quite 80 kilos). Aside from the daily fights that he undertook against his colleagues during the performances, fights that were naturally not very serious, he met in great bouts of genuine fighting with some wrestlers who never got the better of him. He thus had some exciting matches with Lefrein, Berger from Agen (whom he beat), and "the Terrible Shepherd" Étienne, before whom he succumbed only after a fierce fight.

Dumortier died in America in the prime of his life, the victim of alcoholic excess, which resulted in a horrible end with delirium tremens.

Marseille the Elder

Lapalud is a little village on the banks of the Rhone not far from Orange that has produced several famous men. Not in politics, it is true. In order to lie really well, one has to have the easy calm of those from the North. But if Lapalud was poor in ministers, it was rich in athletes, and among the most illustrious of those that

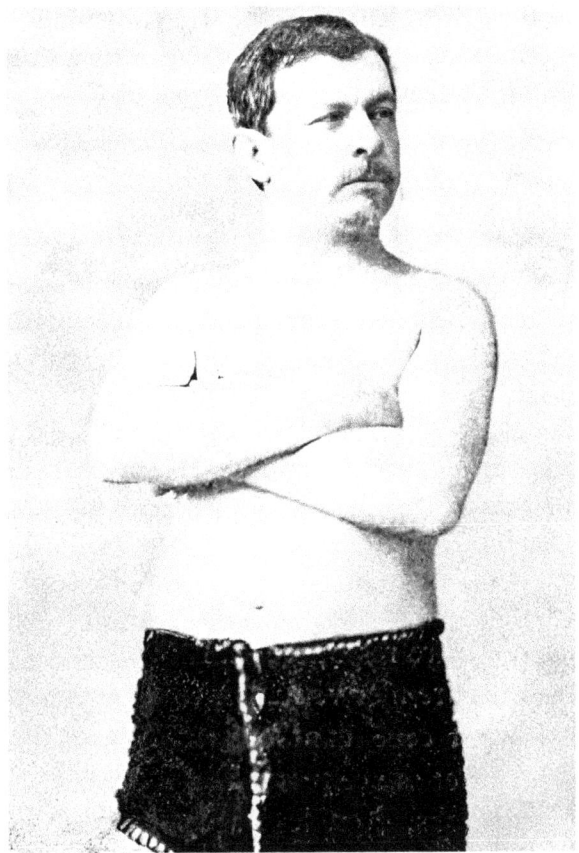

Feisty and short, Dumortier was especially combative when he had a "little shot of syrup" in him. He died in alcoholic misery in America.

Europe has ever seen in the previous century, one can cite [Henri] Marseille the elder [1821?–1897], this uncontested master of a career in which one rarely gets fat and never earns enough money to pay the taxes.

If Marseille had lived 2,000 years ago, the Greeks or Romans would certainly have erected a statue of him. And in our days if he had put on the costume of a gladiator, he could have been a model of physical beauty, and almost certainly more interesting than one of [Adolphe] Thiers or [Léon] Gambetta in a frock coat.[56] By erecting this statue on a granite plinth, France could certainly place its memories in a worse place, because this compatriot of [military hero, Louis] Crillon has demonstrated for many years, and in all countries, that the descendants of the Gauls are today still the strongest as they have always been the bravest. And Marseille the elder was not only a brave man; he was also an honest man—double qualities that are rare enough these days.[57]

Alas! This famous athlete died several years ago, having hardly any other resources in his old age than from time to time to offer up his octogenarian torso, bent by rheumatism, to the wrestling holds of the first comer. He had, however, retained almost until his final days his physical beauty and his agility. For he looked rather frail, not in the manner of our young snobs, whose English-style overcoats, long and narrow like dresses, greyish, yellowish, greenish, resemble those serge sheaths in which fencing masters carry their foils. But he was slender relative to most of his former adversaries like Creste, Étienne, Richoux, and Rivoire, whose shoulders invariably seemed so broad that they could only fit through double doors. In the fierce battles he so often fought chest to chest, skin to skin, where the bodies, entwined and confounded by the embrace, twisted like vines; where tense fingers sank into straining muscles; where arms were entrapped as if by pincers; where heads were crushed as if in a vise. Frequently, Marseille, would almost disappear under the masses of flesh, as he seemed to be crushed by the sheer weight of his adversaries, but it was he who, thanks to his prodigious skill, tossed these colossi weighing 300 pounds over his head or his shoulder. This is not even to mention the famous masked man (who was not Prince Napoleon, as had been claimed).[58]

However, at the time the arena on Rue Le Peletier was flourishing, our hero was almost an invalid by then because of age and injuries. He was approaching his fiftieth year; he had a dislocated knee, five or six useless fingers, and several broken ribs; but what could all that matter to this athlete whose heart was as impervious to fear as his muscles were insensitive to fatigue? His ribs had more or less healed, he was going to get back in the ring despite his knee when it was dislocated once again, and those fingers that remained to him were as strong as steel.[59] Even so, old as he was, he still made the others tremble before he utterly defeated them; we well knew that with him the game was always a battle, and the battle was never a game.[60] Only death could defeat this wrestler, and he had never been defeated.

It was almost sixty years ago when he first arrived in Paris; he left his mill (he had been a miller's apprentice) in order to fight Arpin the Terrible Savoyard, the famous wrestler whom everyone thought would never be defeated since he seemed invincible. This was so certain that every Parisian in the know at that time came to the Montesquieu Hall to see the foolhardy young man who dared to fight the colossus of Savoy. We can read in *l'Illustration* from the year 1852 the account of that memorable day when the two champions met one another. I know of no better way to tell the story than to reproduce the article in its entirety.[61]

> Twenty-year-old Marseille is slender, supple, wiry, and beardless. Arpin is at the height of his strength; he looks like a Titan. He finds it difficult to control his laughter. Is this adolescent really serious about challenging him? He will send him back to his wetnurse in no time at all. It is as if a huge bull sees a little cat and offers to fight him. But then the fight begins.
>
> The Hercules discovers in the first holds that the child is a man, and a man who knows how to wrestle. Even so, he grabs the young man; one would think he was going to crush him; he gives him a tremendous jolt; an oak would have been uprooted; the mill might stand its ground, but the miller slips away and escapes from the embrace however powerful it may be. The crowd roars loudly.
>
> The maneuvers multiply; hip locks move to headlocks, shoulder locks revert to hip locks. Thirty-five minutes have elapsed. Arpin is drenched in sweat, and he no longer considers

laughing. Marseille is dry, and he is smiling. The two adversaries release one another simultaneously. They catch their breath for a moment, and then they pull themselves together. This time it is Marseilles who attacks; the cat is astounding the terrified bull with his incredible audacity. Eight minutes later, the titan touches his two shoulders to the floor. The arena erupts in frenetic applause.

The English give their boxers funerals fit for kings; we do not ask that boxers should be treated like kings of wrestling, but more than ever we need to encourage strength. Numbers are evermore against us, but strength can overcome numbers.

Marseille had a brother [Jean-Baptiste] who was called "the Lion of Lapalud," and he is the father of those two Mar-

The Marseille Brothers were both strong and ambitious. Elder brother Henri (left) had become legendary after he defeated Arpin in 1852, and Jean-Baptiste eventually became the most famous and prosperous of *baraque* owners.

seille brothers who have a fair booth at the Neuilly Fair, the Trône Fair, and others.[62] On the front of their fairground booth, they still display a painting on canvas that absolutely represents the portraits of the two famous Marseille brothers, "the Miller" and the Lion of Lapalud, in a standing wrestling pose.

One final anecdote about Marseille. The Miller of Lapalud was introducing his wrestlers at the Neuilly Fair and was trying to get the passersby to come and wrestle because he did not need to resort to using accomplices to fight against his colleagues. "Who will claim the trunks?" shouted Marseille. Poet and playwright Joseph Glatigny (1839–1873) accepted the challenge. Since Glatigny had a tall and thin physique and an appearance so unlike a wrestler, Marseille was alarmed to be confronted by a man like that because certainly this person who dared to accept the challenge looking like he did must have something up his sleeve. All the same, the famous showman wanted to get the better of the unexpected adversary. He braced himself with all his strength and threw himself on Glatigny whom he lifted like a feather and laid him on the ground with an ease that even he himself could not believe. Then, quite solemnly Glatigny announced, "Ladies and Gentlemen, I will not hide from you that this gentleman is much stronger than I." The public doubled over in laughter, but Marseille had been unnerved.

André Christol, known as "the Little Hunter"

André Christol [1846–1908?] was a very fine wrestler, similar to Lacaze known as "Pietro II," whom he resembled a little. He had his hour of fame around twenty years ago and was part of the Rossignol-Rollin troupe. Soon after, he left for America where he triumphed under the pseudonym of André Christol André. His real name is unknown to us.[63]

Juge, known as "Sunshine of Lyon"

Juge, called "Beau Soleil" [Sunshine] of Lyon was also a wrestler in the Rossignol-Rollin troupe, as we can see from his photograph, there was nothing really remarkable about him from the athletic point of view. He was fat and rotund, and he did not give the impression of having great strength.

André Christol made a name for himself in America and Australia where he was a popular wrestler (collection of Michael Murphy).

Toby

Toby took part as a wrestler in the troupe of Pietro Dalmasso whose brother-in-law he was at that time. He had a share of success about twenty years ago. He died around 1900.

Left: The wrestler Juge was described as round, fat, and unimpressive. **Right:** Toby was the boss's brother-in-law, and he was unremarkable as a wrestler.

Bonnet "the Ox of the Alps"

Bonnet, known as the Ox of the Alps, was born in 1830 and was a mountain dweller endowed with a strength that was without equal, and he possessed a remarkable suppleness despite his titanic proportions. He measured 1 meter 88 in height, and he weighed 130 kilos. He was big and thick but well proportioned. He was a very skilled wrestler. He was honest and good; he never sought to harm his adversaries and avoided all the blows that might have presented any danger for the one with whom he was wrestling. Rossignol-Rollin had hired him as a heavyweight wrestler. He fought with all the most famous men of the era: Arpin the Terrible Savoyard; Bernard; Pujol; Vincent the Iron Man; Dumortier; Lacroix; de Lyon; Richoux the Rifleman of Bugey; Étienne "the Shepherd," etc. He was not an easy man to defeat, and more than one champion had to admit that he was beaten by the Ox of the Alps. He took part in all of Rossignol-Rollin's tours as well as those of Coudol, another director from the same time period, and he often had some very good bouts.[64] Despite his good character, when he was not in a good mood, this had to be taken into account, because then (like Pujol) he became unbeatable.

His principal matches took place in the in the cities of the South of France, but he also toured in north and central France. The most remarkable of his matches was that with Garelli, the colossus of Genoa. Garelli was a giant who was 2 meters high and who could lift on his shoulders a weight of 1,000 kilos. It was Rossignol-Rollin who organized the match, and he was actually very curious to know who was the better wrestler. And realizing that the two athletes were very interested, he offered a superb gold ring as the prize for the victor. The match took place in Bordeaux. The two adversaries offered a striking contrast: Garelli was taller, thinner but more muscular. He had a dark complexion with skin that was nearly the color of bronze; he was a superb example of the race of the south. Bonnet was not as tall, but he had wider shoulders, and with his enormous chest, his bull's neck, his incomparable arms and legs, and his skin that was as white as milk, he looked like an imposing and majestic representative of the ideal man of the north. Both men radiated strength and confidence. The winner was Bonnet the Ox.

Bonnet the Ox traveled a good deal, especially in Belgium. He appeared in fairs at the booth of Rabasson, a French wrestler who was for his weight a man of the first rank whose strength and agility were unsurpassed. Bonnet wrestled until he was seventy years old; he died around 1900 on the Isles of Hyères where he was a caretaker.[65] He was a fine man who was honest and good, and he achieved a well-deserved success, even in Germany and in Russia where the Rigal Brothers took him on their tours.[66]

The Ox of the Alps, Bonnet was pale but muscular, and he made a great impression when he wrestled with olive-complected Garelli.

A Student of Arpin—Lacaisse

Lacaisse was a student of the famous Arpin. He debuted in 1862 on the Place Maubert for Bertrand, director of wrestling in the fairs.[67] At the time, he was eighteen years old. Slender, lithe, and having surprising agility, he united these qualities to an uncommon muscular strength. At twenty-four years he did an arm extension with 25-kilo weights. Unscrupulous in his choice of methods to fight an adversary, he was as dreaded as he was dreadful.

In 1866, Eugène Paz organized a large wrestling tournament in his gymnasium at 34 Rue des Martyrs. The names of the greatest French champions of the era appeared on the poster. We recall that at the first show, Deligne and Lacaisse wrestled together and just as they were ready to enter the arena, Crest, the manager of the matches, told the latter to let himself be defeated, and Deligne would lose the next time. Lacaisse bluntly refused to lend himself to any deal settled in advance, adding that he would rather be defeated legitimately many times than to take a fall to an opponent even once in a faked fight. The two rivals had barely begun when Deligne put his adversary's head in a stranglehold; in order to make him let go, Lacaisse put his fingers in his opponent's eyes. The second round was in all respects similar to the first and Paz had to intervene. In the third round Deligne got his opponent in another stranglehold, but this time Lacaisse poked his fingers in the man's eyes hard, and Deligne let go and left the arena. Since a stranglehold is not admitted in a legitimate fight, the wrestler actually has the right to use any means at his disposal to get out of it.[68]

Joseph Arpin demonstrates a unique headlock on his pupil Lacaisse. The student later became a mighty fighter and was known as "the Wrestler of Steel."

Not long afterward, Lacaisse was seeded among the top champions of wrestling and he was nicknamed "the Wrestler of Steel," because he defeated the terrible Boulanger every time he wrestled with him. Lacaisse later became an impresario for the Folies Bergère, and he introduced Pietro [Dalmasso] in 1884, Tom Cannon in 1889, and the Turk Yusuf in 1895.[69]

Pujol "the Pillar of Porte-Neuve"

Pujol was a colossus weighing 120 kilos, measuring 1 meter 80 high, and endowed with an amazing strength. He was one of the handsomest men of his times.

He had curly chestnut hair that was long and which fell onto his shoulders. His face was virile and expressive with an enormous neck balanced atop two very wide shoulders. His gait was slow and proud, and his gaze was assured; all of this made him resemble a lion. We can cite several feats that testify to his phenomenal strength. Here are a few of the many:

Pujol did his national service in the navy as a gunner's assistant. One day when they had a review by the admiral, Pujol performed a "present arms" with a small cannon just as the officer was passing in front of him.[70] The admiral was amazed at seeing such prodigious strength, and he had Pujol step out of the ranks where he congratulated our hero warmly.

Pujol lifted enormous weights on his broad shoulders, and he hardly seemed to notice them. The piece that he preferred lifting most was a ship's anchor weighing 400 kilos. Because of its shape, this anchor was an extremely unwieldy burden. Here is how he lifted it. He had the anchor placed on two trestles between which Pujol placed a thick pad for his shoulders. He lifted the weight, made a half turn, and replaced it on the opposite side from where he had taken it.

Pujol wrestled a long time under the direction of Rossignol-Rollin and Coudol, and he fought with all the celebrities of the mat.

Pujol was strong and he used this trait to his advantage in the wrestling arena. Desbonnet claims that he was "the handsomest man of his time."

He did not invest too much egotism into these matches, but when he did not want to be defeated, he was a veritable Rock of Gibraltar, and the champions never managed to touch his shoulders to the floor. He was not a refined wrestler, but he substituted science for strength and weight. He often wrestled with Bonnet "the Ox of the Alps," and when they both arrived majestically in the arena, Rossignol-Rollin sounded out a call to arms, and made sure that the audience realized that this was no joke. It was a truly imposing spectacle to see these two examples of Hercules Farnese as they walked in, looking like living statues as they prepared to confront one another in Olympic wrestling.

The most memorable of his bouts were those that he had against the Ox of the

Alps in the arena in the Rue Saint-Sernin in Bordeaux. They remained there for three days without being able to claim a clear victory over each other, even though they wrestled for an hour at each session.

Pujol also fought with Creste "the Bull of Provence," who weighed 130 kilos and who had been the victor in several wrestling tournaments in Nimes. Creste, who joined the Rossignol-Rollin troupe, had an argument about a card game in a café with Pujol. The argument degenerated into a fight and the two athletes could only be separated after a great deal of trouble. Eight days later, after Pujol requested it, Rossignol-Rollin let the two men wrestle together and offered a superb watch as a prize to the victor. This match was not to be done in a "scientific" way; it was to be a bullfight where strength would dominate over skill. As soon as the two men shook hands, they threw themselves at one another, shoving and shouldering each another savagely. Creste was heavier, but he was smaller and could do little more than defend himself when he encountered the strength of his adversary. So, despite his weight and his experience, he was brought down by a superb front waistlock with his arms pinioned. He was lifted from the ground, and he fell backward in a heap, crushed under the weight of Pujol.

Pujol died in Marseilles at the age of seventy-eight where he was a dock worker.

Catin of Lyon

The photograph that illustrates this brief report represents an athlete named Catin of Lyon from the Rossignol-Rollin troupe. Catin is the person who is shown with a pipe in his mouth and a cap on his head at the top of the image. This is the only photograph that we have been able to find of this athlete. Like many other athletes in the Rossignol-Rollin troupe, he was a wrestler and a weight lifter, but unfortunately it has been impossible to get a precise measure of his strength

The man in the center with the pipe is Catin of Lyon. He had powerful muscles, but it is difficult to know just how strong he was. The other two men are unidentified.

Bernard Mangelle, "Old Bernard"

Bernard Mangelle was born in 1820 in Sarniguet, 10 kilometers from Tarbes.[71] He was quite well-known in his day (as later was his son, Félix Bernard), and he became one of the most ferocious wrestlers in the Rossignol-Rollin group. Old Bernard was a "street fighter" who was fierce and loyal but very brutal as often wrestlers are who do not like fakery. He retained the title of champion for many years, but Faouët "the Wild Beast of the Jungle," won this title from him, which had so justly been earned in a famous tournament. He wrestled up until the age of sixty-seven years, fearing nothing, not even the end of his life. He was forever jostling for first place among younger wrestlers who were then in fashion. The number of his years had no effect on his intrepidity or his endurance. His long career was full of sensational wrestling matches.

In 1874 Étienne "the Shepherd," from Bourg St. Andéol, was jealous of Old Bernard's laurels, so he issued a challenge that put the man's honor at stake. Bernard had heard a great deal about the strength and dexterity of the Shepherd of St. Andéol, who went through life with his head adorned with his legendary cap on which was written in gilded letters the following inscription:

> *Étienne the Shepherd, The King of Wrestlers*
> *I offer 500 francs to the one who defeats me.*

However, confident in his experience and courage, Old Bernard took up the challenge. He was at that time fifty-four years old. Even so, this match did not fail to worry him a bit—so much so that he said to his friends, "There's a young man who is very strong, and if I do not take him down at the start, I will be the one to be taken down."

The match took place in Bordeaux at the Louis Theater, which was at the time the largest establishment in the city and could seat more than 3,000 persons.[72] In the event, the hall was packed and it was necessary to turn away 2,000 people.

The fight proved to be very thrilling; for a few minutes Old Bernard put his adversary in danger, but after seventeen minutes, the Shepherd beat him in a manner that was indisputable. Old Bernard's take-down was unfortunate in another way, for in falling he tore the muscles of his shoulder. But the public did not realize the accident that had occurred during the fight and made a terrible uproar because they did not want to accept the defeat of brave Old Bernard. They were so insistent that Bernard had to resume the fight despite his injury; in the end, he let himself fall without defending himself.

Another time at the Bordeaux Fair he had an adventure that was greatly discussed. Old Bernard had erected his booth on the Place des Quinconces.[73] One

The Fair on the Place des Quinconces in Bordeaux was the location of Old Bernard's wrestling booth. It was also the scene of a brutal and bloody fight between the wrestler and a cocky sailor.

evening he was shouting out his usual spiel, and he ended it by asking if there might be any in the audience, apart from wrestling amateurs, who would like to participate in the fights with the cane, baton, fencing foil, saber, and English or French boxing—which were at the time, classic sports in the wrestling booths. At that very moment a group of sailors who had just come ashore gathered in front of the booth. One of them asked confidently for a challenge glove for English boxing and French kickboxing. "Whom do you want to fight with?" asked Old Bernard.

"With you!" replied the sailor.

"That's fine, my friend. Come forward. Here's a glove." All of his comrades followed him into the interior of the booth, not without a bit of eager pushing. The show began with weight lifting, and then came the wrestling, but the English boxing and the kickboxing, that is what everyone wanted to see. Old Bernard cared very little about the fight, and he was even less enthusiastic since he was completely ignorant of this kind of sport. If he had advertised boxing and *savate* (French boxing) to the audience on the outside, it was only because he wanted to attract as many people as possible into the interior and not to box someone in person. Old Bernard whispered into the young sailor's ear, "This will have to wait until the next show. As you can see, the program is already a bit long."

The sailor would hear nothing of it. He parked himself in the middle of the arena and declared, "You have given me a glove so that I can have a bout of boxing and *savate*. I want to have the fight that you promised me!" And the whole group encouraged the recalcitrant seaman not to leave the arena without boxing. Old Bernard understood that the sailors would be stubborn and that it was better to comply than to cause an inevitable scandal.

"All right! That's fine with me," he said, "Let's hurry up. Let's begin!"

As soon as the sailor made the traditional salute and then brilliantly executed a demonstration of the first position with a grace and agility, he won hearty applause from the audience. Of course, his partner did not give him a proper response to the second position for the very good reason that he did not have the slightest idea of what he was doing. Every time the sailor raised his foot to deliver a kick to the body or the face, he let it be seen that the soles of his shoes were studded with large pointed hobnails. Old Bernard sensibly pointed this out to him and he added, "You have a pair of shoes with which you can injure me; take them off and I will give you a pair of court shoes instead."[74]

"No! No!" shouted the sailor's team in a chorus. "Don't take off your shoes!"

"Fine. Keep them on. I am not afraid of him because of that," replied Old Bernard. And the match began immediately. As soon as the sailor had readied himself, he launched a hail of punches and kicks at his hapless adversary, which the unfortunate man seemed to respond to quite badly—very badly—since his entire role in this unequal assault was limited to dodging blows as well as possible and to assuming the most prudent defenses. After a short while, poor Old Bernard's arms were flowing with blood after all the pummeling given him by the cleated shoes of the dishonorable sailor.

The audience wanted to end this savage fight, but Old Bernard himself refused to do so. Maddened with anger and pain, foaming and covered with blood, he was a terrible sight to see. It was like a fight between a tiger and a bull. In the end Bernard gathered his strength, rushed at his adversary, and dealt him such a terrible blow on the head that the sailor rolled unconscious in the middle of the bloodstained arena.

This fall was the signal for a general melee with the sailor's group taking the side of the brutal seaman (who had only been dazed) and the audience defending Old Bernard. Without the intervention of the police, the scuffle would have ended up taking unfortunate proportions, but everything was limited to exchanging a few nonlethal punches.

Well, it was just a little family misunderstanding.

Old Bernard's last wrestling match took place in 1887. At the age of sixty-seven, Bernard had a match with the Negro Abdullah at the Landaise Arena in Bordeaux. It was a true triumph for him, and the ticket receipts rose to 4,500 francs. A four-way partnership formed that was made up of Old Bernard, Abdullah, Mangematin, and Paul "the Miller." The winner of the partnership would win a bull owned by Old Bernard or 500 francs. Of course, it was Bernard who won the prize.

Old Bernard was one of those rare wrestlers who never experienced poverty. He died at his home in Sarniguet on January 20, 1893, at the age of seventy-three.[75] His house still features a gate that is crowned with a representation of an athlete wrestling a lion. He was an excellent wrestler and an honest director, and all his former employees sincerely miss him.

Milhomme, "Pitiless"

Milhomme was one of the handsomest wrestlers from Bordeaux. As a student of Old Bernard, he was known by the name of Milhomme "Pitiless." It was he who devised the "side waist hold." The first time that he visited Paris was in 1864 when he appeared in the Trône Fair along with Old Bernard and Emile Jentien "the Spaniard," and he had put up a poster on his booth with the following notice:

> ON YOUR FEET, PARISIANS!
> The Girondins Are at Your Gates![76]

Although he had fought with François le Rouget, Lacaisse (the Man of Steel), with Alfred (the Parisian Model) and others, Milhomme had never been defeated. He would die quite young in 1876. Among the various adventures that marked the life of Milhomme, here is one of the most interesting.

In 1875, he was working in a vast booth on the Place des Quinconces in Bordeaux; there were also many impressive athletes like Faouët who were defeated when it was their turn, or pitilessly defeating a few amateurs who were as strong as they were inexperienced. At one of the shows the famous mime Marcellin (who had studied with [Paul] Legrand, [Jean-Gaspard] Deburau, and Rouff) was present. Marcellin shouted the word "faked" while the wrestlers increased their antics as they performed on a carpet laid over a thick layer of sawdust. Milhomme found this exclamation not to be to his liking, and that same evening, he went to the Alcazar where Marcellin was performing. During the pantomime, Milhomme called out some offensive words and some inopportune whistles so often that the famous Pierrot lost his temper and publicly challenged the unwelcome spectator by inviting him to meet him at the artist's entrance after the performance. A half hour later, the two adversaries, accompanied by a crowd of friends and curiosity seekers, came together a short distance away on the Avenue de Paris in a remote place and faced each other.

Right at the start of the fight, Marcellin jumped forward and planted his two feet on Milhomme's torso, which greatly startled him. Before the wrestler recovered from his surprise, the mime kicked him in the side and flattened him on the ground. Milhomme, however, got up and rushed at Marcellin with outstretched arms to seize and crush him, but Marcellin dodged the holds and redoubled his acrobatics with kicks to the shins, to the flanks, to the chest, and in the face. It was for real and not faked. Milhomme had to be taken home in a carriage.

Several days later in front of the booth of this selfsame Milhomme, a young artilleryman who was admirably built accepted the trunks that were thrown by the barker, and he entered the arena. Milhomme saw at once that he would have to deal with an aggressive fellow. Without losing time with a lot of extravagant moves, he went right after the artilleryman with great forcefulness and little "fakery"—so much so that the unlucky sometime-wrestler had his spinal column broken and died on the spot. The indignant crowd demolished the booth, reducing it to shreds and setting fire to what was left. When the crowd in its turn gets angry, it is not faked; it is for real.

Rabasson "the Little Peasant"

Rabasson [1824?–1854] was a native of the Pyrenees, and he was a man of short stature (1 meter 54), and he has very wide (though sloping) shoulders, very long arms, and although he hardly weighed 75 kilos, he had an incomparable strength and agility.[77] In a region famous for its foot races and its jumping contests, he was the best in these two sports. As a wrestler, he was a master, and in his day he justly held the title of "King of Wrestlers." He must have surprised the audiences in every place he visited—even in Paris where he competed with the strongest and most adept athletes, he always emerged victorious. This is how at the Montesquieu Hall he took down the famous Rivoire "the Cannon Man," who weighed 130 kilos and who was considered the strongest man of his time. He also beat the famous Spanish wrestler Blas as well as all the wrestlers who dared to compete against him. Unfortunately, while wrestling against men of huge stature and whose weight was infinitely superior to his own, he exerted such effort that he contracted a hernia, which must have bothered him considerably from then on.

At one point he heard that there were to be great wrestling tournaments presented at Bordeaux that would be under the direction of Auguste (Rossignol-Rollin's predecessor) and Coudol.

The only known image of Rabasson is this rather crude cartoon from the humor magazine *Le Journal pour Rire*, 3 July 1852. It purports to show Rabasson taking down Arpin.

Rabasson went to this city and found that the circus in the Rue Saint-Sernin had advertised, *Old Bernard, "The King of Wrestlers."* Rabasson went to find Auguste, the director, and complained to him for giving Bernard his own title. Auguste tried to make him understand that this was a matter of advertising, that the receipts depended on it and that Bernard was the best-known wrestler in the region. Rabasson then asked to wrestle with Bernard, and this was agreed to.

When the match between these two men was announced, the price of for the seats was doubled, but spectators still flocked to the arena to such an extent that it is said that it was necessary to turn away more than 4,000 people. It was therefore before a packed arena that the two men fought for the famous title.

The wrestling was extremely heated and very active; actually, at that time if a fighter were knocked down, he did not have the right to remain on the floor for more than a minute before being declared the loser. The only style was upright "Olympic wrestling," which the Greeks called perpendicular wrestling—and, by the way, it would perhaps be desirable that we return nowadays to this custom which would very rightly favor technique to the detriment of weight. Be that as it may, Bernard was thrown to the ground, and he wanted to get up immediately, but Rabasson grabbed him by the waist from behind in a move that he himself had invented and pinned him on both shoulders.

After Bernard had his title taken from him, he announced that his revenge would take place the next day, and Rabasson accepted. He was asked if his hernia did not bother him and if it might be better to wait two more days after such an effort, but the brave athlete replied that he had no objections to make. However, two days previously, while trying to carry Rivoire's cannon, he had hurt himself so badly that his hernia had emerged again.

The second match therefore took place on the very next day, before an audience that was even larger. After more than half an hour of wrestling during which the adversaries showed proof of an equal knowledge and courage, once again Bernard found himself on the floor and Rabasson tried another reverse waistlock. But forewarned by his misadventure of the previous day, Bernard put up great resistance to the move, so much so that Rabasson, not wanting to let go of his grip, had to make a terrible effort to lift Bernard up and throw him on both shoulders. But Rabasson immediately sank down with a groan and collapsed almost unconscious; his hernia had bulged out, and it was now strangulated.

Rabasson was taken to his residence, but at that time, surgery was poorly equipped against accidents of this kind, and the unfortunate Rabasson died eight days later as a result of this strangulation of the hernia. It was a sad end for this excellent and courageous wrestler whose weak point was his light weight, but it had not prevented him from defeating the heaviest of men. Rabasson was barely thirty years old.[78]

Bergez "the Indomitable Agenais"

Bergez was a native of Agen, a town where everyone loves wrestling as well as all athletic sports.[79] He had two brothers equally gifted with strength and agility, but they both perished in a brawl; the first was stabbed in the chest with a knife, and the second was thrown into the Garonne River and drowned.

Bergez was of medium height but very stocky. He had a neck like a bull, arms that were short and enormous, a chest that was hairy and barrel-shaped, very strong thighs, and very muscular calves. He started wrestling early in the fairs around Agen, and from the age of eighteen, he began to acquire a reputation (especially in wrestling and weight lifting) that only grew with the years. He soon succeeded in getting a little fair booth in which he performed in the surrounding area. He operated this concession with several friends, in particular with Gaspard "Little Lacoque" from Toulouse, and a very good wrestler named Garibaldi.

One day he went to Bordeaux with the company he was working with, and there he joined forces with a wrestler named Lagriffe; Bergez was so successful that he was hired by Old Bernard, and after his stint with Bernard, he was employed by Milhomme and Ricard. He then undertook great wrestling matches against Milhomme, Dumortier, Émile the Spaniard, and others. After this, Bergez ventured on his own with a booth, making the rounds of the fairs in Bordeaux; he then traveled around the neighborhood of Agen and Toulouse. The little company of which he was the principal actor could be found at all the fairs. At the same time that he was wrestling, he also lifted weights. Toward the end he featured a bear who wrestled with amateurs, and he even pitted it against dogs in a spectacle that was quite popular in certain regions.[80]

Probably following the custom of most carnival athletes of that time, Bergez cut short his life with all sorts of overindulgences, and in particular with excessive alcohol. He died young and in poverty.

Ambroise "the False Arpin," also known as "Little Pip"

Ambroise Little Pip, was a man of tall stature (1 meter 80), who was very knotty and wizened with limbs that were very thin but muscular.[81] He had an enormous neck, shifty-looking blue-green eyes, sharp features, and a slow gait. In short, he was not well built; however, he had a Herculean strength and he was a good, tough wrestler. He had been a member of the famous Rossignol-Rollin troupe for a long time, and he was the most ferocious adversary of the champion of the troupe, Faouët "the Beast of the Jungle."

The two wrestlers wrestled each other in very hard-fought matches in Bordeaux eight times in a row in the same month. On these occasions Ambroise put up a resistance that the champion Faouët was not used to. Two times a draw had to be declared; it is true that Ambroise was defeated in the other six matches, but with such an adversary, a result of this sort would be anything but humiliating.

Ambroise Little Pip, also wrestled in sensational matches with Milhomme; Béranger "the Elegant Parisian"; Pujol "the Pillar of Porte-Neuve"; Bonnet "the Ox of the Alps"; and others. This man was comparable to Yusuf and could have become the best wrestler in France, but unfortunately, he did not have enough character to make his way in life, and while still young (he was not yet fifty years old) he died in darkest misery of exhaustion in the Bordeaux hospital.

Mathieu "the Colossus of the Loire"

Mathieu was a blacksmith by trade, and from a very early age he had worked in forges up and down the Loire Valley. He was known for his tall stature and his muscular strength. At the age of nineteen, he measured 1 meter 90, possessed a massive build, and already weighed more than 100 kilos. He had enormous, heavily muscled arms and legs.

One day he entered the wrestling booth at a fair in Saint-Étienne in order to measure his strength against the weights and barbells; after he had easily lifted all the fairground athletes' equipment, he wrestled in rigged matches. Considering his lack of familiarity with the specialized field of wrestling, it was obvious that he was extremely gifted and that he could have done much more had he been guided correctly. The booth where he had tried his hand belonged to an old wrestler named Coeur-de-roi [Royal Heart] who had broken his leg in an earlier bout and had been left with a limp as a result of that accident. Very cunning and very intelligent, Coeur-de-roi was an accomplished Barnum who knew his business exceedingly well. He kept Mathieu with him for a time, then he passed him on to the famous Rossignol-Rollin troupe, which was always eager to find exceptional men.

Rossignol-Rollin was a

Visual representations of early wrestlers were quite rare in the days before the easy transmission of photographs and engravings. This generic wrestler can stand in for the many hundreds of grapplers whose portraits we will never see.

practical man, and he had Mathieu exercise seriously, especially with weights. The young man then began to appear in the larger cities: Paris, Marseilles, Lyon, Bordeaux, Toulouse, etc. Each time that Mathieu's tour arrived, Rossignol-Rollin made a special announcement, saying, "Gentlemen, I introduce here a man who can be called 'The King of Human Strength.' I will give two thousand francs to whoever repeats one of the two feats which he will perform before you!"

The first of his feats consisted of lifting an enormous barbell with only one hand. At first, he lifted it in two stages, then after having allowed it to descend without letting it touch the ground, he snatched it up in a single movement; finally, he tossed it into his left hand. The second lift consisted of raising with one hand the end of a four-meter-long steel rod with a 1-kilo weight attached at the other end.

Mathieu remained for a very long time with the Rossignol-Rollin troupe, but he was very quarrelsome and often got into fights. Eventually, he tangled with his employer who finally sent him packing. Mathieu then organized a fair booth of his own. He teamed up with a woman unique in her field who lifted weights and barbells with him and even wrestled with occasional amateurs. She was called "Rouge" [Red], but she was never known by any other name but "Mathieu's Rouge." She had both the bearing and the physique of a man: tall, tightly muscled, strong, and hard as nails with reddish blotches all over her body and hands covered in warts.

At one point things got so difficult for Mathieu that he was forced to sell his canvas tents and even the carriage that allowed them to follow the fairs transporting his weights. He was then forced to walk with Rouge carrying two 20-kilo weights on a plank and with Mathieu following with the large barbell on his shoulders. It sounds incredible, but they were known to have journeyed to all the ancient fairs in southern France in this way. Mathieu and Rouge often walked 20 and 30 kilometers like this, going from place to place and from fair to fair. Mathieu had quite a number of additional adventures in his nomadic existence as a carnival performer.

Mathieu usually enjoyed making others fear his great strength; he consequently found himself embroiled in many dangerous quarrels. That is how he became associated with Deligne. One day, when the takings were good, he attempted to swindle his partner when the money was being divided up. When Deligne protested, Mathieu's only reply was to strike the man five or six times in the face with his fist, thereby doing him considerable injury. Deligne was nearly as good a fighter as Mathieu, and he fought back. The two men parted only after giving each other a thorough hammering. But that evening Mathieu was enjoying the company of Mr. John Barleycorn, and when he staggered back to his wagon, Deligne was waiting for him. The drubbing Mathieu received was truly magnificent, and he carried the marks of it for a long time afterward.[82]

Another time, in Agen, Mathieu tangled with a crowd of peasants who had drunk with him, and he ended up throwing about fifteen of them out the second-story window. All went well for him until one of the last people in the room, a young man of around eighteen to twenty years old, slashed his attacker twice with his knife. Mathieu was in the hospital for a month, but this did nothing to improve his disposition, and he began acting up again a little later in Blaye.

It was the feast day for the surrounding countryside, and Mathieu lifted his weights with Rouge on the main square. After two successive performances with what he considered to be unsatisfactory receipts, Mathieu began to berate the crowd. Then in the midst of the furor, he cold cocked three or four villagers. At first his adversaries said nothing, but a half hour later they returned with cudgels and commenced beating Matthieu and Rouge. Though at first surprised, Matthieu recovered quickly, as did Rouge, and the two of them fell upon their assailants. The police arrived, and separated the combatants, but made sure to throw Mathieu and Rouge in the calaboose where they remained for the night. The next day when they came to free the little birds from their cage, the authorities discovered that the two had already flown the coop. Mathieu had broken down the door by beating it with his shoulders and his fists!

Mathieu and Rouge traveled all over France with similar mishaps—sometimes on foot and sometimes in wagons, but always in very wretched circumstances. In fact, they did everything they possibly could to end up in this way. Part of the reason for his difficulties was that among his other qualities, Mathieu was a phenomenal drinker; he often downed more than ten liters of wine in half a day!

About twenty years ago Mathieu found an engagement as a weight lifter and wrestler in Bordeaux. He arrived about twelve days before his appearance, still accompanied by Rouge, and he asked for an advance of seventy-five francs. But the night before he was to make his debut neither Mathieu nor Rouge were to be found. They had both disappeared as if by magic, and since that time no one has heard a single word from them.[83]

Étienne Garnier "the Rock of the Loire"

Étienne Garnier was born in the Department of the Loire. He was the son of miners and had an exceptional constitution; he measured around 1 meter 70 was very muscular with a pleasant (some might say sweet) face and a neck that was remarkably developed. As a young man he did exercises to develop his strength and enjoyed handling heavy paving stones and masses of iron with his friends. Since he never had a teacher, he naturally showed more strength than skill, but he nevertheless acquired a great reputation in Saint-Étienne and the surrounding area. But one day some fairground entertainers passed through this town, and they were under the direction of a Spaniard named Pedro. The troupe included a remarkable athlete named Bainaize.

In accordance with custom, during the parade of athletes the director invited the amateurs of the town to compete with his men if they had the heart for it. Étienne's friends urged him to accept this offer, and although he was very modest, he had to accept. Pedro quickly sized up his stature and suggested that he go up against his champion Bainaize, but young Étienne thought that this would be a very difficult debut, and immediately declined this honor. Pedro complied with his request and consented to fight the young amateur himself. This Pedro was not a man to be discounted although he was light in weight, but despite his know-how, he had to yield to Étienne. But perhaps in this circumstance Pedro put his interests as a manager ahead of his pride as a wrestler; because the victory of the Rock of the Loire was welcomed by his compatriots with delirious enthusiasm, which Pedro took advantage of to announce that he was matching him the next day against Bainaize.[84]

Naturally, there was a full house on that evening. Bainaize was a wrestler of the first order and Étienne could not take him down, but neither was Bainaize able to triumph, and after two hours of wrestling, the conclusion of the match was postponed until the next day. That day the two men again tied and afterward Pedro took his troupe elsewhere. Aside from the excellent receipts in Pedro's ticket booth, the result of the match was that Étienne made up his mind definitively to devote himself to wrestling and weight lifting; he acquired a serious reputation there and ended up performing in a fair booth himself.

As he grew older Étienne gained weight, so much so that at twenty years he weighed nearly 115 kilos, and he had become a fearsome wrestler whose successes were countless. After he had succeeded in vanquishing the famous Ambroise, "Little Pip," it was suggested one day that he might fight the famous Félix Bernard at the Alhambra in Bordeaux. Despite the difference in weight (Bernard only weighed 82 kilos), the wrestler from Bordeaux accepted. This caused Pietro Dalmasso to exclaim these memorable words, "That's very good, Félix. You always have to be aware! Men don't have roots under their feet!"

The two men fought to a tie on the first evening. On the second day after an hour and a half of wrestling, Étienne was pinned using a side hold, which the renowned Bernard was able to give him by taking advantage of a moment of inattention. It was at the same Alhambra where Étienne wrestled the Negro Abdullah. The fight was remarkable in that the public and the wrestlers desperately wanted a result, but the session was excessively prolonged without success. So much so that at midnight the police issued the first fine for not closing down; at one o'clock, they issued a second, and at half-past one, they began to expel the spectators and wrestlers. The Negro Abdullah was the last to go, thrashing about like the very devil. He later eluded the police in order to return to the center of the darkened arena, where he called loudly for Étienne to continue the game, babbling, "This no good! This no good! Must be the winner!"

Sometime later Étienne's wife died, and he fell into a deep depression. Perhaps in his despondency he surrendered to some excesses—excessive drinking having, it seems, the property of drowning sorrows—so much so that he died of a lung disease at the age of thirty years.

The Wrestlers Mordon and Rivollon

Not even counting Faouët, Rossignol-Rollin possessed in his troupe a whole string of famous wrestlers. Among these were Mordon, the champion from Provence who weighed 102 kilos. Mordon excelled especially in the wrestling style known as "hook wrestling," which greatly resembled Swiss wrestling.[85] Next to him was Rivollon "the Eel of the Loire," a wrestler weighing around 90 kilos. Rivollon distinguished himself in particular by his agility and is today over seventy years old. He lives in Perpignan where he raises horses.

Faouët "Beast of the Jungle"

From 1868 to 1878, Faouët [1850?–1879] was the star of wrestling. He had practiced the trade of baker in Langon, his native region.[86] While quite young he had already demonstrated an exceptional vigor, and he soon became a formidable opponent who terrorized the best wrestlers for ten years. From the beginning to the end of his career he was only beaten on three occasions. One time at the very start of his career by Richoux; the second time he was accidentally taken down by the Negro Laperle; the third time by Pietro Dalmasso. Here are the circumstances in which this last meeting took place.

For quite a while Faouët had heard a lot about a new Italian wrestler named Pietro Dalmasso. All the professionals who had gone up against him were unanimous in declaring him to be unbeatable. Despite his great renown, Faouët had not as yet wrestled him. To tell the truth, he was suffering from a serious illness which was to kill him a short time later. He hardly traveled or wrestled any more, which did not facilitate the meeting of the two athletes.

The great Faouët had a muscular physique, an unruly head of hair, a shaggy black beard, an olive complexion, and cruel eyes (collection of Michael Murphy).

But if Faouët's strength had diminished, his courage and his will had remained the same.

To his great joy, one day he learned that an athletic arena under the direction of Marast had just been installed at the Rosière Fair in La Brède (a little village near Bordeaux) and that Pietro Dalmasso was listed among the wrestlers of the troupe. Faouët arrived just as Marast, who was doing the introductions, had just thrown gloves to the amateurs. Faouët asked for a glove for Pietro. Although he had been immediately recognized, there was no difficulty in giving him one. As he was going up the steps to go into the interior of the arena, he said in a low voice to Pietro who was standing near the ticket table, "I did not come for a fake bout; I came for the real thing! You'd better watch out."

The encounter was terrible; Faouët increased his attacks with ferocious energy, but from the start of the match, Pietro had shown a strength and an endurance that was superior to that of his adversary, so much so that at the end of twenty minutes, the courageous, invincible Faouët found that he had underestimated his opponent's strength, and he ended up out of breath. This was his last wrestling bout. Several days later he was admitted to the Saint-André Hospital in Bordeaux and he soon died following an operation for a liver cyst. He was twenty-nine years old.[87]

Faouët was 1 meter 84 tall and weighed 104 kilos—all of it muscle. There was never seen a wrestler with a more masculine and energetic figure. Rossignol-Rollin had nicknamed him "the Beast of the Jungle," and to tell the truth, when Faouët was in the arena facing his adversary, he absolutely had the look of a wild beast who was about to spring on his prey. He made a huge impression with his tall stature, his powerful and slightly arched back, his enormous head supported by a very short neck that measured less than 50 centimeters around, his mop of hair and his shaggy black beard, his olive complexion, and his cruel eyes.[88]

When he wanted to give an idea of Faouët's value, the athletic impresario Doublier, whom he knew quite well, said one day while speaking of him, "I have never met a stronger man than my poor Yusuf. No other wrestler could honestly resist him; well, I believe that Faouët might have beat him."[89]

We want wrongly to attribute to this wrestler the athletic prowess which consists in snatching four weights of 20 kilos, but this is a completely inaccurate assertion. Faouët *never* exercised with weights. In his time there was only one man capable of accomplishing this extraordinary feat of strength, and that was Vincent "the Man of Iron," who it seems snatched four 20-kilo weights while bent-pressing five. Since then, this record has passed in an official way into the hands of Apollon, who seems to have kept it for a long time.

Jean-Pierre of Montastruc

The carnival barker yells at the crowd with his hoarse voice, "The Academy of wrestling is here, the kingdom of muscle, the empire of savages who are on the attack!

We have the strongest men in the world." Observe, here is Pierre the "Rampart of Caudéran"; Valentin "the Torch of Saint Nicolas"; Tony "the Publican"; Paulin "the Apollo of Chartron. If there are any amateurs in attendance who have some biceps, let them raise their hands! Who wants a glove?"

And in the audience, a cavernous voice intones, "I will!"

A head emerges from behind the other heads, and this head makes a sensation because of its abnormal proportions, because it is yellow and because it is hideous. The man to whom this head belongs raises his hand—an enormous hand.

And everyone whispers, "It's the giant of Montastruc."

Giant as well as a man and a monster. Although malformed by an accidental disability, he towers a head above the public—better to say an entire body, and when he climbs the steps of the fairground booth, he reveals a bizarre humped back and a cartoonish appearance.

Jean-Pierre de Montastruc was a "giant" who suffered from acromegaly, but he was also extremely strong. As he grew older, he began to look increasingly deformed.

The barker continues to throw the gloves to the right, the left and in front, and the athletes enter the stall followed by a multitude of fans.

This scene at which I was present twenty years ago in Bordeaux—that shows my age—is still present in my memory, and I will never forget it.

This is how Paul Puy in the now defunct *Journal des Sports* introduced the giant of Montastruc.[90] Jean-Pierre Mazas, "the Ploughman," was born in Montastruc (Haute-Garonne) in 1848 of very tall parents, though not of gigantic proportions. Around the age of sixteen he suddenly began to grow in an abnormal way. When he stood before the draft board, he had attained the height of 2 meters 12, which he later surpassed, for he measured 2 meters 22 a few years before his accident.

For twenty years, his health was excellent and the best response to those who claim that he came into the world deformed, is to recall that he was part of the Regiment of Mobiles [national guard] during the War of 1870 where he also behaved with great bravery. At that time Jean-Pierre weighed 160 kilos and his strength was proverbial, and we can cite numerous feats attributed to him. He undertook to learn wrestling under the direction of Rossignol-Rollin who used him in faked matches from which he always emerged victorious, and he thus managed to make a great reputation for himself. But in 1878 he was the victim of an accident that led to a progressive deformation of the spine.

Forced to bend over, Jean-Pierre saw his height decrease to 1 meter 86. What was the cause of this accident? Some claim that it was a fall from the top of a tree, others that he hurt himself by carrying a load that was too heavy (a field roller). Because of the place and the nature of the injury, the first hypothesis is much more likely. The fact remains that Jean-Pierre of Montastruc had to give up his career as a wrestler and he was happy and satisfied to earn his living by exhibiting himself at fairs as a freak. More than one of our readers must remember his booth where canvas posters showed him in the costume of a wrestler and another pushing a plow.

His measurements were as follows:

Biceps	36 centimeters
Forearm	32 centimeters
Wrist	25 centimeters
Thigh	59 centimeters
Calf	40 centimeters
Ankle	38 centimeters
Foot	35 centimeters long

His hand was monstrous; its shape was regular but immeasurably enlarged in all its dimensions. It was 26 centimeters long and the middle finger 15 cm 6. Jean-Pierre could completely cover a five-franc coin with his thumb. As for his voice, it was extremely deep and muffled. Jean-Pierre died in Bordeaux on 5 November 1901, a victim of acromegaly.[91]

My friend Professor [Georges] Dubois reported an anecdote to me, which he had heard from Dr. Mouls.[92] When the doctor was still quite young, he was witness to the following extraordinary performance, which gives an idea of the astonishing strength that Jean-Pierre of Montastruc had. The hay had just been mown but not all of it had been brought in. One evening the weather had turned, and it began to storm. "Jean," said the farmer who had employed the giant, "Go take a cart and go look for the harvest that remains."

"Bah!" said the colossal farm boy, "No need for a wagon!" and he left after having taken a number of ropes. Less than an hour afterward, a large haystack moving on its own power was seen coming toward the farm. With a skill that only peasants possess, Jean-Pierre had piled up and secured what remained of the hay, he had slipped under this enormous mass and with slow steps, in spite of the friction of the uneven ground, carried this little haystack back. Despite knowing his strength, everyone was astounded. The hay was weighed, and it totaled more than 500 kilos. Doctor Mouls said that he has remained stupefied by this for his entire life.

Lépi the Giant

Lépi was a colossus originally from Normandie (?) who at 2 meters 6 centimeters tall was as wide as an armoire, and all of it muscle and bone. He was a perfect

No images of the "giant" Lépi have been preserved, but the artist Gustave Doré used Lépi's head as the model for this engraving of Goliath and David. The artist was touched by Lépi's melancholy expression.

example of an acromegalic giant, like Jean-Pierre of Montastruc; that is to say, that he had a very tall stature, a huge nose, a very long neck, low forehead, and feet and hands that were so large that in spite of the man's tall height they seemed disproportionate.[93] His voice was muffled, his gait was especially heavy—and there was an excellent reason for this: Lépi actually had legs covered with varicose veins that at this point formed a network similar to that of the ivy on the trunk of an oak. As a result, the giant willingly leaned, when he did not have a cane, on the people who accompanied him. But if the honor of supporting him was not small, the task was painful enough for everyone who was aware of his mania of prudently avoiding others.

Lépi was fairly clumsy except when he juggled weights, which he did with great ease. In wrestling he owed his success to his height and to his great weight, which exceeded 300 pounds! His tactic when confronted by a worthy adversary was simple: he confronted them with his force of inertia and, in the greatest danger, got down on his knees, a position in which he was unbeatable. Even so, in a training session at Old [Henri] Joigneret's I saw Pietro flip him over like a crêpe.[94] After a while he got the better of his exhausted opponent quite easily; only top-notch scientific wrestlers such as Pietro Dalmasso and Achilles "the Colossus of Mount Ventoux," could beat him at that game.

Alongside his triumphs as a wrestler, Lépi reaped success as a freak. He performed as a giant in Paris and Bordeaux, and everywhere he was a hit. The famous artist Gustave Doré even used him as a model, particularly because of his head which was extraordinary because of its tragic expression.[95] But if Lépi accepted being considered a curiosity when he was hired for hard cash, he was less tolerant of being followed in the street, where his singular appearance never failed to gather a few gawkers. The good people who followed him around were more than once terrified when the giant turned on them, swearing terribly, waving his long arms and hurling abuse at them like a Homeric hero! They then fled frantically before this savage anger, unaware that all they had to do to appease him was to take up a little collection for the benefit of the object of their admiration. Lépi the Giant retired to Aix-en-Provence where he died several years ago, around 1900.

Laperle the Negro

Laperle was a wrestler who was a bit mysterious. We can never know who he was—neither his real name, his age, nor his birthplace. We suppose that he arrived in Bordeaux on a merchant ship coming from the colonies and that (for reasons that he never wanted to reveal) he never returned. Laperle was in Bordeaux around 1865 and was employed as a dock worker unloading ships. His strength and courage were such that all the stevedore bosses fought over him; he could do the work of four men all by himself, lifting the heaviest burdens with extraordinary facility.

Summer and winter, his only clothing consisted of a jacket and a pair of trousers. For him, a shirt, shoes, and hat were conspicuous by their absence. Laperle did not seem to be any the worse for it, and in the harshest weather, as well as in the hottest weather, he took off his coat and invariably worked with a bare torso, and quite an admirably muscular torso it was too. It was this circumstance that brought him to the notice of Lagriffe, a wrestler and director of an arena who was walking near the port one fine day, and he was smitten in admiration for this young fellow. The black man's athletic appearance had drawn his attention, and he quickly calculated the advantageous and remunerative advantages that he could draw from our hero.

He took him into his service and began his employment as a boy to clean his fairground stall. Meanwhile, in his spare time he began to teach him the rudiments of wrestling, which the Negro quickly assimilated. At the end of several months, Laperle could already confront the most powerful wrestlers successfully. One year after his engagement by Lagriffe, he had become unbeatable. His manager then decided to feature him, and Laperle began to be admired by the Bordeaux public (which is so fond of wrestling). Laperle was perhaps the only wrestler who never wanted to take part in fake bouts; none of his managers could ever persuade him to go down in defeat. When they wanted to tease him, the wrestlers in the booth where he worked just had to say, "Today it's your turn to lose!" Laperle became furious and stubbornly repeated, "I always on the level. Me not lose—never lose!"

Only one man could flatter himself with having defeated him regularly, and that was Faouët "the Beast of the Jungle." Laperle had unlimited admiration for this famous wrestler whom he considered to be practically supernatural. But despite the veneration that he had for Faouët, our Negro did not fail to wrestle honestly and conscientiously each time they found themselves paired up. It came to the point that the directors of the wrestling arenas avoided engaging Faouët and Laperle as often as possible because the matches between these two were interminable. It was for this reason that Laperle never became part of the troupe of the famous impresario Rossignol-Rollin.

One day at the Bordeaux Fair he managed to take Faouët down by surprise. It would be impossible to describe the joy the Negro felt. He attempted to manifest his enthusiasm by turning a somersault, but as he had never practiced this kind of trick, instead of landing on his feet, he fell headlong into the sawdust. He got up dazed and with a sprained wrist, but his satisfaction was such that he paid little attention to his accident and began religiously to wipe the sawdust that Faouët still had on his shoulders. Faouët was vexed at his defeat, and it was only after he glared fiercely at his opponent that the good Negro's exuberant transports of joy were calmed.

Laperle also performed weightlifting exhibitions, and his favorite feat was to hold a 100-pound weight between his teeth by a ring and biting into the iron. Another 100-pound weight was placed on his head, and in each hand a 25-kilo weight, which he held very firmly like an "iron cross"; and thus loaded, he circled the arena, receiving the applause of the audience with the most manifest satisfaction.

But his most astounding feat of strength was his work with a barrel. A barrel full of water with a capacity of 288 liters was placed in the middle of the arena; it was upright and without any support, and Laperle's hands were tied behind his back. This done, the Negro advanced close to the barrel, spread his legs ever so slightly, seized the upper edge of the barrel between his teeth, drew it onto his belly, lifted it and held it horizontally for a few seconds, then put it down again without anyone's help. When it was performed under such conditions, this feat meant that it was done by a veritable Hercules who had neck and jaw strength that surpassed imagination.

Only two athletes are known to have imitated Laperle's work. They were two brothers who were phenomenally successful in repeating our Negro's strength feat—at least in appearance, for they had faked it in an ingenious way. In reality, they had taken care to introduce into the interior of the barrel enormous rubber balloons, which once inflated, took the place of an equal volume of water.[96] Each time, before lifting the barrel with their jaws, and in order to convince the public of the sincerity of their performance, they uncorked the barrel and let a little water flow out, thus giving convincing proof (Oh, how little!) that all trickery was alien to their athletic prowess. The audience was ignorant of this hoax, and they were not sparing in their applause for these artists.

By 1896 Laperle was very old, but he still wrestled in fairs around Bordeaux. Eventually, the wife of the famous Marseille, "the Miller of Lapalud," took him in to employ him to work in the fields. Laperle had qualities rare in a professional athlete; he was very sober and unusually dispassionate. He often gave away part of his earnings to the less fortunate, keeping only that which was strictly necessary for himself. For all of these reasons, it is obvious that Laperle was as interesting from an ethical as a physical point of view.[97]

Baby "the Cavalryman of Reichshoffen"

In Rossignol-Rollin's troupe there was a wrestler known as Baby "the Last Cavalryman of Reichshoffen."[98] Yes, he was an authentic cavalryman from the famous charge of Reichshoffen, a brave man who had come back from facing the enemy ranks, and he owed his survival to his horse. The noble beast had served as a shield for his master, and a hundred Prussian bullets had been found in the animal's entrails. Rossignol declared that he had the very projectiles and that they were at the disposal of the incredulous; actually, he never had any such things. Besides, if he really had any, Rossignol would simply have bought the necessary bullets.

The Last Cavalrymen was successful, and he had never been beaten. However, a vigorous farm boy, encouraged by his employer, once challenged the former soldier. The fellow was extraordinarily built, so Rossignol thought it useful to have a private confab with the boss. The latter was won over to the promoter's cause; he then gave the boy his instructions but it was clear from the lad's grimaces that he did not like them. In the end, the cavalryman beat the farm boy with surprising ease. The audience responded with rapturous applause.

Unfortunately, feeling a surge of egotism, the cavalryman made the mistake of issuing this disdainful exclamation. "He can't even stand up!" Then the young man who was already humiliated by the applause given to his vanquisher, stood up, and in a voice shaking with rage cried, "You want to do it over?"

Rossignol tried to intervene, but the boastfulness pleased the crowds, and the promoter had to withdraw in the face of such cries.

"Revenge! Revenge!" shouted a thousand voices.

The cavalryman prepared to fight, and so did the young man. Suddenly the older man was seized round the body by the farm boy, and flattened on the carpet without any childish flourishes. This time it was not faked, and the "Last Cavalryman of Reichshoffen" was never again seen in the troupe of Rossignol-Rollin. Baby wrestled once more in Bordeaux in 1874 in the Jeantien Arena in the locality that witnessed his defeat.

Paul "the Porter"

Paul the Porter, of Bordeaux was a contemporary of Bernard, Arpin, Rabasson, etc. He was of medium height and he stood a little stooped; he had acquired this posture because of his profession as dock worker. All day long he carried loads on his back as he unloaded ships in the ports of the river Gironde. Paul had a remarkable natural strength, and the habit of carrying had developed in him a great power in his lower back and legs. He was also well known in the entire region because of the feats of strength that he performed. Thus, it was that in the warehouse he would load a full barrel or a couple of bags of sand onto his back and offer a prize of 200 francs to anyone who did the same. Many stevedores, porters, or athletes tried in vain to imitate his example.

Paul worked all day at his trade; he only visited the fair stalls in the evening, thus giving proof of an extraordinary resilience and courage. Even though he came at the end of his day, he was still able to make considerable exertions either to fight, or to perform various feats of strength from his repertoire. But if he did not disdain to add a bit of money in this way to what he earned as a longshoreman, he mainly practiced athletics because he liked it; in wrestling, he was always honest and never agreed to a fix.

One day at the Bordeaux fair, he asked Old Bernard to hire him, but Bernard refused, probably because his troupe was full. Paul was annoyed, and that evening he came back and stood in front of the booth; during the parade when Bernard (following the custom) issued a challenge to amateurs, Paul requested a glove to wrestle against the boss himself. The two men fought honestly, and their combat was Homeric. The first evening there was no result. The next day, after being injured quite badly by falling against the railings, Bernard managed to put the Porter in a terribly tight headlock. He was nearly strangled, and after Paul gasped for breath and begged for mercy, Bernard only consented to let him go after his opponent had been pushed down and both shoulders touched the mat. Paul had been punished so much that he had to enter the hospital for a few days! Back then, fights were not always fun and games.

The Porter wrestled until a fairly advanced age. Currently he lives in an out of the way corner of the province where his old age is comforted by his memories of his former prowess.

Rambaud "Resistance"

Rambaud, who went by the name Resistance, was a remarkable athlete. He was a boxer, javelin thrower, wrestler, and weight lifter. He maintained a gymnasium in the Rue des Écuries-d'Artois, where he gave lessons in boxing.[99] Tall, well formed, and intelligent, he had been admired and well paid in the court of Egypt. "Blessed be the womb of the mother that bore you," remarked the Khedive Ismail Pasha [1830–1895] one day. He had been taught by Henri Joigneret, an old-time Hercules who had operated a wrestling and weight-lifting gymnasium for many years in Montmartre. Later this establishment passed to [Paul] Pons and has been replaced today by apartment blocks. Joigneret continued to have a limitless admiration for the athlete Resistance.

In 1876, Resistance was in the Swiss town of Chaux-de-Fonds, and here is his verbal portrait made by [boxing expert Joseph] Charlemont the elder according to one of his friends, Mr. Coeurderoi, who knew Rambaud at this time.

"He was no longer young but looked a little tanned and slightly bloated." He enjoyed life a great deal. He had returned from the Levant where he had wrestled in Greece. He remained in Switzerland for two years—drinking well, hunting well, and eating the game he had killed; he did not return until all his money ran out. When Mr. Coeurderoi met him coming from the station at Chaux-de-Fonds, Rambaud was dressed as a sailor and exhibited something amazing to this population of watchmakers most of whom had never seen the sea (we are 1,000 meters above sea level). What did he reveal to us? An ordinary, dried up, stuffed fish that he called "a shark." Naturalists would have a hard time calling it a shark, but Resistance did not find the problem so sticky. Occasionally, he lifted weights in a style that was entirely correct and graceful. "He still remained a vigorous man."

A short time later Charlemont met him on his tour of Belgium. At Antwerp he occupied a booth at that city's fair, but by then he had difficulty recognizing in him the superb male specimen that he had once been.

Rambaud had demonstrated French boxing at the Montesquieu Arena with Vigneron, "the Cannon Man." The two men demonstrated remarkable power and physical beauty, giving the audience an unforgettable impression. In 1850 Rambaud fought against Bernard in Bordeaux at the Casino des Arts under the direction of Leboucher, the professor of boxing. Bernard was the father of Félix Bernard and (as everyone knew) was a strongman and a wrestler. Like his adversary, he was big and well proportioned. In the South of France, Rambaud was known as "the King of Wrestlers," and as a teacher of boxing, he enjoyed a great reputation in Bordeaux.

The match was most interesting. From the start to the finish, the two

Sculptor and artist Alexandre Falguière created the painting *Lutteurs* (Wrestlers) in 1875, and it was first published as an engraving in the weekly *Le Monde Illustré* in May of that same year. It represents the wrestlers Rambaud "Resistance" (left) and Blas "the Proud Spaniard" at the Montesquieu Hall.

champions fought with equal ardor, and it was difficult to predict how it would end. It was Resistance who brought this memorable fight to a magnificent conclusion. Bernard was hit in the chest and fell to the ground to the great surprise of the spectators who nevertheless applauded excessively.[100]

Another match that was no less sensational took place at the Montesquieu Arena in 1853 between Arpin "the Terrible Savoyard," and Resistance. Arpin had been defeated by Marseille the elder for the first time as a wrestler in the previous year, and he hoped no doubt to make up for it in boxing. At any rate, he had chosen his adversary poorly because he was soundly defeated.

Rambaud was originally a baker's helper. He remained the darling of the public until the day Louis Vigneron appeared and quickly got the better of Resistance, supplanting him in the eyes of the contemporary sporting public from then on.

Achille "the Colossus of Mont Ventoux"

With his height of 1 meter 80, Achille the Colossus of Mont Ventoux, was an enormous mass of flesh and bone. He was uncommonly strong, and he began to wrestle with his friends when he was relatively young, then he began visiting the little stalls that traveled around the fairs of his region. When he was twenty years old, he already weighed more than 100 kilos, so from that time on, it was no small matter to roll him on his back. He was soon taken with enthusiasm for wrestling and weights, and he began his tour of France starting with the regions of the north where he quickly became known and appreciated. Hearing of him, the wrestling managers of the south fought over who would get him, and Jeantien and Dumas the elder presented him to Bordeaux where he earned a great and legitimate success by defeating the best amateurs and even some professionals.[101] He carved out an unrivaled reputation both for his strength and his skill, for, despite his formidable appearances, he fought with great skill. On several occasions he also took part in the fairs of Bordeaux and was the hero of some rather remarkable incidents.

One day in particular the boxer of the troupe to which he belonged was absent when an army provost sergeant had just asked for a glove and insisted on having an opponent, although he had been warned that the boxing master was not there. To satisfy the public, Achille offered to replace his comrade at short notice, and this gave rise to a sensational encounter. The sergeant who was quick, light, and quite skillful, circled around the fat Achilles who coolly took many low kicks with his opponent's clodhoppers, the boxer's friends applauding frantically each time the colossus announced in a formidable voice, "You got me!" Unfortunately, success encouraged the sergeant to become a little too reckless—and believing his opponent to be completely helpless, rushed at him without precaution. With a single punch in the face, Achille sent his rival over the ropes of the ring and back into the middle of the audience, his nose a mass of bruises and a few loose teeth, while announcing in the same thunderous voice; "I got him!"

There followed a great uproar and a lively altercation between the colossus and the sergeant's friends, which caused Achille to descend into the street. Without hesitation, our hero who was still riled up thanks to the soreness of his shins, followed them into the square and urged them to come together in a group and prepare to get a beating, since individually they were all in his opinion "too puny." He engaged in a terrific fight where the colossus no longer had to observe the conventional rules of boxing, and so he seriously injured three or four opponents. The affair ended at the police station but at least it made an excellent advertisement for the booth where fat Achille worked.

Another anecdote about this formidable wrestling protagonist comes to mind. Relations were strained between the Colossus of Mont Ventoux and the giant Lépi, and one day when they were wrestling together (and let us admit it right away, they were fighting quite brutally), and Achille carelessly dropped the Italian giant on a spiked dumbbell.[102] It is easy to imagine what resulted from this. But on another occasion Pietro was wrestling with him, and it was a real match with absolutely nothing faked. The terrible champion gave Achille as good as he got. Moral of the story: Clear away the furniture when you wrestle for real.

At one time the Colossus of Mont Ventoux was one of the best French wrestlers. At the time when he was at the height of his form, he got the better of Étienne "the Shepherd," among others, and fiercely resisted Faouët "the Beast of the Jungle," the king of wrestlers.

Dubois

The strongman, Dubois, was born in Saint-Denis [near Paris] in 1830. Around the end of the Second Empire [1870] he was the director of a wrestling arena. He played at all the carnivals and fairs with his company, and he was a past master in the arts of trickery and chicanery. His accomplice was a strongman named François Villier. Both were of a corpulence that bordered on obesity. It is true that although they exercised the profession of Hercules, they took enormous pains to avoid fatigue. The manner in which Dubois and Villiers pulled off their deception deserves to be recounted.

Well then, after having amassed a modest fortune by lifting phony weights on public squares, Dubois resolved to purchase a secondhand carnival booth. From that time on he hired several accomplices to lift and wrestle with, but whose real talents consisted of fooling the public and working with the bogus "20-kilo" weights. He then took on a stevedore of Herculean appearance to act as a shill. That man was François Villier.

When the athletes (?) of the Dubois arena stood before the public, Villier's job was to mix in with the crowd and to act like an amateur who wanted to try his skills against those of the men in the booth. The discussion between Dubois and Villier very quickly degenerated into an argument. The latter bounded tumultuously up the staircase to the stage and threw himself onto Dubois as if he wanted (according to his own expression) to "grind him into sausage meat." This travesty was played to perfection, and the crowd rushed inside, never doubting for an instant that they were going to see an amateur pin the mighty wrestler's shoulders to the sawdust-covered floor.

After several uninteresting intervals, the crowd began calling for the main event, the match between Dubois and the "amateur." The two actors took their places. They lunged and attacked one another with ferocious-looking energy. Suddenly, Dubois was grabbed in a hold and he rolled to the ground, nearly touching both shoulders on to the floor. But at the same time, he let out with a cry of pain and escaped from his adversary's hold while screaming loudly. Villier had bitten Dubois on the shoulder, and he asked the audience in the front row who now roared with indignation to act as witnesses. Chaos ensued, and the other wrestlers had to step in to keep Villier from being torn to pieces by the crowd. It was decided to take the dishonorable amateur in front of the official in charge of the entire fair. But after a few moments, Dubois appeared and intervened in favor of the prisoner. "What can we do, your honor? This sort of thing is simply a calculated risk. In the heat of the wrestling match—when it is for real—we often forget our training. This would never have happened if, like so many others, the match had been faked."

In short, the official was touched by this gesture of generosity, and he released Villiers. As soon as Dubois and Villier left the judge's post, they began to argue once more, much to the delight of the audience who stood at the door in order to see the climax of this incident.

Dubois had a foolproof way to keep customers coming back to his wrestling baraque; it involved a phony but convincing rivalry with an accomplice named Villier. The image shows the rotund wrestler with his wife who did fencing demonstrations.

Seeing with satisfaction that the quarrel had picked up once more, the audience followed the two men back to the booth, but by this time the crowd of followers had naturally grown as passersby saw and understood the cause of this gathering. Everyone wanted to see the end of the piece.

Arriving at the foot of the arena, Dubois assured the audience of his courage: "Despite having been bitten by him," the wrestler bawled, "I want to take him down. You can watch my revenge. Ladies and gentlemen, you will see how I deal with him."

"I accept the challenge!" shouted Villier, and as he said so, he clambered up the stairway with terrible and aggressive intent. And the dupes in the audience had been taken in again. With that, the fierce, inexorable, but above all, well planned match began once more.

Thanks to an impressive hold, Villier was taken to the floor. He was about to have both shoulders pinned when the director suddenly burst forth with his awful scream of agony once more! Villier had bitten the wrestler again!

There were cries and insults thrown at the amateur and his duplicity, then a new procession to the official during which Dubois followed his unscrupulous adversary all the while heaping insults on him because of his injuries.

The judge was annoyed at being bothered once more but was about to give his decision when Dubois intervened as before and got his brutal opponent off the hook. The judge then had both men escorted to the door, and they went back to the booth during which Dubois shouted to Villier, "I will get you tomorrow! I'll chew you up and spit out the pieces."

This farce went on several days and the booth was never empty anymore. When Dubois and Villier transferred their props and devices to another town, the little scenario began all over again. Obviously, the bites were superficial and since the employer was able to throw many a gold coin into his cash box, he did not complain a bit. This little swindle lasted several years before it became too well known. Dubois thus made a good living practicing what he termed "honest wrestling."[103]

Picard "the Agile Bordelais"

Picard the Agile Bordelais [native of Bordeaux], a contemporary of Milhomme, Ambroise "Little Pip," Old Bernard, and others, was fairly short (1 meter 60) but thickset, potbellied, nimble as a goat; despite his paunch, he was as pugnacious and irascible as a gamecock. He had been in Bordeaux for a long time and he was the director of a wrestling arena where he partnered sometimes with Émile "the Spaniard," and sometimes with Jeantien. He frequently lifted weights, and thanks to the short length of his muscular arms he was able to perform very nice arm extensions quite easily. As a wrestler, he was not to be sniffed at and he performed masterfully the moves that require speed, such as a shoulder throw, a flying mare, etc. He was excessively combative and hardly ever admitted defeat. When he found himself lying on his shoulder blades, he usually challenged his winner to a personal fight, wanting at least to prove his superiority with kicks and punches.

One day after losing a bout with someone called Beaufort, a large young fellow who was extremely skilled at wrestling; as was his custom, Picard, went out into the street to demand his revenge by fighting with fists and feet. Beaufort was quite resourceful, and he made Picard take a few serious blows, but the Agile Bordelais, in the height of fury, suddenly stooped after a feint to the face and grabbed his opponent's two legs and brutally unbalanced him. Beaufort fell back and lay on the ground unconscious. Picard was convinced that he had killed him. The little man tore his hair in despair, swearing never to fight again as long as he lived. But Beaufort soon came back to life, and everything ended for the best in the world at a nearby wine bar.

Following this violent episode, Picard took the firm resolution of satisfying his belligerent instincts henceforth in less dangerous combats. He developed a passion for billiards and became very skilled at it; but in billiards as in wrestling, defeat made him fly into a terrible rage. One day when he had lost more than 300 francs, he returned home maddened with fury. He hastily drank two large bowls of hot milk and retired to his room to fulminate at his leisure. When his wife thought that he was a bit calmer, she came in to check on him. She found him dead, stretched out fully dressed on the floor. In his anger he had been struck down by an apoplectic fit. He was barely forty years old.

Bainaize

Bainaize was the dean of wrestling veterans. After sixty-eight autumns, he was still wrestling. His parents were from Ariège, but they traveled around with the fairs. "I must have been born around 1834 in Montignac (Dordogne)," he says, "however, I had not really settled down at that point." As a boy he was a baker, and at the age of nineteen his eyes were scorched by the oven. He then turned to wrestling. He anticipated the blows of his adversary without seeing them, and he became one of the most terrible men of his time, so much so that he was nicknamed "the Wild Beast," since he brought real passion in his desire to win. "I know neither pity nor pardon," he repeated recently, "Look at my fingers. All the joints are broken." And to tell the truth, his fingers were bent in all directions. "When I grab a man in a waistlock from behind, his only recourse is to break one of these so that I will let him go. And my ears! Aren't they

Bainaize was a tough old bird who survived over sixty years in the wrestling business. He ended in misery and poverty, but he had an exciting life.

nicely done? It was Béranger who detached the right one and Lacroix who did the left one."

Bainaize belonged to the legendary Rossignol-Rollin troupe, and he still has fond memories of the old impresario. "Ever since the boss died," he often repeats, "real wrestling—that also died." After the war [of 1870] when the famous troupe was disbanded, Bainaize went here and there, following the fairs working for this one and that one. He visited the whole of France, Switzerland, Belgium, and Lorraine. But freelancing wrestlers did not earn much money, and he became acquainted with atrocious poverty. One day he had three sous, and the next day nothing. He did not even know where he could stay. He slept in cemeteries. What an epic tale was the life of these nomads! And he spent nearly thirty years like this!

In 1898 he was in Toulouse where he was appearing in various fair booths when the first wrestling championships were created in Paris by Mr. de Lucenski.[104] Then an invincible obsession, the desperate love of his profession, perhaps even visions of glory invaded the brain of the old athlete.[105] Let us let him tell of his adventures.

Bainaize, my old man, I said to myself, there are lots of young people here who work. You think you know what you are worth. Go show them how their papas worked.

He did not have a penny. His faded trunks and his wrestling shoes were tied up in a handkerchief. This is how Marseille elder arrived from Lapalud to challenge Arpin, and also how Bainaize arrived in Paris. He was immediately taken to Gangloff Hall, where the regulars gave endless ovations to the old lion, who had a hairy chest that was completely gray, and he wheezed furiously when he was surprised by an adversary's waist hold.[106]

Here is an anecdote showing that Bainaize had all the resourceful craftiness of the Gascons, and who more than once got out of a bad situation, or got his comrades out of it by one of those particular tricks that constitute the genius of the race. In 1875, a Spaniard, Don Ramon, an athletic-tour entrepreneur, hired him for a series of performances in Catalonia. Four of them departed: Gallivet, Baby "the Cavalryman" of Reichshoffen, Mathurin of Lyon, and Bainaize. They had to join the impresario in Barcelona. They left from Montpellier and stopped at Cette, where they earned a few coins. But owing to the misfortunes of the road, they did not have a single penny by the time they arrived in Barcelona.

Don Ramon was not yet there. Since the men did not exactly look like millionaires, hotel owners refused to put them up. None of the four could speak Spanish. Bainaize took the situation in hand; he went to the square and harangued the crowd in gibberish that skillfully jumbled his native dialect with Arabic and French so that the Catalans half understood and applauded. The "Wild Beast" did feats with weights and the audience threw a few pesetas, which was all he needed to get an inn and a meal for the evening. Don Ramon joined the group the next morning and he had them wrestle in the Pre Catalan region of Spain.

Another typical anecdote is as follows.

In 1878 Bainaize "the Wild Beast," traveled to the East [of France]. At this time he had a little carnival booth that was "well painted and quite pretty," which he exhibited on the fairgrounds. He arrived in Besançon, and there he found a terrible competitor, Achille Mouchon (1855–1900?), a man of the greatest strength.[107] The Wild Beast moved his booth opposite that of Mouchon, but the citizens of Besançon wanted only Mouchon, swore by Mouchon, and would only patronize Mouchon's establishment. Mouchon got all the nice receipts of the evening and the afternoon. Bainaize was left as the unwanted visitor at his neighbor's party. He challenged Mouchon to wrestle him in front of the entire town. He enhanced his challenge with a bet of twenty francs. One of the two booths will kill the other. Mouchon accepted the challenge. Bainaize took him down in two minutes. The bet was won. The people of Besançon now know the value of the Wild Beast.

Described as "a man of the greatest strength," Achille Mouchon was a tough adversary, but he was defeated by Bainaize. Despite this, the two men remained friends (collection of Michael Murphy).

Mouchon did not hold a grudge, and it is necessary to hear Bainaize tell the end of the adventure. "Happy as gods, proud as Indian braves, Achille and I went to have a pint together. We embraced at the pub. Since then, we've remained great friends, but we never fought each other again."

There is also the story of the Tyrolian giant that Bainaize defeated in Madrid; there's the one about Vuillod, "the Cannon Man," now a senator, whom the old Wild Beast got the better of at Lyon and how many others, all full of heroic or comical details.[108] When Rossignol-Rollin saw Bainaize appear on the mat, he shouted to the other men in the troupe, "Step aside, you reeds! Make way for an oak."

The old wrestler managed to amaze me one last time. One day when I was cycling around Fontainebleau in the summer of 1907, I felt like going for a swim. I was heading toward the Valvins bridge when my eyes fell on a circle of onlookers. I approached quickly. I saw an old athlete with a Homeric countenance, a beard and white mane blowing in the wind, and old glasses on his nose. He performed a double arm extension masterfully with weights of 20 kilos. I saw him from behind, and when he threw his weights behind him, they rolled down near my feet. I hefted them immediately. They were real! When the old man turned towards me, he recognized me immediately and, smiling, he said to me with a certain coquetry, "Not too bad for a man of seventy, eh?" My only response was a heartfelt handshake. When the performance was over, I took him to a wine shop, and we shared a bottle of old Bordeaux while I took many notes for the present volume. We talked about those who had come before and their athletic prowess.

Bainaize was 1 meter 82 tall and weighed 100 kilos. In 1907 he lived in Héricy near Fontainebleau. After that I completely lost track of him.[109]

Another of Bainaize's opponents was Jean-Baptiste Vuillod, who performed as a strongman and wrestler before going on to serve as a senator in France's Chamber of Deputies.

Abdullah Jeffery

A coffee merchant had known a very strong Negro in America and, considering the public's enthusiasm for the wrestling matches that had just taken place at the Folies Bergère under the direction of Pietro, he obtained the Negro's address in America and brought him to Paris. Immediately after his arrival he handed him over to François the Bordelais, who is a fine wrestler that all Parisians know.

The Negro was named Abdullah Jeffery. He was born in the Cape of Good Hope, and when he came to Paris he was thirty years old. He was of gigantic stature and possessed colossal strength, and in just a short while he became a fearsome adversary. After two months of lessons, he was presented to the public in several fights, and the wrestlers were convinced that he was a competitor whose future would be out of the ordinary. Now, one day when a public match was being given for him at Aubervilliers, the wrestlers were not keen to go up against the Negro, so it was agreed that a prearranged match should be held. Abdullah was to wrestle with Joseph Schilling, the only wrestler who seriously stood up to Tom Cannon, and who only got the better of him by nearly throttling him with a rear stranglehold headlock (a hold that is forbidden in wrestling). Abdullah therefore had to wrestle with Joseph Schilling and defeat him. Nicolas Guitchen, "the Butcher," who had fought at the Follies Bergère a few months before, had to fight with François the Bordelais and also lose.

Supposedly from the Cape Colony of South Africa, Abdullah Jeffery was a forceful fighter. He accidentally killed an opponent and thereafter suffered from a possibly suicidal fit of melancholy.

François and Abdullah then had to pretend that Abdullah would win.

The first part went well. True to what had been arranged, Joseph Schilling was defeated after a quarter hour of wrestling; then it was the turn of François the Bordelais and Nicolas the Butcher who wrestled just as they had agreed. But suddenly Pietro entered the hall and came to watch the fight. When Nicolas saw Pietro, in whose troupe he had been at the Folies Bergère, he decided to wrestle with the Negro "for real," first from pride and then out of a kind of animosity against Abdullah, whom he had insulted a few days before.

After realizing that Nicolas was changing what had been agreed, François wanted to get it over with as quickly as possible and easily let himself be pinned. Abdullah understood nothing of what had just happened; he only supposed that François had slipped (which often happens), and that finding himself under a move that involved rather heavy pressure, he was pinned. Nicolas took about a quarter hour of rest, and after that the match began between the two victors. Abdullah wrestled unwarily and calmly, but suddenly he realized that there was nothing civil about the fight and, remembering the disagreement that had happened between them a few days before, he realized that Nicolas wanted to take him down. Furious at this lack of good faith on the part of his adversary who had not warned him of this change in conditions, he increased his efforts and using all his Herculean strength he astonished the wrestlers present, because Nicolas was not an ordinary adversary. The spectators saw nothing of what was happening and yet the life of a man was at stake in the match then being played out, because Nicolas had decided to do anything to bring down the Negro, who on his side, did not want to lose.

The match went on for twenty minutes. Suddenly a few blows were struck with great force, and before the other wrestlers had time to realize it, Abdullah had grabbed his opponent in a rear waistlock with such force that Nicolas was sent rolling on the floor, his back broken. They took him to the hospital where he died on arrival.[110]

One evening three months later at eight o'clock on the track of the central railway near the Avenue de Villiers, Abdullah's body was found; his forehead split and his right arm severed at the shoulder by the wheels of a train.

Auguste and Nicolas Guitchen "the Butchers of La Villette"

Nicolas and Auguste Guitchen were born near Metz, Auguste in 1849 and Nicolas in 1856. Both worked in the abattoirs of La Villette where they enjoyed a very great reputation for strength. Every day after their work, they trained seriously at wrestling. In addition, the wrestlers of the time often asked them to come to their fairground stalls, where they always attracted a large crowd, especially when the match took place in La Villette or La Chappelle.

In 1879, Joigneret the strongman organized a great tournament at the Concert Perrot, Rue de la Chapelle; Auguste, the Butcher and his brother Nicolas emerged victorious. That evening, Tournier "Iron-Head"; Joseph "the Vise"; Louis Schilling—and others who were wrestling stars at this time—all experienced the bitterness of a defeat to which they were unaccustomed.

This was the first glory for our two butchers, especially for Nicolas who decided at that point to go on the road. That is how he wrestled for a very long time with Marseille the younger, "the Lion of Lapalud," in the principal fairs of Paris and its suburbs. He then worked in different establishments in the capital. He also traveled to Bordeaux where he fought with renowned wrestlers such as Bernard the younger; Jules Renaud "Pug Nose of the Abattoir"; Little Pierre; Paul "the Miller"; Paul "the Hulk"; Trillat "the Barrel Man"; Mazin; Jules; Montey; Jeannot "the Bear of Tourny"; Toby; and Pietro Dalmasso.

Nicolas was a tall youth whose height was around 1 meter 80 with a manly face and full of energy. He spoke very correctly, a rare quality (very rare, alas!), among professional wrestlers. Nicolas made his debut in Bordeaux with Jules Renaud, a

The brothers Nicolas (left) and Auguste Guitchen were butchers by trade but wrestlers in their spare time. The younger brother Nicolas was killed by Abdullah Jeffery, and Auguste was terribly distressed by this turn of events.

wrestler of the highest quality. He defeated him two times in a row—the first time very normally at the Alhambra of that city and a second time by a very lucky move. Renaud grabbed his adversary in a rear waistlock, but he slipped on both heels and fell backward on his own, which proves that one should never wear boots with heels in a wrestling bout since you risk committing a very serious error. Nicolas was also the winner over Paul "the Hulk," but after a very hard and very long wrestling match.

In short, Nicolas was only very rarely defeated since he was a wrestler of great finesse. He united a tall stature with sizeable weight and great endurance. After a long stay at Bordeaux, he returned to Paris where he once again took up his trade as a butcher and only wrestled now and then. After their success of 1879 the two brothers appeared in Paris with Old Bernard at The Two Cannons, Rue de Flandre, at the Winter Alcazar, and elsewhere.[111] They were hired by the Folies Bergère to fight against Pietro Dalmasso, but they were not able to defeat the famous champion. Only Auguste the Butcher, opposed him with a terrible endurance which required several rounds, but finally he only succeeded in having his own shoulders pressed against the mat.

Despite their ever-growing success, Auguste and Nicolas refused all the brilliant engagements abroad; they did not want to abandon their profession as butchers at any price. It took a most tragic event for Auguste the Butcher to leave the slaughterhouses and turn professional. This was the death of his brother killed in a wrestling match by Abdullah Jeffery. [See previous section]. The Butcher was deeply saddened by this catastrophe. From that moment he turned his back on the slaughterhouses and resolved to leave Paris; the sight of Abdullah in the wrestling tournaments in which he took part was too painful for him, and constantly reminds him of poor Nicolas.

But before leaving, he wanted to pay one last tribute to the memory of Abdullah's victim by presenting a big wrestling tournament for the benefit of his brother's widow and children. All the wrestlers were happy to participate in a charitable work, and they lent their support to this tournament that took place at the Chaine Hall, Rue d'Allemagne, in the presence of a huge crowd packed into this overly crowded room.[112] More than a thousand people were turned away at the door. In addition to wrestling, the program featured an extraordinary feature. Suspended by his knees from loops of rope, Auguste had chosen to lift the heaviest ox from the slaughterhouses; but this feat of strength almost cost the brave athlete's life since he had overestimated his own strength. The lifting straps were of unequal length, so at the decisive moment of the lift, only the animal's forequarters were lifted, and it began to struggle furiously to such an extent that that its frantic jerks and jolts threatened to tear the Hercules apart. The audience shouted to Auguste to drop everything, but the courageous butcher would not hear of it. Marshaling his strength in one supreme effort, he ended up causing the animal to lose its footing, and he kept it suspended for a few seconds, thus bringing the spectators' enthusiasm to a fever pitch. The bravos of the audience as well as the generosity which they showed toward the widow and the children of Nicolas soon made our hero forget the danger he had run.

The day after the performance, Auguste the Butcher, set out for Bordeaux. He then traveled through all the major cities of France and abroad, defeating most of the wrestlers who were then in vogue as he passed through. He returned to his abattoirs, which he had left with regret. From time to time he went to the Butchers' Athletic Club in the Rue d'Allemagne to give some advice on wrestling.[113] There were other superb athletes in this club, in particular Auguste's employer, nicknamed Alfred "Chest of Steel" who did an iron cross with 60 pounds in each hand and snatched a very heavy weight with one hand. The following measurements help us to understand his remarkable performances: biceps 44 cm and 46 cm calves. Nigoux, another member of the club, could do a one-handed swing lift of 140 pounds. He could also sit in a chair and do an arm extension using a 25-kilo weight while drinking a stein of beer with the other hand. We should also mention Charles Lecomte, a colossus who weighed 260 pounds but who was a nimble as a roe buck deer, and as proof of this he issued a challenge with a stake of 100 francs, for any athlete to race down the Rue d'Allemagne (1,820 meters) in as little time as he. Then there was Pinssart, who could lift a barbell of 220 pounds and do a superb arm extension. The club's collection contains, among other curiosities, a great number of weights and barbells that belonged to several famous athletes. Professor Arasse was a great friend of the Guitchen brothers.[114]

Don Ramon

Don Ramon, who took over Rossignol-Rollin's business, was a wrestler whose talents were not extraordinary. For the rest, nothing is quoted about him that is worth recalling. He had, like Rossignol (though to a much lesser degree), the gift of making extraordinary pitches that never failed to attract a crowd to his fair booth. He lived on it until 1902, when he died (May 30). He was then sixty-eight years old. He had become remarkably obese. This man who for nearly fifty years had thrown out the gloves, praised muscles, had seen many a waist hold or headlock, but he had not enriched himself. He died suddenly at the bar of the Museum in Saint-Étienne just a stone's throw from his trailer, which at that time was parked in the Cours Victor-Hugo. Don Ramon (whose real name was Franc) appeared for the last time on a stage worthy of the name in Saint-Étienne at the time when the famous Turks and the incomparable Yusuf were exhibiting. It was at the Eden. We can say that he died fighting, because despite his obesity, he retained a remarkable activity until the end.

Don Ramon took over the *baraque* of Rossignol-Rollin, but he had little of his predecessor's charm or panache, and he never enjoyed great success.

Raulin "Toothless"

Toothless was born in Paris in 1847, and he was a strongman of the first order but a mediocre wrestler. In his book, *A Wrestler's Memoirs* [Johannès] Gravier [1869–1929] recalls Toothless in the following words.[115]:

> Everyone in Paris knew of the extraordinary Raulin Toothless. Everyone had seen him at some time or other, whether in his fair booth, on the public squares, or in private courtyards. He was always dressed in the same way, winter or summer: a red, sleeveless shirt and

trousers that came down to his calves. He was invariably escorted by his wife, his dog, and his horse. For all that, he was one of the strongest men in Paris, but additionally this Hercules was quite a philosopher! And what of his valiant consort, then? At one time she had been an extremely beautiful girl—one of the best lady wrestlers—one who was fearless and virtually insensible to pain. With any other husband, today she would have a pretty little shop and lots of money instead of dying "in harness." Despite that, she deeply loved "her big fellow" as she called him.

He had a great love for the theater. I am certain that he has tried every seat in the house at the theaters of the Château-d'Eau and the Ambigu.[116]

"The Arena of Toothless," as he pompously referred to it, was nothing more than a patchwork of old canvas,

"Toothless" Raulin usually lived on the edge of poverty, but he was much loved by his audiences and could usually count on a good crowd at his wrestling arena.

one piece stitched to the next and each one having a different color, origin, and history. He had a box of hay that he spread out to form a ring.

His troupe consisted of his wife, me, and a Negro named Bamboula. Oh, not the famous wrestler! This was some poor devil whom Toothless had found who knows where, and whose only distinction consisted of an abysmal ignorance of all the rules of wrestling. Toothless never worried about his parade of athletes since it was always the same.

Mrs. Raulin rode back and forth in front of the fair booth mounted on the piebald horse that we nicknamed "Old Barrel Staves" because we could count all his ribs. When all this marching about had attracted enough of a crowd, Toothless began his pitch.

"Ladies and Gentlemen, in this performance you will see for the very first time the lifting of a horse." Fortunately, the proprietress's legs hid the hoops that encircled the old nag and without which a smart aleck might suppose that no horse could float up on its own. "At this show, ladies and gentlemen, we present the celebrated Negro, Bamboula! Bamboula! The King of wrestling in New York! As you well know, I stop at nothing to engage worthy men! So I have paid for his travel expenses—even though it cost me an arm and a leg—for the sole purpose of presenting this admirable man to you."

Oh, the shows with which we hoodwinked the public! I will laugh at them for the rest of my life. They took place with such dizzying speed that the last to enter arrived just in time to pay his two sous but to miss the performance. This is how we bamboozled the audience: As soon as there were a few people inside, Toothless advanced toward the two peculiar weights that were resting on a chair. He never lifted barbells or dumbbells.

Just before he got to them, he stopped and eyed the audience scornfully. "Oh, I see that you are saying to yourselves," (remember that no one had made a peep), "'Feats with weights. We've seen that hundreds of times.' You want to see some wrestling. Well, then, have at it." He proposed two matches without further ado. Before the black man wrestled, Raulin would seat himself and announce gravely, "Ladies and gentlemen, I implore you to follow the American's movements very carefully. In him lie all my hopes."

The match had hardly begun before Bamboula went onto his two shoulder blades without having even attempted any resistance. Then Raulin announced with comical sarcasm, "I, who have spent so much money to get you here.... I now have to watch you lie down like a cow!" There were gales of laughter from the audience at this. "One more wrestling match to say thank you, ladies and gentlemen!"

Sometimes hecklers would call for the horse lift. Raulin then seemed to have a brainwave. He showed them the animal as it chewed a few miserable shafts of hay with its worn, dull teeth. "Have a little pity for this poor beast.... At this time, anyway, can you tell me what would be gained from the experience... ? but at the next performance, he will have a fuller belly, and he will be heavier." And so on, up to the midnight show, it was always the same patter.

Toothless died in Paris at the Lariboisière Hospital in November 1899 at the age of fifty-two years.[117] He was buried in the Pantin Cemetery.[118]

Louis Mazin

"The classic wrestler Mazin" is what he liked to be called, and the man's competence in wrestling was indisputable. Mazin was born in Bordeaux in 1847 where he had begun as a strongman. One fine day he abandoned weights and barbells and became a wrestler, and later the understander in several acrobatic troupes, but this type of profession did not suit him very well.[119] He then became a comic singer, a clown, even a boxer before he became a wrestler again. Mazin held the title of Champion of Bordeaux for ten years in a row. He wrestled almost

A former strongman and acrobat, Louis Mazin later became a wrestler. He also helped Desbonnet to research this book (collection of Michael Murphy).

everywhere. He remained as quick and nimble as a youth of twenty years, but he had the vanity not to confess his age or the length of his career. He was the pupil of Old Bernard, the father of the well-known champion Félix Bernard, and Mazin was a champion himself; he despised brutal wrestling where bulk was more important than strategy.

Here are some technical details. He was from Bordeaux, measured 1 meter 68 in height, weighed 160 pounds, and had a chest circumference of 1 meter 16. He died in April of 1907 at the age of sixty. Mazin was a striking example of what training could do for a man; in particular, he retained a remarkable agility and vigor right up until his death. Mazin was a friend to everyone, and he greatly helped me in the construction of this book, for since 1863 he knew all the wrestlers and strongmen, and his recollections have been particularly precious to me. He was an excellent man whom we could shake hands with confidence, because he had always known how to stay away from pseudo-athletes whose morality is too often questionable.[120]

He triumphed over the famous Milhomme "Pitiless"; Picard "the Bordelais"; Emile "the Spaniard"; Hervas and Toby. Mazin had wrestled with all the great champions of his era: Étienne "the Shepherd"; Bonnet "the Ox"; Pujol "the Pillar of Porte-Neuve"; Marseille "the Miller of Lapalud"; Dumortier "the Agile Lyonnais"; Freysinet "the Crimson Snatcher"; the Miller of Darnetal; Faouët "the Wild Beast of the Jungle"; Achille "the Colossus of Mount Ventoux"; Deligne; Rambeau "the Serpent of Ariège"; Bernard; Pietro "the Master of Masters"; Fénelon; Sabès; Gambier; Pons; Laurent of Beaucaire; and Aimable of Calmette.

He had met with such foreign wrestlers as: Tom Cannon; Antonio Pierri "the Greek"; Carl Abs; George Green, "the Englishman"; Joe Carrol; Petroff the Bulgarian; Nurullah; Kara Osman; Mehmet; Mémich; Yusuf; Schmelling; Pytlazinski; and many others.

Paul Fournier

Fournier was born in Lyon in 1854, and he was one of the wrestling veterans who had an enormous reputation around 1890. Fournier took part in several world championships, and he was always classed among the best. Such kings of wrestling as Tom Cannon, Pytlazinski, Sabès, and Félix Bernard had all fought Fournier, and the last two were even defeated by him.[121]

Despite his age, his weight (85 kilos) and his height (1 meter 70), Fournier was still one of the most prominent French wrestlers in 1900, thanks to his endurance, his strength, and his knowledge of wrestling. Fournier was from Lyon; when he was in his prime, he measured 1 meter 18 in the chest, 41 centimeters in the arms and 34½ centimeters in the forearm. His son [François] promises to be a worthy replacement for him.

 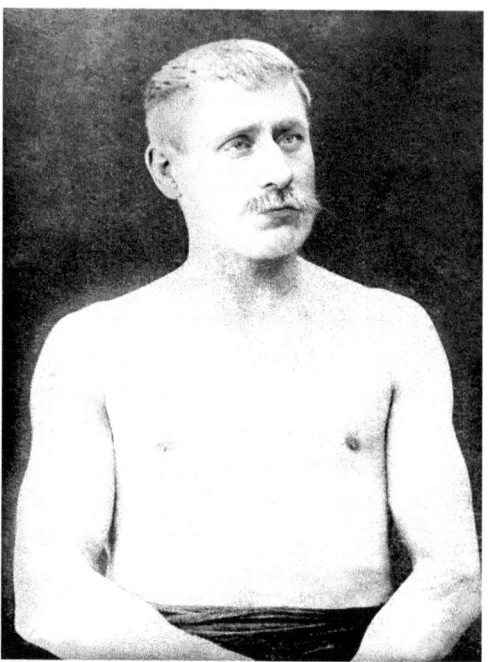

Left: When it came to wrestling, Paul Fournier valued experience and technique over brutality, and he was much respected for this quality (collection of Christian Gaildraud). *Right:* Trillat was credited with almost unbelievable feats of strength, and he was also a talented wrestler who defeated some of the finest grapplers of the time (collection of Michael Murphy).

Trillat "the Savoyard"

"The Barrel Man" is the name that he was given because he once carried a 175-pound cask on his back on top of which sat Paul Pons. At that time Pons weighed 100 kilos, Trillat thus supported a total weight of 275 kilos, and he made several laps of the track in this way without appearing inconvenienced by his burden. Later, Trillat was able to transport a millstone weighing 510 kilos on his shoulders. Jean-Pierre de Montastruc did this astounding feat but with 500 kilos, a weight that was difficult to surpass in similar conditions.[122]

Trillat the wrestler was equal to Trillat the strongman. He defeated Paul Pons at Toulouse in 1897, and at the end of that same year in a booth at the Neuilly Fair, he delivered the same fate to Sabès "the Bordelais."

Trillat was born in Savoy at Romagneux in 1863. At the Roubaix [weightlifting] Club he achieved a swing lift and a snatch of three 20-kilo weights at a time when he was no longer the Trillat that he once was. Indeed, an unfortunate addiction to drink brought him to a rapid decline, and he died in Paris in 1908 in direst poverty. Around 1900 he was 1 meter 79 tall, 1 meter 15 in the chest; 38 centimeters in the arm, 39 centimeters in the calves; he weighed 92 kilos.

François "the Bordelais"

The astonishing little wrestler who, despite his white hair, would still give a hard time to more than one crafty devil, was born in Orléans. The real name of François the Bordelais is Paul Levacher, and he began to wrestle in 1874. He was the pupil of the famous Frank of Montmartre (now passed away).[123]

From 1874 to 1887 François wrestled all over. In 1874, he was seen wrestling against the famous Negro James ["the Terrible Negro of Jamaica"] who was part of the Rossignol-Rollin troupe. He could be seen working the ticket table of the Étaux brothers' wrestling arena.[124] François wrestled with the best experts of his times. No matter what the circumstance, he knew how to oppose brute force with a marvelous agility and an artistic finesse that has always made him sympathetic to the public. He was a marvelous teacher, and the Negro Abdullah Jeffery was one of his pupils.

François le Bordelais knew how "to oppose brute force with a marvelous agility and an artistic finesse that has always made him sympathetic to the public" (collection of Michael Murphy).

Raoul "the Bordelais"

Raoul Guimberteau was the real name of Raoul, the Bordelais, and he began his wrestling career at the age of eighteen with Félix Bernard; Pietro Dalmasso; Auguste, "the Butcher"; and others. His first victories were those he won at the Bordeaux Arena against Picard, Rambaud, and Boyer of Marseilles, and they were certainly not ordinary triumphs. At the age of twenty he defeated C[h]ristol, the American champion in fifty seconds at the Crystal Palace in Marseilles.[125]

After his military service; Raoul, the Bordelais, returned to Bordeaux and acted as director of the Great Bordeaux Wrestling establishment. Many of our best wrestlers were coached by him. Raoul the Bordelais, was born in 1855.[126]

Left: Although he was an excellent wrestler, Raoul le Bordelais achieved his greatest success as an organizer and referee of matches. *Right:* Belgian wrestler Henri Péchon possessed great strength and a noble head.

Henri Péchon

The heavyweight Péchon was 1 meter 80 tall and weighed 103 kilos. He was born in Belgium in 1850. He wrestled with the illustrious Félix Bernard, Old Pietro, Hans Beck, and Pytlazinski. Péchon once did a one-handed swing lift of 92 kilos. If his knowledge had been proportional to his strength, he would have been an extraordinary wrestler. His arm is featured in my gallery of plaster casts.[127]

Pietro Dalmasso

Hail to the illustrious Pietro! Even though he has been retired for fifteen years, this man's name has remained in the public memory as a symbol of strength and skill. Indeed, while Pietro (nicknamed the "Rampart of Turin") occupied the mat, there was no athlete in the world who could compete with him. His knowledge of wrestling, his muscular strength, his lightning speed of execution put him above everyone else. Tom Cannon, Félix Bernard, Muldoon, Gambier, Sabès, Carl Abs, Fournier, and even Pons himself had to bow before this extraordinary man who really had no equal.[128]

Pietro was born in 1852 in Chieri (Italy), and he weighed 95 kilos and was 1 meter 76 tall.[129] His strength was very great. I have seen him snatch a barbell of 152 pounds very easily and afterward he picked up two 50-pound weights from the floor, which he turned flat and held with outstretched arms as if he were playing.

One day we played a little trick on Apollon.[130] We let him believe that he had become a very good wrestler and that Pietro would not survive in a match with him. On the other hand, Pietro was told that the terrible Hercules was claiming that he would make short work of him. Pietro jumped up in outrage. At last, we brought the men together. A tiger jumping on a rhinoceros, that was the impression imagined by the privileged spectators of this little match … for a laugh. Two slaps aside his head, followed by a masterful neck choke hold, and the champion of strength rolled on his broad shoulders. Apollo never knew what hit him, and we still laugh about it.

The great Franco-Italian wrestler Pietro Dalmasso was a major talent in wrestling, but he also managed several companies of wrestlers (both male and female) who performed in Europe and America (collection of Michael Murphy).

Pierre Desbordes

Pierre Desbordes, "the Rampart of Limousin," was born in 1817 and died 19 June 1896 at the age of seventy-nine years. In spite of his great age, he remained excessively robust, and until the last few years he did not cease to exercise his spry and victorious old age in matches with renowned athletes who passed through Limoges from time to time. We remember, in this connection, the introductory patter spouted by [Don] Ramon, the director of an athletic arena, who said, "Since Desbordes has been fighting, he has never been defeated by anyone, but among all his adversaries, there is only one he has not been able to pin to the mat, and that is I, your humble servant." Not to have been defeated by Desbordes was, for this professional wrestler, the height of glory.

Here are some unpublished details about this man who was so popular in Limousin and who had retained his extraordinary strength until a very advanced age. Dr. [Ferdinand] Lagrange [1846–1909] has noted this last fact in one of his works on physical exercise.

Desbordes was the son of a miller from near Limoges and was employed in the

Pouyat firm as a carter for almost his entire life.¹³¹ He began as a wrestler very young, and for forty years, no athlete could beat him when he wanted to fight seriously. It often happened that he let himself be defeated either out of complacency or for a more selfish motive, but even then he always took care to show his superiority by some feat which was not within the abilities of his adversary regardless of the latter's strength. For example, he might bring him to his knees just after the traditional handshake, by not releasing his adversary's hand and jerking him violently to the mat, or he might toss the man over his shoulder several meters behind him.

Not fifteen years ago we could see Desbordes carrying a cannon on his shoulder which would then be fired. Despite his great age, he engaged in this feat with an eternal smile on his lips and with a comfort and ease that surprised professionals of the genre.

He had a sister who was just as strong as he; she died young under singular circumstances. To satisfy a bet, she crossed a frozen stream laden with two sacks of flour; the ice cracked and after taking a very cold bath, the unfortunate woman succumbed to an inflammation of the chest.

Pierre Desbordes was a much-loved figure in Limoges, and when he was not wrestling, he worked at one of the porcelain factories in his hometown.

Old amateurs of Limoges remember the happy days of Desbordes at the Salle de Plaisance; the terrible members of the Rossignol-Rollin troupe looked like children next to this enormous fighter, who recalled the Hercules of marble left to us by ancient art.

Pierre Desbordes lived in Limoges where he was greatly esteemed.

Here is the biographical article that was dedicated to him from the newspaper the *Petit Centre* from Saturday, 20 June 1896, the day after his death.¹³²

> The *Petit Centre* announced yesterday evening the death of Pierre Desbordes, the old wrestler that everyone in Limousin knew and loved. He died at the age of seventy-nine years in the

little house where he lived with his family at number 4 Rue du Calvaire, in the middle of the neighborhood of Les Ponts.

Despite his great age, he still possessed Herculean strength. To everyone who encountered him it seemed that the ordinary events of life were powerless to destroy his vigorous constitution, and yet here he succumbed to the consequences of a heart ailment aggravated by the after effects of minor mouth surgery three days ago. We did not want to let this event (so newsworthy here in Limousin) pass without devoting a few lines to the invincible champion, to the legendary Hercules whose death will certainly leave a void in our city where he was popular and where, until recently, he led by example and contributed to spreading the taste for athletic sports so powerfully.

The "Rampart of Limousin," as he was fondly called, was not one of those athletes who rely mostly on their corpulence and an exaggerated amount of adipose tissue; on the contrary, he absolutely resembled the academic type and an admirable musculature on a sturdy framework. He measured 1 meter 95 in height and no less than 85 centimeters wide in the shoulders. The rest was proportional; he had huge hands that were strong as a vise, and his feet were renowned—his shoes were size 50.

When he began to wrestle, he worked as a laborer at the Pouyat factory in the Place des Carmes, and his comrades often enjoyed having him perform extraordinary feats of strength. His employer, Mr. Pouyat, who had a great affection for him, also took pleasure in having him compete with the fairground wrestlers who passed through Limoges from time to time; he even gave him money for it. The young people from the best families in Limoges were also very fond of the brave Desbordes. They encouraged him in his wrestling matches, supported him with their bets and no doubt, at the present time, several of them (now old men) will read these lines about the death of this wrestler with sadness since it will remind them of the prowess of their poor companion of the olden days.

We were told of this occurrence which is very amusing. Like all really strong men, Desbordes was a good person, and he was regularly the dupe of the showmen who used him to attract the crowd to their fair booths. They loudly announced their bouts against the Rampart of Limousin with stakes of 500 or 1,000 francs for the victor. The public crowded around the "athletic arena" where the matches took place, and Desbordes overcame his opponents and went away without touching any money, because the wrestlers who were always very poor had managed to make him feel sorry for their sad lot. Our good giant had been hoodwinked several times this way, when one day his employer, Mr. Pouyat put an end to this unscrupulous exploitation. In a fight that has become famous, he had the stakes placed on a table, had it guarded by two gendarmes, and he did not leave the stall until he was sure that the money had been transferred into the pocket of the invincible champion.

If Desbordes was good when treated honestly and when he was dealt with gently, he became terribly brutal when he had to encounter an adversary who showed ill will. One day, wrestling with an individual who had tried to use an injurious hold, he seized him with his hands by the left arm just at the level of the biceps and squeezed it so hard that under his iron fingers the skin of the arm burst and the blood spurted out. In a similar situation at the Alcazar where he was then wrestling, he took his adversary in a massive bear hug and crushed him against his vast chest and let him fall back almost fainting and spitting blood. On the Place de la République we ourselves have seen him throw a first-class wrestler down onto the mat with all four limbs in the air with a violent thrust because the opponent had used a controversial hold.[133]

When it was necessary to entice the public, and especially when his adversary gave him a "large sum" varying between five and twenty francs, Desbordes sometimes let himself be taken down, but almost always these fights of convenience were followed by superb revenge matches.

They tell of him this episode which shows that he was a veritable wonder of nature. One day he left the fairground and went through the wood market. There, he asked a peasant what price he wanted for a cartload of wood that required two oxen to pull. The peasant having asked an exaggerated price, Desbordes replied that this price was not in proportion to the "little bit" of wood that was on the cart.

"Little bit of wood!" said the annoyed peasant. "If you can load it on your shoulders, I will give it to you." Before you could say it twice, Desbordes got under the cart and lifted it with its load to the great amazement of the merchant and all those who were there.

He himself sometimes told the story that one night in Paris he had been attacked by twelve thugs, almost all of whom he had beaten up. We are convinced that there is nothing exaggerated in this episode considering that when he was young, Desbordes was as agile as he was strong. As he grew older (around 1875) Desbordes suffered mild attacks of rheumatism and had lost much of his agility. He no longer had much confidence in his legs and fought only on his knees [i.e., in referee's position]. In this position he was unshakable; he was a rock, a knotty trunk welded to the ground.

Even though he was still invincible despite his sixty years, he was no longer the good fighter that he once was. His fights were devoid of the thrilling interest that attaches to hotly contested matches. He had only to lay his hand on his adversary for him to be knocked down; nothing resisted the formidable pull of his enormous muscles. It was at this time that his famous struggles against Stiernon took place. Henri Stiernon [1838–1918] "the Northern Hercules," was not only a very strong man; he was also a showman who thoroughly knew all the tricks of his trade. He had understood all the advantages he could derive from Desbordes thanks to the fame attached to his name, so he exploited it to the fullest.

The fair booth on the Place de la Republique was comfortable, and from this headquarters, issued every day on the city a troop of poster hangers loaded with marvelous placards announcing continuously the assaults of a "rampart" of an "eel" or whatever "lion" was available against "the Indomitable Rampart of Limousin." What triumphant posters one could read at that time and how the public hastened to respond to their call! Generally, it was Stiernon, who fought against Desbordes, and Desbordes always emerged victorious from these wrestling matches that were worthy of the Olympic Games. The director of the athletic arena consoled himself for his successive defeats by contemplating the crowd, which packed his establishment at each performance; but in the long run, his self-esteem as an athlete was hurt, so he finally decided to present to the Rampart of Limousin a sensational challenge. Desbordes claimed that he wrestled on his knees because he had no strength in his legs; however, the challenge was to lift an old bronze artillery piece weighing more than 500 pounds.

The meeting took place at the Plège Circus, located then as today, on the Place de la Republique.[134] The cannon was placed horizontally on two trestles. Stiernon got underneath and lifted it on his shoulders. Desbordes went next. Not only did he lift the cannon, but he also walked around the ring carrying it on his shoulders, while the spectators, standing on the benches, applauded with delight. That same year, great wrestling matches were organized at the Plège Circus, following which Desbordes who had beaten all those who had come up against him received a large silver medal with the arms of the city emblazoned with these words: "City of Limoges, prize presented to Desbordes, the wrestling champion on 19 August 1877 at Limoges," and this inscription in the patois of Limousin: "Lou aï tou foutu per terro, lou aï tou bien roulas," which means "He knocked the heck out of them. He pinned 'em all." Desbordes was well over sixty at that point.

He wrestled again at the Café de Paris against Rabasson—if memory serves—in famous matches of the time where the winemaker Léon Noilhas received the nickname of "the Cannon Man." He also fought at the Alcazar, while Garemin was the manager, against the wrestler Robin.[135] Finally at the age of seventy-six, he fought in a number of fairground booths, still undefeated, still invincible. Managers of athletic arenas had respect for this giant whose reputation stretched far and wide in the world of wrestling; they had deference for him since he alone sufficed to attract the crowd.

One cannot imagine beautiful shows without Desbordes. "Strong as Desbordes" was a phrase commonly used to characterize an exaggeratedly strong man. Finally, we had become so used to seeing him contrast his victorious old age with the youth of all the athletes who passed through Limoges, that many of us would not have been surprised if on the eve of his death he might be seen subduing the superb bodies of the young Turks currently wrestling at the Plège Circus by his eighty-year-old muscles.

There would still be a lot to say about this poor old brave man whom all our fellow citizens will sincerely miss; but as this article is already very long, we will limit ourselves now to recalling that with him it is not only an original and thoroughly Limousin personality who dies, but also a good, loyal, honest man who takes with him to the grave the esteem and sympathy of all those who knew him.—Jean Couzeix

Félix Bernard

Félix Bernard had a very eventful life; he was born in Maubourget (Hautes-Pyrenees) in 1857 and died in Milan on 17 April 1900. His youth was somewhat turbulent. His father, known as "the King of Wrestlers," raised him in the open air just as the Duke d'Albret did for Henri IV.[136] When he was eight or ten years old, he was brought to Bordeaux where he spent his school years. Later, when he was around eighteen, he worked at clearing the moors in the of the Department of Landes—a miserable task which was very repugnant to him.[137] Fortunately, every Sunday he could enjoy himself by wrestling in the fair booths.

One feat reveals it all. Here are the details: during 1882, the fairground wrestler Charles presented a troupe of sixteen wrestlers in different towns in the South, and Bernard was hired by him. His comrades received the word that for his introduction to the public they should let the

Félix Bernard was son of a wrestler, but he won renown in France, England and elsewhere on his own. He was known for his pleasant and likeable personality.

newcomer win. Those who were jealous of him exclaimed, "To be defeated by this kid, under the pretext of advertising. Well, really! No way."

Charles warned Bernard of the state of mind of his companions. "Let's have at it!" he replied. "Since these gentlemen want it, we'll fight without trickery." And so it was done. Bernard defeated the sixteen wrestlers one after the other, and they later regretted not having allowed themselves to be beaten a bit more obediently. "Trumpet-tongued Fame" spread the story far and wide. The echo of it arrived all the way to Paris, and a Parisian sportsman, Mr. Lacaisse, a former wrestler, went to Bordeaux to search out the hero of this adventure in order to introduce him to the capital. Bernard thus appeared in Paris for the first time in 1882 on the stage of the Folies Bergère where he went up against Pietro who succeeded in defeating him after forty minutes of a very exciting match.

From 1882 to 1888 he lived in Bordeaux where he wrestled—continually wrestled from one end of the year to the other, formulating that valiant school of aggression and experience that was championed by Paul Puy in the now discontinued *Journal des Sports*.[138] For Bernard, the year 1889 consisted of a series of triumphs. It was on that date that his famous match with Tom Cannon took place—a much disputed match that was at the Folies Bergère and which unleashed such a violent tempest among the spectators. After he valiantly won a round, Bernard was taken down by the Englishman. The public were convinced that Cannon had won dishonestly, and they vigorously booed the Britisher and in the ensuing rampage they caused 10,000 francs worth of damage to the building and the gardens. It was an infamous evening.

English wrestler Tom Cannon called himself "the champion wrestler of the world," and he was adept at both Greco-Roman and freestyle forms of the sport. He frequently appeared in France (collection of Michael Murphy).

Bernard was at that time in the prime of life. Lacaisse then took him to England where he fought frequently at the Aquarium against Pietro, Tom

Cannon, and Steedman—and always and always successfully. This tour of the land of fog lasted six weeks. Bernard soon returned to Paris and fought with Apollon, Crest, Eugene de Paris, and Pytlazinski in the Arena at 24 Quai Debilly. In 1890 he returned to Bordeaux for a match with his old adversary, Tom Cannon. Toward the end of the year, both men fought again at the Casino de Paris. It was in 1891 that he began as a wrestling teacher at the Piazza Gymnasium, and after a few months, he sponsored Cesari, Piazza's father-in-law at the Sorbonne gymnasium.[139] In both establishments he had many students who wanted to be taught by him. Among them, I will mention Mr. Semitchoff, son of an aide-de-camp to Emperor Alexander III, and Mr. Bonvalot, the intrepid explorer.[140]

In 1894, Bernard won a brilliant victory at the Folies Bergère against the Englishman Bob Marshall, who was believed to be unbeatable.[141] His compatriots had bet outrageous sums on him. Imagine their surprise and their confusion on seeing Marshall taken down five times in ten minutes by the valiant Bernard. It was a disaster for the sons of Albion. The stakes for this meet were 5,000 francs in total.

Mehmet, the Turkish wrestler, was not happy with his match against Bernard in 1895.[142] It might be remembered that the fight took place at the Folies Bergère. Petroff the Bulgarian, was also beaten by the son of the "King of Wrestlers." Toward the end of 1895 after a rest of several months that he took in Bordeaux, Bernard left again with Pons; Leitner "the Chain Breaker"; and Eugène de Paris for a tour around the United Kingdom.[143] It was during this trip that he contracted the germs of the malady to which he eventually succumbed.[144]

As soon as he was back on his feet, he left for Russia the following year where he won a few more matches. In 1898 Constant "the Butcher," succeeded in defeating him at the wrestling championships in Roubaix. It must be said that Bernard was dealing with an unparalleled athlete who was tireless and who was victorious by sheer strength rather than by the knowledge of wrestling because at that time Constant was not the fine wrestler that he is today. Since that time Bernard has, as it were, abandoned active wrestling. His tour of Europe was a great success, but these frequent journeys affected his health once again, and he came to Milan to die quietly like a lamp whose oil is gradually consumed.

What a misfortune that a man who was so gifted should die so prematurely! These were the kinds of exclamations of those who had known him. Bernard was the very incarnation of likeability.[145] He was not conceited, not at all boastful, not smitten with himself; he was simply excited by a good wrestling match, and he liked to tell about his previous exploits plainly but always with modesty! He diminished his victories, and he sometimes lingered over his defeats with a very sincere embarrassment. He embodied the smiling and friendly wrestler, and even at the height of the fight, he still retained the look of a statue; in a word, he was an artistic wrestler. At first sight, he was hardly impressive. He was not a Hercules, but thanks to his expert knowledge of wrestling, to the rapidity of his holds, to the natural grace of his movements, he managed to disconcert and then to defeat formidable adversaries—and to us that seems to be ideal.

It is reported that after he was defeated by his pupil [George] San Marin at the Piazza Gymnasium, Bernard's father disinherited his son.[146] Unfortunately, he could hardly have done so. Father and son always fought for the sake of fighting; they made a lot of money in the ring but they died poor. Félix Bernard never loved money. He did not know the value of it; he earned it easily, and he was free with his money when touched by unfortunates. To strength and power, he combined tenderness. This wolf on the stage was a lamb with his friends.

Clovis Citerne

Clovis Citerne (called Clovis) was a great big blond fellow who would have become extraordinarily solid if he had a little less love of gambling, wine, women, and tobacco. He wrestled at fairs, and he is recorded in Lille as "a strongman," but to tell the truth, no one ever saw him do anything to deserve this title.

Clovis died young, done in by the life that he led; he did not even reach his forties. One can notice on his left ear the stigmata caused by wrestling, when the ear is broken by a turn of the head or a stranglehold around the head; moreover, many wrestlers display an example of this professional deformation. In 1899 it was the subject of a doctoral thesis by Dr. [Gaëtan Henri Alfred] de Clérambault [1872–1934], *Contributions to the Study of Othematoma*.[147] This disfigurement can be found on the ears of certain Greek wrestlers.

Clovis Citerne died young thanks to his dissolute habits. His melancholy expression and cauliflower ear testify to his rough life.

The Negro Bamboula

Anytime a Negro wrestles, he is called Bamboula, but the real Bamboula—the very first one—was actually a very skilled wrestler, and it is he who is shown in the accompanying photograph. He is moreover recognizable by a mark on his right elbow. This deformation was caused by a type of cyst that caused a projection that was three centimeters thick. This was all the more annoying because Bamboula's arm, like the rest of his body, appeared remarkably fine.[148]

At this time Bamboula was twenty-five or thirty years old, and he was in top condition.[149] The photograph that we have of him was taken in Roubaix in 1898 when poor Bamboula, aged around forty years, was plunged into a dark depression when he rarely ate his fill but often drank more than he should have. However, he still had the remains of a fine body, and it is obvious that he must have had an impeccable physique.

Bamboula was married to a white woman.[150] We do not know what became of this poor wretch![151]

Although many others took his name, this is the original Bamboula. The name came to be attached to any Negro wrestler, but the real one is distinguished by his genuine skill as a wrestler and a deformation of his right elbow (collection of Michael Murphy).

Laurent of Paris

Laurent of Paris was born in Vesoul [Burgundy-Franche-Comté] in 1854. He was a dangerous wrestler who was rascally, and full of tricks with an opponent who refused be defeated. Fat, short, and adorned with an enormous belly, he did not look much like a fighting gladiator. I saw him for the first time around 1887 in Lille. I saw him again in 1906 in Paris at a fairground on the Boulevard Rochechouart.[152] Since then, I do not know what became of him because Laurent of Paris (a native of Vesoul) never performed in any major championships.

Marseille the younger (left), Bazin (center), and Laurent of Paris (right) all try to look fierce. Laurent was an unscrupulous and crafty wrestler, and Bazin "the Artilleryman" was remarkable only for his death in a knife fight.

Bazin the "Artilleryman"

Bazin was born in Paris in 1863, he was an ordinary wrestler who did little worth talking about. He was assassinated in Lyon by an individual with whom he had fallen into a quarrel. A stab wound that perforated the intestines of this young wrestler (he was thirty years old) put an end to a career that nothing he had previously done would predict a brilliant career. He should not be confused with the real [Adonis] Bazin, the strongman and weight lifter whom we discussed elsewhere in *The Kings of Strength*. [pp. 167–68 in that book]

The Kings of Wrestling
Contemporary Wrestlers

THE CONTEMPORARIES

I adopted no particular order for the listing of contemporary wrestlers. In these random memories I noted what I knew about them, alternating the mightiest men with athletes of lesser importance, but whose sporting value gave them a well-deserved place in this book.

Zbyszko

Zbyszko (whose real name is Stanislas Cyganiewicz) was born in Strij (Galicia) in 1883 [died 1967].[1] He belonged to the Windobona Club in Vienna where he began to participate in athletics—and before he began any serious training, he quickly performed feats that were out of the ordinary.[2]

Here are Zbyszko's exact measurements that were taken in my anthropometric office in the faubourg Poissonnière. 1 meter 75 in height, 51 centimeters neck circumference, 130 centimeters chest

Stanislaus Zbyszko was active from the turn of the century to the 1950s. He was intelligent and an accomplished linguist as well as an extremely competent athlete.

(expanded), 124.5 chest (normal), shoulder circumference 152 centimeters (a record!). His left arm is 47 centimeters (bent); his right forearm (extended) is 39 centimeters; forearm bent at a right angle to the arm measures 42 centimeters; his left forearm is 37 centimeters. His waist measures 1 meter in its normal state and 93 centimeters when the abdomen is retracted. Zbyszko's thigh measures 72 centimeters; his calf is 46 centimeters. His fist circumference is 21.5 centimeters; his deltoid circumference is 58 centimeters. His weight (stripped) is 110 kilos; and his shoulder width is 61 centimeters.

Zbyszko's strength is no less extraordinary than his measurements; without being trained, he cleaned 120 kilos two times with two hands and jerked it to arm's length without moving his feet; he bent-pressed 115 kilos without resting it on his shoulder, and at the Weightlifting Club of France he registered 125 kilos in his first attempt on the Régnier dynamometer (normal position). We note that Zbyszko currently holds the world record for biceps circumference, but his forearm is smaller than that of our French champion Apollon, whose forearm measures 44.5 centimeters.

Zbyszko has carved out a good reputation for himself in wrestling, and we don't see anyone except Poddubny standing up to him at the moment.[3]

Van Tol

[J. E.] Van Tol was born in 1879, and he is neither tall nor heavy, but he has surprised all the experts at the time of the great championships. His comrades and his adversaries have nicknamed him "the Earthworm," because Van Tol has extraordinarily suppleness, stamina, skill, and energy. This young wrestler knows how to attract the sympathy of the audience by his pleasant appearance and by his honesty. Van Tol who is Dutch, measures 1 meter 68 tall and weighs 78 kilos.[4]

Dutch wrestler Van Tol was nicknamed "the earthworm" because of his ability to wriggle out of almost any hold.

Jean-Pierre Pierrard

This man is the heavyweight record holder; consider this: he weighs 155 kilos and is 1 meter 83 in height. Even so, his weight does not prevent him from fighting with great skill. Jean-Pierre Pierrard, who is Belgian, has always been recognized in his country as a very strong man and he once triumphed in a strength championship organized in Liège.[5]

He can easily carry three sacks of flour on his back and he can walk with it 200 meters; he can lift equally well the axle of a tram that two ordinary men are incapable of moving.

Lassartesse

The South of France is where [Gabriel] Lassartesse was born and where he acquired an athletic education as a wrestler from Sabès "the Bordelais." He continued to make his way in life until (at the 1899 championships) he pinned Tom Cannon in no time at all.

Lassartesse registered 172.5 kilos on the Régnier dynamometer (free position), he snatched 70 kilos three times in a row without releasing the barbell, and 75 kilos two times. One day he performed five squats with 135 kilos on his shoulders. In 1903 at the championships, he established the record for the snatch with 173 pounds in his right hand, and this was at a time when he only weighed 159 pounds. He was able to hoist 160 pounds in the swing lift. He is a wonderful wrestler of the Bordeaux school. His measurements are remarkable. He is 1 meter 71 tall, and has arms of 41.5 centimeters and forearms of 34 centimeters.[6]

The Turk Cotch Mehmet discovered that he was a tough adversary. His relatively low weight is the only obstacle that prevents him from triumphing over the heavyweight champions, because Lassartesse has a strength and a knowledge that are difficult to equal.[7]

Gabriel Lassartesse was a lightweight wrestler at a time when there were no weight divisions, but he managed to use his natural aggression to overcome many opponents (collection of Michael Murphy).

Sossiko Essebona

Sossiko Essebona is a wrestler from the Caucasus who is 2 meters 6 centimeters in height and weighs 145 kilos.[8] He is extraordinarily strong, and he is particularly fond of belt wrestling, so named because after putting on a kind of jacket equipped with a leather belt passing around the waist, the two wrestlers try to take one another down by grabbing this belt. It is said that Sossiko Essebona is so powerful that a man with the strength of Pons, for example, could hardly resist him for a quarter of a minute. All those who have wrestled with him could not do better than resist for half a minute.

Sossiko Essebona enjoys a well-deserved reputation in Russia, but he is completely unknown in France. Let us hope that some enterprising impresario will decide to bring this famous athlete to a wrestling championship at the Folies Bergère or the Casino de Paris. The photograph shows Sossiko Essebona in his early twenties; he is now thirty years old and in the prime of his muscular power would allow him to stand up to all our French champions, even in Greco-Roman wrestling, a style he barely knows. His weight, his height, his measurements, his strength make him almost unbeatable. Will we see Sossiko Essebona in Paris? We hope so![9]

The regions in the Caucasus mountains in central Asia has long been home to a number of belt wrestlers like Sossiko Essebona.

Léon Dumont

He was born in Havre on 30 December 1867, and he began in athletics as a weight lifter, and he achieved superb results; he was also equally devoted to wrestling where his weight and strength made him a fearsome adversary.[10]

Dumont weighs 115 kilos.[11] He became an impresario and introduced many worthy men in Paris—men like Ahmed Madrali, Siegfried, and others. He was a good wrestler who was hard to pin, and he is not much easier to take down as an impresario.[12]

Crest

Crest was born in 1860. He is a wrestler of considerable merit who was for a long time the bodyguard of Max Lebaudy (he is not to be confused with Creste, "the Bull of Provence" who died a long time ago).[13] During the performances of *La Prise de Troie* [The Siege of Troy] at the Opera, he was responsible for organizing the wrestling matches that figured in this work.[14] It was on this occasion that he had calling cards made thusly.

Léon Dumont was an excellent wrestler, and then later in life he became the manager of a group of wrestlers who traveled around western Europe and North Africa (collection of Michael Murphy).

CREST
Professor of Wrestling
at the Opera

Which he soon replaced with others that were, shall we say, simpler.

CREST
of the Opera

It is said that next time the printer, a former typographer who was an incorrigible practical joker, gave him a hundred cards with the following wording.

CREST
Professor of Lute at the Opera

In the end, the good man may have believed that it was a printing error, but this one was a corker.[15]

Left: Crest began as a wrestler, but he was proudest of his work as technical advisor of the Paris Opera. *Right:* Alix the Negro seems to have inspired little admiration as a wrestler. He was described as "slender, fairly knowledgeable, but not having enough stamina."

Alix the Negro

This wrestler who had his hour of fame is well known in Bordeaux where he wrestled in the fair booth of the Etaux [vise] Brothers so called because of the strength of their hands. The climate did not suit him well and he died young of tuberculosis. How many unfortunate Blacks have thus found in our country a miserable end for which our climate was not always solely responsible.[16]

Anton Zaremba

Zaremba was born in Vienna, Austria [in 1866, died 1937], and he was one of the strongest Austrian athletes. He debuted as a strongman in 1881 and here are several of his records: one-handed snatch 130 pounds; without bending his knees and keeping his body erect, he pressed 200 pounds with two hands six times in a row, and 268 pounds in the two-handed jerk.[17]

Zaremba is 1 meter 84 tall, chest circumference 1 meter 34, 72 centimeters in the thigh, 1 meter 15 waist, 47 centimeters calves, and he weighs 268 pounds. If such a man were to train for wrestling, he ought to be in the highest levels, but at the present moment Zaremba's knowledge does not seem to be equal to his athletic ability.

Raoul "the Butcher"

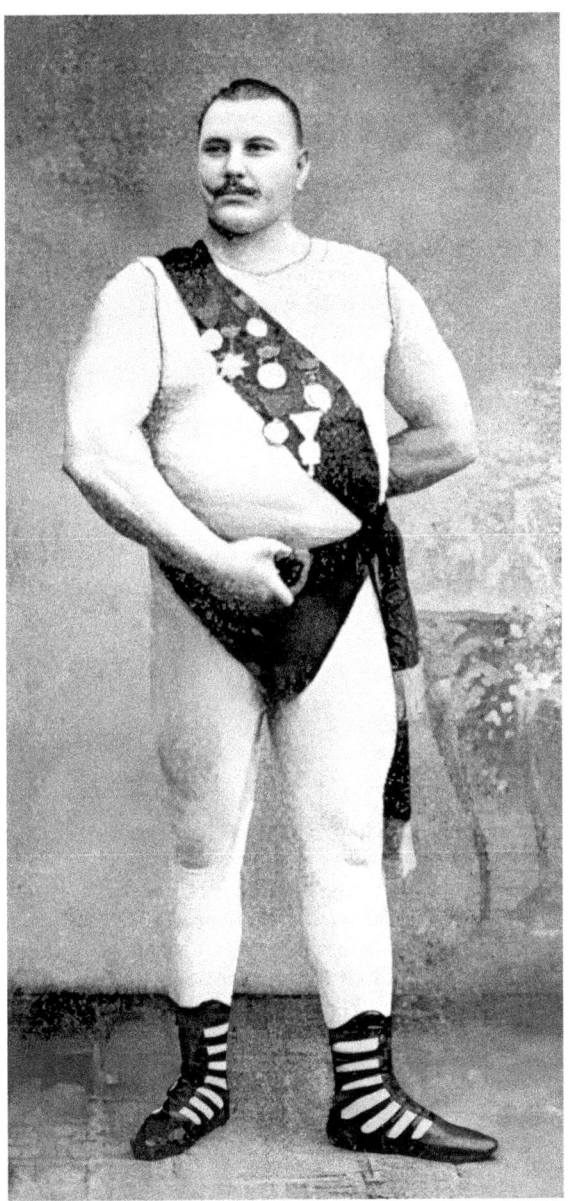

Austrian athlete Anton Zaremba could have been a great wrestler, but he had not learned enough technical skill to attain the heights.

Raoul the Butcher's real name is Raoul Musson, and he was born in 1883 in Chatillon-sur-Loire (Loiret). While still very young he came to Paris, and he was placed by his parents with a butcher for whom he was supposed to take over. Young Raoul was athletically built, and he was quickly smitten by strength exercises, and when he was barely thirteen years old, he was one of the most noted customers of the Pons Gymnasium on the Avenue des Tilleuls in Montmartre.

He devoted himself to wrestling and soon excelled at it. We know that many in the butcher's profession have always practiced wrestling as their favorite sport and that this craft has already given us a great wrestler, Constant le Boucher. After having taken down the best amateurs, he took on professionals and amazed his instructors. His public debut took place in 1899 at the Hippodrome; he was sixteen years old. But it was not until 1901 when he was eighteen years old that he revealed himself as a great wrestler, rising to fourth place in the world championships [in Vienna]. In the world championships of 1902 [in Vienna again] at the age of nineteen years, he was second behind [Jess] Petersen and had in the course of this tournament met [Ivan Maximovitch] Poddubny [1871–1949] who was there for the first time. Neither of the two men could pin the other, and after many long hours of wrestling the judges granted the victory to Raoul by a single point. In the same year he took part in the first Gold Belt championships, and took third place behind Pons and Laurent of Beaucaire. In 1903, again in the Gold Belt, he took third behind Pons and Petersen, but he pinned Laurent le Beaucairois [1867–?].[18]

In 1904 in the third and final Gold Belt contest, he was second, defeated only by Pons, then he entered a contest in Buenos Aires during which he pinned Paul Pons several times conclusively. In November of 1905 we find him at the Folies Bergère, still not having an opponent capable of troubling him except Pons who became in the meantime a close friend and partner. This was the last time that he was to wrestle in Paris. After a new tournament that was long and successful, Raoul had amassed a certain fortune and bought a nice piece of property in Maisons-Laffitte that had once belonged to [wealthy horse breeder] M.E. Fischoff.[19]

Raoul the Butcher died prematurely in 1907 on the day of Mardi Gras at eight o'clock in the morning at the Villa Sainte-Marguerite in Nice. Raoul had been on the Riviera for about three months. He lived at the Fournier Hotel on the Cap d'Ail and had come from Paris by motorcar with his brother-in-law. Both men frequently went to Nice where the winter visitors soon recognized the figure of the famous wrestler.

Raoul the Butcher was an extremely talented grappler, but he died prematurely after refusing to give up his unhealthy antics while on a vacation to the French Riviera (collection of Michael Murphy).

Raoul the Butcher contracted a bad case of influenza, and he should have remained in his room, but despite his sickness he felt full of life, and he had never wanted to keep to his bed. Typhoid fever began to set in and a short while later he contracted meningitis. Soon he was out of his mind, refusing all the medicines that Doctors Prons and Péguin (who had been summoned in great haste to Cap d'Ail) had prescribed for him. In his fever, the athlete wanted to wrestle, to wrestle against everyone or to leave immediately in the automobile for Paris. "I have to leave at once," he raved. "I have an engagement to fulfill, and I will be disqualified for life if I do not defeat them all, one after the other."

Summoned by telegram, his mother and his two sisters had to act quickly, and have him driven to Nice by devoted members of the Nice chapter of the Green Cross.[20] It took five muscular young men to hold the wrestler down and, half an hour later, to carry him to an open motorcar which took him to the Villa Sante-Marguerite, the clinic of Dr. Fossé. But the fever still raged and poor Raoul's condition soon became desperate. On Mardi Gras at five o'clock while all Nice was in the midst of carnival, Raoul the Butcher fell into a coma, and at eight o'clock he was dead! He had been struck down by meningitis. Raoul the Butcher's body today rests in Maisons-Laffitte.[21]

The measurements of this unforgettable wrestler were amazing: arms 44 centimeters, forearms 36 centimeters, thigh 72 centimeters, calf 48 centimeters, chest 1 meter 36, waist 1 meter 7, height 1 meter 86. His feats were no less remarkable: press of a 200-pound barbell; one-hand snatch of 140 pounds; arm extension of a 20-kilo ring weight (25 kilos with a slight lean of the body). He deadlifted 443 pounds and stood upright with it.

Kuhlo

Kuhlo, the Indian wrestler, is the brother of the famous wrestler Gulam, for Gulam is not the only one in the family to possess great muscular strength, and all his brothers, like him, have extraordinary vigor. From the point of view of strength, Kuhlo comes immediately after Gulam, and he made a deep impression when he appeared on the stage of the Hippodrome during the 1900 World's Fair. In less time than it takes to say it, he fell upon his adversary who was opposing him and pinned him instantly; it is perhaps more accurate to say that he crushed him as a giant would a pygmy. Since a serious opponent to Kuhlo could not be found, he did not really give the full measure of what he could do, but we believe that if he was not quite of Gulam's strength,

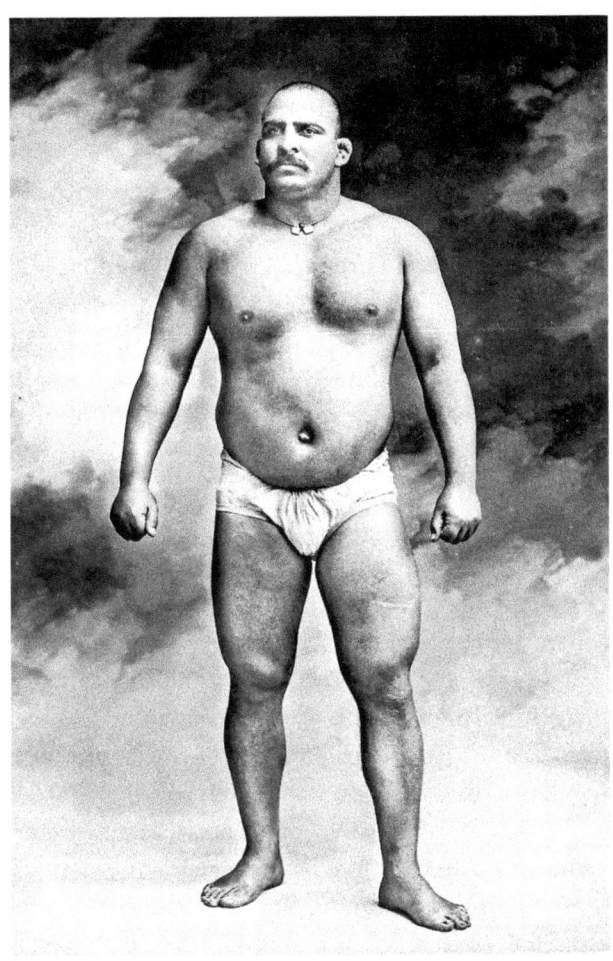

Indian wrestler Kuhlo possessed tremendous strength and speed, and he was a powerful adversary in the ring (collection of Michael Murphy).

he is not far from it and that a match between the two brothers would be really exciting.

In 1900 Kuhlo's measurements were as follows: height 1 meter, 72, neck 40 centimeters, chest 1 meter 32, arm 44 centimeters, forearm 33.5 centimeters, thigh 73 centimeters, calf 42 centimeters, weight 110 kilos.

Kuhlo combines astounding strength with unforgettable agility. As soon as the referee blew his whistle, he fell upon his adversary and pinned him so quickly that it was impossible to see which hold he had used. We can count Kuhlo among the kings of wrestling—those whom we can justifiably call super-athletes—men like Gulam, Yusuf, Faouët, Pietro, etc. Here is what one of my students and friends told me about Kuhlo.

It was when Yusuf was reigning at the Folies Bergère [around 1895]. Pons was among those who were defeated, but he did not say much, however Pierri and Tom Cannon wanted revenge.[22] These two were very good friends at that time, and they vowed to Yusuf that they would find someone who could overcome him. "On that day," said the Terrible Turk, "I will cut my own throat"; in fact, neither he nor his family would ever admit defeat.

Doubtless Pierri and Tom Cannon said to one another, "This will be even better." The two sanctimonious friends went to Turkey where the only one who responded to their inquiries was the brave Kara Ahmed. But he had hardly arrived in Paris when he repented, knowing that Yusuf had decided to kill him during the match; he therefore pretended to be sick and it was the courageous Ibrahim who took the beating. As it had been predicted, Yusuf emerged victorious from the encounter, but the hero was still Ibrahim. It was necessary to look elsewhere if Yusuf were to be defeated; he himself had imprudently declared that the men he feared most were the Hindus. Therefore, despite the distance, Pierri and Tom Cannon set off across the seas and arrived in Calcutta on a festival day. All the wrestlers of northern India, all the stars of the kingdom of Lahore were there. It could not have fallen into place better, as we say in Brussels.

From their first appeal, the two partners made it clear to their hosts that their trip was very expensive and that they wanted to make no mistake about their choice. "But since you are European champions," they were told, "it is up to you to try the wrestlers. You will not lose much by defeat and, if you win, you will be rewarded as never before." Pierri and Tom Cannon were very tempted to accept the match; a tribal chief from the Punjab presided. He lined up his wrestlers in order of size, and had Kuhlo come forward, at a time when he was in his true environment and in splendid shape.

"That fellow surely won't know the American-style arm flip," said Pierri to Tom Cannon, "You can take him down easily." And Tom Cannon undressed quickly so that he could confront his adversary. He did not have to wait for long. Kuhlo clapped hands on both sides of his body, lifted him, spun him around, and threw him over both shoulders with a speed and force that stunned the European champion. "I don't know how he took me down," said Tom Cannon, "but it has never happened to me like that before."

"Now, let's have the second one," shouted the chief of the tribe, and immediately he brought Gulam forward. When he saw this fellow who was a fifth larger than Kuhlo step up, jumping like a child and grinning with happiness, Pierri could only murmur to Tom Cannon, "If the younger one dealt with you as he just did, what will the older one do? Let's get back on the boat!" They did not bring anyone back with them because they had to pay too much for these Hindu masters of wrestling.[23]

Janos Czaia

The Hungarian champion Janos Czaia left me with a particularly intense impression. It seemed that he knew neither pain nor fatigue. He possessed an extraordinary strength, and resembled Petersen a little. He weighs 105 kilos and is 1 meter 74 tall.[24]

Paul Belling

Here is another colossus, Paul Belling. He is a German by birth, but he became a naturalized Englishman.[25] He was a former lifting champion. He snatched 80 kilos

Left: Hungarian fighter Janos Czaia had great strength and endurance, but he never had much success (collection of Michael Murphy). *Right*: Paul Belling was reportedly "a handsome and well-built Teuton" who was successful in both France and England. He later fell afoul of the English authorities for running a bawdy house (collection of Michael Murphy).

with one hand, swing lifted 82 kilos, and lifted 125 kilos with two hands. Belling measured 1 meter 82 in height and he weighed 120 kilos. He earned a well-deserved reputation in Paris where he performed in wrestling championships.[26]

Reiber

Leonhard Reiber is a Tyrolian colossus who came to Paris to challenge Poddubny, but despite his extraordinary strength, he had to return to his country without having been able to defeat the formidable Russian champion. Reiber is a man who is 1 meter 84 tall; he has arms that measure 43 centimeters; calf 44 centimeters; 68 centimeters thigh; 1 meter 28 chest; 48 centimeters neck; and he weighs 123 kilos. Reiber is thirty-two years old and he was born in Ismaning [near Munich in Bavaria]. This man has not made his abilities clear to me, but I have been told that he has gone back to train once more and that we will certainly see him again. These colossi always manage to surprise us.[27]

Tyrolian colossus Leonhard Reiber was a huge man who poses here in lederhosen and alpenstock (collection of Christian Gaildraud).

Michael Hitzler

In wrestling as in running, there are two distinct categories of competitors: stayers and sprinters. Sabès can be considered a sprinter, but Michael Hitzler can be rightly considered like the long-distance man, the one who will be able to resist any champion for whole days, while sometimes succeeding in terrible counterattacks.[28]

Hitzler weighs 90 kilos and is 1 meter 68 in height. No one better than he is capable of taking on the tallest of wrestlers with a hip roll. Hitzler was world champion in 1899 when he wrestled against Gambier for three days (ten hours of wrestling total).

Jacobus Koch

This superb German athlete [Jakob Koch, 1870–1918] whose successes are too numerous be counted, is also a former weightlifting champion who snatched 80 kilos with one hand. This is something that those who are interested in wrestling, whether near or far, should certainly never forget.

For a long time, we have hoped to see him compete with our French champion, Paul Pons. Koch is capable not just surprising us, but of putting our "big man" through his paces, and maybe even of triumphing over him. Koch had in turn once expressed the desire to participate in the famous Gold Belt Tournament, and due to some unforeseen obstacle, this desire was not to be realized. Koch is 1 meter 79 in height and weighs 100 kilos.[29]

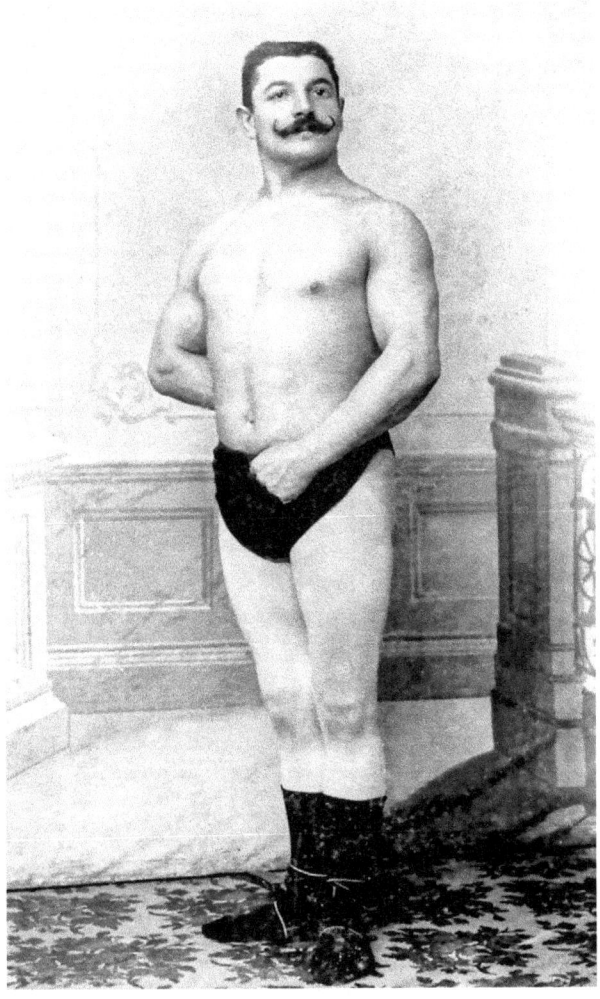

Michael Hitzler had great staying power as a wrestler; he once endured through a match that lasted ten hours and forty-four minutes (collection of Michael Murphy).

Paul Bahn

Not since Apollon [Louis Uni] have I seen legs that were as powerful (48 centimeters calf) as those of Bahn. This colossus is 1 meter 85 tall; 45 centimeters arm; 37 centimeters forearm; 1 meter 30 chest; 48 centimeters calf; 46 centimeters neck; and weighs 118 kilos. In France we know only of his reputation, and we can confirm at present that Bahn is a man of prodigious natural strength and that people will be

Jakob Koch was "the perfect type of German athlete: big, corpulent (but not excessively) and very well-muscled" (collection of Michael Murphy).

talking about him in the next championships. Bahn was born in Germany.[30]

John Pohl "Abs II"

Karl Abs is synonymous with strength in Germany.[31] He was a famous strongman from the other side of the Rhine, and the nickname Abs II given to John Pohl [1867–1914?] proves that this man's strength is extraordinary. Pohl is 1 meter 85 tall and weighs 118 kilos. He is an excellent wrestler who enjoys a great reputation in Germany.

German-American Paul Bahn had a great career in the 1920s as a heel (a bad guy) in French wrestling rings.

Vervet

Another former weightlifting champion who was able to achieve superb results thanks to the muscles acquired by using dumbbells. Like Gambier and Pytlazinski, [Emile] Vervet has his admirers. He is a wrestler who attracts crowds because he knows how to wrestle wonderfully. He is a fine wrestler above all else because he knows how to discipline himself to do serious training.

John Pohl borrowed his stage name from that of famous German strongman and wrestler Karl Abs (collection of Michael Murphy).

Emile Vervet began as a weightlifter, and the muscularity he gained from that endeavor served him well as a wrestler (collection of Michael Murphy).

Vervet has been wrestling for nearly ten years. The German [Heinrich] Weber eliminated him at the first international wrestling championship. Two years after he began training seriously, Vervet managed to place third behind Constant "the Butcher" and Hitzler. Since then he has never been beaten by any lightweight. In 1903 he had no luck; he was forced to abandon the world championship due to a knee abscess. The same year in Antwerp he beat his former victor Weber, the lightweight world champion, in twelve minutes. Shortly afterward the two men fought to a tie at the Gold Belt Tournament.[32]

Vervet measures 1 meter 73 in height; 42 centimeters arm; 32.5 centimeters forearm; 67 centimeters thigh; 41 centimeters calf; and he weighs 92 kilos.

Bech-Olsen

Denmark has a magnificent representative in this man. He weighs 120 kilos and is 1 meter 90 in height; he appeared in Paris where he earned a place in the finale, but he was defeated by Petersen and Poddubny.[33]

Left: Danish athlete Magnus Bech-Olsen wrestled all over Europe and America, and in this photograph, his chest is adorned with medals earned mainly in the United States (collection of Michael Murphy). *Right:* Oskar Schneider was from Austria, and he was famous for his handsome face and muscular physique (collection of Michael Murphy).

Schneider the Austrian

The Austrian [Oskar] Schneider weighs 100 kilos, and he is very strong and very adroit. He is a superb model of physical beauty—a second [Cyrill] Wetasa—with an impeccable physique.[34] He is 1 meter 79 tall; 1 meter 26 chest; 45 centimeters neck; 2 centimeters arm; 35 centimeters forearm; and 42 centimeters calf.

Anderson

The champion of Stockholm who holds the new world's record in the two-handed barbell lift of 298 pounds is [Arvid Anderson] a magnificent man of 1 meter 82 in height and weighing 116 kilos. He is a fearful competitor for the veteran wrestlers who had to reckon with him. Anderson was born in Stockholm in 1873 [died 1954].[35] It was at the Montmartre Athletic Society where he succeeded in breaking the record in the two-handed barbell lift.

George Strenge

Strenge is a Berliner who is extremely strong and a wrestler who is fairly knowledgeable. He is 1 meter 78 tall and weighs 110 kilos.[36]

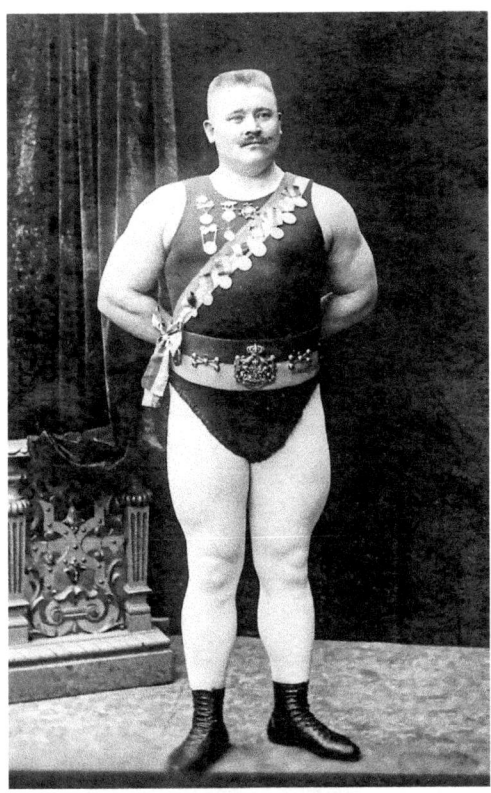 

Left: Arvid Anderson could earn more as a fighter than a strongman. With his profits he opened a restaurant in Stockholm (collection of Michael Murphy). *Right:* Jos Šmejkal gave up wheel making in his native Bohemia to become a wrestler (collection of Michael Murphy).

Jos Šmejkal

Šmejkal is the strength champion of Austria-Hungary and was born in 1880 in Cesky Brod.[37] His father intended him to become a wheelwright, a trade which he learned in Nusle near Prague. He is 1 meter 85 tall and weighs 118 kilos. Here are his other measurements. Chest 1 meter 34; neck 48 centimeters; waist 96 centimeters; biceps 44.5 centimeters; forearm 35 centimeters; fist 24 centimeters; thigh 73.5 centimeters; calf 47 centimeters. It is easy to see that such a man would be an adversary to reckon with.

Nicolas Petroff

Petroff the Bulgarian, was born in Shumla (Bulgaria) in 1872, and he is very experienced and very solidly built.[38] His upper torso is incredibly powerful. He has the neck of a bull (50 centimeters). The Bulgar weighs 105 kilos and is 1 meter 77 tall. He was a student of Doublier and Robinet whom he met in Romania and who convinced him to embrace the career of a wrestler. He has since become a marvelous athlete because he has weight, strength, agility, and flexibility. He has wrestled against the best, and rare—very rare—are those who could boast of making his shoulders touch the mat. He was also a good weightlifter; he can still snatch 65 kilos very easily and he can jerk a barbell of 100 kilos five times in a row.

When he was twenty-five years old, he was one of the handsomest men that one could find, but since he has specialized in wrestling, he has gained weight and no longer has the same elegant physique that he had in 1896. On the other hand, thanks to his weight he has become more formidable in Greco-Roman wrestling.

The Two Raicevich Brothers

Giovanni

He is the youngest and strongest of the three brothers. The strength of his muscles is almost equal to that of the famous Russian Lion, Hackenschmidt.[39] The young Italian champion is in the

Nicolas Petroff was born in the Ottoman Empire, and he played a significant role in bringing Turkish wrestling to France. He was also a powerful and skilled wrestler (collection of Michael Murphy).

unanimous opinion of his adversaries, the finest, the most perfect and the deepest connoisseur of the secrets, tricks, and resources of the fight. His specialty is the bridge; in this position he can resist any human force and all the champions who have fought against him have been convinced of this. Otto Nowozielski [a.k.a. Otto Arco], the Russian [Polish] wrestler (lightweight 65 kilos) is unbeatable for this same reason in his category while being only mediocre at pinning a man. This defense has even made Giovanni Raicevich a pretty much unbeatable wrestler, as long as the rules don't require wrestlers to get up after a set amount of time.

Ruggiero (Emilio)

He closely follows his brother Giovanni in muscular strength and for the finesse of his style.[40] He has defeated many champions of undisputed skill. His passion for sport caused him to abandon the career of naval engineer which his parents had intended for him, but he knew how to retain in this often-brutal sport, a correctness,

Giovanni (right) and Emilio Ruggiero were two of Italy's finest grapplers, although Giovanni was the star of the family (Emilio from Collection of Christian Gaildraud).

an honesty, and a courtesy that made him very sympathetic to all his adversaries.

Aimable of La Calmette

What a dreadful fellow is this man who is otherwise full of strength and skill in combat. He wears a large sombrero, which on occasion can serve as an umbrella; his legs wrapped in immense baggy trousers and his hand armed with an alpenstock as heavy as it is gigantic. Aimable is proud of his muscular power and inexorable toward everything that bothers him, and he inspires respect wherever he goes. "I am handsome! I am lively! I am superb!" he replies in a satisfied and mocking tone to the friend or curious person from Nimes or La Calmette who questions him respectfully about his health.[41] Aimable, indeed, is not wrong to consider himself handsome, spry and superb, for he is still as well-built as ever a man was.[42]

Aimable Béchard of La Calmette weighs 100 kilos. His broad form and his colossal build make him a difficult wall to breach. Also, woe to them whom fate puts face to face with him in a championship! "Bibbidy, bobbidy, boo!" he yells loudly when his bile is up, "I will take them down and flip them over like a crepe!"[43] Nevertheless, he was forced to admit defeat with Hackenschmidt and Pytlazinski, but there is no dishonor in that.

So far Aimable has wrestled with all the stars of the sport and none of them, including the most formidable Turkish wrestlers, ever impressed him very much. It is true that Aimable combines courage and admirable energy with his strength and his great wrestling abilities. "Let me have the Turks or the biggest of the others!" he always demands when the opportunity presents itself during the events he participates in. When he is willing, nothing can resist him, but unfortunately for him, Aimable is one of those who goes through life without considering that they are also compromising their health and diminishing the power of the physical efforts that they may have to provide.

Aimable was born in 1873 [died 1934] and is 1 meter 76 tall. He is a fellow you don't trifle with. If you pass through the South, ask in this land that appreciates wrestling, what people think of Aimable. "Mercy! He's a dear who is certainly worth two of you!"

Aimable is the champion of the entire Gard region in general and of his hometown La Calmette in particular. A special addition to which is the wrestler's son. Go ahead and try to deny atavism.[44]

Aimable de la Calmette may have been an excellent wrestler, but he was also vain, combative, and eccentric looking; few of those qualities are obvious in this portrait (collection of Michael Murphy).

Charles Fengler

He is one of the champions from Central Europe. This athlete was born in Neumarkt (Silesia) in 1868 and is now an American citizen.[45] Fengler is distinguished in boxing as well as wrestling; in the latter sport he was the favorite pupil of the American champion William Muldoon. He is a tall, well-built man measuring 1 meter 78 in height and weighing 95 kilos. He has won the most surprising successes in wrestling; in this way he famously beat the German champion Pohl. Fengler has traveled much. He has stayed longest of all in America.

The Cossack Ivan Poddubny

Today the Cossack Ivan Poddubny (Zaporozhian) can be considered the strongest of the Russian wrestlers.[46] He won first prize at the wrestling championships in

Left: Charles Fengler was a German-speaking emigrant to the United States, and most of his career as a wrestler was spent there and in Australia (collection of Christian Gaildraud). *Right:* Russian wrestler Ivan Poddubny poses proudly with the sash that he won at the Paris wrestling championships of 1905 (collection of Michael Murphy).

St. Petersburg. He was never defeated in Paris; at the time of the world championships in 1902 his adversary was Raoul "the Butcher," and he was unable to overcome him after more than an hour of wrestling. Poddubny was defeated by the famous points system.[47] His last success was in Moscow where he won the title of champion. He is currently the world's champion in wrestling and no wrestler can boast of having pinned him. Only Zbyszko could oppose him.

As we can therefore judge from his photograph, Poddubny is a very well-proportioned man, and he possesses extraordinary measurements. Here is his anthropometric chart, which was taken by me at my school of physical culture, Rue du Faubourg Poissonnière where this athlete was measured upon his arrival in Paris. Height, 1 meter 83.5 (stripped); weight (stripped) 112 kilos; chest in normal state 1 meter 30; chest inflated 1 meter 34; arm 43 centimeters (both left and right); forearm bent at a right angle to the arm 40 centimeters; left thigh 68 centimeters; right thigh 67 centimeters; left calf 44.5 centimeters; right calf 44 centimeters; neck (under the chin) 48 centimeters; neck at the base 50 centimeters; shoulder circumference 1 meter 44!!! (record); waist (normal position) 1 meter 04; waist with abdominal retraction 91.5 centimeters; fist 21 centimeters.

At the Weightlifting Club of France while he was just playing around, Ivan Poddubny very easily lifted a cone-shaped kettlebell weighing 428 pounds. He could do much more. Poddubny was born on the 26 September 1871 in Zolotonosha, Russia.[48]

At present, he is an athlete who produces the greatest impression of strength and who truly possesses masculine beauty in all its magnitude. He is tall, with a long and thick neck, an energetic and characteristic head, excessively broad shoulders, a slender waist, strong legs, and arms. When Poddubny is dressed as a Cossack in a suit that fits his form, he is a man who leaves an unforgettable impression. He defeated his compatriots Kascheff, Zaikine, and Schmelling.

Antonitch

This "little fellow" lights his cigarette with gas lampposts—an easy thing to do if, like him, you are 2 meters 16 in height. He weighs 130 kilos.[49] [Simon] Antonitch was one of the heroes of the great Gold Belt Tournament. Everyone still remembers his Homeric wrestling matches, which he underwent with Laurent, Pons, and Raoul "the Butcher."

The giant is Serbian and is naturally very gentle, but he is terrible when wrestling, especially when he is fighting for a title or for an important prize. Antonitch is not conventionally pretty; he represents the peak of deformities caused by acromegaly. His neck, which is 50 centimeters in circumference, is distinguished by the extraordinary size of his anteroposterior diameter. His arms which seem thick by reason of their length have a biceps circumference of 42 centimeters and 37 centimeters in the forearms. His chest measures 1 meter 29.

The Serbian giant Simon Antonitch stood over 7 feet in height, and despite his striking stature, he never really had the requisite aggression to become a great champion. Still, the public loved him (collection of Michael Murphy).

The giant Antonitch made his debut in Bulgaria. He was then taken to France by Doublier, the same person who brought us the Turks.[50]

Kuschke the Saxon

[Emile] Kuschke is extraordinarily strong. He is 1 meter 83 tall, weighs 105 kilos, and he exudes an extraordinary impression of strength and stamina. He is a remarkable wrestler who can look forward to a wonderful athletic future.[51]

 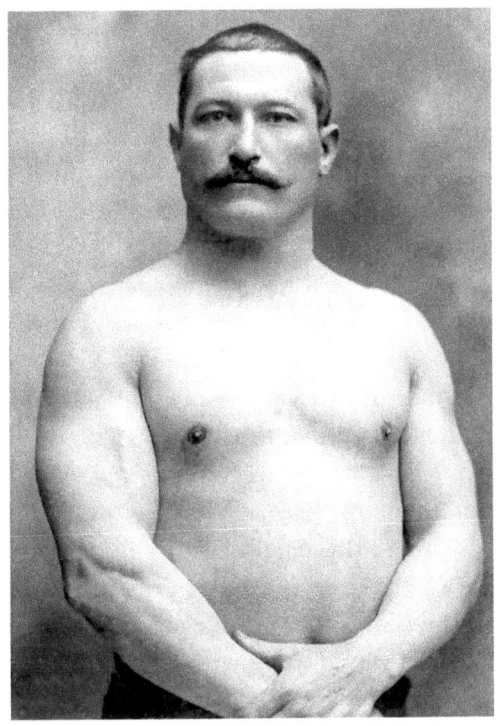

Left: German wrestler Emile Kuschke cut a dashing figure on the mat, but he never rose to the highest ranks (collection of Michael Murphy). *Right:* Maurice Gambier was a much-loved wrestler, especially in his hometown of Bordeaux. He was the overall victor at the first international championships in Brussels (collection of Michael Murphy).

Gambier

Gambier is the most admirable of contemporary wrestlers. He is a veteran grappler; he has been performing arm rolls for twenty years. Small, light, solidly built, lively eyes, a bit roguish in appearance—this is Maurice Gambier, the most famous wrestler from the city of Bordeaux.[52] He hardly weighs 86 kilos and is only 1 meter 67 tall, and this is a little short when trying to pin giants, but Gambier never holds back from anyone, and he proved it to us during his long career as a wrestler.

I do not believe that we will ever see such a lively, agile, and experienced wrestler again, for Gambier carried out his attacks with extraordinary speed of execution, without losing his composure, and when he found himself being pulled down in a back waistlock by a man much heavier than he, Gambier never let himself be bothered by so little a thing. Oh naturally, it is easy to throw him down on the ground since he is so light, but it is extremely difficult to pin him, and to achieve this result it will be necessary to provide for an athletic power much greater than his own, because otherwise, at the very moment you believe you are certain of victory, the little Bordeaux native often finds a way to bypass you with a twist or an irresistible arm roll.

Gambier earned his stripes almost twenty years ago, when he defeated the famous Pietro Dalmasso in two minutes and thirty seconds. This unforeseen victory created a sensation in the world of wrestlers since Pietro had wrestled for twelve years without ever being pinned. Maurice Gambier was therefore immediately considered as the best wrestler in France. He continued his series of victories by triumphing over Robinet, Petroff, Buisson, Toulon, the terrible Tom Cannon, and the Turk Mehmet.[53]

In 1897 Gambier won the world championship, held in Brussels, thus placing ahead of the 118 competitors who had participated in this excellent tournament, which I attended as a member of the judge's panel.[54] In 1898, Gambier participated in the world championship. He ranked third behind Paul Pons and Pytlazinski. His match with the former Russian champion had great repercussions throughout the whole world. Gambier surprised everyone by holding his own against his terrible opponent for three consecutive evenings.

These three fights were splendid and Gambier, although beaten, was applauded for a long time. The entire press was unanimous in praising his knowledge and skill. In 1899 Maurice Gambier won the world lightweight championship and since then he has always fought with the same ease, with the same vigor.

Limousin

Emile Bruyère "the Limousin" [from the French district of Limousin] is no longer a very young man [1860–1910], and he was nicknamed "Papa Limousin," but he nevertheless remains the finest and the most skillful of all our wrestlers.

Limousin weighs 90 kilos, is 1 meter 74 tall, measures 43 centimeters in the arm, 35 centimeters forearm, and 1 meter 24 chest. He is a purebred Bordeaux native. Limousin is also very strong in weightlifting; he snatched 143 pounds with his left hand, and did a swing lift of 145 pounds.

Emile Bruyère was better known by his nom-de-ring "Le Limousin." By the time Desbonnet knew him, he was a bit long in the tooth (collection of Michael Murphy).

Peyrouse "the Lion of Valence"

Peyrouse the Lion of Valence was born in Montélimar on 26 June 1872, and he is amazing because he exudes natural strength. He is tall as a giant (1 meter 87), with wide shoulders, bulging and arched hips. His enormous limbs seem like they have been hewn with an axe. The Lion of Valence is prodigious, it weighs 118 kilos. He is a giant who grew even larger thanks to acromegaly.[55]

Pytlazinski

[Wladislaw] Pytlazinski is a marvelous athlete, 1 meter 84 tall, weight 100 kilos, 1 meter 20 chest circumference, 41 centimeters arm circumference, 35 centimeters forearm, 67 centimeters thigh, and 44 centimeters calf. He defeated Pons on 26 April 1897 at the residence of the Count de Ribeaupierre in Saint Petersburg.[56]

He was born in 1863 in Warsaw in Poland [died 1933]. He has lifted 134 pounds in a swing lift and snatched 148 pounds with both right and left hands. He snatched 205 pounds with two hands and cleaned 197 pounds with one hand.[57]

In 1889 he pinned Karl Abs at the Cirque d'hiver. In 1892 at the championships

Left: Thanks to acromegaly, Peyrouse was a tall and impressive wrestler, but he was not particularly reliable or overly intelligent (collection of Michael Murphy). *Right:* Polish wrestler Wladislaw Pytlazinski was both impressive looking and an excellent wrestler (collection of Michael Murphy).

in Saint Petersburg he was awarded first place. He fought Robinet and Pierri in Budapest at the Ciniselli Circus. In Paris in 1898 he defeated Gambier. At the Grand Prix in Paris he triumphed over Laurent le Beaucairois, Petroff, Sabès, and Constant "the Butcher." At the championships at Namur he got the better of Aimable and de la Calmette. Pytlazinski has pressed down the shoulders of the giant Antonitch.

Petersen

[Jess] Petersen [1879–1946] who is considered by some to be the current champion, is a very strong man. He is 1 meter 78 tall and weighs 103 kilos. He made his debut in our capital in 1901; at that time he had completely shaved his head; the ladies thought he was a wild man, and the jokers nicknamed him "the Bull Dog," because Petersen fought brutally, like many athletes who lack experience, and it was with great difficulty that the "old-timers" managed to take him down.[58]

In 1903 he came back to participate in the world championship. Still not very skillful, he none the less managed to triumph over Raoul "the Butcher," thereby sealing the title of world's champion. During that same year, the terrible Dane took part in the Gold Belt Tournament, and in the course of that memorable championship, he was able to pin the giant Antonitch, Raoul the Butcher, the Negro Anglio, and Laurent le Beaucairois, world champion from 1901. He finally succumbed (??) to Paul Pons after two memorable rounds of wrestling.

Jess Petersen was born in Denmark, but he lived most of his life in France where he was a popular figure as a wrestler (collection of Michael Murphy).

Sturm

A superb man! The most beautiful of wrestlers![59] Measurements: arm 40.5 centimeters,

He might not have been a top-notch wrestler, but Albert Sturm was renowned for his shapely physique. Nude images of this "most beautiful of wrestlers" were sold in many photograph shops (collection of Michael Murphy).

forearm 35 centimeters, neck 47.5 centimeters, chest 1 meter 14, waist 86 centimeters, shoulders 1 meter 27, thigh 58 centimeters, hips 1 meter, fist 19 centimeters, calf 39.5 centimeters, height 1 meter 81, weight 86.5 kilos. These measurements were taken by me on the occasion of Sturm's arrival in Paris.⁶⁰ [Albert] Sturm was born in Berlin in 1884 [died 1946].⁶¹

Ibrahim Mahmut

Among the men who have stood up to Yusuf Ismaelo, one must mention Ibrahim Mahmut.⁶² After Tom Cannon retired from wrestling (in an active sense of that word), he became an impresario and the successes of Doubler, Yusuf's manager, must have disturbed his sleep. Because of this he saw fit to take a little junket to Constantinople, and he returned with two Turks in his vest pocket, Kara Ahmed and Ibrahim Mahmut.

The reader will also see that Tom had a winning hand, since Kara became world champion. As for Ibrahim Mahmut, it was he who had the honor of competing with Yusuf in a match that remains famous and was conducted at the Cirque d'Hiver. I will say right away that Yusuf could not defeat him and, even though he used all his means, since the two Turks were fighting in the style of their country, so thrusting their fingers into their nostrils to cause asphyxiation, twisting their organs, and doing a thousand other "kindnesses" sanctioned by these "delicate" sportsmen.⁶³ Nothing could make Ibrahim give in. The combatants were separated with cudgels, and Yusuf was dragged away to the organizer of the match, because his brutal maneuvers had gone too far.

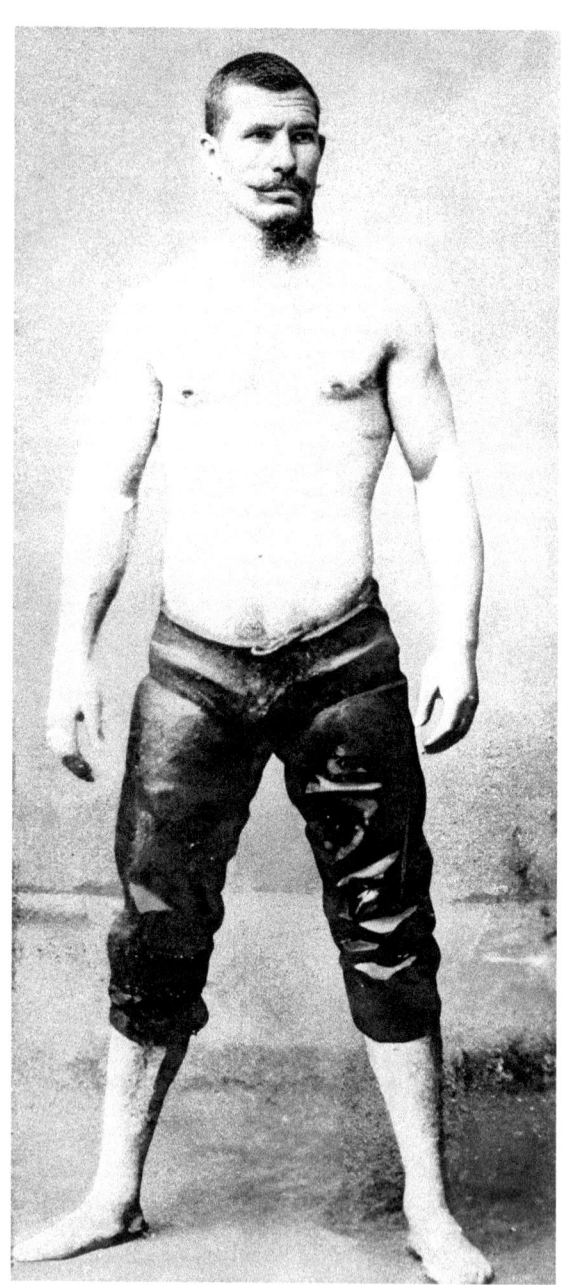

Turkish wrestler Ibrahim Mahmut fought a notoriously brutal match with fellow countryman Yusuf Ismaelo in 1907 (collection of Christian Gaildraud).

When the magistrate asked Ibrahim if he lodged a complaint, he replied, "On the whole we fought properly in Turkish fashion," and he added with that fatalism that is incomprehensible to us Westerners, "In Turkey, when men wrestle, women weep."[64]

Ibrahim was very handsome with less fat enveloping him that the famous Yusuf, and his musculature displayed powerful and wide contours. He was 1 meter 85 tall, 1 meter 24 chest, 90 centimeters waist, 42.5 centimeters arm, 34.5 centimeters forearm, 41.5 calf, 62 centimeters thick, and he weighed 100 kilos. His courage and endurance excited the general admiration and won him the approval of everyone in the audience.

Mourzouk

Another man of color, but what a carcass! Mourzouk is the handsomest negro wrestler that one can imagine. He is 1 meter 79 tall and weighs 112 kilos. He has been wrestling since he was five years old, and he has participated in numerous championships in Algeria, France, Germany, Russia, Holland, and Belgium. Mourzouk can certainly not be classed among such fine wrestlers as Gambier, Sabès, and company, but he is a courageous man (a rare thing for a Negro).[65] He is an athlete in every sense of that term.

Mourzouk came from the North African French protectorate of Tunisia. He was reportedly "the handsomest Negro wrestler that one can imagine" (collection of Michael Murphy).

Weber the German

He is a champion who is very well known in France as someone who has been considered for a long time as the world champion in his category. [Heinrich] Weber [1879–1958] is a wrestler of the very first order. He has a great deal of cool calculation, and he learned a lot during his encounters with our famous Bordeaux champions.

It was in 1901 that Weber made a reputation for himself in France during the world championship held at the Casino de Paris.[66] Although he was unknown at the time, this man managed to beat the famous Bordeaux man Sabès in seven minutes fifty-eight seconds with a brilliant front waistlock. During the Gold Belt Tournament in

Most German wrestlers in France were not well loved, but Heinrich Weber was an exception. He was justifiably proud of his constellation of medals shown in this image (collection of Michael Murphy).

1902 Weber truly became popular; he was the great favorite of the public, and everyone still remembers the splendid wrestling matches he gave against men who weighed 40 kilos more than he. Weber was remarkably handsome.[67]

Nurullah

He was one of Yusuf's companions who came to Paris around 1894. Nurullah was born in Schoumla [Schumen, Bulgaria] in 1870, and he is 2 meters tall and weighs 150 kilos.[68] He has a chest that measures 1 meter 30 and 49 centimeters in the calf. We have all noted

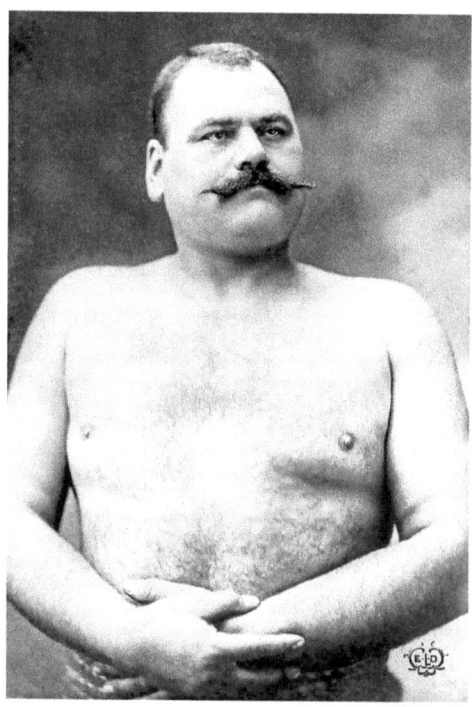

Nurullah (sometimes called Nurlah) came to Paris with the first group of Turkish wrestlers (collection of Michael Murphy).

that he has not participated in any championship. ??? Mystery. Four years ago, he was engaged in a summer café concert, and he challenged anyone. No wrestler of any standing accepted, so he was forced to pin "celebrities" who were completely unknown.[69]

Kara Osman

The handsomest of the Turks who came to Paris. He had olive skin and eyes shining like carbuncles. Kara Osman was a splendid athlete measuring 1 meter 80 in height, 1 meter 21 in the chest, 49 centimeters neck, and he weighed 100 kilos.[70]

Winzer

The German wrestler [Heinrich] Winzer weighs 105 kilos and is 1 meter 78 tall. He is tough and knowledgeable.[71]

Left: Kara Osman had a successful wrestling career in both Europe and North America (collection of Christian Gaildraud). *Right:* If Winzer's wrestling career were as magnificent as his upturned mustache and noble cranium, he would have become a household name. Alas, it was not to be.

Anglio

To discuss Anglio in an interesting way might seem difficult after Edouard Pontié [1877–1940] published his account under the title *Histoire de la lute* [History of Wrestling], so I will transcribe it below.[72]

> There could be volumes of anecdotes to write alongside sport, and sometimes the detailed history of a champion is arranged according to the taste and emotion of popular novels, but often these provide only an account that is despairingly banal. There are however adventures touching certain athletic personalities highlighted during a tournament, which deserve to be rescued from the shadows, unless (according to the popular saying) we can see Negroes in the night.[73]
>
> Do you remember Anglio Anastase? Anglio Anastase who got to the final rounds of the Gold Belt Tournament, and who sent the Folies Bergère crowd into raptures by the hard work he demonstrated to some of his opponents before laying his broad shoulders on the mat or forcing those of others down in his oily grips. Here is Anglio Anastase's story just as it was told to me.
>
> In a time not long ago when Martinique was peaceful, Anglio Anastase lived out his pleasant and indolent existence at the foot of Mount Pelée in a flimsy hut under the beautiful sun of the Antilles. Then there came a terrible moment when the volcano awoke from its slumber, and Anglio Anastase, among other good Negroes, fled distraught toward the shore, while behind him his fragile roof was consumed in ashes and smoke.[74]
>
> Also, like so many other good Negroes, Anglio went from the state of a simple citizen to that of a disaster victim seeking help. He thus did better than most, for he crossed the seas and came to take refuge in France where national emotion and both private and governmental subscriptions made the people of Martinique feel welcome. Within a year, the future champion of Negro-Roman wrestling recovered his peaceful and useless existence at the expense of those poor souls who were moved by pity.[75] But everything comes to an end, and one fine day, tired of constantly finding the same face for such generosity, the relief givers decided to repatriate Anglio Anastase to his sugar cane and coconut palms. He was therefore sent to Le Havre, provided with a ticket for the distant islands. But when he arrived at the port, he hesitated so much when he contemplated this return since he now preferred to live in the place that had grown so near and dear to his heart—the beautiful land of France. And he might also have been terrified of Mount Pelée mixed with the regrets of having to abandon so ungratefully all that public generosity. So Anglio stayed in Le Havre.
>
> He lived there as well as he could, worse rather than better for a time. He made himself busy with minor port jobs, and one fine day after descending into complete poverty, he met the wrestler [Léon] Dumont who was from Le Havre. Dumont is the general of an army of wrestlers and an excellent director of arm rolls, headlocks on hips in all the music halls of France and abroad. He needed a Negro in his troupe; Mourzouk had left, and the "champion of Martinique" could replace the one from Tunisia. So Dumont hired Anglio Anastase on the spot. His stature and his face pleased Dumont, and he sent him to Agen to board with Limousin who would have the task of training him. As everyone knows, Limousin is a former wrestler who is now retired from the wrestling mat, and he knows all the moves. He received Anglio Anastase, and for two months he taught him all that he could. During those eight weeks he trained him to withstand all the blows and to bear up under the most painful holds. Nothing is as tough as a Negro's skin, and Limousin knocked him around very

Opposite: **Anglio Anastase was originally a refugee from Martinique, but he quickly made his mark as a wrestler. Here he poses with his Junoesque French wife in a photograph taken by Desbonnet around 1913 (collection of Christian Gaildraud).**

conscientiously. Then he patiently instilled in him all the tricks of the trade, the art of going to the mat gracefully, of letting himself be hit, to defend against it or making an opponent succumb to it.

After that, Anglio Anastase admittedly never did have a brilliant attacking game—oh, far from it—but he knew how to hold his own and to look convincing. This is the most important thing, and the disaster victim of Martinique appeared in the Gold Belt Tournament. From that time on, his story is known to all.

And now Anglio Anastase follows Dumont, and he travels from town to town. He has found a social niche; he is a wrestler. We will find him wherever they wrestle using waist headlocks in front of an orchestra. Let us hope that the latter only blasts out triumphal marches for him.

* * * * *

I can only add that the champion from Martinique first wrestled in 1903 during the Gold Belt Tournament. He is a very fine athlete who weighs 120 kilos and is 1 meter 88 tall, arm 46.5 centimeters, and forearm 37.5 centimeters. At the time of his debut Anglio was a sensation. He defeated all the men of the second order who opposed him with unimaginable ease and then went on to defeat the strongest men in the world.[76]

Gulam

Gulam is a man who is so extraordinary that I cannot resist the desire to reproduce the article published on him by *La Culture Physique*.[77]

A great wrestling contest had been announced on the occasion of the Exposition of 1900. Three Indian wrestlers who enjoy an extraordinary fame in their country were charmed by the stories of the feats of their European rivals and were long envious of their triumphs. When they learned of a tournament that would take place in Paris, they made a huge decision; they would leave their native country and would go over there to France where they would show that no one in the world could claim to equal their strength, their knowledge, and their courage.[78]

And that is how the three brothers Gulam, Kuhlo, and Rahmani came under the direction of a manager, Mr. Janki Nathschak. But the wrestling tournament did not take place, and the unfortunates wandered aimlessly. They had come to Paris to fight against rivals, but they found that they had only to combat the difficulties which rose up before them at every step. No tournaments, no wrestlers! What would become of them?

By chance they met Mr. Motilal-Nehru, a millionaire lawyer from Amritsar, north of Lahore (home of the three wrestlers). Mr. Nehru is a sportsman in every sense of the word. Physical exercises interest him, but wrestling is his passion. The famous Gulam told him of his troubles, and Mr. Nehru said to him, "Gulam, challenge all the strongmen of the earth; I will support your chances against all of them, no matter what it will take, 5,000, 10,000, 15,000 francs—more if necessary. I have confidence in your wide shoulders, your courage, and your knowledge."

Gulam was thrilled and delighted, and accompanied by his sponsors, he paid into the hands of the administrator of the newspaper *Le Vélo* the sum of 15,000 francs. This way of proceeding was the correct one; it was the one used by the English and the Americans. Here are the terms of the challenge as they appeared in the newspapers of the time.

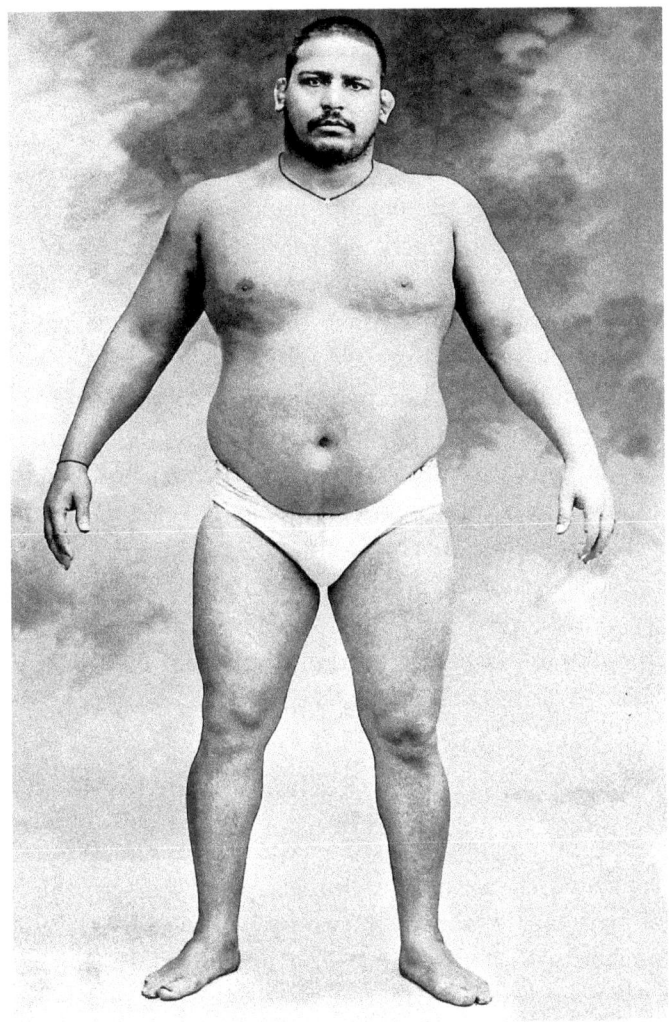

Punjabi wrestler Gulam was proclaimed "Hercules of the Indies" for his great strength and skill. He had a famous match with the Turk Kurtdereli, but the results were very unsatisfactory (collection of Michael Murphy).

> I the undersigned in the name of the wrestler Gulam, champion of Amritsar, issue a challenge to all the wrestlers of the world for a catch-as-catch-can wrestling match. To support this challenge, Mr. Motilal-Nehru has deposited in the account of *Vélo* the sum of 15,000 francs in one lump sum as a guarantee of the sincerity of the challenge and as collateral for all the wagers that Mr. Motilal-Nehru is willing to take. The challenge must be taken up starting today July 29, 1900, until the deadline on 10 August. Replies should be sent in my name to the Theater of the French Indies, located at the Exposition near the Trocadero.
> Signed, Janki Nathschak

The response was not long in coming. The Viscount [Auguste] de Chambure [1865–1943], director of *l'Argus de la Presse* answered the challenge by proposing to match Gulam against the Turkish wrestler Kurtdereli for the sum of 5,000 francs.[79] Kurtdereli against Gulam! A fan could never imagine a better match. If Gulam was an unknown for the majority of the public, Kurtdereli had an athletic reputation that made him out to be one of the Turkish champions. He was a man of weight, strength, and knowledge.

Let us now introduce Gulam "the Hercules of the Indies," the wrestler who issued the audacious challenge. Gulam is a native of Amritsar in the Punjab; his father was a wrestler; his son will be a wrestler. He is part of a dynasty of kings of muscles. His father was never defeated and ever since Gulam succeeded him, his wide shoulders have never touched the ground. But what a man he is! His height is only slightly over the average, but his midsection is fantastically powerful. He has an impressive chest, which contains the most energetic heart that a tenacious and resolute will has ever sustained. He has the neck of a bull. It bears on magnificent shoulders, a dark head with a dark and enigmatic face from which two sparkling eyes and teeth of dazzling whiteness are the only things that shine. His chest is incredibly broad, and he has an arched back. His robust legs are truly impressive pillars which form a base revealing the forces accumulated in this astonishing bronzed mass as they support with dignity an extraordinary human construction.

Gulam is forty years of age, he is 1 meter 74 tall, his chest circumference is 1 meter 45 (record), his biceps measure 50 centimeters, his forearm 35 centimeters, his neck 52 centimeters (record), his thigh 80 centimeters (record), his calf 46 centimeters, and he weighs 130 kilos. All of his sinews are as hard as steel. The muscles do not protrude too much. The strength of the individual is revealed only by his entirety, which is formidable.

Gulam's Training Routine

Gulam arises at three o'clock in the morning and he immediately begins his training with exercises to limber up. For an hour the Hindu champion performs the following little maneuver: two steps forward, and bends his knees on the tips of the feet, the posterior coming into contact with the heel; back to standing position, two steps back and continuation of this fairly monotonous exercise, although it seems excellent. Gulam does about 50 knee-bends per minute, so this hour of flexibility represents 3,000 bends.

Gulam next proceeds to limbering exercises with his hips on the ground. Here is how he does it. He lies facing the ground, resting on the tips of his feet and on the palms of his hands, and, carefully avoiding putting his forearms and elbows in contact with the ground, he executes a plunging movement for an hour from top to bottom and from bottom to top, the result of which is to limber and strengthen the midsection and shoulders.

That is not all! For a quarter of an hour, the Indian champion develops the pectorals with the following system: he leans alternately on the wall with his right hand and then his left hand and by twisting his torso makes his shoulder touch the hand, moving it away from the torso as fast as he can.

The session ends with a quarter of an hour lifting light dumbbells. Then Gulam rests for half an hour and eats his first meal, always consisting of liquid (bouillon), chicken, and a dairy product. After he finishes his light meal, the Indian champion wrestles. He wrestles with six men which he defeats one after the other. This session lasts around two hours. It is finished with a vigorous massage with perfumed oils and a relaxing bath.[80]

Then it is time for lunch. Gulam possesses a huge appetite, and at this meal he eats a chicken or a rabbit. Never sheep or beef unless they are killed according to the rites of his religion, that is to say, bled for a long time, the slaughter being accompanied by traditional prayers. Since these formalities are impossible in Paris, Gulam contents himself with rabbits and chickens. The Indian champion drinks only milk or pure water; never wine, beer, or alcohol.

After his luncheon, Gulam has a siesta, and this is a long nap that can last for three hours. He interrupts it only to grapple once again with his wrestling sparring partners. Then, when they are tired, he ends his athletic labor with the following little exercise: He plants himself solidly on his legs and one by one his adversaries who recently practiced with him, strike him with their forearms and on his sides and especially on the neck. This exercise is done to strengthen the neck—Gulam has a bull's neck, by the way—and to accustom him to this attack that Kara Ahmed revealed to our French wrestlers: the famous clout that knocks a man down!

Gulam's day is now over. He has a solid meal—once more a rabbit or a chicken—to keep up his strength, and then the champion of the Indies retires to his bed to get some rest which no one can doubt that he certainly earned.

So this is Gulam's schedule. With such a training method, you will therefore be amazed at his power and endurance!

Gulam and Kikar Singh

Gulam is known as *Rustam'e Hind* [Hercules of the Indies], and he was a stranger to defeat; never has his back failed, never have his legs stumbled for the fatal fall.[81] Gulam's exploits are countless. Here is one tale among many—the best known of them all. Very far from Amritsar lived a man who was quoted everywhere as the modern Hercules and as the personification of strength itself. He had been dubbed Kikar Singh, for he had one day embraced a ten-year-old tree of the Kikkar species which had roots stretching far into the earth, and which clung like claws to the soil; and he uprooted it in a victorious effort.[82] Word of this exploit reached Amritsar. After that Gulam, who never shied away from a possible threat when his reputation was at stake, he went on a long journey to defy Kikar Singh. And Kikar Singh was defeated; nothing of his glory remained, and Gulam was considered a god.[83]

From that time on, Gulam was rich. He was sent magnificent gifts from all over. Indian princes came to visit him, leaving him with elephants, horses, and rich jewels. And now this wrestler had a veritable palace with women, slaves, and gifts from the Maharajah of Kashmir who made him his favorite. There in his palace he lived in abundance, and he knew all the splendors of oriental luxury.

But, as he did for Kikar Singh, he left everything, he crossed the seas to compete at the championships at the Exposition of 1900 which only ever existed on paper. Gulam only learned of his disappointment when he arrived in France. As soon as the first plans had been scrapped, the organizers began looking for a place [for the fight with Kurtdereli] and chose the Hippodrome in the Boulevard de Clichy. The presidency of the panel of judges was offered to the Maharajah of Cooch-Behar who accepted it. The Prince of Cooch-Behar was an outstanding sportsman, and he was himself is an excellent wrestler of remarkable vigor and knowledge. He was particularly fond of wrestling shows. He also maintained a whole regiment of wrestlers, seventy men chosen from among the finest and most vigorous athletes in his realm.[84]

The majority of these wrestlers were recruited from the Gurkhas who are indeed the most vigorous among the Hindus. They are extraordinary mountain climbers.[85] The men of the district of Sialkot are also renowned for their Herculean strength, they are specimens of what nature can produce, untouched by the attacks of civilization.[86] Their method of physical development is quite primitive but effective. They make use of large tree trunks that are roughly fashioned into shapes like barbells that weigh about 50 kilos, which they handle with extreme ease. To make these giant dumbbells, they use a special wood chosen for its weight and density. The character of the wrestling practiced by the Indian wrestlers of the district of Sialkot is that of freestyle wrestling, much like the "catch as catch can" of the English, but stripped of the complications which characterize it.

Hindu wrestlers oil their bodies before wrestling. They consider it a defeat when the opponent's shoulders have touched the ground. The extraordinary strength and endurance of the natives belonging to these primitive tribes is a further argument in favor of a natural life. They are products of physical culture brought up in the school of nature. Their diet is very simple and they do not need to resort to eating healthily to be well, because rice already forms the basis of their food.

But let us return to the match between the Turk and our Indian hero.

The Match Between Gulam and Kurtdereli

The bout between Gulam and Kurtdereli took place at the Hippodrome on the Boulevard de Clichy, currently the Bostock Hippodrome. From the start of the match, Gulam showed an overwhelming superiority over the Turk, Kurtdereli. As soon as the whistle announced that the two adversaries could come to blows, the Hindu, agile and quick, leapt on his adversary and took him down with a masterful armlock. His two shoulders touched, but as this fight involved great financial interests, after interminable discussions, Kurtdereli's pin was not allowed and the fight started again.

Several times the Hindu passed his terrible armlock, and each time Kurtdereli rolled over on both shoulders but immediately got up. Finally, feeling that he was dealing with too strong a party, the Turk decided to crouch down on the mat and did not move from this position for at least an hour and a half. He was content to defend himself from the attacks of Gulam. The Indian was tired, and invited his rival to stand up, and to show his contempt for his opponent's incorrect attitude, he punctuated his invitation with a few kicks in the backside. But Kurtdereli who decided that he was probably fine where he was, did not want to get up when the referee signaled to him; Kurtdereli seemed nailed to the mat throughout the hard match. Finally, we had to resort to the points system and to avoid harming the interests of which we spoke above, the bets were canceled. Kurtdereli was declared not to have been defeated and Gulam was declared the winner, but the bets were refunded.[87]

Be that as it may, Gulam was obviously superior to the Turk. Although he wrestled for the entire duration of the match with a sprained left arm, he dominated the fight from start to finish, knocking his opponent down three times.[88]

I witnessed this memorable wrestling display with the late Dr. Krajewski of St. Petersburg and Noël le Gaulois; we occupied a box at the level of the platform, and no detail of the fight escaped us. Dr. Krajewski was enthusiastic about Gulam, whom he had examined a few days earlier when he had been photographed in the pose we reproduce. It was at the photographer Waléry where we got Gulam's exact measurements.[89]

In our opinion, no current wrestler could last five minutes with Gulam if it is a fair wrestling match, that is to say, without squatting on the mat, a system of defense that should be prohibited as unsportsmanlike.[90]

Schmelling

In 1898, at the time of the amateur championship of Russia organized by the Athletic Society of St. Petersburg under the presidency of the Count de Ribeaupierre and Dr. Krajewski, [Alexander] Schmelling [1870–?] was bedridden because of severe bronchitis, but he did not want to give up his championship title, so he summoned all his strength and jumped out of bed. He told his friends, "I want to fight tonight; given my weakness and my gasping breath, I cannot defeat

Alexander Schmelling was a proud and well-educated Russian who began as an amateur wrestler and later turned professional (collection of Michael Murphy).

Hackenschmidt, but no one else will be able to defeat me." He kept his word and after an hour of wrestling, the judges saw that even if it went on indefinitely, it would never result in a decision. Taking account of the state of fatigue of the two adversaries, the directors decided to postpone the fight until the end of the year. By that time Hackenschmidt had departed for his military service, and the match did not take place.

The two adversaries did not meet again until 18 May 1899, and this time Schmelling had to lower his flag before the terrible Russian Lion, who got the better of him after twenty-five minutes of wrestling. That same year, Schmelling won several important victories fighting among others, over Petroff the Bulgarian, Adamschewsky, and John Pohl "Abs II," all men of the first rank. On 4 May 1897 he defeated Félix Bernard and Paul Pons in four minutes each. Then Schmelling fell ill and as soon as he had recovered from his sickness, he participated in the world wrestling championship in Paris in 1908.[91] In his first match he had to fight with Poddubny, and it resulted in a loss. Because he had been injured, he had to withdraw from the championship without having given a real indication of his strength.[92]

Schmelling is 1 meter 93 tall, 1 meter 27 chest circumference, 42 centimeters biceps, 34 centimeters forearm.

Fernand Sabès

You don't have to look at Sabès twice to guess that he is from Bordeaux. Ah! He is a hearty fellow. He's a perfect example of an athlete from the South of France. Very solid shoulders, arms like iron girders, and with all that, he has keen eyes—really keen! If he never spares his adversary, he does not spare himself either. There is no waiting game; he takes down his rival or he is taken down, and all this in the space of a few minutes. This is how it was done in 1899 by Tom Cannon and in 1900 by Weber.

Sabès is 1 meter 71 tall and

The Bordeaux native Ferdinand Sabès had a fiery character, and he was imbued with a strong musculature and a fighting spirit.

weighs 88 kilos. He defeated the Turk Cartanji, Constant the Butcher, and quite a few other champions.[93] When we pronounce the name of Sabès, we have said everything and even those who are not initiated into the workings of wrestling know that he is considered as one of our most famous champions. Along with Gambier, Sabès is one of the most popular wrestlers in Bordeaux. His popularity is well deserved simply because we can affirm that he rarely suffered defeat even though he fought with wrestlers from all over the world.

As for his physique, he is an athlete in every sense of that word. He is of medium height, but stocky; just looking at him it is easy to believe that he is always ready to attack an imaginary adversary. His eyes are greatly imbued with this fighting spirit, and this distinguishes him from other wrestlers. He is of a fiery character, and Sabès sometimes loses his temper; but at heart he is none the less an excellent lad, always ready to oblige his friends, so that his comrades profess for him not only affection, but real veneration. Even so, once in the ring he no longer knows anyone, and Sabès would never resolve to spare an opponent no matter who he was. Full of self-confidence, he takes the offensive and multiplies his attacks with lightning speed, without thinking for a moment that fatigue is waiting to defeat him in a few moments if he cannot triumph over his adversary from the very start.

Sabès has taken on Yusuf, Mehemet, Nurullah, Pietro, and a host of others; but his most resounding victory was that which he won over the famous English wrestler Tom Cannon.[94] He took part in the Grand Prix de la Ville de Paris. In this tournament, he easily triumphed over the Turk, Cartanji; a few months later in Bordeaux he came up against Constant le Boucher whom he took down in fifty-nine seconds with an armlock around the waist. In this wrestling match, which made an enormous noise, Sabès triumphed over brute strength by his knowledge and experience.[95]

Sabès was also capable of prodigious feats in weightlifting. He was the first in France to snatch 75 kilos with both his right and left hands. He even snatched 80 kilos with his right; he is a man of real talent. It is regrettable that his man has been retired from the ring for several years. Sabès was born in Bordeaux in 1869 [died 1928].

Louis Chappe

Otherwise known as "the King of the Dockmen," Louis Chappe was born in Toulouse in 1864. He had made a specialty of foot racing while carrying a load of 100 kilos on his back. Chappe triumphed over many flour merchants in this sort of feat, and one day he won a race going from Paris to Versailles.[96] He also beat a number of cyclists in the same way, including Bordas and Klotz.[97] These contests were thus mixed. Chappe carried 100 kilos and received a 50 meters handicap on 100 meters from his opponent. Chappe was 1 meter 72 tall and weighed 92 kilos.

He took part in different championships as a wrestler.[98] Chappe died at the

Left: **Before he became a wrestler, Louis Chappe won a foot race from Paris to Versailles carrying a hundred kilos on his back (collection of Christian Gaildraud).** *Right:* **Kurtdereli Mehmed was born in what is now Albania, and he had great natural strength. He used that strength to win many wrestling matches (collection of Michael Murphy).**

age of thirty-seven of tuberculosis in Paris on 27 September 1901 at the Lariboisière Hospital.

Kurtdereli, "the Wolf of the Shore"

The Wolf of the Shore is a faithful and picturesque translation of Kurtdereli's name.[99] Kurtdereli is Turkish, or rather Albanian, but for a long time this terrible fighter has made his abode in Asia Minor five or six hours from Balikesir in a wild and mountainous region where his family cultivates the land and raises their herds.[100] While his family goes about their lives as farmers and shepherds, Kurtdereli packs up his wrestler's breeches—leather breeches they are—and goes to Constantinople, and beyond, to wrestle. Then, laden with victories, money, and booty, he returns to join his tribe.

Kurtdereli was born in 1869.[101] He is a colossus who is 1 meter 92 tall. The man is superb when stripped, but he is even more impressive when he is dressed. Made to look taller by his tall turban, and made to look wider by his ample Albanian costume, with a coat of goatskin negligently thrown over his shoulders, everything about him breathes strength—prodigious and natural strength; this strength makes one think of a bull.

Kurtdereli is an implacable wrestler. He is not afraid of pain. On the contrary, it stimulates his courage, his valor, and his ardor. His motto is that of all Turkish wrestlers: "When men wrestle, women weep."

According to the custom of his compatriots, Kurtdereli accompanies his efforts with the war cry popularized by Kara Ahmed, the resounding "Hoah! Hoah! Aïde!" Kurtdereli has already wrestled in Paris where (like the cat with the mouse) he toyed with the colossus Daumas, "Pique-Planque" (138 kilos), whom he defeated by one of those astonishing front waistlocks whose secret is known only to the Turks.[102]

It was at the time of the Grand Prix of the City of Paris (organized by the magazine *Vélo*) that an unexpected incident put Kurtdereli out of the tournament. On the evening of his bout with Petroff the Bulgarian, he was naïve enough to agree to spare his adversary, who feared his rival's terrible embraces, and to make the match last thirty to thirty-five minutes to safeguard the Bulgarian's self-esteem and reputation. Petroff was able to take advantage of his rival's inexperience, and while Kurtdereli unsuspectingly laid himself open to the Bulgarian, who used a headlock from below to pin the Turk on both shoulders.

It is useless to describe the terrible anger which seized Kurtdereli when he realized his defeat. Petroff slinked off, and it was well that he did so. In the evening at the editorial office of *Le Vélo*, the Turkish colossus protested against his treacherous adversary. He wept like a child at the thought of the shame which the undeserved defeat would bring him. Kurtdereli next issued a challenge to all the wrestlers of the world, but no one dared to accept it. They had seen his work in the ring, and the few examples he had given of his strength had sufficed to convince them all that the wisest of proverbs is "Words are silver, but silence is golden."

Kurtdereli did not forget his dubious defeat, and he came to Paris in 1900, attracted by these famous and illusory world wrestling championships whose echo had circled the globe—and to take a dazzling revenge. But the tournament did not come to pass, and Kurtdereli was already in despair when Gulam's challenge and the resulting match came along. Unfortunately, Kurtdereli had to deal with a terrible man and he was in Gulam's clutches, and this was like being a child in the arms of a grown man. It is always true that even the strongest can always encounter someone who is stronger.

Doublier

The honor of bringing the first Turkish wrestlers, Yusuf, Nurullah and Kara Osman, to France fell to the wrestler [Jean-Claude] Doublier.[103] For several years Doublier had been a teacher of Greco-Roman wrestling in Turkey, and his knowledge of the Turkish language gave him the idea of being the impresario for a troupe of Turkish wrestlers that he would bring to Europe.[104]

Doublier introduced Turkish wrestlers to the Parisian public. Here he sits with three of his burly protégés behind him. Left to right: Kara Osman, Nurullah, and Yusuf.

Although only of ordinary strength, Doublier was himself a keen wrestler, well acquainted with the finer points of the trade. He traveled a lot in Germany where he trained many students such as Hans Beck, Hitzler, and others. Doublier died in deepest poverty on 5 November 1901 at the Lariboisière Hospital following a chest ailment. He was born in Lyon in 1844; he was aged fifty-seven.

Omer de Bouillon

Omer de Bouillon, who is Belgian, has been considered for a long time as the equal of his comrade, Constant "the Butcher." He is a very courageous man who has learned to take advantage of the lessons of his elders and who has thus become a wrestler of the very highest order in just a few years. Omer de Bouillon's real name is Omer Garitte, and he was a foreman at a foundry. He is 1 meter 72 tall, weighs 98 kilos. He was born in Bouillon in 1874 [died 1936].

In Belgium, he has triumphed over Pietro [Dalmasso], [Ignace] Nollys the Belgian, P. Lenoir, and even Van Den Berg. In 1900, after three long sessions, he was able to defeat the famous Bonnelli. In the tournament finale of the championship, he fought to a tie with Cotch Mehmet and was pinned only the second time after four long rounds.

The German Sauerer

This athlete became a wrestler after he left the Bavarian artillery when he completed his military service. After a magnificent match against Apollon II at the

 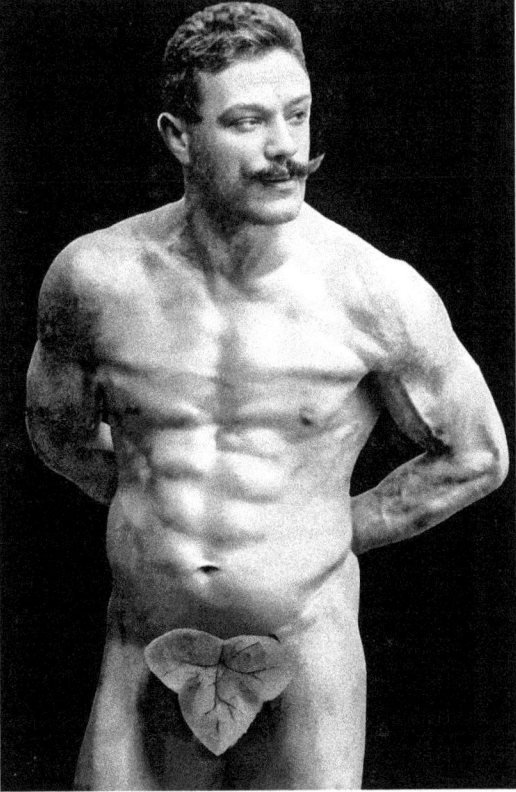

Left: Belgian wrestler Omer de Bouillon was originally the foreman of an iron foundry in his native country (collection of Christian Gaildraud). *Right:* The wrestler Sauerer was from Bavaria, and he was well trained in the techniques of his chosen sport.

championships of 1900, Sauerer had to lower his flag before Constant "the Butcher." In 1901 he was defeated on points by Celestin Moret.[105] In 1902 he beat [Jacques] Roumageon.

Sauerer has remarkable muscular strength. He has achieved splendid performances with a globe barbell in Piazza's Gymnasium. He weighs 82 kilos and he is 1 meter 73 tall. In wrestling, the men are divided into only two categories, heavyweight and lightweight. Multiple divisions exist only in boxing.

Chalzet, "the Thrasher"

Once again, a pureblooded Bordeaux man was one of the revelations of the 1899 championships. He was born in Bessèges (Gard) in 1875. Chalzet is very well known in the South of France, and it was there that he beat Limousin, Quercy, Laclampe, and many others. He was the champion of Toulouse in 1899. Chalzet was defeated in 1899 by the Turk Cotch Mehmet. He weighs only 85 kilos, but his strength is extraordinary. He can do a snatch of 70 kilos in his right hand with a 20-kilo weight in his left hand.

Chalzet originally came from the south of France, and he contended with most of the famous grapplers of the day (collection of Michael Murphy).

Clément "the Navvy"

To say that he is the brother of Constant the Butcher is to say it all. Certainly, Clément Lauvaux (his real name) does not shine with skill, despite the notable progress he has made in recent years. Above all, he is an extraordinarily strong and marvelously constituted man.[106] Clément is Belgian and is 1 meter 72 tall and weighs 85 kilos.

François "the Flour Miller"

He is a fine-looking fellow: he is a well-built man with superb legs. François is a market porter by profession, and he is an athlete of the first order. He is Swiss, but

Left: Clément worked as a wrestler in his more famous brother's shadow (collection of Michael Murphy). *Right:* Swiss wrestler François "the Flour Miller" was renowned for his ability to carry heavy sacks of flour up flights of stairs (collection of Christian Gaildraud).

this does not prevent him from wrestling in all the rules of Greco-Roman wrestling. He has fought with all the most famous wrestlers like Pytlazinski, Petroff, Alphonse Henry, and others.[107]

Now, would you like to have some details on this solid young fellow's strength? Yes? Well, all those who know him (and they are numerous) know that Francois can carry two sacks of flour weighing 318 kilos up to the first floor. Francois weighs 99 kilos and is 1 meter 74 tall. He was born in 1871.

Kara Ahmed

The famous Turkish wrestler Kara Ahmed was born in 1870; he died at thirty-two years of age in Constantinople on 24 May 1902 from a heart disease caused by overtraining.[108] He was one of the best wrestlers from Turkey, not just because of his knowledge, but also because of his strength and his stamina. His countenance was constantly illuminated by a broad smile which was most pleasant. He was a Hercules as well as an excellent fellow.

He came to France for the first time in 1897, at the time that his famous compatriot Yusuf was at the height of his glory. Kara Ahmed accepted the challenge issued by Yusuf to any wrestler in the world, but on the day of the match a boil on his arm prevented the more famous man from wrestling, and it was another compatriot

Ibrahim Mahmut who replaced him. Since he was unable to find a match in Paris with French wrestlers, Kara Ahmed went to Lyon where he made short work of the opponents he went up against. Then he went to Lille, Liège, Antwerp, and Brussels, where for two months he never had a defeat. From there he went to St. Petersburg, but he was not able to wrestle with Pytlazinski who was already very famous; and finally he went back to Turkey, victorious on every leg of his tour. He then returned to Paris for the world championship where he emerged victorious.[109] Spectators of this tournament still remember his sensational wrestling match with Laurent le Beaucairois.[110]

Kara Ahmed was 1 meter 80 in height, 1 meter 24 chest, 50 centimeters neck circumference, and he weighed 105 kilos.

Turkish wrestler Kara Ahmed had great strength and stamina, and he toured all over western and eastern Europe before his death at age 32 (collection of Michael Murphy).

Laurent "le Beaucairois"

Laurent is "the King of Beaucaire," and when he walks around in his hometown, he is pointed out and greeted respectfully. Laurent is a colossus. His form is pleasant; he is of middle height, a little head buried in vast shoulders, enormous arms, a rounded chest and, for legs he has veritable posts. There, that presents in a few words the famous Laurent who is ordinarily called le Beaucairois. Laurent is a Hercules—a mass of muscles, but his weight does not prevent him from being uncommonly agile and flexible. To speed in execution, he joins extraordinary strength and a great deal of composure.[111]

But what a fine young man is this Laurent! Nothing is more amusing than to see him opposite his adversary, multiplying his attacks with a vertiginous speed, not even giving him the time to recognize himself; always good natured with the weak and comically serious with those who resist him or make him work harder. No one knows better than he how to pirouette on his head and jump from one end of the ring to the other.

The Kings of Wrestling: Contemporary Wrestlers

Laurent is one of our best-known wrestlers. He was born in 1867 [died 1935], and he is 1 meter 73 tall and weighs 112 kilos. In his long career as a wrestler, he has fought with men of the highest renown; he has defeated Pons, Gambier, Sabès, Gérardy, Kara Ahmed, and others. Here is an anecdote about Laurent that deserves to be told and which demonstrates this athlete's character.

For around ten years, Laurent le Beaucairois and his friend Aimable de la Calmette had a fairground wrestling booth in the South of France. They were particularly loyal to returning to the St. Michael's Fair in Nimes. One year, some other wrestlers who were younger and less well known moved in to the place where their booth usually stood. Driven by force of habit, one fine Sunday, Laurent (who had just returned from Liverpool where he had defeated Tom Cannon) came to take a look at the fairground and mingled with the crowd listening to the patter of his successors on the stage. When the manager had finished, Laurent said to him, "And what will you give to the winner?"

Laurent le Beaucairois was immensely strong as well as being a skilled and much-loved wrestler (collection of Michael Murphy).

Fairly pleasant but a bit nonplussed, the other one answered, "A bottle of wine."

"That's not much," Laurent replied.

The director saw the interest that the people of Nimes took in this colloquium, since they all knew Laurent, took a risk and said, "and five francs."

"That's pretty modest," said Laurent.

"So, what do you want, then?" shouted the director.

"Everything in your money bag, which I see hanging right there," answered the famous wrestler. Since this proposition seemed very serious, and the director who saw Laurent's potential, hesitated. Yet egotism and the prospects of good receipts encouraged the showman to exclaim, "Done! If you can defeat me, I will give you the contents of the money bag."

"Show me a little of what it contains. I am quite convinced that there are hardly any banknotes in it." The director complied and inside were copper coins and a few rare silver coins that were emptied into a hat. These were the day's receipts, perhaps fifteen or twenty francs. Then Laurent, remembered his own early years and considered the trouble that this modest amount had cost these young showmen, said, "Ah, my poor fellows, you do not know me if you think me capable of touching these few coins that were earned with such difficulty by your comrades. I want no other recompense; I will wrestle for nothing. It will be good training for my next big wrestling match, and you won't be the worse for it."

It was easy to judge the astonishment and the joy of the wrestlers in the booth. Laurent gave them three bouts in a row—causing the booth to be full for every one—and wrestling admirably and seriously; they did it for real and not fake. "It's also because," he said, "everyone has his own pride. If you see me being defeated, here, in this booth—it is I, Laurent le Beaucairois." But his opponents were all brilliantly defeated.

Le Beaucairois was also a very strong weight lifter. At the Robert Gymnasium he lifted, without much training, 140 pounds in a right-handed snatch, did a 50-pound arm extension with the arm kept at the side of the body [i.e., a curl], correctly deadlifted 459 pounds, and he lifted 472 pounds to the height of his knees. In front of Maspoli he brought 160 pounds to arm's length ten times without using proper form, but Maspoli estimates that Laurent could snatch this weight quite easily.

Schackmann

Above the average size, but very heavyset; he has a face with an energetic and dark expression. Despite his unprepossessing physiognomy, his appearance is hardened even more and made almost fierce by enormous drooping, auburn mustaches. But thanks to his openness and his courage, which is quickly obvious, he attracts the sympathy of those who admire his wrestling.[112]

Schackmann is 1 meter 71 tall and weighs 83 kilos. He has fought with Fénelon, François the Flour Miller, Bonnelli, Mazin, and others. He has taken part in the championships of the Meuse at Namur. In this meet he placed second in the lightweight category. In the overall ratings, he obtained a third prize after having beaten Clément the Navvy, brother of Constant the Butcher. He was nicknamed "the Strangler" quite wrongly because all those whom he strangled are presently doing quite well.

Bonnelli

Joseph Bonnelli, winner of the jousting tournament, is a colossus with an extraordinary strength.[113] He carried off the second prize at the championship of

Left: The German Schackmann was nicknamed "the Strangler," and he was one of the most popular (if that is the right word) bad guys in early French wrestling. In reality, he was a kind and gentle soul (collection of Michael Murphy). *Right:* In addition to being a wrestler, Joseph Bonnelli was also a porter at Les Halles, the main food market in Paris (collection of Michael Murphy).

strength in Brussels in 1897 where he especially distinguished himself by carrying 500 kilos on his back and lifting 115 kilos with two hands in two movements.

Bonnelli is a market porter at Les Halles, and this young fellow is impervious to fatigue.[114] If Bonnelli had the time to train seriously, he would be one of the champion wrestlers of the world, but his trade takes up much of his time, and he only does athletics as an amateur.

Joseph Bonnelli weighs 120 kilos and is 1 meter 72 tall. I will add that he is a happy and lively person, and he is a hearty eater.[115]

Halil Adali

Here is another famous Turk who is 1 meter 87 tall, weighs 115 kilos, and has a chest circumference of 1 meter 25 and 50 centimeters around the neck.[116] He was born in Adrianople [now Edirne] (Turkey). His strength is such that he could bend the famous wrestler [Jacobus] Koch like a reed. When Adali clasped him in a front waistlock the German shouted, "Kaput! Kaput!" The unfortunate man thought he

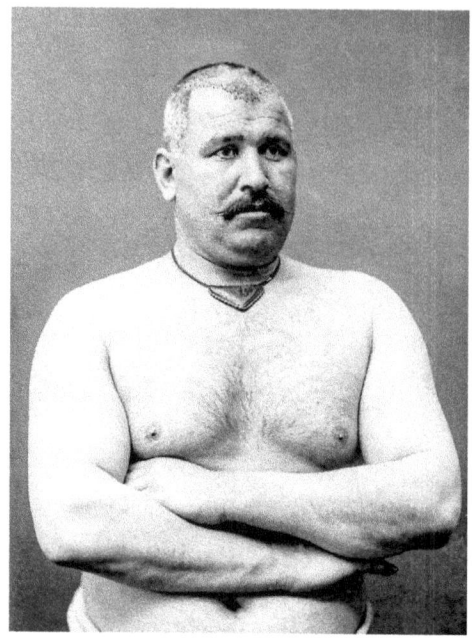

Halil Adali was another formidable Turk who came to Paris to wrestle. He was particularly adept at using the front waistlock (collection of Michael Murphy).

Dieckmann was renowned in both Germany and France as an excellent grappler (collection of Christian Gaildraud).

was dying of pain when he felt himself gripped by such strength.

Dieckmann the Bavarian

He is also a man of the very highest order who is highly rated in Germany and France. Dieckmann is not only a terribly strong man, but he is a perfect wrestler.[117] He is as knowledgeable as our most famous wrestlers from Bordeaux. He is 1 meter 83 tall and weighs 92 kilos.

Paul Pons

Pons is man who cannot walk down the street without making passersby (both male and female) turn around and look. He is a giant, but a handsome giant. The man is no less than 1 meter 97 tall, 1 meter 31 chest circumference, his biceps and calf measure 43 centimeters around. He weighs 236 pounds. Let us add to this portrait that Pons is certainly not potbellied as are certain of his colleagues. His physique is nothing but aesthetic.

Pons is a southerner. He was born in Sorgues (Vaucluse) in 1864.[118] Before becoming a wrestler prior to 1888, he was employed as a blacksmith and machinist. He took part in several contests and there he encountered Pietro who hired him to go to Bordeaux to wrestle. The famous champion saw in his young colleague a man capable of succeeding him.

He soon became a star, and Pons went to Paris to wrestle at the Folies Bergère in company with Bernard, Apollon, and Robinet. He admits to having profited a great deal from these matches, thanks to the knowledge and experience that he acquired. Pons still boasts of copying Bernard a great deal because he considers him the finest wrestler.

It was on the stage of the Casino (in 1891) that Pons defeated Tom Cannon, who had been invincible until then. This victory hardly benefited him, because our champion remained inactive for three years because he could not flush out an adversary who dared to wrestle him. In 1894, the Turkish wrestlers came to Paris, and Pons fought with Nurullah and managed to pin him after an exciting match.

In addition to being one of the finest wrestlers of his time, Paul Pons was intelligent, literary, and articulate (collection of Michael Murphy).

As far as physical strength is concerned, Pons is gifted by nature, for he does a one-handed swing lift of 150 pounds—and this without any serious training. Pons has wrestled for twenty years, and it can be said that he has never had very many defeats. For fifteen years he was the incontestable champion of France. In my presence Pons registered 126 kilos on the Régnier dynamometer, regulation position (13 October 1902).[119]

Van Den Berg

He was a butcher by profession, but one day he abandoned the butcher's stall for the ring. Then after gaining a reputation as a cycling trainer, he turned entirely to wrestling. He was born in 1875 in Holland.[120] This wrestler had an irreproachably

The Dutchman Dirk Van Den Berg had a "harmonious musculature," so it is perhaps fitting that he is celebrated on the cover of sheet music (collection of Michael Murphy).

athletic physique, and in a short time he acquired the greatest reputation [as a wrestler].[121] [Dirk] Van Den Berg is 1 meter 74 tall and weighs 94 kilos—all of it harmonious musculature.

Julius Cochard

As an introduction to an athletic career, Julius Cochard [1868–1902] distinguished himself simply by traveling the distance which separates Paris from Reims, that is to say 180 kilometers—with 100 kilos on his back.[122] Encouraged by this success, Cochard devoted himself to wrestling, and he fought with the famous Turk Kara Osman.[123] A little later in the salon of one of our great courtesans, the Bulgarian Petroff found in him an unbeatable adversary.[124] Julius has arms that measure 42 centimeters, forearms of 36 centimeters, and he is 1 meter 80 in height.

Handsome Julius Cochard began as a "flour-sack racer" but soon turned to the more lucrative profession of wrestling (collection of Michael Murphy).

Willy Stalling

The champion of Holstein, Willy [Wilhelm] Stalling weighs 96 kilos. He is a magnificent specimen of physique beauty with very fine forearms and a muscular harmony that one rarely encounters in professional wrestlers.[125]

Constant "the Butcher"

Constant is a perfect specimen of an athlete. A calm face, eyes that seem, despite their coldness, to scrutinize the depths of your soul; tall, well-built, a shapely physique; here, sketched in a few lines, is the portrait of Constant Lauvaux, known as the Butcher.

He is muscular all over, and this marvelous man is free from those masses of fat which characterize some of our wrestlers. He unites to his strength the skill and endurance which has always astonished those who admire his style of wrestling. In his private life he is a superbly serious man who always has the sense to avoid excess. Very few wrestlers can say as much. With such strengths in his game, Constant cannot help but become a top-notch wrestler no matter what happens.[126]

Constant was born in Florennes (Province of Namur) in Belgium in 1877 [died 1961]. He is the son of honest farmers. From his earliest youth, after a few years devoted to school, Constant dedicated himself to working in the fields until his seventeenth year. Later, around his twentieth year, Constant came to Paris to practice the profession of butcher, from whence he derived his surname. In the meantime, to kill his leisure time, he went right and left to wrestle in *ad hoc* places which were pointed out to him. This is how one day he ended up at Pons's gymnasium where his first matches and his prowess caused a sensation.[127]

The victory that definitively made him a star was that which he won over Félix Bernard and the wrestling championship at the velodrome at Roubaix on 30 May 1898, a championship which

Constant "the Butcher" was "a perfect specimen of an athlete." He later became a brewer in his native Belgium. This photograph is a formal portrait, not from the Roubaix velodrome (collection of Michael Murphy).

I attended and acted as a member of the panel of judges. Since that time, Constant the Butcher has only gotten better, and he is currently one of the best European wrestlers.

Constant is 1 meter 76 tall, 1 meter 16 chest circumference, 40 centimeters biceps, 34 centimeters forearm, 40 centimeters calf, 44 centimeters neck circumference, and he weighs 93 kilos. Without any special training, he snatched 130 pounds with only one hand and jerked 210 pounds with two hands.

The previously unpublished snapshots that accompany this chapter were taken at the Roubaix velodrome during Constant's wrestling match with the late Félix Bernard, who died in Milan in 1900. They show the rise of one star and the fall of another, and if the victory was sweet for Constant, the defeat was very bitter for poor Félix Bernard.[128]

Jules Quéniart

Eighty kilos, 1 meter 74 tall. Quéniart was born in Verneuil in the Oise in 1874 [died 1911].[129] This athlete lifted 250-pound globe barbell in two stages with both

Left: Jules Quéniart's body was "a marvel of physical beauty," and whether he won or lost, he was always a crowd favorite (collection of Christian Gaildraud). *Right:* Fénelon was a popular wrestler especially in his native Bordeaux. He was also the proprietor of a bar that was frequented by his sporting friends (collection of Christian Gaildraud).

hands, naturally, and he lifted 150 pounds in a one-handed swing lift. His body was a marvel of physical beauty, and his torso was especially remarkable for its vigor.

Fénelon

Everyone knows the Bordeaux native, Fénelon [?–1925], the king of the headlock, the technically knowledgeable wrestler par excellence, the perfect example of a Bordeaux. The man is solidly built, has a slender waist, is hardy, courageous, and endowed with a lot of spirit. He is a first-rate wrestler who pleases wrestling fans, he is a fellow who knows how to infuse his audience with enthusiasm because he thoroughly knows his job as a wrestler. No one knows better than Fénelon how to apply a headlock, an arm hold or a waistlock. Fénelon weighs 89 kilos and is 1 meter 70 tall.[130]

He is the owner of a very popular bar on the Place des Capucins, he has a brilliant sporting past. He was trained by Félix Bernard, and he made his debut in 1889. Among his numerous victories, I will cite his match with Buisson, the champion from Toulouse. The champion from Bordeaux defeated [Georg] Jägendorfer; he beat Petroff the Bulgarian for the first time, and the second time with the same adversary in Bordeaux at the Palais de Flore. Jean "le Lyonnais" was beaten twice by Fénelon. Many other powerful professionals have also found their master in the terrible Bordeaux man.

Émile Deriaz

He was born in 1879 [died 1940] in Baulmes in the Swiss canton of Vaud. Deriaz is certainly one of the most famous strongmen in the athletic world. There is an excellent reason for this; it is because Émile Deriaz has brothers who spread his name by their own personal prowess. All of them are remarkable, whether as wrestlers (like Maurice) or as strongmen. I should say that these two qualifications apply to all the brothers, because, similar to the eldest, these men practice both weightlifting and wrestling.[131]

Émile Deriaz is the tallest, heaviest, and strongest of the four brothers. I clearly got this impression five or six years ago at an event organized by the Club Américain in the Rue Notre-Dame-des-Champs.[132] There were English boxers; the Frenchmen [E.] Antoine and [Lucien] Chabrier; my friend and collaborator Georges Dubois, who made a comparative demonstration of foils and fencing. Finally, the Deriaz brothers were there; Adrien and Maurice wrestled. Émile Deriaz had had the nerve to go up to the second floor where he demonstrated his weight lifting skills in a huge workshop that served as a reception room. He dared to work with a 250-pound barbell and a 160-pound dumbbell.

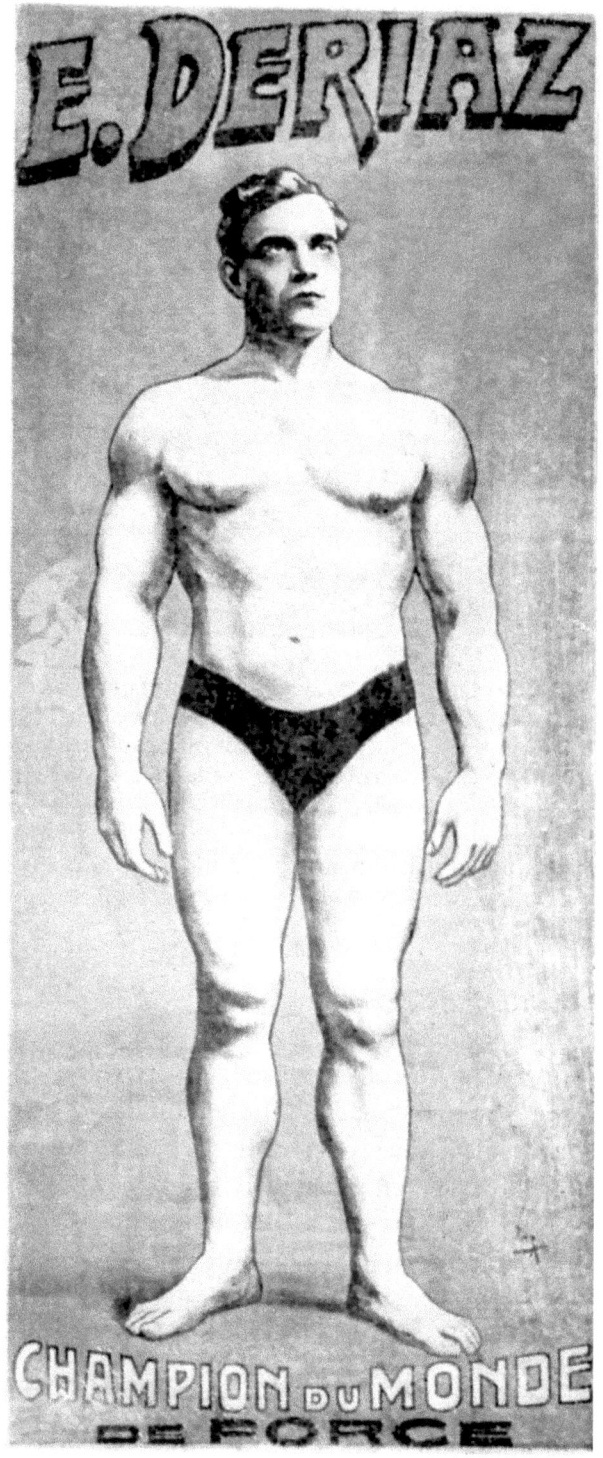

Swiss strongman and wrestler Émile Deriaz came from a family of athletes, but he was the tallest, heaviest, and strongest of his brothers.

In his powerful hands the devices rose quickly, and he put them down gently and noiselessly.

Deriaz worked almost naked, I saw him in profile, and the great symmetry of his muscular masses and the purity of their lines plunged me into deep admiration. He was a Hercules in all his beauty without exaggerated protrusions, without depressions, without muscular bumps, which from the first glace I found to be superb. The musculature that I observed on Émile Deriaz is, however, less beautiful and expresses strength less when compared for example, to the immense pectorals that are apparent in the Borghese Achilles in the Louvre.[133]

As a wrestler, his energy is prodigious. Who does not remember the magnificent way that he pinned the Turkish wrestler Achmed Madrali two times in a row with an irresistible and unstoppable front waistlock?[134] In a recent match with François le Breton, Deriaz just won the title of world champion in strength, a title that Bonnes no longer defends.[135]

Deriaz is a moderate man; I do not see there the explanation of his strength, but I draw from it the hope that he will keep this quality for a long time to come and that he will serve as an example for the generation which immediately follows us. One point which increases our esteem of Deriaz is his revulsion of all the compromises of honor in the wrestling championships. Émile Deriaz does not want to sell his shoulders. Well done, Deriaz!

Yusuf

Yusuf Ismaelo was a formidable Turk whose memory will long remain as an irreplaceable man in the world of wrestling and wrestlers. He had come to Paris accompanied by two other Turks, and we must trace the cause of the introduction Turkish athletes into French wrestling arenas due to rancor—perhaps it is better to say a grudge—of a wrestler beaten by Sabès. At one time Sabès was the king of wrestling, and no one could defeat the hotheaded Bordeaux native.

But among those who had been beaten without hope of a rematch was Doublier, a wrestler from Lyon. On the spot, this man got the idea of going to Turkey to find three men and, one fine day, he landed at the Folies Bergère accompanied by three colossi:

Kara Osman, 100 kilos, 1 meter 80, 1 meter 31 chest
Yusuf, 120 kilos, 1 meter 88 (47 centimeters neck and 1 meter 31 chest)
Nurullah, 150 kilos and more than 2 meters in height

"You'll see," said Sabès to one of his friends, "how I will get the best of these fat fools." The "Turkish idiot" that fate had designated to fight with the terrible Bordeaux man was Yusuf. "So, bring him on!"

Sabès began confidently with his front waist lock, his irresistible attack. Yusuf, both hands in front, absorbed the shock and with one hand, he crushed the nape of Sabès's neck in such a frightful way that it brought him to the mat. The Turk then turned him over and pinned him with astonishing ease. "Yusuf, the winner in four seconds," proclaimed the referee.

Kara Osman and Nurullah finished off their adversaries in similar times. The "fat fools" were renowned as unbeatable. The man from Lyon, Doublier, was avenged and his revenge, all in all, was very correct since he fairly opposed his conqueror who was too much in love with himself with men who were stronger than they were technically skilled.[136]

Yusuf carved out a great success for himself in New York by nearly beating Roeber (who called himself American but was actually German). Roeber had beaten Pons, and he seemed in a condition to overcome any champion and even to beat him; at least that was the opinion of the Americans. We might not be surprised when I say that the Madison

Yusuf Ismaelo was probably the most powerful and most brutal of all the Turkish wrestlers who came to Paris in the mid–1890s. Desbonnet clearly did not have much affection for the man despite his wrestling prowess (collection of Michael Murphy).

Square establishment where the Yusuf-Roeber match was to take place was packed on the evening of the match. This match was organized by Pierri the Greek and old Tom Cannon.

The Turk stuck to his system, and as soon as they were face to face, he began his attacks on the back of Roeber's neck. The German went down to the mat, but every time he immediately got back up again. The Turk got angry and soon the fight became so savage that Roeber panicked and ran around the ring in order to escape the brutal clutches of Yusuf, who pursued him while roaring like a lion. Finally, Yusuf grabbed him and with a howl all the more terrible because he had become maddened with rage, he threw Roeber among the spectators outside the ring that had been elevated above ground level by 1 meter 50.

Yusuf was disqualified and the match was ended. Roeber was thus not defeated. And this judgment is in my opinion correct because wrestling is not a battle, it is a sport. This way of demolishing people by throwing them outside the ring cannot be accepted. If a wrestler is injured during a fight and chooses to abandon it and is declared defeated, we can admit his defeat. But we cannot accept the principle of first injuring a man who will then return to fight. It would mean the end of wrestling and the triumph of brutes and ignoramuses.[137]

After this pseudo victory, Yusuf got $10,000—in gold. The Turk had refused any other form of payment. This heavy load, which he carried in his belt, brought about his downfall. We remember the sinking of the *Bourgogne*. A few passengers escaped death. If we are to believe these survivors, Yusuf behaved like a wild beast; armed with his dagger, he cut a bloody passage through the crowd of panicked passengers, pressing against the railings near the lifeboats. One of these little boats, which was already overloaded, had just gone down to water when Yusuf jumped into it despite the pilot's orders and the cries of the other passengers. His enormous weight and the brutality with which he threw himself into it caused the frail skiff to tip over and its human cargo was submerged under the waves.

Yusuf was a good swimmer; he could have survived for some time as he waited and clung to an illusory piece of wood, which alas too often only prolongs the agony of shipwreck, but the 50,000 gold francs weighed heavily in his belt; they had to be sacrificed. Yusuf clenched his hands on his fortune, and implacable death clutched with its gnarled fingers the formidable throat of the colossus. And he was asphyxiated as quickly as the delicate misses, who a few hours earlier had entertained the passengers of the *Bourgogne* with their joyous laughter. Thus ended Yusuf, the only man who might have gone up against Gulam.[138]

Émile Maupas

He was born in Evreux in 1874 and was the student of Paul Pons. Maupas is a wonderful athlete and a model at the Ecole des Beaux-Arts. He swing-lifts 150 pounds. He is 1 meter 78 tall. On 15 September 1904, he registered 160.5 kilos on the Régnier dynamometer (free position).[139]

P. Jankowsky

Jankowsky "Ursus" is a Polish strongman who began as a weightlifter, but then he devoted himself to wrestling, and for his debut defeated all the German wrestlers who went up against him. Jankowsky is 1 meter 93 tall, 48 centimeters arm, 38 centimeters forearm, 48 centimeters calf, 75 centimeters thigh, 136 centimeters chest,

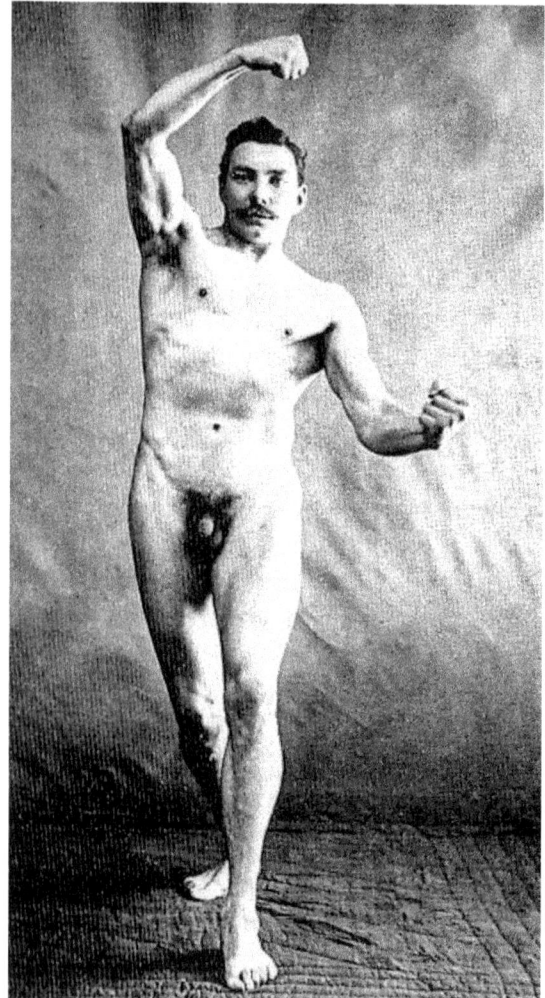

Left: Émile Maupas was a wrestler in France and Canada, but before that he was a model for the École des Beaux-Arts in Paris. Perhaps that is why he posed for this nude photograph. *Above:* Polish-born Jankowsky's greatest asset as a wrestler was his tremendous physical strength (collection of Michael Murphy).

and he weighs 300 pounds. Jankowsky snatched 160 pounds at the time when he was training with weights, he lifted a 135-kilo barbell with two hands and worked with weights that were very difficult to handle because of the thickness of the bars. An ordinary athlete could not have lifted a 270-pound bar from the ground. One wonders as a result if phenomenal men such as Faouët, Pietro, and Laurent de Beaucaire could have triumphed over such monsters of strength.

Ignace Nollys

Ignace, or "Nasque," as his good Brussels neighbors call him familiarly, began his wrestling career sixteen years ago in the South of France. This is how he found himself in company with the great French wrestlers, Sabès, Hefty Paul [le Mastoc], Boyer of Marseilles, Laurent le Beaucairois, and others. It was thanks to contact with them that Nollys acquired that finesse and knowledge that made him one of the best champions of Belgium.

Nollys particularly distinguished himself in 1900 in the Grand Prix of the City of Paris where he wrestled with Hefty Paul, a young fellow who weighs 110 kilos. We remember that Nollys kept Hefty Paul in suspense for almost an hour, and the victory would probably have been his if an imperfection in the ground had not caused him to lose his footing resulting in a broken leg.

Nollys is very generous, and all his comrades know it. He knows how on occasion to defend his friends with energy. Whoever attacks them is to be pitied because Nollys joins his wrestling talents those of a former boxer.

Nollys was born in Brussels in 1870. His height is 1 meter 72 and he weighs 76 kilos. Nollys is just as remarkable as a strongman as he is as a wrestler. He correctly snatched

Ignace Nollys ("Nasque" to his friends) was a strength acrobat before turning to wrestling.

65 kilos and he could certainly do much more. He did a two-handed lift with a barbell weighing 114 kilos, as well as other feats. He performed along with Joseph Wattée under the name of the Ignace Brothers in the act, "The Gladiators."[140] Ignace was also an excellent acrobatic jumper (with his feet together).

G[eorge]. Hackenschmidt

For many sportsmen, this powerful man represents strength united with physical beauty. He was born in Yourief (Baltic provinces, Russia) [now known as Tartu sometimes Dorpat in Estonia] on [1 August] 1877. He studied at the school of practical arts and professions in Yourief, and while quite young he devoted himself to the practice of sports.

This extraordinary athlete was nicknamed by his compatriots "the Russian Lion" and trained under the direction of Dr. Krajewski who wanted to test the value of his method applied to such exceptional individual.[141] Hackenschmidt worked out with medium weights two times a week so that he could develop his natural strength. On the other days he only exercised with light weights. Dr. Krajewski put him on the following diet: no alcohol, no tobacco; for drink, milk, and one time each day a bit of wine at lunch. The Russian Lion took all his meals with his trainer, who could thus make sure of the strict observation of his prescriptions. It was in large part due to his professor that the famous Russian wrestler owes his strength and especially the harmony of his physique.

By harmony, I mean the surprising equality in his power; in fact, taken separately, the various muscular regions of this man offer an equal aspect of strength. Hackenschmidt is of the pale type of athlete; we know the fierce energy of these men as soon as they fight.[142] They accumulate all their will in the effort of a second and when they possess the force of a Hackenschmidt or a Deriaz, the result is appalling. We still remember the match between the Swiss champion and the Turkish wrestler Madrali Ahmed. Infuriated by the way this match had been presented to him, Deriaz took down the Turk twice in a row with an irresistible front waist hold. [See section on Emile Deriaz for details]

George Hackenschmidt "united strength with physical beauty." He also united wrestling skill with uncommon intelligence, and he became (and remains) one of the most famous grapplers in the world (collection of Michael Murphy).

The Russian Lion has extraordinary measurements which one can judge by the following figures:

Weight	97 kilos
Height	1 meter 74
Chest	1 meter 37
Biceps	45 centimeters
Forearm	36 centimeters
Calf	42 centimeters
Thighs	68 centimeters
Neck	47 centimeters

In April 1898 when he was then twenty-one, for his introduction to wrestling Hackenschmidt defeated the amateur champion [Alexander] Schmelling and since then he has marched on from victory to victory.[143] His adversaries fear to wrestle with him since his grips are so appallingly harsh. Alexandre Cayol, a colossus from Marseilles weighing 133 kilos seems but a child when he is caught between his powerful hands, and the enormous wrestler himself confessed that when confronted by such a man, he could do no more than put up a prudent defense.[144]

His weight lifting performances are typical. Lying on his back, he pressed a 144-kilo barbell with two hands. While shouldering [cleaning] a 122-kilo barbell (in the German style) with two hands, he finished by bent pressing the weight with one hand.[145] At the competition in Vienna, Austria, he snatched 171 pounds, but despite all his efforts he could not increase that weight that the French champions [Alexandre] Maspoli and [Pierre] Bonnes that snatched in his presence.

This man is and will remain in the thoughts and memories of sportsmen, one of the finest specimens of an athletic wrestler. The fact that he defeated Pons in one hour and twenty minutes on 8 May 1899 in St. Petersburg, despite the difference in weight, is not one of his lesser feats.

The Cossack Zaikine

[Ivan] Zaikine is a Little Russian [i.e., Ukrainian]. Enticed by the fortunes that some of his compatriots had made in the wrestling tournaments of the great capitals (like Hackenschmidt and Poddubny) he dreamed of acquiring one day the glory of his elders and also of their banknotes, so he began to train.

Zaikine is young; he is twenty-eight years old. He is a splendid athlete whose measurement we have recorded as follows: 1 meter 86 tall, shoulder circumference 1 meter 43, chest 1 meter 28.5, biceps 43

Ukrainian wrestler Ivan Zaikine was a new star in the wrestling firmament when Desbonnet described him. He later turned to aviation (collection of Michael Murphy).

centimeters, forearm 35.5 centimeters, thigh 67 centimeters, calf 43 centimeters, neck 49 centimeters.

Just now Zaikine's star is shining with particular brilliance among the constellation of wrestling. At the Paris championship in 1908, he beat Giovanni Raicevich and all the other men with whom he wrestled. He was defeated only by Poddubny.[146]

Romanoff the Russian

This colossus weighs 116 kilos and is 1 meter 93 tall, 45 centimeters around his arm, 1 meter 27 around his chest. Romanoff made his debut in 1902 and the second Gold Belt Tournament. He made it into the finals with Pons, Laurent, Petersen, Antonitch, Raoul, and others. At that time, he was not very well built; currently, he is a superb athlete.[147]

The False Rabasson

I cite "the False Rabasson" specially to avoid all confusion between him and the famous wrestler with the same name.[148] The False Rabasson was a good boxer and a fairly good wrestler. He toured mainly in Belgium and in the east of France. He was born in Saint-Étienne in 1857.

The Russian athlete Romanoff was a tall and muscular colossus (collection of Michael Murphy).

Constant the Sailor

Constant "the Sailor" is Belgian.[149] He is a powerful strongman, built along the lines of Raoul the Butcher, and the only one who could possibly replace him today. He is twenty-five years old. He is a thoroughbred wrestler who delivers his blows

Left: The man known only as the False Rabasson exhibited as a wrestler and a boxer primarily in the late-nineteenth century. *Right:* Constant le Marin (the sailor) was a popular wrestler, particularly in his home region of Belgium. He was later a great war hero in the First World War (collection of Michael Murphy).

with prodigious rapidity. Most recently in London, he went head-to-head with Poddubny during a match that lasted a quarter of an hour, and he was not defeated.[150]

Constant the Sailor is a likeable man, with an agreeable face and of proud bearing. He is 1 meter 86 tall and weighs 112 kilos.

Appendix
and Metric Conversions

The following pieces help fill in the early history of Greco-Roman wrestling in Europe, and they are presented in chronological order. Desbonnet's *Kings of Wrestling* was compiled and written in the early twentieth century, and his source material was very limited. He kept newspaper-clipping scrapbooks, but these could only supply a fraction of the information. The following works are taken from roughly contemporaneous books and newspaper articles, and they show the great enjoyment that French, Germans, and Italians took in the sport and spectacle of wrestling.

The longest work in this section is an excerpt from Paul Pons's excellent book *La Lutte* (1912), which expands and corrects many of the errors that Desbonnet made, and which tells the stories from the viewpoint of one of the greatest wrestlers of his age. Pons does not always divulge to readers the source of his information, but it must have been from talking to either the men who appear in the stories or to those who knew them. He also expands the details behind the arrival of Turkish wrestlers in Paris and their subsequent successes all over Europe and America. Assuming that his account of Doublier and his adventures are accurate, they reveal many incidents that were almost certainly conveyed directly to Pons himself. The chronology of events is likewise murky, but at least the anecdotes have survived, and they give modern historians a unique perspective into this long-gone world.

One of the things that is apparent from reading the following accounts is the rapid internationalization of sport. As wrestling grew in popularity, it attracted participants and audiences in all the major population centers of Europe. The only other major wrestling regions that are not represented here are Russia and Eastern Europe. Most of the best athletes in the early twentieth century visited and competed in tournaments in the Czar's territories, and there were many wonderful magazines and newspapers that have preserved this prerevolutionary ardor for grappling. Unfortunately, linguistic difficulties make it difficult for me to include any of them. Perhaps someone will one day accept the Slavic wrestling gauntlet and head into this particular arena.[1]

If nothing else, these excerpts from books, newspapers, and magazine confirm how deeply wrestling had penetrated French (and later European) popular culture.

Appendix and Metric Conversions

To paraphrase the great impresario Rosignol-Rollin, wrestling and muscles were quite clearly in the air.

Since the metric system is still not familiar to most people in the United States, I provide the following chart for weights used most frequently in the text.

Kilos	Pounds (rounded)
1	2.2
10	22
20	44
25	55
30	66
35	77
50	110
65	143
70	154
80	176
90	198
100	220
110	242.5
120	264.5
200	441
400	882
750	1,653
1000	2,205

In length measurements, a rule of thumb is that 1 meter is a little more than 3 feet.

Centimeters	Inches
5	1.9
10	3.9
20	7.8
30	11.8
40	15.7
50	19.6
60	23.6
70	27.5
75	29.5
80	31.4
90	35.4
95	37.4
100	39.3

Here are some frequent measurements of height:

Meters	Feet and inches (rounded)
1 meter 50 cm	4 ft 9 inches
1 meter 65 cm	5 ft 4 inches
1 meter 70 cm	5 feet 6 inches
1 meter 80 cm	5 feet 9 inches
1 meter 85 cm	6 feet 0 inches
1 meter 90 cm	6 feet 2 inches
2 meters 16 cm	7 feet 1inch
2 meters 22 cm	7 feet 3 inches

Appendix 1:
Timothée Trimm, "Truly Strong Men"

Although he signed this piece with his more famous nom de plume, it was actually written by the journalist and humorist Antoine Joseph Napoléon Lespès (1815–1875). He was a cofounder and editor of *Le Petit Journal*. The article was written as entertainment as well as instruction, so there are several places where the author exaggerates for humorous effect.

Timothée Trimm
Le Petit Journal
Thursday, 31 May 1866

Truly Strong Men

Yesterday as I was walking down a boulevard, I felt someone grabbing my arm with an extreme vigor. Only a creditor or a shop guard could have used such ardor in restraining me. Turning around, I saw that I was mistaken. It was Rossignol-Rollin, an old friend who had been missing from the Parisian asphalt for fifteen years.

Back in the day my old friend had been an artist at the Variétés and the Vaudeville where he had played alongside Arnal and Odry.[1] Then he departed the Parisian stage and left for parts unknown. When I saw him yesterday after a long absence, I thought that he might have become a potentate, a Quaker, a Trappist monk, or a miner in California. He was accompanied by two men, a brown-haired person and the other a blond who both gave me a very friendly greeting. "They are artists," he murmured to me. "They are artists in my troupe."

"Oh, so you are a director?"

"Impresario, my friend, nothing but that. With successes at haranguing the public that would put Demosthenes to shame."

We all entered Peter's Tavern to dine.[2] There, good old Rossignol Rollin ordered a sole normande, a beef paté, a salad of green beans … and two twenty-kilo weights.[3] I must confess that this last stew intrigued me a little. It was not on the menu.

As soon as the soup was served, one of the artists took a 20-kilo weight and raised it by the ring in an arm extension. Then he began to juggle with the 80 pounds of weight represented by the two masses of iron as if they had been a child's playthings.

As for the other, he lifted the fully set table with one finger; he wanted to lift the waiter, who was serving us, in the palm of his hand, and then he was about to knock down the column which supported the ceiling of the room like Samson, when we threw ourselves between him and the pillar. "Don't worry," said Rossignol-Rollin, "if he moves the column, he'll put it back."

I had the honor of having two celebrities who were unknown in the capital as guests: Marseille the younger "the Peasant of Lapalud," the king of wrestlers from the south and Bérenger, "the elegant Parisian Strongman."

I write these lines for the thousands of my readers who rightly feel that the physical strength in a man is equal to the beauty of a woman. It is only in wrestling that strength reveals itself without using offensive arms or dangerous blows.

Rossignol-Rollin was a wise, crafty, bigger-than-life, and slightly ridiculous character. He loved wrestling and wrestlers, and his men returned the compliment.

The ancient wrestler was called *palestrite* when he was a mere amateur and *athlete* when he was a professional wrestler. The Greeks and Romans had three types of wrestling: perpendicular wrestling, horizontal wrestling, and *acrochirisim*. Perpendicular wrestling is performed most often, and it consists of overcoming one's adversary and of pinning him to the ground. In horizontal wrestling, the two adversaries fight on the floor, rolling one on top of the other and interlacing themselves in a thousand ways until one of the two is underneath and can force the other to surrender. Finally, acrochirism was wrestling in which one does not touch either the arms nor the body except by fingers, hands, and fists. These are twisted, and in this way one tries to turn the opponent over.

Modern wrestling has neglected acrochirism since it resembles the ancient perpendicular wrestling. The wrestlers wrap their arms around each other, launch themselves with the express prohibition of bringing their hands below the belt; they rise from the ground, they fall back, they let go, they pull themselves together until both shoulders of one of the combatants have touched the dust of the arena.

Fifteen years ago the man who fell with anything other than a flat back was released and he got up. A wrestler, the famous Rabasson, whose memory Paris has preserved, created a school by continuing to wrestle on the ground. He unknowingly revived the horizontal wrestling of the pagan eras.

I knew Rabasson [1824?–1854]; he was shy just a few centimeters in order to become a soldier. He was fat, squat, and moved in face to face with the adversary; he let himself be grabbed around the waist without resisting and when the opponent tried to lift him from the ground, he pushed him back with a snap, sending the man to fall down in the sand. Rabasson died like a bourgeois a few years ago—in his bed.[4] If death had assumed visible form, a body, a palpable form, Rabasson would have pinned him.

I knew Rabasson at a time when there was still wrestling at the Montesquieu Hall. Then, there was Marseille the elder, a miller from the Vaucluse who was big, thin, lean, hairy as a panther who wriggled out of the hands of the wrestlers like a monkey.

There was Creste "the Bull of Provence," who at that time could resist the efforts of all the force of inertia; you could have shaken him by the shoulders, by the neck, by the head, and it was as if you had tried to shake one of the towers of Notre Dame.

There was also Arpin "the Keystone." Who performed ironic pirouettes and entrechats in the air and then into the arms of his enemy who always landed tails, never heads, in accordance with rules of the game.

Then little Anthèlme [Baboula of Lyon], a wrestler with the body of a child, who clung to the arm of a colossus, never let go of him, made a pendulum of this limb which he paralyzed by his embraces, and suddenly brought him over his shoulder by what in wrestling is called a perfect flying mule; he laid his man on his back, making him float like a feather over his head.

Then there was also Blas, "No Quarter," a hero out of [epic poet Tarquato] Tasso, and Rivoire "the Invincible Lyonnais." Blas, who was a fine looking fellow, was one day asked by a sculptor if he wanted to have his portrait made in plaster. Blas consented for the price of twenty-five francs to be paid to the sculptor. A month after the commission and multiple posing sessions, the sculptor brought him a medallion. "That's my portrait, is it?" said Blas.

"Certainly!"

"You want twenty-five francs for that?"

"We agreed."

"But this is rubbish! I don't owe you anything. You have only done half of my face." The good wrestler did not understand that it was a portrait in profile. Blas, the bold fighter was felled in Toulon by cholera in 1856.[5]

Some prominent people were seen among the audience at the Montesquieu Hall (which has today become an outlet for Duval's Bouillon): a minister, Mr. Léon Faucher; a member of Parliament, Mr. Granier de Cassagnac; a member of the Institute, the Count de Nieuwerkerque; the British ambassador; and famous actors and artists of the stage.[6]

Among the wrestlers that they applauded, we must cite "Resistance" who wrestled missing one finger; Jules Le Marin who was straight as a mast; Louis the Mechanic who had lifted the locomotive which he drove on the Northern Railroad; Charpentier, "Friendly," an athlete from our neighborhoods, and Pierre the Savoyard.[7] This Pierre drove a hackney carriage on the square, and he was a coachman—and quite a faithful coachman he was.[8] He was strong as a horse, and if one of his wheels broke, he would, if necessary, carry his passenger to his destination on his shoulders, dragging the three-wheeled coach with one hand and the unharnessed horse with the other. When there were wrestling matches, Pierre no longer cared. He made it his practice to park his coach in front of the wrestling hall after telling his fare that there was an accident that had to be repaired. He then entered the arena, fought with a rival, and (whether he won or lost) resumed his seat in the coach and tried to calm his furious client.

Wrestling—even flat-hand wrestling—was banned in Paris following an accident that happened to Dumortier, even though he did not suffer from it very much since he still wrestles under the name of "the Agile Lyonnais."[9] Wrestling has become one of the distractions of the provinces, and especially in the departments of the South. And under the direction of Rossignol-Rollin, it has produced a new generation of wrestlers who are unknown to Parisians, and it is they whom I wanted to introduce in this article.

With my two dinner guests, Marseille the younger who lifts a barrel with his teeth that is straddled by two men, and Béranger who carries 300 in a basket on his back, there is Alfred, "the Pretty Model," a Parisian and former Zouave, and Lacroix "Good Heart," who is strong as an oak but limber as a reed. Let us not forget Vincent, "Iron Man," and "the Shepherd" Étienne who was one day defeated by a sweet little inn keeper's daughter, so he got married and abandoned the arena. He was lost to this art.

A first-class wrestler earns 600 francs per month; he is hired for the year, and he generally wrestles twice a week. Aside from these fixed emoluments, a wrestler will (like jockeys) receive certain gratuities coming from those who bet on him. He must wrestle against all comers, even against a masked adversary who is generally an athlete from the city where they find themselves; he is a Milo who wants to try his chances under the veil of anonymity.

The wrestling manager, Mr. Rossignol-Rollin is a combination orator, thinker and writer. In his harangues to the turbulent wrestling audience, he gets lively repartees. "Shut up," one of these hecklers said to him the other day in the Arena of Nimes, "because you're only witty on the posters."

"And you," replied the impresario of physical strength, "you who cause a disgrace here, you have no wit at all especially when you're showing off."

Sometimes his posters seem like official proclamations. In one of these posters he announced a show with the generous participation of the band from a regiment. I reproduce it here:

Latest Show of Messrs. Crest and Vincent
YOU ARE RIGHT, CITIZEN OF LYON!

And your severity was correct; in your justifiable anger, you did not want to hear me, perhaps you will deign to read me. Yes, you are right, a wrestler whom I was happy to call famous and invincible, one day, only one—yesterday—forgot his duties; today, he is no longer part of my troupe, and if you could have believed for a moment that I, Rossignol-Rollin, could be an accomplice in this felony! Well! People of Lyon, you misunderstood me!

You were wrong, and Rossignol-Rollin is still worthy of you, and do not think that because one man one day fought poorly that wrestling is dead because of that. No! No! A hundred times No! Do not think this because you will be wrong, and wrestling is real. And now, to you, wrestlers, whom I consent to exhibit, since you cannot be responsible for the faults of one of you, wrestle on, ah! I advise you to wrestle! Seriously! For the punishment which has been visited upon your colleague is waiting for you, and if you are not careful, it will get you.

For shows in the smaller towns, the poster ends with an admirable comment.

The Wrestling Matches Will Take Place on a
MAGNIFICENT AUBUSSON CARPET
Having a Value of 20,000 Francs!

For all those inhabitants of rural communities who do not know what an Aubusson is, they should hasten to see this additional curiosity.

As a thinker, Mr. Rossignol-Rollin has invented maxims like La Rochefoucauld for the wise use of those who calmly encounter them. He has written:

> Muscles are flowers that must be watered with wine.
> However, the first muscle is equanimity.
> It is only an awkward or a weak man who is brutal.
> A truly generous wrestler embraces his defeated enemy.

I dined with the two greatest modern wrestlers, and they were gentle, polite and well-mannered guests. Young Marseille could have turned the salad upside down with his feet in the air. He didn't. Béranger could have taken the counter and the cash register lady with a toothpick. He had the good taste to refrain. They left at the earliest hour for Agen where they value strength as much as they love poetry. My best wishes accompanied them.

And I want my old friend the director to collect enough gold coins to fill even his Aubusson carpet, which is one of the attractions of his piquant program.

Appendix 2:
Jules Vallès, Excerpts from *The Street*

Although he was a revolutionary firebrand for most of his life, journalist and novelist Jules Vallès (1832–1885) retained a love of Paris and a lively sympathy for its poorer inhabitants. The following section is from *La Rue* (The Street) a work that shows what Parisian street life was like, and it is found in the section on "les saltimbanques" (carnival performers).

Jules Vallès
Excerpts from *La Rue*
The Street
Paris: Achille Faure, 1866

Boxers and Wrestlers

Now to the wrestlers!

They are the most popular, the best known, and this fairground attraction appeals to everyone. It is the common man's Coliseum for two pennies a ticket. The Montesquieu Hall highlighted men of wrestling and transformed a few obscure athletes into heroes by the next day—men whose names we know today: Arpin, Rabasson, Marseille, Dornier, Balandrin, Bonnet (from Lyon), Blas, Rivoire, Leboeuf, Bernard, Anthèlme, Carcassonne….

We know how Rabasson ended up; he died after a match in Bordeaux with Bernard. I was told that Carcassonne went mad with love and that he ended his days in an insane asylum. Several years ago, I attended an honest wrestling match between him and Pierre the Savoyard at the Gingerbread Fair.[1]

He issued his challenge from the stage of his booth, "I always offer 100 francs!" Pierre the Savoyard was a former wrestler at the Montesquieu Hall but at that time he was a coachman who was on his day off, and he asked for the trunks.[2] They fought, and it was horrible. Pierre the Savoyard wrestled well, but Carcassonne, like men of the South was somewhat heavier, fatter, two times stronger, and when he elbowed him with his knotty forearms, the Savoyard's courage crumbled and broke. He even got him from below when his head was caught in a chancery hold (that is to say, gripped firmly under Carcassonne's shoulder), the man then used his arm to exert pressure on the neck and the intrepid fighter's face. And this is how it ended, with the man's face taking a beating. Pierre said nothing and he continued in this way since he thought he was holding his own, so he let himself be bruised in order not to lose the match. He did his best, but Carcassonne was heavy, and weight triumphed over courage.

The two adversaries, victor and vanquished, were furious. "I'll throw you over this wrestling booth!" shouted Carcassonne.

"You are nothing but a cow!" Pierre yelled, and the gasping crowd urged them on. A revenge match was promised, but nothing came of it. One time was enough.

On another day at the same fairground near the old tollbooth of the Trône at the booth of Cadet of Moissac (that is the one I described just now). Carcassonne was still wrestling there. On the other side there was another arena that operated under the banner of "Albus and Ramon, Finest wrestlers in the world."[3] They also challenged strongmen, but their lineup was a little threadbare, the music a bit weak, the wind was not blowing on their side, and they had not earned a penny. All of a sudden at two o'clock on a Sunday just when at Cadet's booth Carcassonne issued his challenge, Ramon who had come down from his deserted booth appeared. He raised his hand and shouted, "A pair of trunks!"

Everyone recognized him as the wrestler on the other side; what is more, he made himself recognized because he spoke loudly and let his indignation and his fury out of the bag. Why was he, Ramon, the hero of Nimes, making nothing while this flea of a Carcassonne (a flea who weighed 300 pounds) make a pile of gold?

"They're going to wrestle!" The audience heard it, they were witnesses. If Carcassonne is defeated, the winner will get 100 francs (which was displayed on a table in the booth). "We might as well go see it!" Carcassonne smiled and said, "Enter!"

The crowd rushed in, and all the other preliminaries were done away with. Ramon asked sarcastically if he could win twenty-five francs by first hip rolling and making the understudy bite the sawdust—this was a scrawny little Negro who rolled around on the ground after the main event. Carcassonne called Ramon a coward, and they started the match.

It was beautiful to see, but for those who knew a little about what they were watching, the results were never in doubt. Ramon was nearly taken down twice. He howled; Carcassonne laughed mirthlessly, and they went back at it. Ramon sensed that it was all over; he had fallen two times, and he was going to be pinned. His shoulders approached the floor. Confused and desperate, he took Carcassonne's ear in his teeth, bit down, and tore it off.

Carcassonne wanted to kill him! They were separated. Ramon had to pay 200 francs for the ear which was brought to court in a glass.[4]

I was told that Blas had died, but the details of his death are so romantic to make me wish that the old wrestler were still alive. Here is the story. It started in Toulon in a tavern near the port. Eight or ten men were gathered together, warmed by the wine, their eyes burning, their hands fingering their knives.

Athletic Arena at the *Foire du Trône*. This illustration captures perfectly the claustrophobic interior of a baraque (engraving by Frédéric de Haenen, *Le Monde Illustré* [21 April 1883]).

A quarrel had arisen over a broken bottle, possibly an overturned glass; I don't know. One of the customers was Blas the Spaniard, called "Pitiless." It was against him that the group of sailors, drunk with brandy and anger, circled threateningly. They grabbed him securely, and they were going to knock him out and commit a crime under the influence of drunkenness. Blas, driven mad by wine, cried out to them, "Stop! There are many of you, and I am alone. I can finish off two or three of you easily enough, but the others will kill me. I have a way to settle all of this. You'll see what I have in mind." And he went toward the window which was wide open. It was twenty feet above the ground. He announced, "Those of you who want to fight can follow me!" As he said so, he jumped out of the window. Because of the fall, he cracked his head, and the narrator said that he died from it.[5]

What became of [Bonnet] Leboeuf?[6] I knew him in Nantes where he earned popularity and affection. He had been called to the honorable functions of Drum Major of the National Guard, and he ran a café that was located first near the town hall, then near the establishment of Old Moreau, our dear former professor of arms, but he later let the café go.

I saw him for the last time at the Theater of Varieties in Nantes where he wrestled against an old wrestler named Turck. Turck had issued his challenge by putting up posters. Leboeuf picked up the gauntlet, and all Nantes was with him. The entire city was at the theater to witness the triumph of their champion. While waiting for the show to begin, Turck was seen prowling the halls and the arena in to order make his final preparations. When they saw him, the people of Nantes laughed! Turck was small, thin, already an old man; his hair was gray, his countenance sad; there was worry, almost pain in his eyes.

The show began. A shudder ran through the assembly when Leboeuf and Turck presented themselves. Turck was gloomy, defiant, barely supported by the encouragement of his attendants, while Leboeuf smiled and waved, shaking hands on the right and left.

They began the match; the whole department of the Lower Loire wrestled. There were ohs! ahs! And cries of "He'll go down!" But Turck was still holding on. The crowd said, "Leboeuf is just playing with him." Leboeuf, in fact, used the terrible mass of his fleshy body to oppose the impetuous attacks of the valiant Turck who was desperate but emotionless. Leboeuf prevented his rival from taking him down. Once, however, he was seized and pinned to the ground, but he said that it was an illegal move.

There was a terrible uproar. You would have thought you were at the Cordeliers or the Jacobins.[7] There was isolated tussling in the audience; some, in spite of their chauvinism, believed that Leboeuf had been vanquished, and in the name of simple justice they stood for Turck; others shouted that both champions had deceived them all; there was a sensation of feverish excitement in the arena that somehow dissipated the threat of armed force. A rematch was scheduled for the following Sunday. I don't know what the outcome was.

Even Leboeuf has his legend.

When he was young in Madrid, one day he announced on his boastful posters that he would wrestle against eight men, and that he (a Frenchman) challenged eight Spaniards. When it was time for the match, eight men arrived to fight him. They were all representatives of the Iberian Peninsula. Leboeuf protested, claiming that he had indeed challenged eight wrestlers, but one at a time—one by one. "No!" said many in the audience. "You said eight—and here they are!" Leboeuf appealed to the referee who did not dare announce to the delirious crowd that they were wrong for fear of a riot and further trouble. The assembly had been wounded by the insolence of the French Hercules. "Fine," said Leboeuf, "come on, then!"

They advanced, and the athlete backed up, and then backed up again until he was finally pushed back against a post; but as he was retreating, he grabbed one Spaniard around the neck, lifted him into the air and crashed him against his knee as if he were a piece of kindling! Two more arrived, and with two blows, he flattened them both. When there were only three remaining, he left his post, and the others left the arena! Vanquished Spain cheered triumphant France.

Wrestlers have gone away: Arpin is old, and he has lost his strength, and the same is true of his great glory. Dornier is a porter at Les Halles, Bonnet is a fisherman, Balandrin (of Lyon) is a baker—this is the Balandrin who endured that famous wrestling match against Arpin when he was grabbed around his body and twirled in the air. In the course of this move, Balandrin caught hold with both hands to the iron framework of a gas lamp; it was as if his fingers were screwed to the gas jet. He resisted all of Arpin's efforts to dislodge him for twenty-five minutes even though Arpin pulled on his tall, lean body without being able to take him down. Balandrin did not give up, and Arpin got tired before his opponent could declare that he was beaten!

Marseille remains as a professional wrestler—reliable and strong Marseille; but Marseille is getting old. He has a wrinkled forehead, a gloomy air, and a pale complexion; he is thin, hairy, taciturn. We can say of him, however, that he is, among all the famous wrestlers, the one who has the most *soul*; the word is from Arpin, I got it from him. All his wrestling colleagues agree and use it. But Marseille is just the owner of a wrestling booth where he works. He also performs with others. Where will it all end?

Dubois is the very personification of wrestling.[8] He is strong—very strong—but he does not have stamina. On the other hand, his weight allows him to resist the most violent attacks by sheer inertia and the solidity of an elephant. Like Leboeuf, Dubois has a reedy voice, and coming from that enormous body emerge the tart and flaccid words of a eunuch.[9] After Wolff and fat Masson, Dubois is one of those who lifts weights the best, and the only rivals that I know of are Rabier and Papillon.[10]

Beneath these celebrities, the teeming world in the land of flat-hand wrestling is not worth a damn.

The *Comtois* are not exactly the flower of French gentry.[11] We know that under the name of *comtois* or *comtois drummers* are designated the accomplices or that each fair booth maintains at the foot of the stairs to animate the game and keep the matches going. We recognize them by the breadth of their chests, the swaying of their shoulders, and the hoarseness of their voices. They are defeated men who make it their business to try to defeat others; one thinks of them as unscrupulous people who are violent, ferocious, and who have no other gospel than the brutal code of the arenas and who only believe in force. They live and sometimes die from it: when, knocked down the wrong way, they have broken their ribs or broken their backs.

You should see them at midnight, when they come to collect the wages of their work. They have sweated, breathed, eaten sand or mud; a few grumble about their bruised limbs. Often they get angry; there is wrestling, wrestling with clenched fists and no longer with a flat hand; eyes light up, they insult one another and threaten each other; there is jostling and struggling! They are going to "eat their noses": a horrible expression which, in their vocabulary, means to cut into the flesh, to break teeth, to crack open a head.

I have seen these colossi continue to drink after having had wounds in their skulls big enough to put their fists in, with the blood dripping into their eyes and even falling into their glasses! A second-year student at the schools of Lecour, Vigneron, or Leboucher can best defend himself against these boors by taking off his gloves.[12]

Appendix 3:
X, "Among Men"

The author of this piece, "Côté des hommes," signs the article with only the letter "X" almost certainly because of the homoerotic implications in it. He goes into rapturous discussions of the wrestlers and their sexy physiques. The magazine *La Vie Parisienne* originally covered literature, sports, the arts, and other related subjects. In the early twentieth century it evolved into a mildly risqué publication, but it was clearly on that path already in 1867 when this article was published.

X
La Vie Parisienne
5 January 1867

Among Men

Madame, we are taking you to the Gymnase Paz. Imagine a building as big as Notre-Dame, encumbered with ropes, ladders, and in the middle which has been left empty, there is a sort of padded platform covered with a thick carpet. All around are rows of chairs and benches, two thousand spectators, an orchestra hidden in the upper balcony, and on the platform are men, real ones, all naked and wrestling.

"Then we can't go."

Pardon me, dear madam, because the nudity of these heroes is discreet. Their legs are encased in blue trunks, and over the trunks they wrap a red calico waist sash. Only the back and chest remain bare. So, you see, you can go there, and you will, because before six months have elapsed, it will be fashionable to have seen the Terrible Savoyard's cutlets, the filets of Creste, called the *Bull of Provence*, and the slab of beef that is Bérenger, nicknamed the *Superb Parisian*.

You cannot imagine what these matches are like—it is exciting. You are moved, you take sides, and I imagine that real bull fights must make you feel something similar. From an artistic point of view, it is quite simply splendid. I don't want to bore you with my descriptions; you really have to go there, you have to see it…. I swear to you that it is not just pretty, but really very beautiful.

You have seen notaries, stockbrokers, seminarians in their suits, it is very pretty I'm sure, but go and see what an agile, robust, well-built man looks like—and just

A wrestling uniform of blue leggings with a sash around the waists leaving the torso bare could be very suggestive (from *L'Illustration*, 17 May 1890).

the way the good Lord made him. If I had any advice for Mr. Eugène Paz, because it was he who had the idea of organizing these wrestling sessions in his splendid gymnasium on the Rue des Martyrs....

Dear me! If this bit of an article can be an advertisement for him, I am delighted to make it so, and the proof is that I am going to give the street address. Grand Gymnasium directed by Mr. Eugène Paz, Rue des Martyrs, 40.

If therefore I had to advise Mr. Paz, I would give him the idea of arranging seats, boxes or something similar, which could be hired in advance and where one would not be too conspicuous. I wager these shows would be wildly successful with the opposite sex.

Personally, I adore these wrestling matches—I quite frankly admit it. In fact, I know of nothing more thrilling and more beautiful than this spectacle. There is a Negro there, James, who is called the *African Farnese*, and who is as handsome as an antique bronze. There is another man—Bérenger, or the Superb Parisian, who is also admirable, although much less elegant and less flexible. The other night these two beautiful beings were wrestling together. It is the last word in strength, skill, and agility, besides that the antique bronze has a particular way of falling on his head without breaking it.

If only such spectacles could finally bring into our ethics and into the education of our children a respect for this poor unfortunate body that we have so long persisted in considering as just a box, a container, a simple hat box! Do you think that the English are any more stupid for attaching such great importance to bodily exercises, and that a man's mind is a fortune precious enough to be lodged in a solid coffer?

Before the fight between the Superb Parisian (who certainly deserves his name) and the African Farnese (in other words James), there clashed two massive gods, two mountains. These were Creste, the Bull of Provence, and Pujol, the Colossus of the Gironde.

These nicknames seem a little comical at first, but when you see these young bucks, you understand that the epithets are not too much. They have a certain fabulous something about them, and their pompous labels suit them well. I will return to the Rue des Martyrs, on my hands and knees if I have to, to see this enormous, this heroic Creste wrap his two arms once more around his adversary and suffocate him under his mass.

You may have never seen the Terrible Savoyard, who contributed to the heyday of the Montesquieu Hall. He was there too. Imagine a hairless bear with white skin, short front legs that are as strong as pillars…. But I am afraid I will bore you by telling you about a sight you have to witness. Go there yourself.

In spite of yourself, when you are putting on your overcoat, you will touch your arm and you will feel a sense of shame. These matches will be repeated twice a week, Thursday and Sunday, at eight o'clock in the evening.

Appendix 4:
Edmond Renoir,
"Wrestling and Wrestlers"

A younger brother to Auguste, the famous impressionist painter, Edmond-Victor Renoir (1849–1944) became a journalist, and his works appeared in various publications. He wrote frequently for the weekly magazine *L'Illustration*, and in this instance, he took some artists along with him to a wrestlers' *baraque*, so we have both the writer's words and the artist's pictures to help us imagine what it was like.

Edmond Renoir
L'Illustration
17 May 1890

Wrestling and Wrestlers

"To the arena! To the arena!" Multicolored posters have spread the call everywhere to see the athletes, now the fair is in full swing, the arena is all prepared, and in its center the square of sawdust is covered with a once fresh carpet as it awaits the fighters. Standing outside on the platform, the master of the establishment, proud of his troupe, throws out the gauntlet to the (more or less) authentic amateurs emerging from the crowd.

"To the arena! To the arena!" The manager's patter is shouted in a strong and convincing voice, and it is listened to in open-mouthed amazement by an essentially gullible audience. They are planted straight in front of the trestles to admire as closely as possible the handsome men of the troupe. These men pose to display their torsos as they banter pleasantries that are a bit too clumsy (at least they are as clumsy as their massive bodies). The parade continues while the crowd, enticed by the promise of a performance "that has never been seen before" jostles into the arena.

"To the arena! To the arena! Hurry up everyone, everyone, everyone, men and women, women and children, come and witness the marvels of valor, these kings of the mat. Do not miss such an opportunity, or you will regret it for ten years. Come in! The champions have made a promise not to be defeated. The struggle will be terrible, fierce, merciless. The valiant athletes will uphold their universal reputations

The director of the wrestling booth, Marseille throws the gloves to those amateurs who wish to challenge one of the professionals standing behind him. The artist for these images is E. Rousseau and the engraver is Abell.

in front of you. Come in! You will see the strongest men of the century, those whose exploits are known in both hemispheres. Enter. You only pay when you leave."

We are in; we are in. What is going to happen? If it is in a booth that is respectable, like Marseille the Younger's establishment, the show could be interesting. He is the same one who is shown in the frontispiece of this article preparing to throw the glove with his fierce and cocky appearance.

Often the most renowned among the professionals wind up at the fair, after having been seen at the Circus, at the Hippodrome, or at the Folies Bergère on occasion. By real good luck, we were able to make some sketches of them in person. The first behind Marseille is Tom Cannon, the hero of those famous sessions at the Folies Bergère, following which their little secret was discovered. He had made some prior agreements with Bernard in which the outcome was arranged in advance and they shared the fee![1]

The second is Pietro, the great, the one and only, the unique, the incomparable Pietro superior to all known wrestlers; he has withdrawn a little from the lists and lives quietly on his income in his hotel in Buenos Aires. Pietro has all the qualities for the job: natural strength, remarkable musculature, skill, speed, judgment; he can make his holds as well and as quickly with his left hand as with his right, and he has a great deal of presence of mind. When he is involved in a serious match, he will relentlessly take down his adversary at the first false move. After him come Fournier and Bernard, both very strong, and who can be put on the same level, but below Pietro who is invincible (except under special circumstances)!

I now introduce to you Mr. François from Martinique who is better known as Bamboula (all Negroes are called Bamboula) and he performs extremely well. He is very knowledgeable, but what distinguishes this excellent wrestler of small stature is that he is more agile and more adroit than he is actually strong. Crest is on his left, he is one of Marseille's students who is tall, agile, one of our good wrestlers. The next is a Swiss Hercules, Muller, a heavyweight.

The isolated wrestler who is contemplating his muscles before the match is the famous Louis de Lyon. He is a glorious old-timer who worked in all the circuses and in every square. As a strongman, he carried cannons and lifted an axle that no one else but he could lift. It is not without melancholy or without pride that he recalls his successes of the past, "We made them jealous, in the old days!" he repeats eagerly. Today, he is reduced to showing off the length and thickness of his massive Indian club when he carries it around like a trophy; that is all.

There are still many others, well known to the public, and warmly greeted when their names are announced in the arena, applauded, encouraged,

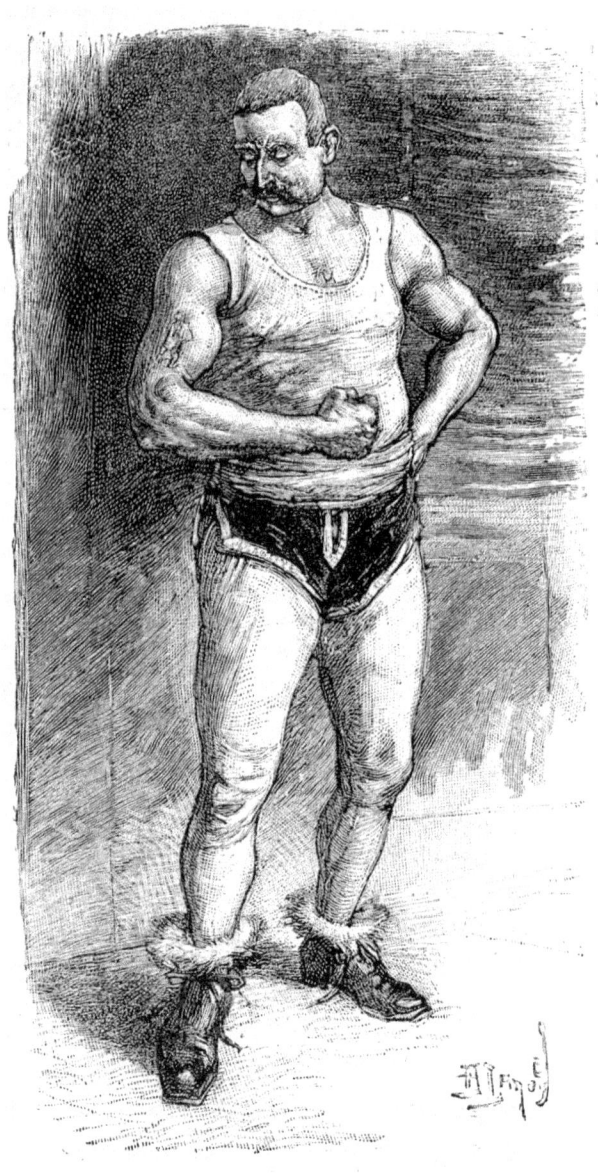

Louis de Lyon flexes his arm before the match.

and also outrageously booed when it is obvious that they are too indulgent and they let an amateur defeat them in order to have a moment of glory.

But wrestling is not only about professionals, as one might suppose, and in a completely different world, there are many athletes capable of competing with them. The true amateur, who must not be confused with the professional in disguise, would not lend himself to combinations of prepared moves, as we have seen too often even in tournaments that seem to present all the desirable guarantees of honesty. You do not find him indulging in his favorite exercise in public. He is too proud of his muscles not to fight hard; then, as he is generally widely known and since he is usually part of Parisian high society, it would not suit him at all to be seen in these places, even in the uniform of the job—one can judge this by our engraving—they look absolutely different from the professionals. Distinguished people always seem so. It is obvious.

Before the [Franco-Prussian] war, it was thoroughly exceptional that an eccentric could be counted among the number of people like him who considered using the muscles which nature had endowed him. Things have since changed; the most diverse physical exercises are in full favor, and this is very fortunate. Running, swimming, rowing, velocipede riding, fencing, and boxing have their followers. Could wrestling, the great and beautiful Roman wrestling, be despised any longer? Young people attending the gymnasium tried it, took a liking to it and finally a serious group of amateurs was formed. This explains in part the public's enthusiasm for the spectacle of wrestling that it had previously neglected. We are only interested in what we know, even vaguely. The amateurs began frequenting the arenas, their friends and the friends of their friends followed them. This explains the formal eveningwear that one sees at the *baraque* of Marseille the Younger!

Amateurs have naturally considered wrestling as a sport and not as a profession, they have pursued the study of wrestling holds with a view to the serious part, the physique poses, the theatrical attitudes are unknown to them—at least they will not indulge in such things. The Sorbonne gymnasium has become their meeting center, and a sort of academy has been founded.[2] Amateur wrestlers generally practice all sports, we can therefore believe them (at least it makes sense for them) when they assure us that out of all sports, wrestling is the most hygienic because it brings into play the totality of our physical faculties. The taste for this kind of gymnastics is spreading day by day; it is the obligatory complement of the other exercises, and it seems that when you have tasted it, the other sports pale in comparison.

The Molier Circus is not a stranger to this activity. Every year during the shows that attract all of fashionable Paris there are always one or two acts reserved for our high-society athletes who have rid themselves of their dinner jackets or tailcoats.[3]

Going from left to right in the portraits that we publish, Mr. Magisson's head is seen; he is an enthusiastic gymnast at the Sorbonne and is excessively strong and very muscular. He is an unparalleled weightlifter and an equally good wrestler. Mr. Pascaud, who is at his side, is an example of a total sportsman; he does everything,

A lineup of amateurs who look as formidable as the professionals.

knows everything, and is always looking for some new challenge. Mr. Pascaud is from Bayonne, and the Orleans Railroad Company would see its shares drop significantly if everyone followed his example: when he comes to Paris, it is by velocipede!

The next man is to amateurs what Pietro is to the professionals, you have put a name to the features of this Parisian from Romania whose exploits have fueled the chronicle for so long. He is Mr. San Marin.[4] We salute him! Hail to him as we remember the epic wrestling of the masked man against the athletes of Marseille the Younger at the Arena in the Rue Le Peletier. So too in the enthusiasm of youth, Mr. San Marin was almost always masked at the Hippodrome. Needless to add that if the establishment had given him a load of money, the gentleman would not have kept enough to buy a cigar. He had with him a beginner, a colossal apprentice whom he fed and clothed and, on top of that, to whom he gave the sort of fees that neither Bernard nor Fournier had ever touched.[5]

At the time when he was training hardest, Mr. San Marin lifted a barbell weighing 250 [pounds]; that is amazing. He wrestled at the Mollier Circle where he competed against Pietro [Dalmasso]—but Pietro is Pietro—he does less training in gymnastics, weight lifting, and wrestling. These days he is more interested in boxing at Charlemont's school.[6]

Mr. Laporte is also from Bayonne and is a close friend of Mr. Pascaud; he is equally very strong, and he is especially elegant and does his wrestling with perfect grace; he lifts 230 [pounds] while smiling all the time thus giving the impression that the barbells is made of feathers! Like his inseparable gymnast friend, he is a cyclist and is very handsome with a great flexed arm.

Next to him is Mr. Van Huyssen, a wrestler of great strength and is distinguished from every point of view. He is an athletic zealot, a practicing theorist, which is the ideal. He is modest, and he can lift 200 [pounds] with ease and without any sign of emotion, as if to say, "What's all this commotion?" He is the kindest and most obliging man one could meet; the day when a real athletic sports society will be created, he will certainly have had something to do with it. The last is Mr. San Marin in his mask.[7]

Paris also has a certain number of amateurs: Mr. Macherel who is thin, muscular, and at the very top of developing his physical being; when he is wrestling, he is adroit. He is included among the best wrestlers along with the painter [Hippolyte] Prat, the young Mr. Moreau, Mr. de Saint-Michel-Rive, and Mr. [Albert] Vazeille, a student in medicine.

We have just seen that the world of wrestlers is divided into two well-defined castes: the professionals and the amateurs who render mutual services. The men of the trade by teaching the methods, the rules and the holds to the sportsmen, and the amateurs by putting the athletic games that have been neglected for a long time back into fashion. Wrestling has survived from antiquity where it was held in the highest honor to us who have practically forgotten it. It might seem that the epochs from then to now might make us think that it would never recover, but in some parts of France it is still known—in mystical Brittany and the South who still love the styles practiced there, but Paris has treated the muscular young fellows who travel in fairs as little more than buffoons.

The sword has dismembered society, and people have been thrown together; plebeian pleasures might be despised in other places. But as deep as was the scorn for wrestling, the awakening is dazzling. The craze for physical exercises has become general, and it is remarkable that it started from the top. Wrestling is currently in the process of reconquering the place to which it has indisputable rights, because, according to practitioners, it is of all sports the most suitable for developing the human machine, for bringing the whole organism to maximum power. Almost all exercises work toward a specific goal: the legs work too much or not enough, certain muscles are forced into immobility, and the overall balance is disrupted. Wrestling, as it is performed in France is not a brawl—not like Switzerland, where tripping as well as gripping of the leg with the hands is permitted; in America any maneuver is allowed; French wrestling is an athletic game par excellence governed by formal conventions that retain a very appreciable character of courtesy. The partners can grip each other only by the upper body, using all their strength, but without resorting to anything that influences sensitivity; a victory must occur but not by moves that will injure the opponent.

Stripped to the waist, the opposing wrestlers will use all the factors that are available to them: strength, suppleness, agility, skill, quick thinking, and stamina. The weakness or absence of one of these six elements gives rise to the different kinds of play observed in athletes; as with the blind, the sense of touch is refined and exaggerated. The wrestler who feels himself inferior by one point tries to use his other assets in greater proportion. The perfect wrestler is the one who brings together all of these physical and intellectual qualities. Take away from Pietro his marvelous presence of mind, and you obtain a person of medium strength; but apart from the fact that he is tall, admirably versatile, heavily muscular, of unequaled suppleness, agile as a feline, dexterous as a monkey, robust, he adds to this rare baggage a nimbleness which allows him to strike right and left, at the right time and with the speed of lightning. Conclusion: it is pointless to stand up to him.

None of today's athletes combine all these qualities together to the same degree, and they need them a great deal. Like fencing (perhaps even more so), wrestling has its strategies and tactics. The holds are catalogued; their judicious use is not. The main ones are very sufficiently explained by name.

The guard position naturally marks the start of the match; the athletes approach each other, they grasp hands, quickly trying to achieve dominance over the adversary (to make an "entry" to use the wrestling term). Often success depends on this first attack, a good grip can follow if the response comes too late. We have also represented the front waistlock with the forearm parry. The wrestlers are face to face, eye to eye, ready for any event, the one who has surrounded his adversary intended to surprise him, to lift him from the ground, or to make him bend over, but the other has quickly crossed his arms, a simple move that removes a point of support from the attacker and prevents him from completing his maneuver.

The hip toss is the most perilous. The man in control uses a side waist hold; with one hand he resists the second's pulling him down, and he wraps his right hand around his opponent's neck to make his whole body turn around in the air in an attempt to lay him out on the mat.

The front waistlock with lifting often ends (as in the sketch on another page) with the parry of the bridge; the man in the waist hold lifts himself from the mat pushing back on the shoulders of the man above him while the latter grabs him by the waist and holds him above the mat. The blocking move that is shown in the bridge; in order to avoid touching his shoulders to the sawdust, which would be the end of the bout, our wrestler has violently thrown his head back, and while his opponent presses with all his weight on him, he tries to turn around. Will he make it?

In this precarious position, big fat Robin (seen here) looks pitiful and contrite, as if to say, "Blast it all! I did everything I could." Undoubtedly, he no longer has enough agility. Robin is now in too bad a shape to wrestle since he has grown considerably; the weight in muscles is supplanted by the excess adipose tissue. Despite his experience, which is great, he is at the mercy of those who are more agile than he. Out of breath, his spine bending, one shoulder at first, would soon approach the mat.

Front waistlock with forearm parry.

This is the critical and passionately awaited moment, bursting with bravos and crisscrossing interjections:

"He's going to be pinned!"

Hip toss with neck hold.

"He won't be pinned!"
"His shoulders touched!"
"I tell you, they didn't!"
"Yes!"
"No!"
"Yes, I swear it!"
"That's not true."

The wrestler's bridge.

"I'm sure of it."

"I saw everything since I was right beside him."

"You saw everything? First of all, you didn't see anything at all, you good-for-nothing!"

We are at the fair, of course, so the wonderful thing is that this is where we struggle the most to control the moves that are agreed to in advance! Among amateurs, we admit defeat with the same smile as when we are fencing and we say, "Touché!" and we shake hands without resentment, ready to start again. These nuances continue through all phases of the wrestling match; the winner who is sketched so skillfully, could say with Musset, "But I who am not of this world…."[8] The joy of the wild beast grasping its prey under its claws can be read in his flaming eyes; this would never happen at the Sorbonne—the gymnasium, that is—one would not see such a countenance, unless it were by way of a joke.

Just because I have spoken of holds that are agreed upon in advance, executed by professionals, one should not quite conclude from this that the fairground athletes deceive the public by not engaging in the fair and frank fight that is so pompously advertised. There are, let us note, two kinds of wrestling, the serious kind, we say then that the fight will be for real, and the simulated kind which only takes place in public representations and which is called "glue matches."[9] Why do glue matches persist despite all the promises? Quite simply because there is no way to act otherwise.

"Serious" fights require time, delays, and sometimes long preparation for each match. They seem boring. So we are content to quickly pass before the eyes of the

The defeated Robin addresses the crowd.

crowd a certain number of holds that make up a performance that is picturesque, varied but that belongs more properly speaking in a theater. This is not to say that professionals never fight each other for real. On the contrary, serious matches frequently take place after the evening's performances out of vanity or to try out and learn new moves. It is like playing for coffee or lunch. Another time, it might be caused by someone familiar with the booth (whose gender I will not mention) who causes a wrestler's strength to be called into doubt. When a challenge is accepted, then it will be "on the level," and always in private. We are condemned, unless we enter into the intimacy of this very curious profession, to know only the prearranged matches. Let us be satisfied with it, for lack of anything better. Besides, the great wrestlers who draw us in with the set pieces that you know, are past masters in the art of playing the crowd and forcing applause.

Where did they come from? Where are they going?

Originally, they were workers in heavy trades, blacksmiths, butchers, porters. One day they gave it all up at the announcement of the owner of the wrestling booth after they accepted the glove, and well built, agile, vigorous, so they fought just for fun with one of the artists (that is the correct word). It was a short and honorable fight, and before he has a time to catch his breath, this would-be imitator of the traveling has been stretched out on the ground. His adversary, however, recognizes in him certain aptitude, and he buys him a drink at the local pub, between the acts. Then they talk. If the workman is courageous, if he sticks to his profession, nothing is done; if the opposite, and he foresees more profits and less trouble by displaying himself in public or if he is motivated by vainglory, he is hired. His first job is to pretend to be an amateur. He is not included among the real champions until after five or six years—sometimes even ten. Once hired, he receives 5 to 6 francs per day—eventually he might earn up to 30, 100 francs, 200 at the circus or at the Folies Bergère if he is worth it.

Then in his turn he will become a professional, and he will wrestle with amateurs. But his satisfaction will only be temporary. When the match is over, everyone will be attracted to him and invite the professional wrestler to recover from his fatigues at the local wine merchant, and some gentleman will then signal to his coachman who will take him back to the arena. But, whether for their own pleasure or for selfish benefit, the attraction of wrestling is so great that though they are separated, socially speaking, by a pit as deep as one might suppose, the two will both have the same thrills and passions when they hear this summons so full of promise: "To the arena! To the arena! To the arena!"

Appendix 5: Léon Ville, Excerpts from *Wrestling and Wrestlers*

Léon Ville was a writer of popular works, and three of them are treatises on the art of wrestling. He also wrote a novel *L'Hercule du nord* (The Northern Hercules) that is set in the world of fairground wrestlers. He presents an excellent tableau of a typical *baraque* and the way that the director induces the audience into the arena and how the wrestlers manipulate their adversaries and the spectators in the bleachers.

Léon Ville
Excerpts from *La Lutte et les Lutteurs: traité pratique*
Wrestling and Wrestlers: A Practical Treatise
París-Imp. G. Chamerot, 1891

A Performance at a Fairground Arena

The wrestlers walk onto the parade [front part of a carnival booth]; some have their hands unpretentiously held behind their backs (these are the rarest ones). The others with their arms crossed over their chests with their hands squeezing between the pectorals and the tops of their arms to make the muscles of their biceps protrude, as if to say, "We're certainly well built."

The manager of the fair booth gives a sign to the four musicians who are at the end of the parade, and soon they begin to play, each one in a different key, the *Père la Victoire* march, while one of the wrestlers rings an enormous bell.

Standing in front of the ticket desk, an idiotic-looking clown with a face painted in black and white begins an absurd choreography accompanied by a girl whose face is painted outrageously. The manager is at the ticket desk where he prepares the entry passes; down below is the crowd all of whose heads face toward the action in order to see better. Several hundred people are there, stopped by the music, the dances of the clown, or the sight of the fat and oversized wrestlers who continue pacing on the parade—except for one or two who lean against one of the posts of the booth, scanning the audience in order to find a face that they recognize in the hopes of later being offered a pint of beer.

Léon Ville, Excerpts from Wrestling and Wrestlers

The speaker at a typical wrestler's booth throws out a glove to an amateur (from *La Vie au Grand Air*, 485 [4 January 1908] by artist, A. De Parys).

The director leaves the ticket table; he makes an imperious gesture, and the music stops; the clown retreats to a corner and the wrestlers line up in a row. One of the wrestlers grabs a gigantic megaphone and gazes out across the crowd, which stops its chatter; then he begins his patter.

"Ladies and gentlemen, let us cut the playing around. What we have done up until now was merely to attract around us a fine and numerous assemblage. We have the honor of offering you a performance at the athletic arena of Monsieur Toulouse, the greatest champion in the world! At this show, Monsieur Alfred de Paris will perform his feats of strength. He will juggle 20-kilo weights on the right, on the left, in front, as well as in back, just as the best jugglers might do with leather balls. He will finish by lifting a barbell of 100 kilos and then 200 kilos!

We will then continue with the wrestling, Roman wrestling, from the head to the waist as it is practiced in the South of France. Wrestling, gentlemen, is the first gymnastics in the world. We have here five good wrestlers, and on the inside of the arena a good bed of sawdust for the safety of the wrestlers and the amateurs. Also, without any excitement, without any provocation—not a bit of it—if there are any amateurs, strongmen, professional wrestlers or not that are in this fine group—anyone, anyone who really wants to participate, we will refuse no one; we will accept everyone.

We will hand out the gloves; if there are any amateurs, raise your hands!" Holding the gloves, the manager addresses the crowd. "So, are there any amateurs?"

A squeaky voice says, "Right here."

"What does he want—that one over there?"

"I want to wrestle."

"You want to wrestle. Are you familiar with the conditions of a wrestling match?"

"I know them better than you."

"Ha-ha! Here's someone who does not seem to be afraid."

"I am never afraid."

"And whom do you want to wrestle with?"

"With the big blond fellow."

"With Monsieur Victor, the Terror of the South?"

"Yes."

"Here's your glove. Is there another?"

"Right here."

"What does he want—that one over there?"

"I ask to wrestle. You asked for amateurs, give me a glove."

"Do you understand the conditions of the wrestling match? Roman wrestling, with holds only from the head to the waist?"

"Perfectly, and I will bet 100 sous against anyone whatsoever."

"We never make bets."

"Because your wrestlers can't stay upright."

The manager, jumped forward, "My wrestlers cannot remain upright! I will prove to you that you do not scare them! You want to bet a hundred sous? I accept. Whom do you want to wrestle with?"

"With the big brown-haired man."

"With Monsieur Louis, the Rampart of Aveyron! You will have a glove. Let's see, are there any soldiers who want to try their luck? If so, you can enter for free."

Two army cadets come forward. The amateur wagers a five-franc coin, and the manager adds another coin; after which the two warriors enter the booth.

Three more gloves are handed out, but without making any wagers. Then the manager picks up the megaphone and announces, "So then, gentlemen, I hope that this will be a wonderful performance! Five amateurs will wrestle! That's something that you don't see every day. Also, at this show the price of seats will be set at a rate for everyone. There are first-class seats at one franc, second at fifty centimes, and third at twenty to four centimes! We will begin in a moment. Come to the arena, to the arena!"

All the wrestlers in unison: "To the arena! To the arena!" The bell is rung again.

The music starts playing *Père la Victoire* once more, the crowd surges toward the ticket desk, looking at the wrestlers' arms and swelling chests as they pass by.

After five minutes the ticket desk is free; that was the first lot; the clown starts to dance once more, those strolling by stop again for a few minutes and the manager makes a second and final announcement that is called by the wrestlers "the summing up."

Finally, the director signals, and the music stops once more, the wrestlers get back into line, and the last announcement is made.

"Ladies and gentlemen! This is the final announcement. Inside there is already a fine and numerous assembly; we will begin momentarily; we have in this performance five wrestling amateurs, but if there are still more some amateurs, raise your hands!"

Two of the amateurs who accepted gloves earlier are in the crowd asking for others to join in.

"Now, gentlemen, the price of seats will be set at a rate for everyone. There are first-class seats at one franc, second at fifty centimes, and third at twenty to four centimes! We will begin in a moment. Come to the arena, to the arena!"

The musical hullabaloo starts again with the accompaniment of the bell, during which the public crowds around the ticket desk.

At last the introduction is over. The musicians enter the booth and go to their places on the upper benches in the last seats, and they begin to play the *Waltz of the Roses* in a slow, sluggish rhythm as the Hercules, Alfred de Paris, begins his feats. Every time he makes a circuit of the arena, he takes a step back, flexing his leg and stretching out his right arm posing with a smile that he supposes to be graceful. Finally, he gets around to lifting his famous 200-pound barbell. A wrestler then puts a tin collection box in his hands; it is locked shut with an enormous padlock, and he announces the following: "At each performance, the manager permits Monsieur Alfred de Paris to go among the audience. I beg you not to forget that this is reserved for just his meager living expenses.

And now, all wrestling amateurs, strip to your trunks!"

A voice from high in the bleachers says, "Here he is, here he is!" A person of average build descends wearing trousers of coarse woolen cloth.

The wrestling begins unenthusiastically and without any great hurry. The wrestler calmly applies an arm lock, the amateur falls to the side, gets up slowly and returns to the wrestler; both are sizing one another up, taking and letting go of each other's wrists without striking a blow, contenting themselves with slapping each other on the back from time to time while holding each other entwined, which makes the spectators laugh. Finally, the wrestler puts a waist hold on his adversary and brings him down without much trouble.

A second amateur of the same type begins with another wrestler; the audience practically goes to sleep, but it is suddenly jolted awake with these words, "Five francs on the amateur!" A skinny fellow descends into the arena wearing blue overalls, and when they see this skeleton, everyone is a bit disappointed.

The bout begins, full of action and finesse; the public, unaware that the amateur is a wrestler, finds him amazing; the amateur has already parried the front waistlock and a hip roll; he grabs the wrestler by the waist and both roll on the ground; but as the wrestler in falling made a bridge and turned around, "there is nothing to be done." They get up, and the struggle becomes intense as sweat flows over the bodies of the two adversaries. Suddenly, the wrestler gives the amateur a headlock and gets up, knowing very well that his adversary has made the bridge, and that his shoulders have not touched the mat.

"Go back and get dressed!"

The audience all shout in protest, "He hasn't lost! He hasn't lost!"

But the wrestler calmly picks up his jersey in order to put it back on without seeming to pay attention to the cries of the audience which protests even louder, really howling with rage.

The amateur turns his back to the wrestler. "What do you think; did I lose or did I not lose?"

"You didn't lose! You didn't lose!"

Taking advantage of the amateur's turned back, he runs over and waistlocks him. The crowd boils with outrage. "He took him when his back was turned! He's a cheater! This isn't right!"

The amateur and the wrestler fall to their knees, still grappling one another. Throwing himself to the side by rolling over onto his back, the amateur drags the wrestler who is lying on his back underneath him, and forces both shoulders to the mat.

The audience stamps its feet, and the applause shakes the booth as the two adversaries arise. The wrestler rolls his eyes in befuddlement and sinks to his hands and knees so as not to burst out laughing when he realizes that this farce is always taken seriously.

The amateur grabs a hat that a friend has handed him, and he addresses the public. "Gentlemen, if you have found that I deserve a pint of beer, I beg you not to forget me."

In order to stimulate the audience, a wrestler says, "We don't take up collections here."

The amateur replies, "Your friend did a fine job just now, didn't he, gentlemen?"

"Yes, yes!"

And in protest to the comments that had just been thrown at the winner, everyone puts his hands in his pockets, while another match begins.

While going through their routine, the next wrestler and the amateur who are wrestling at this moment, watch for their comrade who is in the crowd with hat in hand, making the rounds, as they say; so they wrestle silently in order to wait for their colleague to finish his collection.

When the collection is over, the wrestler pins his adversary as the previous amateur finds his way to the top of the tiers where he is sheltered from indiscreet gazes, and in the presence of two or three friends he can count the results of his "rounds" which one of the two writes down on a piece of paper because all of these collections will be shared that evening with everyone.

The manager bends forward into the booth, and addressing the crowd, says, "Gentlemen, I have the honor to thank you."

The audience exits slowly as the members gaze at the wrestlers and indicate their impressions.

Appendix 6:
Bertrand Fauvet,
"Fairground Performers"

Figaro Illustré was a lavishly illustrated monthly supplement published by the prominent French newspaper, *Le Figaro*. Each issue contained a combination of articles on news, personalities, literature, and fashion. Some, like the one excerpted below, were devoted to a single subject: fairground performers at the Fête de Neuilly. The life of the carefree aristocrats is contrasted with the much less opulent wrestlers and fair participants. The author Bertrand Fauvet was the pseudonym of journalist Daniel Bertrand de Laflotte (1864–19?).

> Bertrand Fauvet
> *Figaro Illustré*
> 1 November 1897

Fairground Performers

Wrestlers

Parisian fads, or if you prefer "fashion" often forces its followers to do very disagreeable tasks. Here is one example among a thousand.

It is summer. You have dined at Madrid or at Armenonville on a skillfully delicate and graduated menu, sampled discreet yet generous wines, enjoyed witty company and shimmering partners.[1] The conversation sparkles with the Champagne wine under the multicolored cabochons of the globes; the tune of a gypsy waltz plays in the shadows, and it sometimes seems to be inspired by the light breeze that agitates the green screen of the leaves, sometimes crackling like a volley of skyrockets, in a flight of notes whipped up by the bow. This is one of the rare moments when we admit that life is perfectly good. How charming it would be to cherish the dream outlined in the last chorus and to walk with it through the alleys of the Bois de Boulogne, all perfumed under the transparent and blue night!

Oh well, fine! You do not believe it! What about the Neuilly Fair? What about the noise, the dust, the firecrackers, the organs, and the smell of the crowds, deep-fried foods and oil lamps? But here is real life—supreme joy! Are we chic, or aren't we? We are chic! Yes. Well, all right then!

"Coachman, to Marseille's booth!"

Under the wailing of the brass band attacking *La Tzarine*, the horses advance with a remarkable and disturbing group.[2] Finally we have arrived! Black clothes and light dresses rush into the *baraque*, stumble over the chairs, run into the benches. We are blind, dizzy, asphyxiated. "Ah, my dear! Isn't this fun?" Have I not put up with these obligatory sessions at brave Marseille's booth! Did I not suffer from these endless discussions to determine if the shoulders had "touched or not touched the floor"? But who cares, we were chic!

It is indisputable that of all the attractions offered to the idle curiosity of passersby at the fairground, wrestling ranks first. This preference is easily explained.

A wrestler tries to collect a few coins from the elegant audience members at a wrestling booth (from *La Vie au Grand Air*, 490 [8 February 1908] by artist, A. De Parys).

Men, whatever their country of origin or their social situation, are apt to be interested in these gymnastics (aside from the fact that it is, or rather should be the exclusive prerogative of their sex). Wrestling requires a whole set of strength, skill, and composure which is not to be sniffed at. The artist, sculptor, or painter can study the play of the muscles and the anatomy of the body as it is subjected to real effort. The chronicler or the man of letters could encounter an original world there. The wealthy clubman and the hunchbacked, dishonest bureaucrat can get a new lease on life there when they make not very flattering comparisons (that alas, are regrettably quite superfluous) between their physiques and those of the men in the ring.

In the countryside (perhaps even more than in the cities) the man constantly struggling with hard work, reserves his admiration for any manifestation of physical strength. Also, in some regions, wrestling is a kind of national sport. In Brittany, for example, there is no real Feast of Atonement without wrestlers.[3] It is the lads of the moor who then take off their jackets; a brutal struggle follows in which the head butts resound against broad chests, like beating granite on a bronze bell.[4] Under Henri II, they were already renowned at Court, and teams of wrestlers often came to bring the wild scent of heather and gorse under the paneling of the Louvre.

Similarly, in several villages in the South of France the mayor presides over the wrestling, arbitrates the holds, and distributes the prizes. Renowned wrestlers enjoy popularity there as much as the much as the *primas espadas* [best bullfighters] in Spain or *pelote* players in the Basque regions.[5] But however satisfied is their self-esteem, they cannot dream without envy of the honors with which the ancient Greeks showered the crowned wrestlers at the Olympic and Isthmian Games.

"One is born a cook, one becomes a chef" says a proverb that is also applicable to wrestling; one is born strong, vigorous, so one becomes a wrestler. Strength is not everything, it takes a quick eye and coolness. The training, the apprenticeship would be wasted if the subject did not start with a solid and resilient foundation based on this triple point of view. Native strength and the necessary nerve are rarely encountered in the big cities; the impassivity of the people of the North hardly lends itself to this *furia*, which is vital for the group. The southern sun, on the contrary, seems to flow in their veins, to puff up their chests, to make them do impossible things like finding the *utdièze*, the rare "white blackbird" of the South, as well as to resisting the suffocating pressures of the waist lock. The majority of well-known wrestlers are also from the South.

From which social class are they generally recruited? Neither from the police headquarters nor from the diplomatic corps, although (especially nowadays) these positions require an unusual flexibility and backbone strength. Accustomed as they are to hard work and continual exertions, laborers and porters provide the most serious contingent, mainly stevedores from the port of Bordeaux. So, few from the lowest sections of society. I can think of only one former lawyer to cite in this category, and I shall have the pleasure of introducing him to you presently.

In England and in America the profession of wrestler has become a career at the exclusion of all others, and a sensational match is often preceded by training that sometimes lasts up to six months. In France, wrestlers content themselves by constantly keeping their hand in (or perhaps it is better to say their body in), so as not to forget the principles drawn from the Piazza gymnasium, Faubourg Saint-Denis, or from the school in Rue Championnet directed by François le Bordelais. This is not far from the "fortifs" and the Boulevard Barbès.[6] Clubmen give preference to Piazza. But, dear me, I understand; around midnight, the approaches to the Rue Championnet are less than reassuring, and too-frequent trips to this district would force neophytes to wrestle, combining practice with theory perhaps sooner than they would like.

Would you like to know the names of the famous wrestlers these days? We have Docquerroy; Sabès; Pietro [Dalmasso], the great winner at the International Tournament of Brussels; Gambier; Pons, the great French champion; Yusuf, the world champion "Turk's head" on whom it would be dangerous to smack your fist.[7] Still others have been given nicknames due sometimes to their origin, such as François le Bordelais [from Bordeaux], sometimes to their psychological qualities, such as l'Amiable [friendly]—could he have been named thus by the wrestling regulars? And finally the dean of the profession, Robin.[8] I don't have to introduce this one to, you already know him. No? You certainly know him, I tell you. He is always at the top of the stairs at Marseille's booth; he is around forty and is always at his post. He is bald and vaguely resembles poor Meilhac from a distance, but a darker and stronger Meilhac with a big black mustache.[9] He drapes his obesity (which he has had since his youth) in the majestic folds of a pink toga and harangues the crowds; he is the announcer of the troupe. One hopes that he has inherited the oratorical qualities of his predecessor, Rossignol-Rollin, the former lawyer, whom I have just mentioned to you.

Oh, this Rossignol-Rollin, what a mark he left on the world of wrestlers. Recalling his former profession, he was not afraid to embark on some very sticky adventures. And what a beautiful performance when, in the midst of his improvisations, he draped himself in his wrestler's toga as he once did in his barrister's robe! In him the wrestler doubled as a lawyer and the lawyer as a shrewd businessman. It was he who had the idea of opening the first arena for wrestlers. One of his favorite students continued the operation: the great Marseille.

Who does not remember this famous showman? Invariably wearing a top hat, torso tightly packed into a black frock coat, Marseille circulated among the wrestlers who feared him like fire—like a lion tamer among his beasts. Once a renowned wrestler, he continued to take an interest in the work and used his megaphone as needed to encourage his men in their bouts with amateurs. When the public—another kind of wild animal—was divided into two camps, stamped their feet, howled, Marseille raised a curtain behind the cash desk and settled the dispute with his trumpeting voice so appreciated by parliamentarians so fond of the eloquence of interruption. "Shoulders touched! Not touched! Yes! No!"

There was nothing but French wrestling in his arena.[10] Bah for English wrestling, Turkish wrestling, or any other—from head to toe, wrestling where strength is subordinated to trickery, perfidious wrestling where one of the two adversaries will stop at nothing to defeat the other.

Marseille died two years ago leaving an unforgettable memory among the community of showmen whose rights he knew how to assert loudly (if necessary), and among the Parisians who have frequented his establishment for so long. The name of Marseille is not extinguished; he survives in the person of his five sons, the eldest of whom has continued to maintain honorably the paternal traditions.[11]

Once his apprenticeship is over the wrestler can appear in public. Thanks to his daily agreement on his share of the proceeds of public collections, his salary varies on average from fifteen to twenty francs per day. The great stars of the troupe earn up to thirty francs, but these are exceptions. In order to earn about thirty louis a month, a man must wrestle three or four times in the same evening, but never more if he wishes to retain a reputation as one of wrestling's serious contenders. Thirty louis monthly! By Jove, you might say, that's a pretty payment that not everyone can get.[12] That's agreed, but you mustn't forget the off seasons (and they are frequent in this profession) and summer evenings when rain closes down the booths—and they are numerous as we well know based on this year. And then fatigue, exhaustion, not to mention old age do not take long to make themselves felt. It is rare for wrestlers to retain the fullness of their powers after forty years. Also, to deal with these eventualities, they willingly seek a remunerative profession where they can exercise their strength. Many are porters in the produce markets, and by unloading bags in the morning they can train for the evening's feats. During the day they rest where they can. Sometimes one of them will pose for a painter or a sculptor wishing to study the anatomy of the human body in full training; but this relative rest weighs on them; this forced immobility is tiring for them. So, there are endless games of cards at the favorite café; the poetic souls—there are even some of these among the wrestlers—go to the country to sit under the arbor, between a traditional venison stew and a welter of painful bruises. I forgot to mention angling which has fervent followers in this fraternity.

To resist the violent exercises of the profession, it might seem that a special diet has to be imposed on the wrestlers. Not at all. They are certainly good trenchermen, but when there is plentiful food on any table, you will encounter others who have similar if not heartier appetites.

In the world of wrestlers, regular relationships are more common than one might think. With a little imagination, this marital picture is not without charm: she, shy and frail, a real little Parisian trinket, leading him, the colossus, who with a flick would pulverize an entire showcase of Dresden porcelain. For, despite his forbidding looks, I am sure he must be gentle and kind; and when the newborn comes, brings back to memory a rather unkind story that is already four or five years old. The scene took place in a small mezzanine near the Parc Monceau.

After an evening spent at Marseille's booth, she cruelly reproached her beau for his slender matchstick arms and his prematurely hunched back. Very worried about this state of mind in his girlfriend, he immediately went to find one of the wrestlers and obtained, for a fee, the promise to let himself be pinned (after a bit of feigned resistance) by the boyfriend. The agreement was reached, and under the eyes of this cruel beauty, things happened as had been agreed between the professional and the amateur. The next day the latter presented himself all proud and perky at his sweetheart's abode. But he soon emitted a cry of astonishment: in the parlor, side by side on a sofa, chatting about the weather was his Little Miss and the boy's opponent from the day before! So Little Miss, in her most natural voice says, "My dear, I am so proud of your victory that I will never be happy until you repeat it here. But this time for real, right, sir?" The wrestler smiled and nodded in assent. As for the boyfriend, he took his cane, his hat, and ran out the door … and kept on running.

It would seem natural and logical that wrestling by its very nature and the efforts it requires should always remain the prerogative of the sex of which Goliath and Samson were the most imposing … stallions. Not at all. The ancients, for example, lovers of beautiful physiques, also wanted women to receive by means of their gymnastics the crowning achievement of a physical education. They would subject themselves for a long time to all the exercises likely to give the limbs elasticity and strength. Perfect forms. In Sparta under the orders of Lycurgus, special gymnasiums were opened to young girls who wanted to exercise by wrestling. In order to allow the freedom necessary for the movements, they had to wrestle absolutely naked! Modern ladies who read that will respond that they were among other women, and because of that it was not much of a bother. But wait just a bit. Lycurgus who was perhaps married (on the point of his conjugal relations, I confess my complete ignorance) but he knew by experience that in order to encourage female emulation, the presence of man was indispensable. Although this seems more logical than moral, he had male wrestlers who had been chosen to equalize the forces enter the gymnastic arena of these female wrestlers. And everyone found this innovation very natural. Touching naivete of the golden age! Other times, other customs! That fierce disciple of Lycurgus, Mr. [Paul] Robin, would he have remembered these ancient customs in the required promiscuity of the orphanage of Cempuis?[13] The chronicle is silent on this point; let us imitate its silence.

Whatever the influence of wrestling from the physical point of view, ladies, do you not think that the exertions inherent in this violent exercise have little in harmony with the delicacy and need for protection that we like to find in the woman? Weakness is not the least of a woman's charms. And yet nowadays a theater has not been afraid to produce women's wrestling matches. You no doubt remember well: it was at the Folies Bergère. The novelty of the spectacle and a certain unhealthy curiosity attracted a crowd to the hall in the Rue Richer; then little by little a reaction took place, inspired no doubt by a rising sentiment of that old French gallantry which suffered from seeing in this way the masculinization of those whose weakness we flatter ourselves to protect celebrate their grace. What happened to all those stars of the biceps? The most famous had names: Rosa, Miss Mariette, Marie la Bretonne, etc.; one is the wife of the wrestler Robin whom we mentioned earlier, and another is supervisor with her husband François le Bordelais of the school on the Rue Championnet.[14] Where are they now? Returned to private life, occupied with the prosaic conjugal pot-au-feu, employing this painfully honed strength to bustle around the corner of the hearth? To be forsaken like this? So phui! You wouldn't like it.

Many of the women then went in search of engagements in fairground arenas. You will see them, their multicolored tiger-skin torsos, their feet laced up in the classic Roman sandals trimmed with rabbit fur, proudly displaying their athletic builds on the platform, provoking the timid "soldier boys" with gesture and voice, throwing the glove to naïve recruits, less eager to face the wrestling match than to be tamed by the exuberance of these ill-contained charms. "Here's a glove for you, dear boy." And to this one. And to that one.

And the poor recruit does not take long to bite the dust as he collapses under this imposing mass, to the great joy of the gallery of his comrades who have come to salute the triumph of the local boy.

"Well, old man…!" repeats the victim returning to the barracks. Ah! the stories in the room after such an encounter! What lovely chapters for friend Courteline![15]

You cannot spend all your time throwing out challenges at the army. There are off-seasons, moments of rest; and then I wonder with anguish what the attitude of a woman accustomed to such exercises may be in her home. Without a doubt, a charitable optimist will expect ideal wives, I wish it to be so. But the others?

When the husband is a wrestler, everything is fine. The chances are equal, hence the easier explanations and the arguments employed on both sides with such success. Otherwise … oh, well….

On the Esplanade of the Invalides last year during the annual festival, an enormous woman invited a triple row of infantrymen, cavalrymen, and artillerymen to fight her with saber, foil, or baton.[16] Not a sound. Finally, one of them, an artilleryman, made up his mind and entered the booth, where he squeezed in close to a small, puny old man with glasses. The clarinet of the orchestra was in full wind.

The baton was the weapon of choice. Usual salutations, then the sacramental formula uttered in a resounding voice by the virago, "Your obedient servant!" And the little old man shaking his head with a bitter sigh, "She is my wife, sir." After a few seconds of painful reflection. "'Your obedient servant!' she said, 'Your obedient servant!' Oh, the hussy! You won't find her at home!"

Appendix 7:
Rémy Saint-Maurice,
"Wrestling and Wrestlers"

Rémy Saint-Maurice was the pseudonym of novelist, poet, and journalist Maurice Diard (1864–1918).

>Rémy Saint-Maurice
>*L'Illustration*
>18 February 1899

Wrestling and Wrestlers

There is wrestling ... wrestling is everywhere: at the Casino, at the Olympia, at the Folies, at the Trianon, at the Excelsior. There is wrestling in Nantes and in Bordeaux where Pons and Gambier triumphed. This season has truly been the season of muscles. The first wave of wrestling in the capital dates from 1848. Arpin the Terrible Savoyard was then the indisputable master of the mat at the Montesquieu Hall. It was there that Marseille the elder, who left home with his bindlestick and savings of 500 francs in his pocket, came to challenge and to defeat him.

From 1852 to 1867 there was a kind of lull.[1] Wrestling began again in 1867 at the Paz Gymnasium then at the Le Pelletier Arena. There one could see Marseille the younger (who later founded a famous *baraque*), Richoux, called "Virgin Shoulders," Faouëtte [sic] the Wild Beast of the Jungle. One of the former referees at the establishment of Paz, Rossignol-Rollin, became an impresario, and he organized a troupe of men who toured around with Bonnet the Ox, Crest[e], Béranger, and Bainaize. It seems that this Rossignol-Rollin had a way of giving very literary carnival spiels: "Ladies and gentlemen, the carpet upon which our artists will frolic was once used by the Greeks at the Olympic Games...."

After the [Franco-Prussian] war, there was a new respite.[2] It was necessary to wait about twenty years before the sort of spectacle was reinstated at the Folies Bergère. This was the era of Pietro [Dalmasso], François le Bordelais, Bernard, San Marin, and Apollon. An Englishman, Tom Cannon, made quite a splash for a long time, and he was only pinned on rare occasions, notably by Pons. One evening, the audience learned that the wrestling matches were faked. On that evening Paul Bernard was matched up with Tom. After two rounds, he came forward toward the footlights and said, "According to our agreement, Tom Cannon should have been pinned by me ten minutes ago. As I see that he does not want to let himself be beaten, I am walking away from the match." After hearing this, there was indescribable tumult; the gas was turned off and everything in the establishment was smashed.[3]

More recently, the presence in Paris of the Turks Nurullah, Yusuf, and Kara Osman, as well as the Greek Pierri brought new popularity to the sport. The Turks wrestled honestly—and with savagery. Their style was unknown to Parisians; the terrible cries that they emitted while attacking renewed interest in the spectacle.[4] They were paired up with Pons and with a majority of well-known champions. Yusuf perished in the wreck of *The Bourgogne*, but it is said, after having knocked out around twenty passengers.

It seems that current wrestling represents a very sensible progress over the earlier styles. The importance of prizes or titles that are to be won and more serious regulation make it possible to correct the abuses that after several brilliant periods brought about wrestling's sudden eclipses. Such a sport will only enthrall the public if it is honest.

Since the Turks have departed, wrestling still happens but only at irregular intervals: at the cabaret of Old Noël [le Gaulois], at the Piazza Gymnasium, or at the wrestling academy of Pons on the Avenue des Tilleuls.[5] Among the secondary establishments that definitively contribute to popularizing wrestling, a special mention goes to Gangloff Hall. This is designated as a café-concert and is located on Rue de la Gaité in Montparnasse.[6] The building belongs to Sajous. All the students of my generation knew Sajous at Bullier.[7] He was a little graying man with a short beard and the face of a macaque; he had an enormous pot-belly, and he always looked happy. Everyone called him "my uncle." He had the job of organizing the cancan, the quadrilles of high-kicking dancers, and he acquitted himself with stunning excellence. Among his "nieces" he created remarkable stars; several were or still are stars at the Moulin Rouge. So "Uncle" became the founder of this profession. One of his nieces—this time a real one—today runs the tavern on the Rue de la Gaité, through which one passes to gain access to the performance hall at the back.

In 1897 Horace Delattre, administrator of a café-concert who was formerly a singer and song writer (we have him to thank for *Coming back from Suresnes*), become director of Mario's theater at Gangloff's.[8] Mario [pseud. of Delattre] had the idea of organizing athletic evenings every Wednesday. The public in the neighborhood demonstrated their support for the idea. The horse and grain sellers on the Avenue du Maine comprised a very attentive audience. The strumpets were fascinated by Bébé's torso or the pectorals of Bibi Poiré.[9] Delattre began with Mazin and Alphonse Henry, two old masters; then he offered François the flour Seller, Favouët the coachman, Rivollon, Schackmann, Chappe and Célestin Moret [1873–1953] (who was already a young but very remarkable athlete). The public was very enthusiastic,

Gangloff Hall was a café concert that featured wrestling matches a few nights a week. Artist George Scott has skillfully captured the loud, dark, and smoky atmosphere as well as the raucous working-class audience (from *L'Illustration* [18 February 1899]).

and the house was packed. It was in popular spots like this where it was demonstrated how much the masses had taken this sport to its heart.

One day last autumn, Célestin took a young and exceptionally muscular butcher of twenty-two years to Delaittre. He was originally from Namur, and he was called Constant Lauveaux. Constant had been victorious over Félix Bernard in Roubaix. He had wrestled in Montmartre with Pons without the older man managing to take a decisive advantage. Delattre hired the butcher, and in just a few minutes Constant had pinned the shoulders of whoever had gone up against him. He got the better of Favouët two times.[10] The boldness of his technique earned him all the sympathy of Montparnasse. People had to be turned away on the evenings when he was advertised. The press wrote about him; he was invincible. Mr. de Lucenski, the very enterprising director of the *Journal des Sports*, saw him at the Gangloff Hall. He saw what an extraordinary influx of passionate spectators these wrestling matches attracted. He thought of transporting them to the heart of Paris. The plans for a World Championship were in the air. Ever since their fights in Russia, Pons and Pytlazinski had a question of supremacy to settle. Gambier, Robinet, Sabès, the Austrian Wetasa would all be invited. Along with Constant, what a nice bunch of participants! The managers of the Casino de Paris, Messrs. Borney and Desprès, to whom Mr. de Lucenski submitted his idea, accepted it immediately. François le Bordelais was chosen as referee. We know the outcome of this championship. Pons and

Pytlazinski once more confronted one another in the finals, and after a somewhat brusque headlock by Pons, the Russian who was complaining of spitting blood, surrendered. Gambier and Wetasa took third and fourth places. Never had such a crowd been seen in the Rue de Clichy.

Soon afterward, the magazine *Le Vélo* mounted on the stage of the Folies Bergère the "Grand Prix of the City of Paris." At the last moment Constant and Sabès defected to the Casino. They were joined by Pytlazinski, Laurent le Beaucairois, Aimable de la Calmette, Daumas, the Turks Kurtdereli and Cartanji, and others. This new series of wrestling matches just ended with the victory of Pytlazinski who finished by getting the better of Constant le Boucher. This final triumph of the Russian champion earned him (other than the glory) a prize of 3,000 francs.

And that is why for the last two months those who frequent the backstage of music halls might encounter strongmen with the neck size of the Farnese Hercules waiting patiently for their turn on the stage with his torso draped in the frilly peignoir of a dancer.

French wrestling requires as much strength as skill. It does not have the brutality of Turkish or American wrestling. It excludes any grip below the belt. The use of the legs, permitted in other countries, is not permitted here. Also prohibited are holds that are too dangerous, such as bending back of the arm, the stranglehold (which should not be confused with the neck hold). Consequently, there remains only a fairly limited number of holds, among which I will mention the front waistlock, the back waistlock, the cross-body hold, the hip roll, the head roll, and the body throw. In order for the man to be defeated, his two shoulders must touch the mat simultaneously. An excellent way of defending oneself on the ground consists of "using the bridge position," that is to say, to arc the body completely, pressing only the head and the soles of the feet to the mat. Constant does a wonderful "bridge."

In addition, those who would like to have a technical knowledge of the various holds can refer to the useful little manual by François le Bordelais, *la Leçon de Lutte / The Wrestling Lesson*, published recently and on sale at the *Journal des Sports*.[11] Pytlazinski also wrote a treatise, but it is in Russian.[12]

A good wrestler must follow a methodical and rigorous training plan. Training will not give you strength. "You either have muscles or you don't," as the good giant Paul Pons says. It provides the endurance without which the strongest are quickly exhausted; to acquire this necessary breath, prolonged walks—or better, running—are recommended. Laurent le Beaucairois who weighs a whopping 122 kilos covers 500 meters running with surprising speed.

The well-trained man will fear nothing from the duration of a wrestling match. His superiority asserts itself there progressively over the breathless antagonist who, at the beginning, however, could have seemed of better dynamic essence. Constant le Boucher, whose weight is 40 kilos less than that of Laurent le Beaucairois, forced the latter to abandon the mat after an hour's fight. At a certain point (in the words of one of their comrades), "his fat heated up Beaucairois's innards." Constant perhaps trained more regularly than Laurent.

It is a mistake to believe that lifting weights and dumbbells is beneficial to wrestlers. This exercise stiffens the attachment of the shoulder to which it is advisable to leave all its flexibility.[13] On the other hand, gymnastics that promote agility such as the trapeze, are an excellent training method. Pytlazinski is an eminent gymnast. The wrestler does not have the exaggerated biceps of the weight lifter. The constant practice of gymnastics, on the contrary, streamlines the biceps and brings more muscle to the forearms, and in waist holds, for example, this is where the principal effort is concentrated.

But the most certain training for wrestling is, in brief, wrestling itself. The wrestler should abstain from alcohol and tobacco. Pons, Pytlazinski, and Constant drink little and never smoke. The secret of many successes and many failures is in the more or less strict observance of this diet. Ask a famous southerner about this (it is not Laurent) who came to compete in the Folies Bergère Grand Prix last month. "Every night he absorbed so many bottles of champagne, so many mugs of demi-sec that (as another professional told me) if you had put all that he drank into a vat, it would have been enough to drown three monks." In most of his encounters he did not live up to his reputation.

If drinks are off limits, a copious amount of food is what a wrestler must have. As opposed to a jockey who must starve himself, a wrestler constantly tries to gain weight. In evidence, here is the menu for a dinner for Constant: three huge slices of lamb, a one-and-a-half-pound beefsteak, two additional (even bigger) slices of lamb.

France is the true homeland of wrestlers. England and in general all Anglo-Saxon countries prefer more brutal sports like boxing. Except for Tom Cannon and [Charles] Green, where are the great English wrestlers? The Spaniard becomes a bullfighter. The Italian is too soft. The German most often lacks flexibility (except Fengler). Belgium has hardly produced more than Constant le Boucher in recent years. Russia, Turkey, and Greece are richer in distinguished men. In Paris we have seen Pytlasinski, Yusuf, Nurullah, Kara Osman, and Pierri.

Certainly, three quarters of our national contingent are recruited from the South. The southeast holds the record. As Daudet says, they are born with double muscles in Marseilles and Tarascon. The smallest holy day festival in Provence or in the Comtat, pits the most robust of the area against each other. The terrible Arpin was from Savoy. The two Marseille brothers come from Lapalud, a Provençal town. Still today, what a constellation! Paul Pons, the king of kings, the world champion, was born in Sorgues (Vaucluse). After him there is Robinet, who defeated the best men of the continent; Laurent le Beaucairois, the imposing and jovial athlete; Peyrouse the Lion of Valence, an admirable Latin colossus; Aimable de la Calmette; [Victor] Daumas, called "Pique-Planque," with his cyclopean shoulders and his missing eye. And how many others?....

Bordeaux can rival Marseille. There is even a school in Bordeaux. The Gascon, less massive than the Provençal but with more nerve, more agility, more endurance, and almost always more technique. "Bordeaux people are riper." They like to attack. Whoever did not see the endurance that Pytlazinski faced from Maurice Gambier last December at the Casino missed an unforgettable wrestling show. The match occupied three evenings, and it required seven rounds. The Russian giant whom the Gascon put in danger several times finally defeated the Frenchman with an arm roll. How valiant was little Gambier! He possesses the essential qualities of our nation. He is a devilish jumper, quick to attack and retaliate, looking for the slightest fault from his opponent, escaping from the most powerful grips with the agility of a clown; one wonders how someone of equal size and weight would end up if he encountered a human mechanism who is at once so hard and so elastic. Gambier is Bordeaux's favorite son. At a championship in Brussels, he triumphed over a hundred and some competitors. Next to him, let us mention Sabès, another artist in the genre, Lacaisse "Pietro II" who is from la Lande, the technician Mazin, Fénelon, Paul le Mastoc, Félix Bernard, Raoul de Cahors—all elite athletes. Even before these men, Bordeaux still had Apollo, Paul Bernard, and others. As for François le Bordelais, whose real name is Paul Levacher and who was the trainer of so many champions, was born in Orleans. His method which is full of brilliance and skill undoubtedly inspired his nickname.

One cannot say that one profession rather than another is a breeding ground for wrestlers. I notice however that there has always been a man in sight who was named "the coachman," "the flour seller," or "the butcher." Favouët (alias Denoix) drives a cab for the Levallois cooperative.[14] François Decrouzas, or "the Flour Seller" who is a Swiss citizen, quite effortlessly climbs up to the first floor with two bags of flour on his back. Constant Lauveaux worked at Edouard's Butcher Shop on the Rue de Montfaucon near the Saint-Germain market.

On the other hand, Pons was a blacksmith and Pytlazinski was a mechanic. At times when sport did not monopolize him exclusively, Gambier was a cooper's apprentice; Sabès was a carpenter. Célestin Moret, with his two-wheel cart and broken-down horse, delivered sacks of potatoes to the convents on the left bank [of Paris]. Mazin, who continues to wrestle at fifty-four (and with what finesse! His recent bout with Wetasa proves it!) intermittently teaches billiards. Before teaching athletic novices some fancy wrestling tricks, he taught billiard balls how to do fancy tricks to many a regular at the Gibelin Academy, Rue de la Sorbonne.[15] He really has an ingenious mind, this Mazin. In a certain year during Carnival, he invented face masks made of gauzy fabric in order to protect ladies' faces from the confetti. The connection between these things is certainly provocative.

In short, we see in most cases muscle resistance or wrist flexibility were already in play in these professions.

Wrestlers from all eras have exhibited the vanity of tattooing. Pons wears two fencers on his biceps; Alphonse Henry, a portrait of General Boulanger; one man has a lion's head, another a laurel wreath.[16] Between his two shoulder blades Jolly has a little naked woman seated, I believe, at the edge of a well. It is obviously the image of truth, the enemy of fakery.

A while ago I spoke of Mazin's fifty-four years. To conclude this chronicle, allow me to tell you the story of Bainaize. He is most certainly the dean of veterans. He can count sixty-five autumns. You will see by him how much love of wrestling can be carried among professionals. I met him at the Gangloff Hall.

His parents were from Ariège, but they traveled around with the fairs. "I must have been born around 1834 in Montignac (Dordogne)," he says, "however, I had not really settled down at that point." As a boy he was a baker, and at the age of nineteen his eyes were scorched by the oven. He then turned to wrestling. He anticipated the blows of his adversary without seeing them, and he became one of the most terrible men of his time, so much so that he was nicknamed "the Wild Beast," since he brought real passion in his desire to win. "I know neither pity nor pardon," he repeated recently, "Look at my fingers. All the joints are broken." And to tell the truth, his fingers were bent in all directions. "When I grab a man in a waistlock from behind, his only recourse is to break one of these so that I will let him go. And my ears! Aren't they nicely done! It was Béranger who detached the right one and Lacroix who did the left one."

Bainaize, "the dean of wrestlers," was sixty-five years old when the artist Scott sketched him here (from *L'Illustration* [18 February 1899]).

Bainaize belonged to the legendary Rossignol-Rollin troupe, and he still has fond memories of the old impresario. "Ever since the boss died," he often repeats, "real wrestling—that also died."

He has wrestled for forty-five years. Last December he was appearing in Toulouse in the fair booths. A friend who reads the gazettes told him that wrestling was starting up again in Paris. They are going to hold a world championship, and this got Bainaize to thinking, "Bainaize, my old man, I said to myself, there are lots of young people here who work." You think you know what you are worth. Go show them how their papas did it.

He did not have a penny. His faded trunks and his wrestling shoes were tied up in a handkerchief. This is how Marseille the elder arrived from Lapalud to challenge

Arpin. "I left Toulouse on 8 December in the morning." I took the road straight ahead, straight ahead, toward the north. I was always pushing forward. G*d d**n it, I would have marched straight to hell if I had to. When I passed through a village, I went to the grocer's or to the marshal's; I borrowed weights or an anvil and although it was not my profession, I did feats of strength in the squares. They threw me some change for absinthe and a crust of bread. And then I continued on my way.

Bainaize arrived in Paris on 24 December, Christmas Eve. The championship was coming to an end. He knocked on every door, but he was turned away. "Bainaize? We never heard of him. Who is Bainaize? The Parisians have forgotten Bainaize the Wild Beast!" His big eyes, discolored by the baker's ovens and by cataracts, were weeping tears of humiliation.

By chance he was put in touch with Célestin Moret who took him to Delattre's place. They gave Bainaize a try. He was still frighteningly strong. And what a classic technique! He contented himself with a weekly salary of ten francs. They paired him up with Schackmann from Metz who appeared honorably in the championship. For two consecutive weeks, Bainaize beat Schackmann, and the regulars at Gangloff Hall gave endless ovations to the old lion, whose hairy chest was completely gray and who hissed so furiously when he was surprised by an opponent's waist hold.

Appendix 8: Frantz Reichel, "Wrestling: A Music Hall Sport"

Journalist Franz Reichel (1817–1932) was also an Olympic athlete (rugby, track and field) and one of the founders of the Olympic movement. As a proponent of clean, honest sport, he obviously had a problem with professional wrestling, and he is not shy about denouncing it. *Le Sport Universel Illustré* ran from 1895 to 1943.

Frantz Reichel
Le Sport Universel Illustré
15 September 1900

Wrestling: A Music-Hall Sport

We are approaching the time when wrestling is about to reappear on music-hall stages which have been transformed into very unathletic and totally inconvenient arenas. A few more weeks of patience and it will be time to gallop around the stage accompanied by drumrolls and ballyhoo to promote the flamboyant title of some world championship or other. Come in! Come in! The posters will proclaim huge prizes and announce the fight between the terrible So-and-so and the famous Such-and-such, the rampart of the Bosporus. The cycle of emotional appeals will begin, skillfully meted out in order to make the incredulous public increasingly interested, until the final wrestling match when the mob flocks to the hall where the admission prices have been raised for this special occasion.

And from then on, we will get to return to all the athletic fakery, the daily revelations of the dubious and endlessly dragged-out rematches that are required (or not) in order to have a lucrative revenge, thus making it possible to play the same song twice for the same price. And it will go like this until the day when disgusted with the vulgarity of some, the cynicism of others, the stupidity of still others, the public will abandon a show that they used to love and which once fascinated them.

We already sensed during the last season that there was some weariness in audience from all the comedies of which it had been the naive victims. We can already see that the unheard-of receipts of the previous year are no longer there. A few

Wrestling at such elegant venues as the Casino de Paris appealed more to the upper and middle classes as this engraving from *L'Illustration* (18 February 1899) shows. Spectators were farther from the action, and the surroundings were as refined as the audience. Author Reichel reminds readers that these matches were all exciting fakes.

tumultuous incidents, mocking laughter, scandal, seat cushions, and small benches thrown onto the stage did more damage to wrestling in an instant than all the good done by a long and favorable campaign in the sporting press. Those who witnessed a few of the uproars last year will not soon forget them.

In such a case, those who must be criticized are not the wrestlers but the organizers, by which I mean the directors of music halls. They readily imagine that the crowd is as stupid as they are and cannot believe that the audience at a sports show is a special audience that knows the underside, the ins and outs of the matches that are announced to them; the typical audience member knows how to appreciate the men, the holds, and however badly placed he is to judge, sees enough to guess fakery when it arises.

Admittedly the wrestlers are quite complacent about this situation; they have every immediate interest in it, and there are many ways of managing equally and concurrently to protect both the interests of the purse and of their reputation! One should not ask wrestlers for more intelligence than is necessary.

Before now most wrestlers had to content themselves with a meager allowance. Many of the men were unfamiliar with anything except the hundred-sou coins that they earned in some fairground booth or in some distant arena in a remote neighborhood. Then came the tournaments launched by the sporting newspapers and organized with imposing prizes by the music halls, and the same men who three years ago were satisfied with a fee of 10 or 20 francs, today demand 500 or 1,000 francs and more per fight.

Even if they had understood that their long-term interest was to work sincerely, to provide good honest sport, but it was too much to ask of them, especially since the directors of the music halls were too happy with an unexpected attraction that made gold rain into their coffers. They then began to go too far. It will be fine as long as it lasts, and indeed, they said to themselves, the day when the public tires of wrestling, we will just find something else.

And we have come to such a pass that it is almost impossible for those who are most skilled and most knowledgeable in the art of wrestling to have a precise idea of what is going on; they must confine themselves to general impressions. I have followed every tournament since 1898, and for various reasons I knew better than anyone what exactly it was all about. And yet, I cannot in all conviction guarantee the honesty of the matches which I witnessed as a critic. I have sometimes seen results so preposterous, such inversions of form that I have become skeptical, extremely skeptical.

There are many ways to fix a wrestling match: (1) By drawing it out interminably, so that it lasts two or three days; (2) by taking a fall for any sum. This allows for revenge matches in which the public lets themselves be taken in. I thus speak of deals made between the competitors with the collusion of the management. I am not talking about the secret agreements made without the knowledge of the organizers—those made just between the competitors who sell their honor as athletes, not for a mess of pottage, but for a more or less insignificant sum. They thus lose all hope of competing for the big prizes, but what does it matter to them, "a little bit of something is better than nothing," and for them that is most important.

For my own part, I know a famous wrestler, the one I consider the best of all.[1] In a few months—from one tournament to another—his expected earnings have become fantastic, rising from 1,000 to 17,000 francs. In the end he became quite wealthy thanks to a contract which guarantees him 1,500 francs per fight. He manages to multiply his fights by an interminable series of draws. He has never agreed to take a fall in France, but as soon as he crosses the border, this athletic coquetry is forgotten, and from then on, he is fine with taking a humiliating fall. He is a smart fellow.

It is certain that it is very difficult to regulate the sport of wrestling, and all the more so since neither in France nor abroad is there any special federative group having authority and power in the matter of distributing penalties and rewards. On the mat, the wrestlers have only the referee in front of them, and he represents an ephemeral power. The only court to which they belong is the management of the music hall where the tournament takes place. So go and ask a manager (who does not know anyway) to choose between his own interests of the moment and sport?

However, there will come a day when the directors of the athletic stages will realize that it is in their interest to provide the public with honest wrestling. Good sport will always have fans; it will always attract a crowd.

It is necessary to form a free, independent wrestling federation without further delay to which the music halls would be affiliated and the representatives would undertake to respect the decisions, suspensions, disqualifications that would be declared by the said federation. Wrestlers would then be just like professional cyclists; they would have an obligatory set of rules imposed on them, and it would already be something satisfying for the public to know that those who make fun of it will not do so with impunity.

Appendix 9:
Paul Pons,
Excerpts from *Wrestling*

Considered to be one of the best Greco-Roman wrestlers ever, Paul Pons (1864–1915) began his string of major victories by winning the first world's championship in 1898, and he continued to be unbeaten until 1900. In addition to being a fine athlete, Pons was also a bright and articulate writer, and in 1907–1908 his autobiography was published serially in the illustrated magazine *La Vie au Grand Air*. This was republished in book form in 1909 as *Vingt ans de lutte* (Twenty Years of Wrestling), and in 1912 he published his finest work, a combination history and manual of wrestling called simply *La Lutte* (Wrestling) from which this excerpt is taken. Although he is not very good about citing dates and sources, Pons recounts the history of wrestling with an air of honesty and candor. Unlike most others in the wrestling fraternity, Pons sought out contacts who still remembered the early history of their sport (he called it "questioning the graybeards"). Pons also operated a gym in Paris that was popular with his fellow wrestlers, and it was here where he must have heard many of the stories that he incorporates into his books. His stated objective in recording the history of his sport was to eliminate "excessively blatant unreality." This is a noble goal for any historian.

Paul Pons
Excerpts from *La Lutte*
Wrestling
Paris: Pierre Lafitte & Co, 1912

Wrestling in France

It has always been extremely difficult to distinguish the truth from the legend in all the histories that have been transmitted to us by the "fathers of the wrestling mat." The history of fairground wrestling will definitely remain nebulous for all that relates to the period of its beginnings. For that was the thankless era of the professional wrestler whose existence was highly precarious, and for many long years the occupation remained highly unrewarding, even for the stars of the sport. Things are better these days for a minority of men who are particularly gifted. As for the others…? We can affirm that they are happier in their profession than the men of second rank who have begun in this career at the present time.

So, nothing specific remains about the very earliest origins of wrestling in France. We know that the Romans who were so passionate about circus games indulged in this sport. But their ways were not ours. Their wrestling permitted holds that our rules forbid, and it was noticeably closer to freestyle wrestling.

For the last twenty years, the development of the sporting spirit in France has allowed us to write the history of the most recent phases of the evolution of wrestling in our country. But beyond this period, we experience a dearth of documentation that would allow us to make order out of the chaos of legends on which we rely to write the history of a sport that for several years has enjoyed brilliant evenings and huge profits. However, by eliminating excessively blatant unreality, we can still glean some truth from the old stories of the past, and by relying on them, we can try to retrace the evolution that wrestling in France has undergone. Perhaps young amateurs will take some interest in it. For it is to them that I am writing here. In fact, I have neither the intention nor the pretension to teach my professional contemporaries things that they know just as well and perhaps better than I. I was able to evaluate them during my twenty-five years in the business; I have also seen the young people come on the scene today who will replace their elders.

That is why I am dedicated to writing a manual that is as clear and complete as possible for the use of novices who want to enter the profession and untried amateurs who already possess certain talents. For the others, it is their own intelligence and their perseverance which must help them to learn. Under the influence of our profession, we form a great deal of our personal ambition, but this is an issue which is premature to insist upon. It deals more specifically with all that relates to training and the most judicious way of practicing it and adapting it to the temperament of each individual. And all one can do if seeking the earliest origins of wrestling in France (even with the best intentions in the world) is to begin its history with the fairground reign of the legendary [Jean] Exbroyat. In short, for us he and he alone deserves to be called "the father." It is impossible to dispute this title. His face might be completely forgotten, even by generations quite past their prime, and he remains completely mythical in the minds of younger wrestlers.

He was a former soldier who had been faithful to his emperor [Napoleon]; he had dragged his steely carcass just about everywhere, following the song on his lips and the flag that led him—he never knew where. When the time came to leave the army, Exbroyat made a few attempts in business and set himself up comfortably as a greengrocer (he had a stall in the Lyon suburbs), but Exbroyat felt that an old vagabond like him could never get used to a sedentary life. Despite his many years of service (he had enlisted at fourteen) he was still in the fullness of his physical strength. His nomadic soul and his past as a soldier adventurer had given him a taste for the gypsy life, which he did not have the power to resist. He enjoyed the open road, the dust thrown up as the stagecoaches passed, the dusty haze in the dazzling brightness of the blazing sun. He needed a feeling of movement; for him it was torture to be held in place by his small business and he had only one dream: to leave. But to go where? It did not matter, he just had to leave. He sold off his business hastily, as one sells off in such circumstances, that is to say to his least favorable advantage, and he disappeared. When he fled, Exbroyat was already known in circles where wrestling was practiced. What was this world of wrestling?

There is no doubt that at the time when Exbroyat lived there were already cabarets in the neighborhoods of Lyon where the customers worked out with weights and practiced wrestling. Although they have a more modern layout, today's athletic cabarets are nothing more than copies of these athletic cabarets of yesteryear. At the time when Exbroyat and his proselytes frequented them, no one spoke of them because the public was not interested in sport, and apart from amateurs who participated, few cared very much about wrestling, and it was as if it did not even exist. By looking carefully, by questioning the graybeards of the Lyon region a few years ago, I ended up being able to shed a glimmer of truth on this prehistoric period, which is indeed the most curious that I know of in the history of our profession. In Bordeaux, I knew an old history buff (who I think is still alive) who was very well informed on all things having to do with sport, and who had extended his investigations to wrestling.

From an indirect investigation carried out in Lyon, it would appear that Exbroyat indeed spent his leisure time wrestling in a tiny gymnasium in the Croix Rousse district.[1] Exbroyat never made much of a reputation for himself as a wrestler. It was as the founder of the first traveling arena that went around France that caused his name to survive in our special world. It is no mistake, however, that the

Jean Exbroyat as a young man (from *La Vie au grand air* [2 February 1902]).

legends did not try to make him an extraordinary wrestler who was specially gifted and before whom no adversary could resist. In fact, today we do not know of a single interesting performance. However, a feat is attributed to him on which there is no need to insist, so ridiculous is the legend on which it is based. But it gained acceptance in France at a time when for laymen everything related to the world of wrestling had something mysterious about it. The fabulous anecdote impressed the public among whom it circulated, and Exbroyat found himself shrouded in it like a halo. Basically, the fellow had the soul of a merchant. Without a word of protest, he allowed people to believe a story that did not have a word of truth to it. In fact, the adventure that he allowed people to attribute to him had not even happened under his name, but under a name quite similar to his own. Did he take a pseudonym? He willingly let people think so.

After Exbroyat sold his fruit stall, he left the country. No one heard from him for a long time. Who then would have taken in this shadowy person? One fine day, we learned that a certain Frenchman, Jean Broyasse, had killed a Negro in the United States in an intense wrestling match by crushing his skull between his hands. O outrageous exaggeration! It was considered a praiseworthy action to kill a colored man in America. No one in the world had ever, ever heard of this Jean Broyasse. Everyone was convinced that it had to be Exbroyat, the former amateur of Lyon. There was a curious coincidence between the absence of the former and the performance attributed to the latter. And then there was the similarity of the names that was rather odd. In short, no more importance than it deserved was attached to the incident at the time. The years passed—quite a few of them passed. Time went on and on, and then one fine day a little old man who was very grizzled, and whom life had tossed around from right to left without taking away his good humor reappeared in the world of wrestling. It was none other than Exbroyat.

How had he amassed a small nest egg in his wanderings? We never thought of asking him. But when we saw him reappear, he had some money with him. He had, moreover, adorned his existence with the presence of a wife. It was she who would take care of the cash holdings for the future Exbroyat arenas. She also took care one evening near Avignon to run off with the receipts. This was an unfortunate incident that Exbroyat took with an accommodating philosophy. "Farewell," he said, "the important thing is that I won't have to listen to her anymore."

But it was said that Exbroyat ended up acting as a wrestling entrepreneur. The few pennies that he had once more amassed were used to have a very rudimentary arena built; it was a classic fair booth made of canvas, planks and naturally little more; and after having recruited a few men able to do some interesting wrestling among the amateurs of Lyon, he made them into professionals, and took them on a tour all over the south of France, displaying his vagabond arena in all the places where there were enough takings to put in the cash box.

It is thanks to old Exbroyat that most of the men whose reputations have come down to us did not remain in the shadows. To young people these old-timers—all dead for many years—seem like wrestlers of great ability, and indeed most of them were athletes of the first rank. It cannot be said that today's men work in a style superior to theirs. Moreover, it is they who invented and codified all (or almost all) of the holds which together constitute wrestling theory.

The Marseille brothers started with Exbroyat, and the older brother later became the director of an arena that enjoyed great success. The name of Marseille is intimately linked to the history of wrestling. The legendary trip on the back of a donkey from Lapalud to Paris, which allowed the elder of the brothers to come and challenge an adversary reputed to be unbeatable, is sufficient to establish his reputation and at the same time, that of his younger brother.

The celebrities of that time whose names were beginning to circulate in the small towns and in the countryside were named Faouët, Arpin, Rabasson, Auguste (already an Auguste!), and Bérenger. Exbroyat was already elderly, tired, and worn out when he decided to travel with his troupe of wrestlers all across the South of France. Oh, they never went far from one point to another. Their travels were done in a horse-drawn caravan. It was truly a gypsy life. "The father" died prematurely, and it was the famous Rossignol-Rollin [1821–1873] who replaced him.

The phenomenal carnival barker that was Rossignol-Rollin followed Exbroyat. He can also claim a sort of paternity: that of *bombast*. He was a former lawyer at the bar of Lyon, and Rosignol-Rollin was an excellent man with a heart of gold; he was a merry deadpan.[2] From his first profession he had retained his style of speaking. The speeches assumed as much importance as the wrestling matches themselves, in the shows that he offered to the public. His rhetoric was uncontrollable, and he had an imagination that was quite poetic. His "appeal to the people" in his profusion of leaflets reached the peaks of exaggeration.

At the wrestling booth, the public was called "miserable dust" or "lowly atoms." It was exquisite, but a trick so ludicrous that it was impossible to do anything but laugh. Who among them would have dreamed of getting angry? He was the king of carnival patter and inventor of the art; Rossignol-Rollin invented himself. No other man knew how to enliven the parade like him. He was the model for all barkers. Was there ever anyone who was his equal?

His speeches were all similar in tone: planting himself firmly on his legs, his hands on his hips, he harangued the crowd.

"Gather 'round you faint-hearts, you molecules!" The terrible men that you see before you will respect your scrawny bodies. The strong should protect the weak. Come closer, we won't eat you. Nature offers exceptional beings for your admiration! Beings who, if they wanted to, could make bronze statues weep under the influence of the pain that they could inflict on them. Approach. Approach imponderable dust. The spectacle that awaits you is well fashioned to stupefy your timorous spirits and make your feeble bodies tremble like a leaf. Approach and enter. Come and pay homage to the triumph of muscle, flexibility, agility and, I dare say, intelligence that is placed at the service of these physical qualities for the great interest of the unforgettable spectacle that I, Rossignol-Rollin, offer to you fragile individuals at the price of 50, 25 and 10 centimes. And it is a steal at that!

The spiel kept going and going in this way, punctuated with amusing flights of fancy which made some laugh and left others dreaming. The price of the seats did not allow either the company or its director to roll in gold at the end of the evening, but at that time, the wrestlers did not expect big fees. The most skillful, the leaders, were satisfied with the meager salaries that Rossignol granted them.

Rossignol-Rollin was always searching for something new, and one day he took it into his head to make a big hit. Business was going well, but not quite as well as it could have. It could be better. And this is what came to his mind.

The public's imagination needs to be shaken up; this is the only condition which he is interested in dealing with. "My men are called Auguste the Sailor, Faouët, Arpin, Bérenger, etc. As names go, they're a bit bland and very bourgeois too. Needless to say, I have to find something else. But what? Something enormous, prodigious, names—or better yet nicknames—that are characteristic, sonorous, and colorful, because after all, a wrestler is a being apart; he is not like anyone else; he has something very personal. And it is this personal side that must be brought out, clearly highlighted. I will unbaptize them, or rather rebaptize them; I will create for them an identity that will distinguish them from the masses."

Since Rossignol-Rollin did what he wanted with his troupe (who all loved him), he did not have the trouble of consulting anyone, and he alone without saying a word then put his little plan into action. One fine day, as the men arrived at the booth to give the first of the shows that had been announced in the town, imagine their surprise when they read the poster that communicated the roster of names to the public. Auguste was no longer just boring old Auguste; Faouët, a simple Faouët; and Rabah, the Negro, a Negro as black as a Black man can be. Every member had his special stamp with Rossignol-Rollin's latest vintage. Auguste the Sailor was "the Terror of the Fleet"!; the limber Tivallon, "the Serpent of the Loire"; Rabah the Black was "Pearl"; Marseille the elder was "the Lion of Lapalud"; Marseille the younger was "the Miller of Lapalud."

The fine wrestler Bérenger with his harmonious physique was called "the Elegant Parisian"; Étienne was "the Handsome Shepherd of the Ladies." There was also another lion; it was Louis "the Lion of the Desert," and still others: Creste "the Ox of Marseille"; Cristal "the Coral Fisher," and finally the smallest of them all, the lightweight Quiquine "Velvet Eye" called thus to commemorate the velvety sweetness of his glance.

The tradition was created. Henceforth, whoever joined Rossignol-Rollin's band, he received a professional title which he never ceased to be proud of. This example was followed for a long time by the successors of the man who had made himself the creator of the genre. This is how they became famous in their time: Raulin "Toothless"; Triat "The Millstone Man"; François "the Miller of Darnétal"; Well-Underway [Va-bon-Train]; Faouët "the Wild Beast of the Jungle"; Lucien "Cri-cri Hoarse-Voice"

[Cri-cri enroué]; Vincent "the Iron Man"; Peyrouse "the Lion of Valence"; Louis "the Boatman," also known as "the Little Wave," who left his oars when he was an amateur to seek the life of a professional wrestler. It is even claimed (but it goes back a long way and is not proven) that it was this Louis who ran Exbroyat's fair booth during the final months of his existence. Really, though, it matters little. All these names no longer mean anything today, and they are completely forgotten by the current generation; only the name of Marseille survived.

When Rossignol-Rollin died, the mourning was general and sincere among the men he employed. The members of the troupe did not want to leave the task of carrying the body to the funeral operators since he had been their director and at the same time their friend. They even had to agree to draw lots to determine which of them would have the honor of accomplishing this funereal privilege.

This stone age of wrestling, which went from Exbroyat to Don Ramon (Rossignol-Rollin's successor), is the picturesque bohemian age of professional wrestling. Don Ramon did not for a moment know how to maintain the reputation of Rossignol's arenas. He imagined that he had only to install himself in his predecessor's place, and let himself get by on the other's good reputation. It did not take him long to realize the error of his ways. In Bordeaux and Lyon a few local traveling shows competed with him. He let his admirable troupe fall apart; its best members dispersed. Some went to Bordeaux, others remained in Lyon; some worked in the booth of the Marseille brothers whose notoriety traveled to the four corners of France.

At this time, which was minus the princely salaries of today, wrestlers and athletes were regarded as beings apart. If wrestling had a few odd attractions like strongmen (weightlifters) who were included among the ranks

Wolff, the Rock of Luxembourg (from *La Vie au grand air* [2 February 1902]).

of curious phenomena, then only a few made a brief appearance in the world of wrestlers. Wolff "the Rock of Luxemburg" was one of the most curious examples of this type. He was an eccentric who must have been ungrateful to his homeland, Germany, because once he was in France, he never showed any intention of ever again seeing the steeple of the church where he was born. It was thanks to him that we owe the importation of phony weights.[3] Wolff had been in Paris for not quite six months before a foundry producing fake weights was created on the slopes of the Montagne Sainte-Genevieve.[4] It did not take long before it was doing a golden business.

The intermediate period, which extended between the demise of Don Ramon and the notoriety of the Marseille brothers, remains in a way uneventful. Faouët and the men of the earliest years were approaching their decline. It was with the arrival of Félix Bernard and Pietro Dalmasso that wrestling shone with a new brilliance.

Félix Bernard and Pietro Dalmasso were the two grand masters of a sport that attained with them the summit of deftness and skill. Neither one of them was exceptionally strong physically, nor of such weight that this alone would suffice to make their adversaries work. On the contrary, they were middleweight men, but what men! Their style was incomparable and their delicacy and skill were unparalleled. No one has worked better than they, and I cannot think of any others except for Gambier, Constant the Butcher, and Sabès (who could have had the finest career if he wanted) who could be compared to them. They had everything: the brilliance, the composure, the presence of mind, the judgment, and a purity—a clarity of execution—such as we may not see again for a long time.

But let us leave behind everything that may have an essentially anecdotal character and that attaches us too exclusively to wrestling's heroic era, so to speak. It was from a sporting point of view, a beautiful period, a period of the great school which saw men whose names we will never forget in its most beautiful time. Wrestling was then a career in which one could not think of getting rich. The best earned their daily living that way, the others … oh my! the others lived sparingly and, in general, badly rather than well.

It is easily explained. Where do you wrestle? In a booth at a fairground. The directors of the "grand arenas" were obliged to work at very low prices. The middle and upper classes stayed away from wrestling, so only small purses fed the traveling performer's cashbox and in order not to frighten the clientele, they should not be pressured. I recall that time, and back then we had to move fast from village to village. When we stopped in a provincial capital, it was beautiful; eight days in a big city was welcome.

At this time the number of professionals was very restricted, and in France one or two booth directors at the most. On the other hand, the clan of amateurs was very numerous. And it was after having graduated from the ranks of amateurs that the majority of those who loved wrestling became professionals. At that time there existed in Bordeaux—for Bordeaux is the city where the public has always been most interested in wrestling—several small athletic gymnasiums where every Sunday and twice a week in the evening, amateurs came to train. One of the busiest was that run by Fénelon on the Route d'Espagne. There, the wrestling was done for glory. The meetings (the bouts) were performed honestly and for real. Everyone brought the best of himself to achieve victory.

The amateur spends without counting. He is quick, he animates the match. He has no interests to defend, so he does not need to be careful. If he is defeated, it is only a small injury to his pride; his reputation does not suffer, his commercial value is not affected by a defeat. He wrestles only for pleasure, and from the beginning to the end of a fight the battle is on the level. It is quite different for the professional wrestler, especially nowadays. In the past, a failure was less serious than today. A defeat was known only to those who witnessed it. Now it is something else. The press brings to the four corners of France—what do I mean? to the world—the results of major tournaments. In the distance, the fallen man is depreciated, and if the failures are repeated, it is the end (or very nearly) for the one who suffered them.

Fake Versus Real Wrestling

And this brings me to talk about this practice that the general public calls "kayfabe." We know the definition of this expression: kayfabe is what consists in setting up a fight between two adversaries the results of which are agreed in advance.[5] The match, therefore, is not honest since the adversaries do not allow luck to decide. The simplistic fan who pays 15 centimes for his place at the booth does not give the kayfabe any further thought. Well, is the public fooled? I dare say no, however strange this claim may seem. Because everything depends on the quality of the work offered to him for his few centimes. Let me explain. Wrestling is a sport which consists of simultaneously touching the shoulders of your opponent on the mat by using means provided for by the regulations, and outside of which any moves implemented lead to the disqualification of the one who engages in them. The means in question comprise a series of well-defined holds that consist of attacks and ripostes. Between them, there must be a sequence, and the more this is harmonious, the more the appearance is varied, the more the bout is interesting.

You do not take down a man by play acting. The expenditure of energy that must be made is proportionate to the resistance that one encounters. Wrestling is therefore an exercise that leads to great fatigue. How do you expect the professional wrestler, who must provide each of the performances of the day without counting those of the evening, to wrestle honestly without stopping? He would be exhausted by the third bout. And then we would always know when a match starts; but when would it end? If neither of the adversaries manages to defeat the other, the show can last all afternoon, and if necessary, occupy part of the evening session. How would the director of the company cover his overhead if he had to settle for just one receipt of.... I suppose two louis! But what would be less amusing for the spectator than this interminable wrestling match itself? Neither of the two men would want to be pinned, so who would use the most caution? No real defenses, pretending to make a vague attack that is incapable of bringing about a result. Do you think that after half an hour the show would not be unbearably monotonous?

The audience at the major championships has sometimes noticed this. This is why we always limit the duration of the matches thereby proclaiming, if necessary, a draw. What is called "phony" can, when it is done between two men who know their trade, give rise to a very interesting demonstration of wrestling. Several holds from the repertoire (and the least odd are displayed there) which demonstrate something to those who know nothing. It is all about the way one of them bears up and how the other responds to it. Doesn't the public get more for their money than if they attended a formal neck and wrist massage of unlimited duration? A demonstration well done and a well-played fight, always affect the audience. And, curiously, there are a lot more yells of "fake" at matches when the men are careful and spare themselves, when they do not want to risk anything, than when they have settled their bout in advance and give the illusion of an "authentic" match.

Wrestling Evolves

It is quite difficult to compare wrestling as it is today to what it was in the past, even in the world of amateurism, although the latter has suffered very little from the influence of the times. The professionals themselves—and I am one of them—have been spoiled by the enthusiasm of the public and by the unexpected benefits, that starting twenty years ago the leading wrestlers were able to derive from their profession. All prominent men of today have been extremely careful to save their reputations. The appearance of the matches has undoubtedly suffered. They have lost the vivacity, the brilliance which they had when Félix Bernard and Pietro Dalmasso were at the top of the tree, especially in the heavyweight category. Many times, in the major championships, the middleweight and especially the lightweight men saved an evening which, without them, would have left the audience with an unfortunate impression of monotony.

A profession that once seemed modest to us and which became—oh how much!—a lucrative profession of unexpected proportions almost overnight. A very understandable exhilaration has transformed us. Who, in our place, would have escaped it! Until 1890, wrestling only occupied a very small place in fairground shows or on the stages of music halls.

The organization of the first world championship surprised a lot of people. There was wrestling everywhere in the great centers of France and in all the important cities of Europe. French wrestlers invaded other lands, and foreign wrestlers invaded France. A time came when there were not enough men to meet all the demands. The situation [of championships] was then put on a purely commercial basis. But since there was only a finite number of professionals and since the profession seemed to be going well, many strongmen came to wrestling.

Far be it from me to blame them. Was the arrival of the new recruits felicitous from a sporting point of view? I leave it to others to judge, but what is certain is that the new recruits, almost all chosen from among the colossi weighing from 110 to 130 kilos, joined the ranks at the expense of middleweights and lightweights.[6] Their technical knowledge of wrestling came up against human mountains. And little by little, they had to withdraw from the ring. Does the public win? It alone can answer.

When the stars Félix Bernard and Pietro Dalmasso shone, it was different. They were two very fine artists in the finest sporting era of wrestling. Bordeaux then had athletic gymnasiums that were something like wrestling academies. Old Bernard, Félix's father, ran the arena in the Rue Rougier where Sabès and Gambier made their debuts. On the Route d'Espagne Fénelon ran a certain athletic cabaret that featured the finest amateurs that had ever been seen. And the Rue d'Ornano! *A la chaussette*, which was frequented by almost all the winery workers who liked wrestling! May I even add, in all modesty, the poor little Pons gymnasium, Avenue des Tilleuls in Montmartre! There we also saw some good matches, but not comparable to those that were seen daily in the arenas of Bordeaux.

I may be exaggerating this fond nostalgia for the past. I know full well that even today, it is in neighborhood athletic gymnasiums where the true amateur can see the best wrestling matches. I do not say the most technically astute. No. These were seen in the past in training sessions between professionals. Nowadays, they are becoming rarer; the professional works less and less and it is the amateur who trains more and more. This explains it.

A professional who makes his living from wrestling from one end of the year to the other is obliged to honor all the engagements that are offered to him from 1 January to 31 December. He usually works in a nomadic troupe, sometimes in one city, sometimes in another. He perpetually changes climate and diet, and he wrestles almost every night with the same adversaries for months and months. When do you want him to train? His work is done in the evening under imperfect conditions, and that is his training. What can he learn? Very little.

Professional wrestlers like Félix Bernard, Dalmasso, Faouët, Marseille wrestle fairly rarely; they have other employees who allow them the leisure of visiting athletic gymnasiums where they go to train of their own free will, I would almost say for their pleasure. When one compares the sport of wrestling in France to that in other countries—in Switzerland, for example—it is easy to see that it is like night and day. In Switzerland, wrestling has remained a thoroughly amateur sport; in France, the men are remunerated and compete for cash prizes that are fought by the big stars of the wrestling mat.

My intention here is not to teach professional wrestlers a trade that they know as well as I know it myself. It is for young amateurs that I have put together the following advice. By taking all the good that my predecessors have bequeathed and by drawing inspiration from what my personal experience has taught me, I hope to

Above and left: The Pons Gymnasium was one of the most important and prestigious institutions of its sort in Paris. Here are some very rare interior photographs from 1903. Above, Simon Antonitch wrestles with Anglio, and below, Raoul le Boucher is toweled off after a practice bout with Vervet (collection of Christian Gaildraud).

succeed in assembling here some advice that will be useful to them. My ambition goes no further.

How the Turks Came to France

The origins of how the Turkish wrestlers came to France is quite curious, even more so since from the very start it focuses on the most formidable man that we have ever seen and who unfortunately passed away quite prematurely. We are speaking of Yusuf; however, he was not the best wrestler that Turkey sent us. Kara Ahmed, who came a few years after Yusuf's death, revealed himself to be much shrewder and much more knowledgeable. But let us take things back to their very origin.

About twenty years ago, a little more perhaps, lived a man named [Jean-Claude] Doublier [1844–1901], a wrestler, acrobat, juggler, man of the circus and the fairground theater, who traveled around eking out a precarious existence in the four corners of France. The profession of a public entertainer that he worked at included feats of strength or prestidigitation, but it was hardly profitable, especially when the work presented to the spectators was not of dazzling interest. And this was the case of the unfortunate Doublier who was reduced to "doing the provinces," which is rarely remunerative, and it was certainly not at a period when he could have traveled off in any direction even if he had wanted to.

Doublier, who had made a family for himself—this despite the shortage of cash in which he systematically found himself from the first of January of one year until New Year's Eve of the next. Doublier's wife was an acrobat who worked on the trapeze and on the rings, and she had combined her poverty with his, but with her husband she worked up a sensational number.[7] At least that is what their posters said. Despite the prestige of this double acrobatic exhibition, fortune eluded them. Tired of vegetating in France, the couple made the decision to go abroad. After living virtually hand-to-mouth in Berlin, very badly in Italy, and barely scraping by in Austria, the Doublier household went to Turkey. This was an unusual idea. Turkey had never been rolling in gold, at least not for a good long while, and it was not a paradise or a Promised Land for acrobats. All the same, to live poorly there or elsewhere mattered little. By what combination of circumstances did Doublier and his wife, who were going from town to town, end up in Chofa?[8] It would be very difficult to say. Somehow it was luck that their wanderings brought them there one fine day.

One fine day—but to call it "fine" is perhaps an exaggeration, for Doublier had an unfortunate adventure there that he had not expected but which forced him to leave as quickly as possible and at night from a place whose hospitality the dignitaries intended to force upon him in a way that was a little excessive. For here in a nutshell is what happened.

Young Mrs. Doublier was very attractive and one evening a certain grand mamouchi of the city thought himself authorized to show the French acrobat in an overly familiar way the admiration he felt both for the gymnastic exercises that she

Mrs. Doublier slaps a cheeky Turk, an action that caused many repercussions, not the least of which was a hasty escape to Constantinople (from *La Vie au Grand Air* [21 March 1908] by artist, A. De Parys).

had just accomplished and for her person, too, which was quite charming.⁹ This happened behind the scenes of the establishment where Doublier and his wife had just given their show. And as the Turk was overstepping his bounds, the young Frenchwoman gave him a slap in the face—the finest one she could give to a gallant who was clumsy to the point of rudeness. This gesture was not the way things were done in the house, since the female staff was generally more welcoming to the blandishments of the local celebrities who frequented it. The rules (or rather custom) preferred that it be so.¹⁰

The scandal was huge. A few gentlemen, outraged by this unprecedented audacity, leaped on the lady and were about to manhandle her, when the arrival of Doublier put an end to the scene, or rather caused it to change direction. Our compatriot quickly settled his account with the most impertinent of these gentlemen. And that is when things turned very ugly. Two or three of Doublier's colleagues managed to shield the couple from the fury of the house regulars. But these customers did not intend to stop there, and they initiated a real manhunt in the labyrinthine corridors of the establishment. The pursuit of the fugitives was, however, without success. A juggler of weights, who was none other than Petroff the Bulgarian, and who was performing a number on the same program for that evening, succeeded in having

Doublier and his wife escape through the skylight of his dressing room and taking the same route, he joined them outside. He led them to a good man he knew, where the couple was hidden and brought to safety. But the Turks did not give up the chase. They set out the next day in search of the fugitives from whom they wanted revenge at all costs. It was necessary to inform the pursued couple of this and for them to get away; Petroff the Bulgarian took care of it.

The following night Petroff came to fetch them in a cart and took them to a nearby refuge, about twenty kilometers away. Protected in a safe place, he returned to Chofa. When the man who was slapped and the one who was beaten and unhappy were convinced that the French had escaped them, they resigned themselves and things calmed down. But Doublier and his wife had left all their equipment in the town. What to do? No need to think about getting it back. The director of the establishment where the incident took place was too loyal to his clients not to confiscate everything that belonged to the people who had caused him so much trouble. Doublier and his family then experienced bitter days. They were reduced to putting together a little street-corner act with which they eked out a living. Going, who knows how, from one locality to another, they ended up arriving in Constantinople. And that is where they counted on recovering from their troubles, but if not that at least to find some way of returning to France.[11]

The sultan's empire no longer meant anything to them. As luck would have it, Petroff the Bulgarian was also in the Turkish capital at the same time. And one fine day on the quays the two men found themselves face to face. It is easy to understand that Doublier was very grateful to the Bulgarian. The two men hit it off immediately, and they soon confessed their mutual distress to one another. Their somewhat shabby appearance spoke for itself. The Doublier couple and Petroff immediately decided to combine their misery. The conditions of this association were easily settled. On the Doublier side, the contribution amounted to nothing, same capital on the Petroff side. But their goodwill was equal. And then, they were still young, so why despair? As one had to live first and philosophize after, they sought and found ways to employ their physical energy on the docks. All day long they loaded and unloaded boxes of goods. In the evening they chatted. By living the life of Turkish jobbers, stevedores, and other laborers, Doublier and his colleagues on the docks had become good friends. And Petroff who was more reserved, followed the activity all the same; he went where his companion decided to go. It was thus that the two were one day drawn into a wrestling contest that was taking place in a neighborhood of Constantinople.

Doublier, who had tried it, loved wrestling; it interested him. As for Petroff, who had already been around a good deal in Turkey and who had seen the Turks fight, did not seem very fond of bothering himself in order to attend a kind of spectacle he knew. However, he followed Doublier, and in a way it was this day that set in motion the course that wrestling was going to experience in France, and it proved to be a trend that lasted for several years. What struck Doublier was not so much the specific way the Turks wrestled as their extraordinary physical strength, and he explained that if these men, who all seemed to wrestle intelligently, could learn to do the same by learning the French method it would be extremely interesting to pit them against the French champions. On the other hand, Doublier felt very firmly that from the moment that the French and the foreigners came to grips in the ring, the public would see from the spectacle that it would enjoy a wonderful attraction. The great task was first, to promote the men whom they would bring to France with a well-made publicity campaign; and second, to make sure that these men justified the reputation that preceded them.

Petroff was not devoid of intelligence either, and he immediately understood all the potential profits offered by a partnership with his companion in misfortune. But how to achieve it and especially how might they profit from it themselves? And he told Doublier that during his travels in Turkey, he had met and seen men fight who were more dangerous than those they had just seen. From then on, Doublier, who had a bit of Barnum in him, was obsessed with only one idea: to bring a quartet of Turkish wrestlers to France and present them on any stage in Paris in order to pit them against the most famous French professionals. But for that, they needed money. Neither Doublier nor Petroff, who were already struggling to survive, had any. But how to get it? The enterprise might seem uncertain to an investor or be misunderstood by him, especially since wrestling as a music-hall show, so to speak, did not exist in France. Doublier was on the point of abandoning his plans for lack of being able to carry them out when an unforeseen circumstance allowed him to meet the hoped-for Maecenas in the form of a sheep merchant.

This honorable businessman was French and what is more, he had been very interested in wrestling when he lived in Marseilles before settling in Turkey. It was during a conversation in a café on the quay where he was sitting at table with Petroff that Doublier's fate was decided. Our compatriot who was talking wrestling with his friend caught the attention of the customer who joined in the conversation. That day it was only a matter of generalities about wrestling and the wrestlers. But a few days later, the men having met again in the same place, Doublier explained his plans and it was not that if he did not follow up on them, it was only for lack of money. The sheep seller oversaw a flourishing and lucrative profession. He could afford the luxury of encouraging a sport that he himself had occasionally indulged in when he was young, and he immediately resolved to learn more about the scheme that Doublier had hatched in his brain. He therefore urged him and Petroff to leave their work in the docks immediately and to follow him the next day to Anatolia where he was going on business. He also had to go to Choumla [now Schumen, Bulgaria] to arrange the purchase of livestock. And he added, "There I will show you a man that no one else in the world will be able to take down." Forty-eight hours later, the three travelers set out at the merchant's expense. It was then that he introduced them to Nurullah who was tending sheep around Choumla. The colossal architecture of the man—two meters tall and weighing 162 kilograms—amazed Doublier. It was obvious that such a man was unbeatable in French flat-hand wrestling. Even in the Turkish style of fighting with the right to grab the legs, the thing was almost impossible. This time our compatriot had found a phenomenal champion, especially since the strength of the Turk was proportional to his fabulous dimensions. But one man was not enough, it was necessary to bring others on the spot and when all the pupils (he needed at least four of them) were gathered, Doublier would begin to give his instructions and teach them how to wrestle according to French rules. But at this point Doublier's troupe consisted of only two men who would be formidable opponents to the French champions: Nurullah the shepherd and Petroff the Bulgarian (who also possessed extraordinary strength).

It was then that, to his great amazement, Doublier learned from Nurullah that there was a man even more terrible than he. It was Yusuf who lived in a neighboring village. Although splendidly tall, Yusuf was smaller than his compatriot, but he was gifted with a strength that was inconceivable to imagine. Finally, he had aggravating character flaws that made him even more formidable: he was cruel, malicious, and pitiless. So they immediately started looking for this famous Yusuf. But finding him was a difficult task. The Turk was essentially a nomad. One day he was there, the next day somewhere else. He worked wherever he could. A legend was circulated around Yusuf that claimed he was the leader of a band of brigands. There was no truth to it. No criminal adventure was ever known of him—except for a few acts of brutality, of savagery even, to which his violent nature had led him. He would not allow anyone to resist him. Although he was liberal with money, it was not without difficulty that Doublier ran around from one locality to another seeking information (and what information he found!) about the man. He finally ended up encountering Yusuf in Stamboul, where he was wallowing in abject poverty because the man was incredibly lazy.

The Frenchman explained to his future pupil what he was up to. But Yusuf saw only one thing: money. He was earning a bit of cash in his homeland every now and then with wrestling, but if he consented to come and exercise his talents in France, the well-being that Doublier promised gave him a glimpse of what seemed to him such an attractive prospect that he could not resist it. And since he was going to encounter his great friend Nurullah, everything was for the best. Doublier therefore brought Yusuf back to Choumla. Our compatriot barely spoke Turkish, while Petroff was fluent in this language. He was therefore unable, during the trip from Stamboul to Choumla, to converse with Yusuf in a coherent way. The Turk, moreover, did not seem very communicative. From time to time, one could barely coax out a few words from him. The impression given to him by his traveling companion corresponded well to what he had already been told. The hard expression, the cruel eye, the wicked grin of the mouth, Yusuf was the living image of cruelty. Ah, it was neither sentimentality nor scruples that would defeat him! But he seemed terribly strong and appearances justified not only what Nurullah had said about him, but also the information given to him by the dock workers of Stamboul confirmed it. Let us cut this account short so as not to linger too long on these preliminaries that we find at the origin of the arrival of Turkish wrestlers in France.

Doublier found himself directing three elite individuals: Nurullah, Yusuf, and his faithful Petroff. It was still insufficient; but recruitment was now easy because Yusuf knew all the wrestlers in the surrounding area. Before going further, our compatriot wanted to find out what the Turks could do in French wrestling as well as their degree of intelligence. Petroff and Nurullah attended the lessons, and it was with Yusuf that he chose to make the first demonstration. Their sheep merchant sponsor, attended this legendary initiation session—and it was certainly not boring.

The first thing that he had to explain to the Turks was that in France it was forbidden to take the legs and either to cross them or to push them apart. They did not conceal their astonishment, and when it was explained to them the particularly precise conditions in which a man had to be taken down in order to defeat him, they could not help pointing out that the French method had extremely curious requirements. Whether the rules were right or wrong, it was always necessary to obey them. Doublier needed great patience to explain to his men the main lines of French theory. Not that they did not understand them, but the overabundance of questions, of "hows" and "whys" with which they bombarded him was becoming really tedious. It must be recognized that the one whose intelligence seemed to him the least lively, the least open, was the good colossus Nurullah. Doublier immediately realized that it would not be necessary to go beyond rudimentary principles in the education of this young man who was satisfied with his natural strength, and despite his initial distress at violence was eventually able to defeat the finest French wrestlers. As for demanding shrewdness of him, that was out of the question. Yusuf was thus the one chosen for the practical demonstrations, and this inaugural session was destined to remain etched in the memory of our compatriot for a long time.

But it was necessary to proceed from theory to practice, and Doublier, happened to be at the same time both the teacher and the trainer of his colts. After putting Yusuf in the guard position, he showed him what a preparatory cuff hold was. Then he grabbed his wrist and said, "There you go." At which Yusuf, without seeming to make the slightest effort, disengaged his wrist and seized Doublier's wrist and said to him, "No. There *you* go." And he secured the hold. It seemed to the Frenchman that his wrist was being crushed under the Turk's grip. He had to signal him to let go immediately because he was experiencing real pain. He explained that since this grip was preparatory to others that would follow, and so it was not necessary to tighten his hands with such force. To which Yusuf replied, "With us, there is no preparatory hold, we hold a man or we do not hold him. If we hold him, we maintain the grip that we have, otherwise there really isn't any point for using that hold." And for his part, he wanted to make a demonstration to prove that he was right. Grasping Doublier by the wrist, in an irresistible grip, he brought him up to him and said, "Now I've got you here." And without finishing his sentence, he grabbed his partner's waist with one arm and bent him over with such violence that the unfortunate man could not help but let out a cry of pain. Then he let himself fall to the ground in a heap. While chuckling sarcastically, Yusuf helped him up and added, "That's how Yusuf wrestles." Although on a personal level, Doublier did not enjoy this short demonstration, all the same it made him realize the fabulous strength of the man he was going to set up against the best French wrestlers. Yusuf, was proud of this first demonstration of his power, but he did not do it again, at least not to his teacher.

The thing that took him some time to get rid of was the temptation to perform leg holds and to use these holds in prone wrestling, but in France these would be considered step-overs. However, a disqualification for this reason would have erased in the mind of the spectator all the really impressive feats that the Turk could do. And that had to be avoided at all costs. Conversely, he and his pupils could not linger on and on at what he pompously called, "The French wrestling school of Choumla." The sheep merchant provided for everyone's needs, but Doublier was in a hurry to make lots of money with his phenomenal Turks.

This was especially true since the troupe had been increased by two men who had been brought in on Yusuf's instructions. One of them was Kara Osman, who professed great admiration for his terrible compatriot, the other was Mehmet who was physically weaker than the others but soon revealed himself as the best wrestler of the band.[12] In reality, Petroff and Mehmet very quickly appeared to be the most skillful in assimilating the rules of French wrestling. Above all, Yusuf needed the lesson of experience and as for Nurullah, he needed nothing at all but to remain "Nurullah the Enormous," for whom the force of inertia was sufficient. But above all it was Yusuf on whom Doublier counted and, after him, on Kara Osman. It was not possible to think of teaching them the finer points of French wrestling in the little time that he had. Besides, Yusuf had clearly marked his predilection for wrestling on the mat and for the forceful moves that use strength and especially double-hold headlocks in the prone position. But there was one maneuver which the Turk naturally excelled at, and that was the drag hold to the neck that immediately brought the opponent to the mat. Yusuf put an authority into his neck drags that few men were able to resist. The move was delivered with such force that one could do little more than to give up and go down to the mat.[13]

The Turk could easily administer his irresistible headlock. This is what Doublier trained him to do most particularly. As for the rest, it was a matter of defense. And for that Yusuf was clever enough to paralyze all attacks. All his defensive tactics consisted (at least at the beginning of his exhibitions) in this: he made sure to take hold of one of his adversary's arms, even if he did not know what to do with it, with the Turk's other arm he attacked the neck of his competitor while watching to see if the man's free arm would attempt a hold. Yusuf had an incredible strength in his fingers which allowed him quite easily to detach the grips that annoyed him. This is why during his debut in France, before he knew all the subtleties of our style of wrestling, when he was put in danger of defeat it was always by surprise or quickly executed moves.

When the members of his team were knocked into shape, Doublier decided to pack up and go to Paris with his troupe. Alas, a dangerous setback still awaited them. A few days before setting out, the sheep merchant, his sponsor died suddenly while on a buying trip. No more money! Doublier had just enough left to meet the travel expenses of his five charges and his own. The critical situation was not, however, hopeless. The correspondence he had exchanged with the management of a music hall in Paris assured him of a well-paid twenty-day contract. But three weeks separated him from the date of the debut. And until then what was he going to do? He did not hesitate; he broke camp and took the road to the capital in which he landed with five men in his group and exactly ten centimes in his pocket. The main thing was that his champions should be in Paris. Once there—well, time would tell.

Was it because he was on his way to the country where he was to make his fortune or because he had taken a liking to his manager, the fact remains that Yusuf, during the trip, showed himself to be less reserved than he had been until then. And it was thus that Doublier was able to appreciate the immense vanity of his champion. Yusuf, in fact, worshiped his own strength. And he let it be seen with a smugness that he in no way tried to conceal: "I have never been, as you have heard it said, the leader of brigands. It is a story that has been peddled in Stamboul, but no one would have dared to take responsibility for such an accusation in front of me. I've been in a few rough spots, it's true, but I was defending my life then. I don't need to tell you whether it was my fault that I was in danger or not. I was defending it and that's all. Why was I risking it like that? The sun runs the risk of being eclipsed by a cloud just by showing itself. My existence was, I admit, quite hectic. It was like that until the day I met Pamongki-Osman.

Never heard of Pamongki-Osman? He was declining when Kara Ibo [1838–?] was in full possession of his physical powers.[14] He was a top-class wrestler. When I knew him, he had already been retired a long time and was no longer fighting. It is claimed that he was even better than Kara Ibo. I saw him wrestle. I admired him but I did not understand him. He was enjoying himself, but he was not fighting, and I am sure that if I had been his contemporary, I would have beaten him. Because, you see, there is only one sun and there is also only one Yusuf!"

When he said things to which he attached a deep value, Yusuf liked to address his manager on familiar terms. "It was Pamongki-Osman," he continued, "who taught me to wrestle. But it was not he who taught me to suffer, and it was from my own suffering that I in turn learned to make others suffer." What preoccupied him, what crowned his astonishment, was the rule in French wrestling which forbade tripping the legs, and when he had discussed the question thoroughly, he concluded with this constant reflection which he returned to frequently: "But what is the point if Muhammad gives you legs, and you can't do anything to do with them! We must use the legs and if necessary, break them when they resist."

Charming conclusion indeed. Basically, all his philosophical and sporting reflections held only moderate interest for Doublier; his thoughts were elsewhere.

He had material concerns too pressing to dwell on Yusuf's remarks about French wrestling. The problem that faced him could be summarized in two ways. The first was not essentially difficult to solve. It was a question of being able to support his men until the moment of their debut in Paris. The second was much more agonizing because it involved the future. How would his champions, who knew virtually nothing of French wrestling, hold up against those who were going to be opposed to them? If they emerged victorious—if not always, at least in most of the matches—everything would be fine. If, on the contrary, they showed themselves to be second-rate, if they were beaten, it would mean the end of everything, the ruin of his experiment. He would find no bookings for them. The European tour he planned after the opening of Paris could not take place. It meant bankruptcy with five men on his hands that he would have to send back home. Doublier worried; Yusuf's rhetoric left him cold.

The arrival in Paris put an end to the promoter's meditations. After having provided accommodation and subsistence for his troupe, he began to look for a room where, sheltered from prying eyes, he could have them work out. Then he asked a few French professionals to come and train them a bit. He found some, and their terms were naturally enough ten times the regular amount to those who agreed to this service. They quickly realized that the Turks had a rudimentary knowledge of French wrestling, but from there to victory in the ring was something else entirely. All were unanimous in declaring that the question did not even arise when it came to the colossal Nurullah. It seemed to them that Kara Osman was the one who, along with Mehmet, displayed the greatest knowledge of wrestling. All that remained was to work with Yusuf. As with other Turks, the issue of training was foreign to Yusuf.

As soon as Yusuf was set up with someone in a training session, he acted in exactly the same way in a private session as in a competition. He neither recognized nor understood the so-called practice sessions. It caused a great astonishment when he was opposed to the first man who was to practice with him. He finished off the match with such violence and so quickly that things almost went wrong. What he did was neither Turkish wrestling nor French wrestling. He simply acted like someone who was confident in his strength and used his brutal, irresistible authority with his opponent. He tackled him to the ground hard, clumsily, but without making him touch the mat with both shoulders and although he was warned of what to do, he did not understand that this victory was challenged.[15] It took nothing less than Doublier's authority to calm the irascible Turk, who was already shouting that he had been taken to France under false pretenses. He had come to throw down men; he threw them down, and that was that. Kara Osman and Mehmet who were more intelligent eventually managed to make him listen to reason. And the following matches (the training matches) that preceded the sensational evenings at the Folies Bergères, were calmer.

This calm, however, came only after a few days. But as in everything there is generally a comic side to the preparations for an exhibition, and it goes without saying that the Turkish wrestlers certainly had theirs. Although Yusuf had little in the way of intellectual education, and he knew nothing of diplomatic organizations, he was nonetheless aware that his country had an ambassador in Paris and that there was also a private individual, a "counsellor" (that is what he called the consul) charged with defending the interests of the nationals he represented. The day after the incident of which we have just spoken took place, Yusuf took it into his head to entrust his interests to the Turkish consul because, if this official was in Paris, he was apparently there to do something about it.

Yusuf demanded to see the consul for a yes or a no to some frivolous question or for some bizarre idea that passed through his head. He was alternately pleading and authoritarian, gentle and threatening. Finally, he made life unbearable for everyone, except his faithful Nurullah who followed him around like a dog, everywhere repeating his comrade's words, "yes, counselor, yes counselor." Finally, it was decided to have him brought to his senses by some of his fellow citizen living in Paris. It was then that he calmed down and bowed to our habits and our way of doing things. The week leading up to the debut at the Folies was calm and filled with good work at the Piazza gymnasium.[16] The French professionals who got a sample of the Turks in the intimacy of the training sessions were unanimous in declaring that it was impossible not to see in Yusuf an opponent who might be beatable for the moment, since he was ignorant of our wrestling style, but after at least six months of living in France he could not be beaten. With Nurullah, there was certainly a draw in store for him. He was judged too clumsy to take down a man who knew his trade well, but because of his strength and his powerful stature he was considered unbeatable for almost all French wrestlers. They saw him as an enormous mass against which they would butt heads, and if a Frenchman had the imprudence to exert himself against him, he would end up exhausting himself and the Turk would inevitably take the advantage. As for Kara Osman and Mehmet, it was thought that, as they would try to fight well, they could be beaten by finesse. In the midst of these appreciations one fact dominated—this was the extraordinary muscular strength of Yusuf. It was evident that he was by far the most formidable. Events were to justify this view.[17]

The first Frenchman who was put up against Yusuf was Fénelon. Fénelon probably weighed 89 or 90 kilos and was noticeably lighter and smaller than his opponent, but he had a very great knowledge of wrestling going for him, and his reputation was quite justified. He was one of the best wrestlers from Bordeaux that anyone knew. At that time he was in full possession of his physical faculties. Alas, all the techniques he deployed were wasted. He did not succeed in putting the Turk in danger, and after having tried all the tricks, he had to lower the flag in front of his adversary. It seemed to him that when he tried an attack on the man, it was like running into a wall. And when he himself was taken down, he really suffered under the terrible iron grip of his adversary. "Never," he said as he walked offstage, "have I ever been squeezed so tightly."

The following evening, Yusuf was pitted against an admirably prepared wrestler who was unfortunately a bit light. He was one of the last who fought according to the theories of the great school of Bernard and Pietro Dalmasso. It was Paul Fournier. Doublier was wary of Fournier. He took him aside in the wings and said, "Don't beat Yusuf, or I'm lost." To which Fournier replied, "Unless I can land a fast hold on him, I don't think I can knock him down. His exceptional physical strength allows him to block everything, he paralyzes all attacks, and wears you down." Then going to his champion, "If you can take down the man who wrestles with you tonight, the future is ours."[18] This was going a bit far and not making much of the men who subsequently had to fight against the formidable Turk.

Fournier made admirable moves with great ability to take down his adversary, but there is little that can be done with a man who does nothing but put up an unbreachable resistance and who gets out of all the holds thanks to the vigor of his arms. And then when Yusuf had been attacked and had let himself be taken in by it, he got out of it by main force—and it was useless to use the same tactic afterwards. It was over; he had a good memory, and he would not let himself be fooled a second time. He got the better of Fournier by dominating him by sheer girth and with his favorite move, the neck drag. When Yusuf had brought him to the floor, he held him so tightly that the Frenchman could not make a single move. Fournier's opinion of Yusuf corroborated that of his colleagues, namely that the Turk knew little or nothing about our way of wrestling, but one could do little but bow before his extraordinary physical abilities. "He will learn all the tricks of our wrestling very quickly," and he added, "and since he is confident in his strength, he will have the advantage of always remaining very calm and of retaining the remarkable coolness he has shown up to now. In any case, he can be beaten by a very strong man of his same size; it will take a better wrestler than he, and above all, one who is very calm and very wary. Despite this, the man is of a superior class. What he will always lack is speed. There will be faster fighters than he, but he is of such a quality that this disadvantage will not be felt very much."

The next evening was historic. That day Yusuf fought against Sabès, one of the most spirited products of the Bordeaux school. Sabès was considered the most gifted of all our fellow Frenchmen, although he was relatively tall and his weight placed him in the category of middleweight wrestler. Yet he was remarkably skillful, knowledgeable, and very fast. Moreover, he had the most heightened fighting instincts and his speed of execution was proverbial. Ultimately, Yusuf had to be wary of these qualities or he would end up in trouble. The two men were brought face to face and exchanged the conventional and traditional handshake. At the whistle of the referee, we saw Sabès attack the Turk with lightning speed with a waist hip roll, he tightened his grip, and before the Turk had time to recover from this human avalanche, he started going over backwards in the direction of both shoulders when … instinctively he grabbed on to one of the structural support posts with his hand, thus avoiding the fatal fall that would spell certain defeat for him.[19] The emotion was indescribable among the spectators, because it was obvious that the Turk was going to go on his shoulders and that he was well and truly beaten.

Can we blame him for the act, since it was thanks to this move that he avoided defeat? Obviously from a sporting point of view, there is no possible dispute. Either the man had to be disqualified or he had to be considered beaten, because in reality if the post that saved him had not been there, Yusuf would have fallen. It was discussed, argued, and finally it was decided that the match between the two adversaries would be resumed two days later. Doublier's role in this discussion was most courteous. Although he had a huge stake in Yusuf's victory, he left it to others to judge the incident and settle it logically as best they could; because, he added, if Yusuf had not grabbed the support post, he would have touched his shoulder against the post when falling and from the outset nothing proves under the required conditions that the victory of Sabès was ensured or that Yusuf was going to hit the ground from that first move. But that was just a personal opinion. In short, forty-eight hours after this first memorable contact, the men were back on the mat together.

A waist hip roll was not going to work. There was no need to think of doing it again, and Sabès, moreover, did not seek to renew it. "Never," recounted Doublier, "had I ever seen Yusuf in a rage similar to that which he showed following the incident which had occurred." He did not admit that a man like Sabès—he called him "the little man"—was capable of putting him, the great Yusuf, in danger. But he swore to take his revenge and, indeed, after his initial encounter, it was difficult to stop him from not taking it.

Things that day were not going so well for Doublier's team. Nurullah had finally been defeated.[20] Kara Osman had done miserably in a match that ended in a draw; Mehmet alone had won a victory to which no great significance could be attached. Quite understandably, the second match with Yusuf and Sabès had attracted a huge crowd. It was hoped that by renewing his tactics of the day (but by using another strategy), Sabès could again succeed in finishing off the terrible Turk.

Unfortunately, Yusuf was on his guard and our representative could not carry out a speedy attack as he had wanted. He did everything in his power to find an opportunity and return at the appropriate time; but Yusuf was wary. It was not in Sabès's nature to temporize, so when his fiery temper was up, he obeyed it; and this is what frequently caused his downfall. Yusuf managed to place a waist hold before his opponent discovered that he had somehow opened himself up, and the hopes of the French camp sank once again with the defeat of our representative.

On the other hand, if the Turk were able to be defeated even though he had been unbeaten up until then, he was learning the ropes at the expense of the French wrestlers. He used each of his matches as a valuable lesson, and he was beginning to be more experienced than he was when he was just starting out. He did not know much more about the skills which our method of wrestling lends itself to than he did on the first day, but he knew how to defend himself better against the attacks that were brought against him, and his wariness was noticeably more pronounced. Doublier, who saw that things were going well, also appreciated his student's progress. Actually, the progress in all his students one might say, because at the same time as Yusuf, the others were also gaining in knowledge. What we have said of Yusuf in connection with the attacks, that opponents should not repeat their same maneuvers applies to all Turks in general. It is very curious to note how the Ottoman wrestlers paid attention at the beginning to all the moves that their French adversaries administered to them. They worked constantly, they had the undeniable desire to get to the top ranks, and nothing could distract them from this thought.

This remark leads us to consider a rather delicate issue, but ultimately one that cannot be passed over in silence. It is that of fakery. We know that (in order to appear "in the know") it is fashionable in certain audiences to view wrestling as nothing but rigged matches whose results are arranged in advance between the competitors. It sometimes happens in matches that are entertainments and not tournaments or in a championship where the winner by the very fact of his victory might imperil too many immediate advantages and too many excellent future engagements so that he does not want to risk his luck until the very end. If he knows that he is going to vanquish all his competitors, a man will not give up all the benefits of fame through deals and accommodations in which he has no interest.

When the Turks came to Paris, it was never necessary to think of offering them an "arrangement." They knew one and only one thing: to take down the man who was opposing them and not to be beaten by him. The champions that Doublier brought to France always fought rigorously in earnest, and when they touched shoulders, it was not out of accommodation, but because they were fairly beaten. Yusuf, Nurullah, and little Mehmet (we called him the little one, although he was 1.75 meters tall) marched only at Doublier's orders. And these orders were very simple. No mercy, and as short an outcome as possible. His instructions were summarized before entering the scene by these two words: "*Tchamouk, tchamouk*," which means "hurry up, hurry up"; that is to say, take the man down as quickly as it was possible to do it.[21]

Later, when the reputation of the Turks was established, it was possible to make them understand that in many circumstances, wrestling was above all a spectacle, and the spectators must be given their money's worth. However, it is obvious that for Yusuf and others, many of the challengers that were opposed to them were not able to hold out two minutes in front of them. It was too simple and less interesting for the public if they defeated them in the blink of an eye. It was therefore necessary to make the match last a few minutes longer in order to keep the spectators' attention. In reality there was no trickery, no deception with this tactic, since it was always the best man who triumphed. The Turkish champion, whose victory was certain, was therefore asked not to rush events and to take down his opponent with a well-executed hold of his own choosing after having put his opponent in danger several times and allowing him to defend himself by getting out of trouble. Finally, they were asked to give the public as full a wrestling spectacle as possible.

When it was necessary to make the Turks understand this, it turned into a major issue. The distrust and vanity of these men did not lend themselves to this innocuous accommodation. They lent themselves to it all the less because Yusuf had had a rather harsh discussion about their pay with his manager, and since then no one knew how to explain to him and make him accept the simplest things. Here is what had happened: it was particularly serious since the Turk possessed an extremely greedy temperament. Although Yusuf and his companions had made formal agreements with Doublier by which the daily fees were established for each of them, the Turk learned the figure that the manager received each day to promote them, and he estimated that thanks to their efforts, Doublier earned a considerable sum if it were compared to the small allowance which he allocated to his troupe every evening. There were four of them and they had been placated with a paltry sum. However, when Yusuf learned that his manager received a large sum, he flew into a tremendous rage, at least we suppose he did because he did not let it show. But he thought that the cake was too good for him not to have his share, and a sizeable slice at that.

One evening after the performance, he summoned Doublier to the room where he was dressing, alleging some pretext or other but likely to incite the manager to take a stand immediately. When the promoter was in the dressing room, Yusuf closed the door with a turn of the key, expressed his grievances, and without giving the other time to explain himself, he leapt on him and seized the 1,200 francs that Doublier had in his wallet. Yusuf liked quick and summary demonstrations of what he considered justice. And so it was that on occasion he used forceful means. This incident was, moreover, the prelude to the separation of Doublier and his champion.

The Turks, who were in great demand because of the success they had obtained, passed into other hands. It was only after a while that they were made to understand that the act of "making a man last" did not mean that they had lost. However, they never really wanted to be stubborn about it, so they sometimes made compromises. Instead of getting it over with as soon as they could by going *tchamouk* they agreed to go *yavasch*, that is to say slowly. Their gentleness was only rather illusory. When they had enjoyed themselves for a minute or two, they felt that was enough and then decided to end it. It was only later, quite a long time after their debut in France, after the Turks had been part of the various troupes that toured the big cities of Europe, that they resigned themselves to adopting the system of giving a "show" to the public who paid for their seats. As for asking them to "lend their shoulders," that was out of the question. "Lending your shoulders" is a term used in the profession that means to let yourself be beaten by an adversary who would be unable to defeat you if the match were on the level; that is to say, if the match were conducted normally.

It should be noted that the first Turks who left their country to wrestle abroad were much more intransigent than those who subsequently imitated their compatriots and contracted commitments in the troupes intended to supply the music halls and major European cities with wrestling shows. The success of Yusuf, Kara Osman, and Mehmet quickly gave added value to Turkish wrestlers. There was no championship or tournament that could continue without some subject of the sultan taking part in it. The first thing asked of a manager responsible for recruiting a troupe of wrestlers to exhibit on any stage was this: "Do you have a Turk?" The Turk was prized in the eyes of the directors because the public wanted to see at least one in the competition. After the Turks, the Negro was good value. And what was bound to happen then happened. The big establishments monopolized the three or four elite figures who were made famous by their stay in Paris, then a certain number of second-class men entered circulation who then had to be "sold" to the public. And here is what that boils down to: to be a Turk and a wrestler, one needed only to be a man of mediocre quality. It must be admitted that Turkey does not have a monopoly on strong men, there are also a few in other countries. The Turks of average quality were indeed forced to admit defeat before adversaries who did not want to lend their shoulders either.

On the other hand, in order to satisfy the public it was necessary to make the Ottoman champion(s) "last," since all the attention of the spectators was concentrated on them. It could not have been admitted that a Turk had been defeated on the first days of the tournament or championship in which he dueled. It was essential that he figured in the finals. Otherwise, the disappointed public would have said, "This is not a real Turk. He is a phony Turk that they are foisting on us." There would be shouts, protests, and indifference by the spectators who would have abandoned the competition matches. The wrestlers would then have performed in front of an empty house, and this prospect did not at all appeal to the directors. Consequently, in order to promote them, their instructions were to spare the Turks. Things did not happen that way in France because the French public only saw the leading men we just discussed, and they did not need most French wrestlers to make concessions to them—far from it. But it was, above all, in Germany, Austria, and Italy that the system of accommodating the Turks shone with all its brilliance. The first quartet, brought to France by Doublier arrived with the sole intention to knock everyone down without any pity. These Turks were not yet assimilated to the way of life of their colleagues from other countries, and it was only later that the professionals from Turkey adapted their existence to that of the foreign wrestlers who worked with them. The adaptation was made in a regrettable way that shows what a difference existed between the character of Yusuf, Nurullah, Mehmet, Kara Osman, and that of their compatriots who left Turkey to come and wrestle in the big cities of Europe.[22]

The sobriety of the first Turks to arrive in France was something curious. They never drank wine or alcohol—only water, always water; grilled meats and vegetables without butter, a little bread, and tremendous quantities of grapes. Yusuf alone ate an average of 7 to 8 pounds of white grapes a day! They were very religious, and since their religion forbade it, they never ate the slightest bit of pork in any form whatsoever. This very peculiarity led to an incident, which quite simply, nearly cost the life of Doublier who had caused it. One could title the anecdote "The facetious manager, the irascible Turk, and the pork chop." And here is the story; by itself it is simple and

A poster (circa 1895) for the Turkish wrestlers at the Winter Circus. The exotic athletes caused quite a stir in Paris, and great crowds came to see them grapple.

ordinary, but the incidentals are quite curious because they are mostly amusing. Doublier, who earned quite a bit of money with his Turks, was put in a good mood and didn't disdain playing pranks (often magnificent pranks!) on those around him. Although he was not unintelligent; he had a mischievous sense of humor and his frivolous comic sense was not always well inspired.

He was as much of an atheist as his men were faithful to their beliefs. But the care that Yusuf and his companions took to avoid eating anything that was pork meat made him smile. He found the thing overstated and ridiculous and he took it into his head one fine day to make them eat pork. It was well understood in his mind that the Turks thus deceived about the goods they had to swallow would never know anything about it. The joke was very nondescript, and all the more silly because one might wonder what inner satisfaction Doublier could have felt at the thought that he had made people swallow pork who, out of religious sentiment, wanted to abstain completely from it. Still, one fine day the manager invited his men to lunch and among other foods prepared a meat dish for them which he told them was veal when in reality it was indeed pork. Careful preparation and a sauce that skillfully concealed the truth helped this culinary subterfuge.

Knowing the appetite of his wards, Doublier had done things copiously. And that day, contrary to their habits, the Turks abstained from the traditional grills which formed the basis of their daily diet. It seems that the dish prepared for his guests according to Doublier's instructions was succulent, for not only did they declare it to their host, but they also refrained from leaving a single morsel on the plate. Yusuf especially declared that he had never eaten anything so good, and when he saw that the dish was empty, he showed regret that there was not more. Impassive, the director of the troupe watched his men eagerly devour the execrated meat with a ferocious appetite, as he thought to himself, "You poor devils, if you only knew what you were swallowing!"

Some time later, Nurullah, who remembered the excellent lunch that Doublier had made for him and his friends, asked him to renew the little party. But Doublier, not caring to start over, replied evasively. And it was Yusuf who returned to the request a little later. The manager dodged the question again; but the Turks persisted, and not a day passed that they did not ask their director for a new feast just like the one which had supplied them with such fond memories. Now it happened that Mehmet told one of his compatriots living in Paris and who regularly followed the wrestling sessions that their manager had given them an excellent dish to eat and that, despite their entreaties, he refused to let them taste it again. At least when asked he turned a deaf ear. But, added Mehmet, Turks residing in France should know what this delicious delicacy of French cuisine is. Doublier is not the only one to have it, and it must certainly be available other than at home. The Turk from Paris resolved to find out what it was all about. And he began his investigation. His amazement was great when he learned that the meat that had been served to his compatriots was nothing but pork.

How did he find out? That is another question. He probably queried Doublier's cook one day after having watched her go to the larder. In short, the fact remains that he learned that what had delighted the manager's guests was skillfully prepared pork. Yusuf and his companions had been duped and although it was not their fault, they had committed a sacrilege. It seemed like a very bad joke to the friend, and he decided to inform Mehmet. When he learned the thing, Mehmet frowned, did not open his mouth, and immediately fell in prayer. Then he waited for the return of Yusuf, who had gone out with Nurullah to inform him of the incident. Yusuf was the one in whom his comrades placed all their trust. Whenever there was something wrong, the Turks notified Yusuf, who dealt with the situation with the brutal and threatening authority that was customary for him.

He was therefore informed by Mehmet of the trap that Doublier had set for them, a trap into which they had fallen because they had unlimited confidence in him. Besides, this Doublier could only have acted with the definite intention of playing a bad practical joke on them. Yusuf and his companions had often expressed to him their revulsion for a food the consumption of which was forbidden to them by the prophet, on pain of incurring a terrible punishment after death and a complete curse during the lifetime of the one who was guilty of infringing this requirement. Yusuf's rage knew no bounds at this revelation. A man in a mad rage, even the most excessive, is something that one might imagine, but Yusuf's anger was something so exceptional, so fantastic, that it became unimaginable. When Yusuf went into a rage, it was frightening. He was a man who was violence incarnate, and nothing resisted him without his breaking it. He had no mercy in those moments. Besides, did he ever feel pity at any moment of his existence—and did he even know what it was? It was said that he was very quick with a knife, and that is what had won him the most appalling reputation as one of the most dangerous men who had ever been given human form. Terror still reigned in the region where he used to live, and everyone was afraid of disturbing him. He was frighteningly cynical and cruel.

Such was the mentality of the redoubtable Turk with regard to Doublier the day he learned from Mehmet that their manager, using a subterfuge had put them in a situation that their religion condemned. Yusuf was no man of half measures; the case was serious, and his first thought was to punish the culprit as he deserved. And yet, ... and yet he retained an old fund of friendship for Doublier; the gratitude he felt for having lifted him out of the mediocrity in which he lived in Turkey, and this troubled his mind to the point of making him hesitate. In spite of these feelings, it was his religious sentiments that carried the day. Leaving aside all scruples, all sensitivity, he was determined to get at Doublier to punish him for his felony. But the way Yusuf came after him was as disturbing as his decision. He had a knife in his hand as he sought him out, a terrible knife that had a sinister past and that he wielded with a powerful arm. The drama was unavoidable. In vain had they tried to make the Turk understand that grudges were not settled in France as they were in the sultan's empire, and the person who took revenge or who carried out his own justice incurred a punishment equal to the significance of the crime. Yusuf had been insulted by Doublier, and this struck him in his religious convictions; he could only regain his peace of mind after having sacrificed an expiatory victim.

And the designated victim was the very author of the misdeed which aroused the anger of the madman, mad at having been thus betrayed by the manager in whom he had placed all his trust. And then if anyone had tried to stop Yusuf, it would have resulted in immediate reprisals that no one cared to incur. The only way to avoid a catastrophe was to warn Doublier and to advise him to disappear until the Turk's fit of rage was over. When the storms of wrath had calmed down a little, he could be reasoned with, and if the terrible wrestler managed to calm down completely, everything would be for the best and Doublier could appear again. Until then, it would be prudent—it would be indispensable—if he were to disappear completely. Doublier was warned, and he found the story of the luncheon to be a good deal less amusing now.

He listened, and without asking for any more (for he knew Yusuf better than anyone), he took the advice he was given and fled, and when the ferocious Turk showed up at his enemy's house, he came up against a closed door. But Yusuf was not a man to give up on his plans so easily, and he swore to recapture Doublier that very evening, because they were to meet him at Franconi's, the director of the Winter Circus who was in talks with the promoter. So in the evening Yusuf set out for the Circus. Although he had already been there once, he did not know where to go, but he still managed to get himself put on the right track several times. Once he had arrived at his destination, he asked for Doublier. He was told that he had not been seen that evening, although he was expected. It was half-past ten, Yusuf resolved to wait too, for he had no doubt that Doublier was coming. They offered to let him sit in the circus so that he could attend the performance, but he refused with a stubbornness that nothing could overcome. He was afraid that his manager would escape him, and he insisted that he be allowed to wait in the very room where Doublier was to be received.

Although Yusuf was obviously a person to be reckoned with and one whom the administration intended to treat with deference, he was made to understand that the room in question was the director's office and that the director needed to use it for himself alone. So the Turk decided that he would stay by the door of the director's office, to which he was refused entry, and that it was there that he would wait for Doublier. Then it was eleven o'clock, eleven-thirty, midnight and the end of the performance arrived, the gaslights were extinguished, and Yusuf was made to understand that the house was closing. In the end, the only thing that did not happen was the arrival of Doublier, who was holed up with friends; there he lay low and did not move, simply waiting for the storm to pass.

But the storm—in this case the Turk's black anger—did not pass. Quite the opposite. Convinced that Doublier had been warned, that he had been driven away, and that he would never see him again, he fell under the influence of an unquenched rage, a thirst for revenge that he could not satisfy. In addition, there was an aggravating circumstance for a mind like his; he had at the same time the vision of his weakened financial interests. In short, in his eyes, Doublier represented a sacred personality because he represented money, and Yusuf's taste for money was considerable. In his brain these two paradoxical hypotheses suddenly collided: "If I punish him as he deserves, my lunch with fresh pork will be forgiven me by the Lord, but on the other hand, if I remove him, it will also be the end of wonderful profits that I intend to make." Cruel dilemma! It was then that Yusuf, torn between his love of money and his religious convictions, felt that he was incapable of resolving such a problem alone. But whom should he have recourse to in order to be told what line of conduct he should follow in order to get out of the embarrassing situation in which he found himself? He had to reconcile two things that were clearly in opposition. The amusing side of this comedy consisted in the contrast which caused Yusuf to alternately fall into prayers with sincere fervor and only get up to seize his knife and examine what a good job he would be doing when directed by a vigorous hand, he would chastise that dog Doublier who had made him fail so treacherously in his duties as a believer.

Unable to satisfy his revenge, Yusuf was quite convinced (actually, he had been fixated on this point) that Doublier was never coming back, and for a moment thought only of redeeming his soul through devotions. This trait, which has only a distant relationship with wrestling itself, nevertheless deserves to be recounted in a work devoted to the champions of this sport because nothing can be indifferent to what affected this most curious human who crossed the world and played a role in the realm of wrestling. All the professionals that were interviewed about Yusuf and who were contemporaries speak of him in such terms that we cannot neglect anything that relates to a man whose premature death prevented him from giving his full potential. Who knows what Yusuf would have done afterward if he had had the time to learn all the tricks of French wrestling thoroughly and how to use them? So the strange, the fabulous Yusuf, having committed the impiety of eating a meat which his religion forbade him, prayed for absolution. This is at least how he began for a few days, dividing his hours between a permanent request for grace from his God and bitter financial reflections on the situation that the disappearance of Doublier created for him. Not that he had no money; the Turks had until then been regularly paid, and their room and board were paid, so they had no immediate material worries.

But that was not what Yusuf had dreamed of when he left Turkey. He thought of nothing less than amassing a small fortune, and the way things were going, he was certain that the bright spot he foresaw would never come to pass. And what about the other Turks whose fate was intimately linked to that of Yusuf? It is very simple, they waited in complete oriental tranquility for events to take the turn that fate was to give them. Their fate was in the hands of their leader in whom they trusted. Whatever he would do would be well done. Apart from that, there was nothing else to say and nothing to do, either; Yusuf acted for everyone. To tell the truth, the religious sentiments of Nurullah and Mehmet were not strong enough to induce them to take the situation to tragic ends as Yusuf did. However, they let their comrade maneuver as he pleased, knowing perfectly well that there was nothing they could say, because he would only do as he pleased and not otherwise. None of them thought of thwarting their terrible colleague who would not allow his way of seeing things to be disputed. Despite his prayers and the prospect of probable revenge, Yusuf decidedly felt doubly worried about both his conscience and his wallet.

Then he lost his head—in a different way, for he saw himself already lost, so great was the disorder of his thoughts—he resolved to put himself and his friends under the protection of the official representatives of Turkey. And it was then that with a great hue and cry, he began to demand help from the ambassador, the consul, the vice-consul, all the big and small officers that were likely to calm his confessional and financial worries. In vain, those of his compatriots who lived in Paris and with whom he frequented tried to make him understand that the Turkish ambassador would not concern himself with giving him an audience concerning the case of conscience in which the Doublier's joke put him, and that in short, the question of financial responsibility did not arise since Yusuf's manager, although invisible, always satisfied the conditions of the contract which bound him to his men.

Yusuf constantly repeated himself, insisting threateningly to reveal his moral distress to the representative of his country. Threatening? To whom? Simply toward those who resisted his demands and did not want to indulge his fantasies. The scenes to which this situation gave rise were sometimes highly farcical. With Yusuf, angry rants were followed by moments of prostration, which were very comical indeed. He fell to his knees, face to the ground, muttering prayers with the sincerest fervor, then he suddenly got up, uttering insults to those who tried to make him listen to reason and whom he now placed on the same level as Doublier, because he saw traitors everywhere. His distrust was becoming untenable.

Finally, someone found the right solution. They introduced him to a compatriot whom he did not know (actually the father of a Turkish law student), and they persuaded him that this gentleman was not the Turkish ambassador, but simply the consul. So, Yusuf made himself agreeable. Suddenly encouraged by the calm approach, he listed his anxieties. The so-called consul then explained that the situation was not as serious as he imagined; because even if Yusuf had committed heresy by eating pork, he had done it only by a subterfuge and without knowing anything about it. It was not done of his own free will. His God would be merciful for a fault which, in reality, he was not the culprit but the victim. Heaven would indeed take care of punishing the author of the misdeed on its own, and it was not necessary for the champion to do the job.[23] This judicious reasoning had the effect of bringing Yusuf back to his senses, all the more so as he was shown the indispensability of a rapprochement between Doublier and himself, a rapprochement inspired by the commercial interests of both enemies.

Piles of gold coins shimmered in the Turk's head—or rather that was the image that was evoked—and all this precious metal could only come from a close association between the two men. The reconciliation between them was therefore quite easy. The comedy had lasted eight days. It was enough; for Doublier it was even too much, since he feared that his competitors would take advantage of the situation destroy his troupe of Turks despite the contract that bound them to him. This fear was realized shortly after the incident which nearly led to a definitive rupture. Moreover, a falling out, or rather a misunderstanding, was soon to disperse the Turkish quartet; Kara Osman, who could not stand his compatriot because he was enormously jealous of him, decided to go off on his own; Mehmet went to Germany; Nurullah, on the other hand, remained at his friend's side. The break so dreaded by the importer of Turkish wrestlers in Paris had occurred. Thus ended the first part of the story of the famous Yusuf's stay with us, a stay that began with the champion's sensational debut at the Folies Bergère.

Appendix 10:
Alberto Cougnet,
Excerpts from *Greco-Roman Wrestling on the Mat*

The most complete and reliable source for early Italian wrestling was written by Dr. Alberto Cougnet (1850–1916). The author was a man of many parts, and in addition to writing two books on wrestling, he also published works on fencing, literature and perhaps most interesting, he became an expert on Italian cookery. His massive two-volume book *L'arte cucinaria in Italia* (Culinary Arts in Italy) published in 1910 became a classic on the subject.

Alberto Cougnet
Excerpts from *La lotta Greco-romana sul tappeto*
Greco-Roman Wrestling on the Mat
Milan: Hoepli, 1912

Pietro Dalmasso

Pietro Dalmasso was born sixty-one years ago, that is in 1850 in Chieri, the strong and ancient city of the [the Celtic] Allobroges and which saw the births of many illustrious families and famous men. In the army and politics, people like [Ernesto] Balbo, [Camillo Cavour, Count of] Benso, [Emmanuelle] Bertone, etc., and also in sport like the well-known billiards player, famous under the name of *vilan de Cher* who in Paris amazed everyone with his innumerable series of carom shots. He won enormous sums in memorable matches, which were not repeated until the time of the contests [in 1882] between the American [George] Slosson and the Frenchman [Maurice] Vigneaux, and several champions who play *pallone col bracciale* or with the *tamburello*.[1] Chieri is also the homeland of the late great physiologist Angelo Mosso [1846–1910], the great apostle of physical education, the eradicator of the "poison of fatigue."

Dalmasso's parents were wealthy bourgeois people who were livestock traders and butchers. From his earliest youth Pietrino was very lively and he would often escape the house to go with others in his own age group to romp in the meadows and even to wrestle, so much so that his mother thought it well to make him wear a woman's skirt instead of trousers in the hopes that he would not dare to run away from home dressed in those feminine garments and which redskin Indians, on the other hand, give to cowards and lazy sloths. But the naughty little boy ran away all the same, but his only idea was to make the skirt into Zouave trousers or a Greek tunic, and like the ancient heroes of Hellas, he went down to the arena to perform feats and the children nicknamed him "the Zouave."

As he grew in years, Pietrino Dalmasso's fighting spirit increased progressively, so much so that at the age of twelve years, his father decided to have him shipped off as a cabin boy on a merchant vessel; but when he returned to Genoa after his journey, Pietro again ran away from home since he did not like the disciplined life of a cabin boy. But he did not stay away long; his passion for fishing and swimming, which was unsurpassed, made him go to Marseilles, where he helped to increase the numerous legions of fishermen and to supply the *maz* (inns) of the Cannebière, with the fat *rascasse*, the scorpion fish, the *fielas* the St. Peter's fish, the *moraines*, the monkfish and other tasty members of Neptune's silent herds to make the succulent *broetti* or *sburrite* and the *caciucchi*, which the Provençals call bouillabaisse.[2]

From a fisherman he became a horseman, and he was a coachman in the service of the House of Rothschild; but after he attended a fairground one Sunday, the various wrestling bouts that he saw awakened in him the old propensity for that violent manifestation of athletics.[3] He thus began to study Greco-Roman wrestling as an amateur and when he felt expert enough, he abandoned the profession of charioteer, for that of a professional wrestler. Although initially he did not have a suitable build, he had *le physique de l'emploi* [the body that he needed] as the French say, more to the point that he

The great wrestler Pietro Dalmasso was claimed by both the French and the Italians. Here he poses with arms crossed and with a decorative sash.

was reduced to skin and bones, and therefore they nicknamed him: *sac à os* or "bag of bones."[4]

His early matches were hard; but with the passion that haunted him, and the truly marvelous determination with which he persisted in fighting, he was able to obtain a surprising agility, and a phenomenal staying power so that he was given the nickname, *Pietro, le rempart de Turin* [the Rampart of Turin].

Having acquired an excellent physique by training to change the "sack of bones" into a "sack of mischief," he wanted to go to Bordeaux. As we have seen, the city is referred to in several places in the book *Vingt ans de lutte* by Paul Pons, as having a population that was very enthusiastic about feats of strength and especially about wrestling. This was so much the case that all the best wrestlers from the middle of the century went to Bordeaux to be recognized as real wrestlers, particularly during the famous fair called the Fair of the *Pains d'épices* (Gingerbread Fair) that lasts twenty days and would correspond to the Ambrosian fair of Porta Genova or rather to the ancient fair of Senigallia.[5]

Dalmasso finally found a carnival booth owner who agreed to enlist him in his troupe during the period of the fair.[6] The following morning after signing the short-term contract, there was already a rumor spread about that a new wrestler of Piedmontese nationality would make his debut in this wrestling booth. He was challenged by almost every amateur wrestler in the square; and from all the surrounding towns, the word had already spread and there was a procession of carriages and char-a-bancs carrying amateurs and other enthusiasts of that athletic sport, as well as all the old and new generation of wrestlers from the Gironde region who had settled there.

The matches took place not in the fair booth because it was too small to contain the enormous number of spectators, but in an open field in the middle of a meadow where with ropes and stakes a ring was formed and the audience surrounded this. The first bout began where the wrestlers "pull their hair out" (*tirer la bourre* of the French) [wrestle for real], and Pietro's opponent could not stand up for more than two minutes before he went down with his back on the ground.[7] A deafening clamor of screams, of whistles, a confused shouting, emitted by a thousand throats, some hoarse, others resounding like little brass pipes. There was an exchange of jokes addressed to the vanquished who had been tumultuously overcome which commented on the rapid fall of the loser; and among those jokes being bantered about was this: "What? You haven't eaten today. Is that why you can't stand up?" alluding to the proverb "an empty sack will not stand up."

To make a long story short, one by one, all those who challenged Dalmasso were forced to grind their shoulders against the grass. From that day, Pietro *le rampart de Turin* became the idol of those from Bordeaux, indeed of all the Gironde, so much so that, after that famous debut, he returned to the square at least a thousand times to defeat all those who challenged him, keeping his shoulders "virgin" for several years—for as many and perhaps more than his French colleague Faouët, nicknamed *épaules vierges* [virgin shoulders].

Even in Paris, the Italian athlete was very well regarded and esteemed because, although he was always victorious in his early years of his prime, he never boasted, he never had the *blague* [boastful nonsense] that others in his place would have filled the world making it unbearable. Modest and taciturn, he never talked about himself, he did not boast, let alone gossip or *débine* [run down] his colleagues. In this he is very similar to our Giovanni Raicevich who is also reluctant to speak of himself as he is of others.

The wrestlers who had to compete with him complained because he never accepted deals of any kind; he fought seriously, properly, without tricks, and "cleanly"; but woe to opponents who were inattentive or who made a mistake; he took advantage of them with lightning speed and defeated his adversaries. Therefore, the audience at the Folies Bergère theater earned a lot of money by betting on him, because he fought honestly and did not make deals or *chiqué* [prearrange the outcome] with anyone, nor did he intend to undergo similar pacts from anyone, be they either impresarios or wrestling *matcheurs* [opponents]. Amazing among his many victories was the one reported of the famous English wrestler, world champion of those times, Tom Cannon [1852–?] whom no one had yet been able to *tomber* [take down]. So too was his victory over Old Bernard [1820–1893] and over Limousin [1860–1910].

Pietro was a good teacher; proof of this is that among his pupils he could count Paul Pons who appreciated his teachers since he also received lessons from Old Bernard. Thus we see in the aforementioned autobiography of Paul Pons, *Vingt ans de lutte* [1909], that the two partners, Dalmasso and Bernard were the ones who arranged his enlistment (*embauche*) and initiated Pons "the Blacksmith of Sorgues" in Mangematin's fair booth, after having seen him work in the weight-lifting competition at Jonquières and later wrestling and pinning the brutal Langlois as well as other opponents like Léger and Big Victor. I have already reported the results, therefore I will not go back to it. I will only mention one detail that many people are perhaps unaware of. During one winter, Pietro Dalmasso had all of Paris rush to the Folies Bergère theater to see a female troupe wrestle—which was made up of twenty of his pupils, and whom he later took with him to America where they earned a considerable sum.[8]

It was also in North America, in California in Chicago and in various other regions that Pietro Dalmasso was able to participate in the world championships over a period of ten years. This was where the wrestling was real, not the usual modern exhibitions where for the most part the manager fixes what and how one has to fall after so many minutes and so on. He also stayed in Buenos Aires for a year. In those days there was a terrible wrestler called Forty Ounces who challenged everyone; and when Pietro arrived in the capital of Argentina, he immediately tried to associate him with a group of scheming politicians who used seductive promises and offers of money if he agreed to "loan out his shoulders" [take a fall], but the proud Italian rebelled against those proposals; he fought with Forty Ounces and was victorious.[9]

Since there were no wrestlers at that time who could justify making a "campaign" or a tour, Dalmasso dedicated himself to lifting weights, but real weights (not phony ones like those called "cooking pots" which are empty inside), and achieved great success. Returning to Marseilles in 1889, he was engaged at the Crystal Palace where he issued a challenge to pay 1,000 francs to whoever was able to equal his weightlifting. No one managed to earn Dalmasso's 1,000 francs. In 1906 he was called to Paris to referee during the wrestling tournament that took place at the Folies Bergère theater, but he reluctantly gave up on it, noting that wrestling was no longer like it was in its day, but

Forty Ounces was a brutal Argentine-Italian wrestler named Paulo Raffetto. In this illustration from a magazine from Buenos Aires (*Caras y Caretas* Dec. 19, 1910), the brutal wrestler bellows, "Bring me another [victim]!"

that often the *tombés* [pins] were already settled in advance, and after so many minutes of academic skirmishes, so that the referee could only say that he had to watch over the perfect execution of the contract.[10]

I will end these brief biographical notes by saying that beyond wrestling, Pietro Dalmasso was passionate about swimming and that he was able to make use of his ability in critical moments in Paris where he obtained the position of swimming instructor at the *Samaritaine*.[11] At the time previously mentioned when he was a fisherman in Marseilles, and when he returned with his companions, he would often get up on the fishing boat and throw himself into the water, swimming ahead of the vessel. He often arrived first, although the stretch between the Chateau d'If and the port de Marseilles was not so short and the crossing was sometimes very difficult.

As for his character, Pietro Dalmasso has always had a heart of gold, always ready to help a colleague; honest, and a gentleman of the finest scruples. As for his physique, I have already spoken of it previously, and it can be seen by comparing the portrait of him in the flower of his youth with that of today. His build has never been anything extraordinary compared to the mammoth giants who today oppress the boards of Music halls and Variety theater stages, but his muscles had and still have a steely consistency.

After all, with regard to these somatic qualities of his, I prefer to hand over the pen to someone who is much more competent than I, a true authority in the field of competitive sports, I mean to allude to my excellent friend and dear colleague "Magno" (Prof. E[ugenio] C[amillo] Costamagna [1864–1918], director of the *Gazzetta dello Sport*) who wrote an article in the columns of this very popular newspaper, on the eve of the tournament that was to take place at the Eden theater in Milan (4 May 1910) between [Roberto] Massimo Raicevich [1878–1915], world middleweight champion, and the giant Antonitch, the massive Laurent le Bordelais, and the sinewy Constant le Marin, to demonstrate that in wrestling, often a heavy somatic mass when it is not supported by an adequate intelligence and assisted by a certain agility and quickness of movements, can be overwhelmed by the flexibility and elasticity limbs that house and are governed by a well-balanced intellectuality. This is an observation which, moreover, Paul Pons, although of colossal height and build, had also made in his very worthy book speaking of his teachers and his colleagues from the first years of wrestling, men such as: Félix Bernard, Gambier, Fénelon, etc. Here is Magno's article:

> Among many lovers of wrestling, even very intelligent people, there is a deep-rooted belief that bodyweight is a *sine qua non* for being a good fighter. If the observation may seem reasonable *a priori*, in reality it is instead proven that the great champions of the Greco-Roman wrestling were never men who weighing more than 100 kilograms. Let us cite for example Dalmasso of Chieri, in France called "the master of masters," who goes by the name of Pietro. He never weighed more than 92 kilograms and made a good living by being invincible for a period of at least ten years as a professional.
>
> His fighting knowledge was based on the observation and study of his opponents. "Every wrestler," he said, "has some hold that he prefers and which, due to special physical dispositions, he manages to use more effectively than any other. Avoid these maneuvers and attack him with a countermeasure and he will find himself completely thrown off. Your victory will be easy."
>
> Pietro Dalmasso was very agile, fast, and resilient. He never opposed his adversaries with useless efforts, instead he forced the competitor to work against an inert mass that stiffened at the right moment to paralyze the opposing action. He almost always attacked his opponents with lightning moves so that it was difficult for the competitor to make a save. The great champions of that time remember the Piedmontese wrestler with true admiration and speak of him as a superior man whose qualities are almost unattainable.
>
> The Frenchman [Félix] Bernard was another very good master of wrestling. Many holds are remembered as "Bernard moves"; yet even this wrestler who had a period of absolute superiority, never exceeded 94 kilograms. Kara Ahmed, the very famous Turk who obliges all the champions of France to bow down before him, did not exceed 100 kilograms, and when he accomplished his first and greatest weight gains in Paris, his weight did not reach 90. Kotch Mehmet never exceeded 84 kilograms and yet for a long time he shattered and defeated all the heaviest world champions. When Hackenschmidt became world champion he weighed just 87 kilograms. Constant the Butcher never surpassed 90 kilograms and managed to beat all the heavyweights and soon became the champion of champions. Gambier, very light, less than 44 kilograms, for a few years he was unbeatable by men of any weight. Wetasa who weighed

just over 80 kilograms was ruined not just conquered by Paul Pons, who after reducing him to impotence, felt the need to break his arm.[12]

Basilio Bartoletti[13]

As Prof. Alberto Zucca writes in his excellent book *Acrobatica e Atletica* (Milan: Hoepli, 1902), More than any other, Basilio Bartoletti [1846–1910] "is an artist who alternately ascended to the apogee of glory and riches and then descended into obscurity and poverty; from the darkness he discovered how to rise again with ever-new and very audacious undertakings only to fall back immediately into poverty and obscurity with ever less probability of avoiding a disastrous end."

"He was an invincible champion in wrestling, an unmatched athlete, a tightrope walker, juggler, gymnast, mime, dancer, manager, and impresario who earned as much money as [circus owners] Renz, Busch, and Ciniselli but has continued in recent years to struggle with poverty by acting as secretary in small companies who, like him, battle against direst depravation."[14]

However, when Bartoletti was in his most splendid form, I remember admiring him in Nice at the circus in the via Pastorelli, who every evening (together with his blonde wife who is also an athlete and wrestler), performed various balance exercises with the ladder (in imitation of the Japanese, particularly that of dancing on the ladder, using them as one would use stilts). He also challenged the strongest athletes of the port and stevedores to wrestling matches. These included such men as the famous Pilastre, who carried an upright piano loaded on his shoulders alone and then climbed up some stairs. He vanquished these dock workers in a few seconds pressing their backs on the mat. It was precisely at that time around 1877 that, after Nice, he performed for the public of Genoa after returning from a long artistic tour abroad where he had remained invincible, conquering glory and riches and the title of world champion.

Italian wrestler Basilio Bartoletti enjoyed great fame and fortune as a young man, but died in misery and poverty. The photograph shows him in his prime.

His rather short but stocky stature tended toward obesity. He was skilled in dexterity and wrestling style more than by the strength of his muscles, he was skilled in dexterity and wrestling style.[15] This is the same style of wrestling that adheres to the faithful confirmation of the vertical or upright wrestling of the ancient Greek wrestlers.[16] The challenge launched by Bartoletti with thousands of public notices, to the *camalli* (workers in the famous Garavan company or stevedores of the docks of the port of Genoa) did not remain unanswered since on the same day of the challenge, other posters were published to announce to the people that the port *camalli* themselves had delegated their companion, a certain Pilota to compete with the world champion. He had a tall and stocky stature, without however being too exaggerated, while his strength was downright phenomenal, and it was not for nothing that he was called by his companions with the nickname of *Brasse Prohibite* [forbidden arms].[17]

Unlike Hercules, he did not tear apart the jaws of lions and dragons, but if they had fallen into his hands, they would certainly have ended up no better off than so many slaughtered oxen who are finished off (as did Milo of Crotona) with a formidable blow to the skull and then collapsing to the ground. At least three companions were needed to carry as many sacks of sugar, grain, or coffee as he carried alone; and when it came to large merchant sailing ships for the transshipment of goods, he towed them alone in a small *gussu* (a light and slender boat whose name in the local dialect means "nut shell"), and when he rowed it, it had the same power as one of those steam tenders which in the port of Genoa are required for this need.

The day in which the fight between this port champion and the famous Bartoletti took place in the Arena of Genoa in the Piazza Galeazzo Alessi, and it was overflowing. An infinite multitude of people who had not been able to enter due to lack of places were crowded outside, eager to hear news at any moment, as if the fate of their family or that of their municipality depended on that challenge. Inside there were hellish screams. They were cries of encouragement to the Genoese champion or of curses and threats whenever Bartoletti had the upper hand of the terrible adversary. The desperate and savage wrestling match went on for two hours, and Bartoletti who was tired and bruised all over, had repeatedly asked for a suspension for that day, protesting loudly against the Pilota's use of strangulation. But amidst the ever-increasing and more threatening howls of the public, he had to continue to be martyred, until, dripping with blood and sweat on all sides and completely exhausted, he was forced to declare himself defeated when he was squeezed under a formidable grip of his opponent's arms just before he would surely have crushed his head under one of his armpits.

Great strength, savage brutality, and arrogance imposed themselves over the mastery of the art, and Bartoletti had to humble himself to the brute who wanted to subjugate him with those muscular arms that were so treacherous and cowardly—however, without ever having experienced the satisfaction of making him touch his shoulders to the floor of the arena.

Lastly, I refer to a short article taken from *Caffaro* of Genoa, regarding the pitiful end (artistic of course, since I believe that Bartoletti is still alive) which he met in Rome (in 1909 if I am not mistaken) in a wrestling match in front of his old admirers: *Habent sua fata!* [They have their own destinies][18]

> The defeat of Pons ended the wrestling championship in Rome [in 1909] sponsored by *Il Messaggero*, and the defeat of the former French champion reminded many of another famous defeat that soured the popular wrath of Rome: that of the Roman Bartoletti. The journalist Mario de' Fiori talks about it in the *Caffaro*.[19] Bartoletti did not give up easily. Whether they were French, German, Russian, or American shoulders, it did not matter, and Bartoletti would force them to the ground. And his supremacy lasted many years. Then the muscles lost their former strength.
>
> Rayos, the famous German who had limbs that were as gnarled as an oak, came to Rome. Bartoletti came up against him on the stage of the popular Manzoni Theatre.[20] The German wrapped himself like ivy around the body of the Roman champion. Bartoletti roared like a lion under the formidable grip and gathered together all the remnants of his glorious youth. But Rayos did not let go. Bartoletti then made a supreme effort, tried to free himself, roared with bloodshot eyes, but the body accustomed to triumphs leaned backwards and the shoulders fell heavily on the stage. The members of the audience, which had been holding their breath for some time, rose to their feet as one man to shout endless abuse. And, above the tumult, a voice hoarse with anguish, the voice of an old Roman, "Traitor, you have betrayed your country!" All those madmen with their mouths open, eyes bulging, fists outstretched, threatened to storm the stage.
>
> Bartoletti saw a whole epic of glory collapse! Like one who was drunk he strode to the footlights, and amid relative silence he muttered, "You must consider that I am fifty-two!" But one of the most furious citizens shouted at him point-blank, "Then don't disgrace the Roman public!" A large crowd then waited outside until dawn to take summary revenge on the man who had tarnished the greatness of Rome, but Bartoletti prudently spent the night on the stage.[21]

Other Wrestlers

I knew Felice Napoli whom I had met in Nice at the Café Americain, and I had the pleasure of seeing him again, even risking letting him gently shake my hand.[22] This was in Paris when I saw him in his phenomenal act at the Concert de la Scala in 1874. I could say many things about him, but little or nothing concerning wrestling. I will only mention that after he had an anvil placed on his chest and then had the iron struck with two hammers; when he was freed from that nightmare (I mean of the anvil), he rose to his feet to wave and then sang, the romance from Flotow's opera *Marta*, "M'appari tutt'amor" in a melodious tenor voice. See the portrait of Hercules with a leotard covering his loins, a large club, and a leopard skin used as a cloak. He wears a mustache and little pointed beard like King Vittorio Emanuele II as shown on his poster from of the time when I met him.

Another very strong athlete and wrestler was the Piedmontese Lancilotti, and many still remember the famous match that took place about thirty-seven years ago, in Alessandria (Piedmont), between the aforementioned and Bartoletti which gave rise to so many wagers, and Lancilotti won. Thus, too, among the famous matches many remember the one between Giulio Sali of the Milanese athletic club La Patriottica, and the famous Sandow which took place at the Dal Verme theater in Milan twenty years ago.[23]

Milan then witnessed the fine fights of the three Rasso brothers, Germans of whom Giorgio was the best.[24] Then came [Antonio] Pierri, a Greek who was the finest wrestler ever seen in Milan up until then. As with very strong athletes (like the aforementioned [Felice Napoli]) they alternated between fair booths and music-hall acts, making tour after tour displaying feats of strength and wrestling matches, we have several among which some come out of the Milanese gyms and who later turned professional, and still travel the world performing surprising exercises of strength and sometimes wrestling on the mat both in Greco-Roman, catch as catch can, or in Swiss wrestling. Among these Luigi Borra, Milo, Nino, Oronte, Osvaldo, Lamberti, and Bellani deserve to be mentioned. Another very strong athlete was Tosoni of Brescia who had hairy shoulders and chest like a bear.

Milo Borra [1869–1955] quickly gained worldwide

One of the earliest Italian wrestlers was the singing strongman Felice Napoli shown here with his signature leopard skin and Herculean club.

fame as a powerful athlete, a gymnast, a weight lifter, and as a decent wrestler. Among his various feats are the kinds that his colleague the French wrestler Dumont performed on the stage at the Dal Verme theater in Milan during the athletic championships organized by the *Gazzetta dello Sport*. We will describe them below. Borra supported an upright piano on his forehead with a lady seated on a stool attached to the piano performing good music in this airy position; Milo then balanced the same lady seated on a chair as he leaned back and gripped the back of the chair with his teeth.[25]

[Francesco] Nino of the Porta Genova [in Milan] was a mechanical artist like

Borra who abandoned the Milanese gyms where he shone as an amateur to devote himself to professionalism. He triumphed on the stage making himself famous throughout the world, performing an act that is worthy of the legendary Hercules and the biblical Samson. Among his various and astonishing feats is one where he assumes the bridge position and uses a winch to load onto himself a colossal wheel using sliding tracks in which six people rotate in a sort of carousel that is put into action by means of a crank which is turned by a seventh person who is also supported on the athlete's body.[26]

Finally Oronte, Osvaldo, Lamberti, and Bellani are four other Milanese athletes who dedicated themselves more especially to wrestling and in this branch as in that of weight lifting. They are highly esteemed and feared, especially Terenzi Oronte, who, as Prof. A. Zucca, in his previously mentioned book, was judged by his fellow artists themselves as one of the most cunning types, since each of his muscles always seems to vibrate in every moment of expectation, while his eye intently studies his antagonist to discover and anticipate his every move using all possible prudence. It is said of him that there are no wrestling holds or dirty tricks in his repertoire that do not surprise or confound his opponent; the headlock, the pincer hold, the stranglehold, the arm hold, finger twisting, the body roll, tripping the legs, strangling the neck, the American arm rotation, etc. These are all holds, however, which he makes use of in freestyle wrestling, which is used in Switzerland, where he prefers to work and where the passion for wrestling reaches the maximum level. And it is certainly not an easy task to grapple with the Swiss champions, whose motto is, "Proud and strong" and that says it all.[27]

Very talented amateurs also emerged from the Genoese sporting societies in athletics and in other competitive games, including wrestling. Among these bold and powerful champions, I will mention the most renowned, such as Masnada, Cereseto, Bauetto, and various others. The first two, writes Alberto Zucca who was

Terenzi Oronte was both admired and feared by opponents. He was said to have muscles that vibrated prior to springing on an adversary.

acquainted with them, later became professional athletes, immediately emerging like many others who then traveled the world. Masnada could carry on his back a sack weighing eight quintali [80 kilos], and in wrestling he had become a terrible competitor of Bartoletti; but an excessive effort left his back partially paralyzed, and today (1902) he is reduced to wandering from town to town, selling bits of soap of his own manufacture which will remove stains.

Cereseto known as the "chicken seller" quickly became a popular artist, despite the fact that his physique had always been anything but an athlete's. He possessed a grip strength that was like a real vise, and of all the strongmen in Genoa there was not one who was able to bend Cereseto's middle finger. Due to a whim of nature, all his strength is concentrated in his right hand, and with the same hand he could have done exactly like the athlete Milo of Crotona who used his hand as a wedge to split a robust oak tree already struck by the axe. A report taken from an American newspaper from that time (1902) says that he had challenged and won a contest with the famous athlete Sandow in handling and lifting heavy dumbbells and iron balls. In another newspaper he was granted the title by the Americans themselves of "The Unrivaled Hercules" and in yet another as "The Modern Samson."[28]

Appendix 11:
Adolf von Guretzki,
Excerpts from *Modern Wrestling*

Adolf von Guretzki (1873–1955) was a journalist who wrote for the German sports magazine *Illustierte Athletik-Sportzeitung* and he was also a wrestling judge and coach. In addition, he published in 1922 the *Lexikon der Schweratletik* on weightlifting. *Modern Wrestling* covers wrestling techniques and history. The first edition of his book appeared in 1907, but the excerpts that follow are from the final edition of the book, so it includes several more modern athletes.

A. v. Guretzki
Excerpts from *Der moderne Ringkampf*
Modern Wrestling
Leipzig: Gloeckner 19226

The first stimulus that was given to professional wrestlers was in the fair booths which at the same time also provided the first and most likely instructors. These professionals, who mostly worked as craftsmen during the day, also founded the first wrestling clubs within workers' societies and used their fellow members to supplement their wrestling staff. Not only amateur athletes trained in this way but also many of the professional wrestlers who still exist today. The former actor Rossignol-Rollin, who in 1848 in Paris in the arena on the Rue de Montesquieu organized wrestling matches that attracted wrestlers from all over France, became extremely famous. Herculean Negroes also made frequent appearances, such as Laperle, Abdullah Jeffery, and others.

During the [Paris] World Exhibition of 1867, the mysterious masked man appeared at Rossignol's for the first time. The year 1872 saw four Frenchmen in the Salamonsky Circus in Berlin: Doublier, Fournier, Cristol, and Rigal in numerous fights, in which especially the Germans Lepp, Kampf, and Grün triumphed.[1]

At the beginning of the 1880s, Karl Abs [1851–1895] appeared as a shining star, and it was thanks to him that the enthusiasm for wrestling spread to all circles and caused the foundation of numerous athletic clubs. The career of the "Low German Oak" was a series of victories over the best wrestlers at home and abroad.[2] His first opponents in Germany were "Iron Wilhelm," Markwald, Sobien, Naucke, Lepp, Kampf, Grün, and Rustov, who sacrificed their glory to him. Through the instruction of the famous Frenchman Doublier, Abs reached the highest level of the technique of the time and, on his extensive travels in Europe and America, he wrestled the Greek Pierri, the Frenchman Robinet, the Japanese Sorakichi, the Americans Bibby and Muldoon, the Englishman Tom Cannon, and successfully against the Pole Pytlasinski.

Félix Bernard, the son of the wrestling king of the same name, fought in Paris in the 1880s and became so firmly established as a master and teacher in the hearts of his students that his name is still spoken with reverence by French professionals today. He also founded the first wrestling school in Bordeaux (École des Bordelais) and became the creator of New French wrestling. Bernard's death in 1899 elicited sympathy far beyond the confines of his homeland.

Pietro Dalmasso shone in Bernard's day, sharing the fame of being the best wrestler in France and wrestling at the Folies Bergère in Paris until the late 1890s. François le Bordelais and Nicolas le Boucher gained a great reputation there. With the death of Auguste Robinet in 1906, one of the most dashing wrestlers of this period was ended. The French achieved the greatest merits in the training of wrestling technique, and who also had a fruitful and pioneering effect abroad. The first to appear was Exbroyat, who toured victoriously in America.[3] The best men of the troupe that he founded were Charles Arpin, Marseille the elder, Faouët, Masson, and Bamboula. Exbroyat's contemporary Jean Dupuis, who was born in Strasbourg, came to Munich in 1841 and found his first conqueror in the beer wagon driver Simon Meisinger. Dupuis was ninety-seven years old when he died [in 1888] in Groß Süßen (Württemberg).[4]

In later years, the champions Heinrich Eberle; Jakob Koch, who had died in the meantime; John Pohl, who had disappeared in Russia [c. 1914]; and Albert Sturm, who had retired in the prime of life, were regarded as first-class wrestlers. Furthermore, the Russians Georg Lurich, Alexander Aberg, and Ivan Poddubny, who have since died, as well as George Hackenschmidt, who has finally given up wrestling. Even the Englishman Tom Cannon no longer works. Nothing has been heard from Bulgarian Nikolas Petroff, Trieste's Giovanni, and Roberto Emilio Raicevich, Belgian Omer de Bouillon, and French Aimable de la Calmette, Laurent le Beaucairois, and world champion Maurice Gambier. The famous Belgian wrestler Constant le Boucher (*le roi de la lutte*) is no longer active on the mat, the extraordinarily talented Raoul le Boucher died in a car accident [*sic*. meningitis], world champion Paul Pons drowned while fishing, and the Dutchman Van Den Berg died of a nervous condition in 1913.

For modern times, the professionals who come into consideration as top-class wrestlers are: Ernst Erlenkamp, Karl Kornatz, Karl Saft, Ernst Siegfried (Reiter), Paul Westergaard-Schmidt, Georg Strenge, Heinrich Weber, Hans Steinke, Hans Schwarz (Germany), Alphons. Steurs (Belgium), Jess Pedersen (Denmark), Stanislaus

Cyganiewicz-Zbyszko (Galicia), and Otto Huhtannen (Finland), as well as the excellent amateurs: Karl Döppel, Franz Reitmeier (Germany), Ahlgren, Johannson, Westergreen (Sweden), Lindors, Bäre, Friman (Finland), and Radvany (Hungary).

Biographies of Famous Professional Wrestlers

The most famous wrestlers owe their dexterity and muscular strength to regular training and a moderate lifestyle. They still prove their enormous energy in wrestling competitions, where fights lasting up to three hours are by no means uncommon. It should therefore be of general interest to hear more about the most important domestic and foreign developments in the following.

Stanislaus Cyganiewicz-Zbyszko

He was born in 1881 in Jolowa in Galicia [now Jodłowa in Poland], height 175, neck 56, chest 125/130, upper arm 45/53, border arm 39, thigh 80, calf 50 centimeters, weight 120 kilos, untrained took 120 kilos with both arms to the chest at one speed, bent-pressed 115 kilos with one arm and mastered 125 kilos on the Régnier dynamometer in a normal position on the first visit to the Haltérophilie Club de France. Besides other successes, He also won the world championship in 1906 in Paris. In recent years, He was mainly active in freestyle wrestling and also won the world championship in 1921.

Josef Hansen-Esch

In Aachen the professional wrestlers have one of their most likeable trainers in Josef Hansen-Esch. From 1904 Hansen trained with Eberle, Antonitch, Petroff, Lurich, and Aberg and soon got to the point where he appeared as a professional wrestler for the first time in 1905 and was able to withstand Ernst Siegfried for thirty-eight minutes. In 1908, at a competition in Russia, Hansen-Esch took third place behind Poddubny and Romanoff and won the Championship of Russia in Archangel. During an engagement in London he got to know the Japanese jiu jitsu masters Akitao Ono and Myake and was trained by them.[5] Soon he was able to reap extraordinary successes as a jiu jitsu fighter himself.

In 1910, Hansen won the German wrestling championship in Gorlitz, traveled to Spain in 1911, and then returned to Russia. In 1914, Hansen joined the army, from which he had to be released after being wounded five times. In 1919, Hansen returned to wrestling competitions and won the Championship of Germany for the second time in Dresden.

Albert Hein

Hein, who is from Berlin, is now forty-three years old [1872–1952]. He is one of the most outstanding wrestlers from a technical point of view and one of the most skilled middleweight wrestlers. Hein won the Danish Championships as an amateur in 1903 and the middleweight world championships in Berlin in 1905. In 1906 he became a professional wrestler, won the championship in Berlin and on 3 November 1919 he competed in the German championships. His physical measurements were: height 173, neck 43, chest 114, upper arm 40, thigh 45 centimeters. Weight 83 kilos.

Karl Kornatz

He was born 7 November 1878 in Königsberg (East Prussia), came to Elberfeld in 1899, and won thirty-seven prizes as a gymnast in the course of two years, about 100 first and second prizes and championships in wrestling and lifting. Later, Kornatz became a student of Emil Bau, then a professional wrestler, won first prize and the honorary belt of the city of Moscow in Russia in 1909, and the world championship in St. Petersburg in 1910 ahead of George Lurich, Chemjakin, Antonitch, Pohl, and Omer de Bouillon. At the 1921 World Championships (Berlin), Kornatz finished second behind Westergaard-Schmidt.

Jess Pedersen

Pedersen was born in 1879 in Odder (Denmark), height 180, neck 48, chest 115/128, upper arm 44, border arm 35.5, thigh 70, calf 43 centimeters. Weight 115 kilos. He came to Hamburg as a young man, became a student of Heinrich Stark, and was very successful as an amateur.[6] In 1900, Pedersen became a professional wrestler, trained with the Turk Halil Adali, won a competition in Munich in 1902 ahead of Kara Ahmed, first prize, 1903 the world championship in Paris and Liege, 1908 in Paris, and 1910 in Paris and Berlin. Pedersen has a powerful build, shoulders of an unusually noble shape, short neck, long legs, powerful thighs, exceptional flexibility of the back, and he possesses great strength and endurance.

Giovanni Raicevich

Raicevich was born 10 June 1882 in Trieste, height 172, neck 49, chest 124/130, upper arm 46, border arm 34, thigh 66, calf 42 centimeters, weight 110 kilos. He became a professional wrestler at the age of sixteen, was initially a lightweight and was characterized by agility, great technique, and a strong neck. In 1902, Raicevich won the championship in Italy; in 1905, the European championship in Liège; in 1906 and 1907, he was victorious at the championships in South America; and in 1907, the world championship in Paris and the championship in Egypt. In 1909 Raicevich defeated the French champion Paul Pons in fifty minutes in Milan.

Karl Saft

Saft was born in Herdain near Breslau.[7] He has enormous physical strength and, without training, snatched 70.5 kilos with one arm and he has cleaned and jerked 123 kilos with both arms. Saft is one of the best heavyweight wrestlers and was the first German wrestler to win first prize in a major competition in Milan (Italy) in 1921. Height 184, chest 123/131, neck 51, upper arm 37/44, forearm 36, thigh 69, calf 43 centimeters. Weight 120 kilos.

Paul Westergaard-Schmidt poses on the cover of this issue of *Sport Biographien* from 1923 (collection of Michael Murphy).

Appendix 11

Paul Westergaard-Schmidt

Schmidt was born in 1887 in Spandau.[8] He was 190 centimeters tall, neck 50, chest 134, upper arm 47, calf 44 centimeters. Weight 125 kilos. He remained in North America for a long time before and after his military service; this is where he became thoroughly familiar with the freestyle and got to know Cyganiewicz, who trained him to be a professional wrestler. In just one year Schmidt had made such progress that he was able to stand up to Cyganiewicz for three quarters of an hour. In March 1913 Schmidt was in Kiev for the world championship and finished ahead of Alexander Aberg, He defeated the Bulgarian Petroff in Spandau on 18 May 1914 and became world champion again in 1921 in Berlin.

Hans Schwarz

Schwarz was born 19 August 1883 in Berchtesgaden (Bavaria).[9] His height is 183, neck 47, chest 128, upper arm 38/43, forearm 37, wrist 20, thigh 68, calf 43 centimeters, weight 117 kilos. He won the Moscow "Golden Belt" in 1907 at the Russian Championship in 1908 and the "Golden Cup" in Berlin in 1909. In the same year, Schwarz took part in a world championship for the first time and won first place ahead of le Beaucairois and Emile Vervet. In 1912, Schwarz won the world championship for the second time in Gothenburg ahead of Iivari Tuomisto,

Hans Schwarz had a muscular physique, and he apparently enjoyed displaying it. He had great success in Russia where this photograph was made around 1910.

and in 1913, for the third time in Vienna ahead of Smejkal (Prague) and Steurs, Belgium.

Ernst Siegfried

His real name is Ernst Reiter, and he was born 7 August 1880 in Königsberg.[10] He measures 188 in height, neck 49, chest 118/129, waist 92, upper arm 43.5, forearm 36.5, thigh 67.5, calf 43.5, wrist 22.5 centimeters, weighs 110 kilos. Siegfried is the son of an East Prussian landowner and became a professional wrestler in 1903 without having been an amateur before. In 1908 he was considered the best German wrestler. In 1908–09 Siegfried successfully toured North America. On 7 May 1909 in Kansas City, Siegfried faced the giant Joe Rogers and won in 1 hour 7 minutes and 8 minutes in freestyle by using a half-nelson and a scissors hold. Unfortunately, Rogers behaved so unfairly that Siegfried was severely injured by a blow to the jaw and two months later he had to undergo a serious operation in Bremen. In 1911, Siegfried gave up wrestling, but returned to the mat in 1912, winning the Championship of Germany in Bremen, but he had to retire again to

The aristocratic good looks of Ernst Siegfried came naturally. He owned a large estate in East Prussia and fought in both world wars as an officer. He was eventually shot by a Russian soldier toward the end of World War II (collection of Michael Murphy).

manage his estates. The East Prussian took part in the World War as an officer. Since 1919 Siegfried has again taken part in competitions, and in 1921 he went over to the boxing camp.

Alphonse Steurs

Steurs was born in 1877 in Oud Turnhout in Belgium.[11] Height 178, neck 49, chest 129, thigh 69, calf 43, upper arm 43.5 centimeters, weight 106 kilos. He won the Belgian championship several times as an amateur, became an understander in an acrobat troupe, and later had good success as a professional wrestler. Steurs defeated Tom Jenkins in 1 hour 38 minutes in North America. Wrestled with Frank Gotch for half an hour without a result, and finished third behind Jakob Koch at the 1908 World Championships in Vienna. Steurs also did an excellent job lifting 75 kilos with his right hand and raising 140 kilos with both arms in a continental press. In the Carl Abs–Memorial 1920 (Hamburg) Steurs was first before Tuomisto (Finland) and Urbach (Cologne).

Heinrich Weber, World Champion

Weber was born [1879–1958] in Mühlheim am Rhein [near Cologne], and had been active in gymnastics and athletes' clubs since he was a youth, but he dedicated

Alphonse Steurs is shown here on a Friedländer poster from around 1910. Although he traveled frequently, he always returned to his farm near Antwerp, Belgium.

himself fully to wrestling after he saw Karl Abs fight in Cologne. While still a member of the Mühlheimer Athletenklub, Weber became German champion (1899) without encountering a conqueror for four years. His professional debut was in Budapest, where he received such a warm introduction to the sport that he endured severe physical pain for days. This did not stop him from energetically pursuing his goal: to demonstrate that he was a first-class wrestler; during a stay in France he made such great progress that he was able to win the world championship in light and middleweight in Paris in 1903.

Gradually, Weber grew into a heavyweight and thanks to his excellent technique in this class he managed to defeat or withstand people like Antonitch, Omer de Bouillon, Petroff, Romanoff, Poddubny (for a full hour), and others. The famous Cyganiewicz was then coached by Weber, and he owes most of his later successes to the prudent management of the Rhinelander. Weber then also made a detour to America, where he also perfected himself in freestyle wrestling and defeated all opponents who faced him. However, he was unable to get together with the big names there because they demanded a "certain concession" from him.[12] He therefore returned to Germany, where he is currently wrestling again with decent success. Weber is a personable and extremely fair wrestler who has a body weight of approximately 220 pounds with a height of 183 centimeters. His measurements are: neck 47, chest 122/130, thighs 70, calves 43, upper arms 40/44 and forearm 35 centimeters.

Handsome Heinrich Weber was a great German champion. He was described as "personable and extremely fair" (collection of Michael Murphy).

Georg Strenge

He was born April 24, 1875, in Prenzlau [district of Berlin]; as an amateur he was repeatedly champion of the Athletes and Artists Association of Berlin and the surrounding area.[13] As a professional wrestler he won second prize in a competition in Aachen in 1900 after a two-hour draw against Jakob Koch. In Berlin, Strenge took third place in 1902 behind Turkey's Halil Adali and the Dane Pedersen. He won the North German championship in Danzig in September 1902 and the world championship in Hamburg in 1911, ahead of John Pohl and Omer de Bouillon. Strict body measurements are: height 174, chest 114/123, upper arm 43, thigh 69, calf 42 centimeters. Weight 101 kilos.

Georg Strenge was active before the Great War, and he was particularly popular in north Germany (collection of Michael Murphy).

Willi Urbach

Urbach was born 1882 in Cologne.[14] He won 158 prizes in gymnastics and wrestling as an amateur. In 1903, Urbach became a professional wrestler, traveled all over the world, and defeated among others Smejkal (Bohemia), Massetti (Italy), Anglio (Martinique), Romanoff (Russia), Aimable de la Calmette (France), and Michael Hitzler (Munich).[15] Urbach has the following body measurements: height 180, neck 48, chest 122/132, thighs 69, calves 45, upper arms 41/44 centimeters. Weight 115 kilos.

Chapter Notes

Preface and Acknowledgments

1. There were a few sports (foot-racing, boxing, gymnastics, horse racing) that had occasional foreign participants, but there were no real international competitions until the very late 1800s. See S.W. Pope, "The origin and diffusion of modern sport" in Murray G. Phillips and others (eds), *Routledge Handbook of Sport History* (London: Routledge, 2022).

2. Many countries had regional styles of wrestling. Great Britain was particularly rich in these styles (Cornish, Westmorland, and Lancashire wrestling are some of the most prominent), but France was alone in first establishing one style, Greco-Roman (sometimes called flat-hand wrestling) as the dominant form of the sport. Soon afterward, Anglo-American catch-as-catch-can (sometimes called freestyle) gained dominance in the United States and the British Empire. France, however, was several decades ahead of everyone else in codifying and regularizing the rules of wrestling.

3. There is a pro wrestling hall of fame in Wichita Falls, Texas, but it is overwhelmingly American-centric and aside to a few nods to Gotch and Hackenschmidt, it mainly covers the eras from the mid-twentieth century to the present.

4. Although wrestling had been included in the Modern Olympics since 1896, in 2016 the International Olympic Committee voted to remove wrestling from the 2020 games. The officials wanted to control the cost and the size of the summer games. *The New York Times* (Longman, Jeré (2013-02-12) "Olympic Fixture Since 708 B.C. Will Be Dropped" www.nytimes.com/2013/02/13/sports/olympics-may-drop-wrestling-in-2020.html) speculatedthat the decision was due to wrestling's lack of any instantly recognizable superstars and its exclusion of women. After a brief but intense backlash, the sport was reinstated.

Introduction to The Kings of Wrestling

1. See the biography of Edmond Desbonnet in *Kings of Strength*, 3–45.

2. Gerald W. Morton and George M. O'Brien, *Wrestling to Rasslin': Ancient Sport to American Spectacle* (Bowling Green, OH: Bowling Green State University Popular Press, 1985), 32.

3. Frédéric Loyer, *Histoire de la Lutte et du Catch en France* (Caen: Presses universitaires de Caen, 2009), 63.

4. Paul Pons, *La Lutte* (Paris: Pierre Lafitte, 1912), 2–9.

5. Quoted in Loyer, *Histoire de la Lutte et du Catch en France*, 61. The rules have been modified a bit in modern times. See William Martell, *Greco-Roman Wrestling* (Champagne, IL: Human Kinetics, 1993) and https://en.wikipedia.org/wiki/Greco-Roman_wrestling

6. In the longest recorded match in history at the 1912 Olympic Games, Martin Klein (Estonia/Russia) fought Alfred Asikainen (Finland) for eleven hours and forty minutes. Naturally, this kind of endurance calls for a great deal from both the participants as well as the spectators. Eventually, time limits for wrestling meets were agreed upon in the 1920s, so marathon matches are no longer an issue.

7. Lee Casebolt, "From Sidebets to Sideshow: The Influence of Gambling on the Development of Professional Wrestling in America, 1870–1911" (master's thesis, University of Northern Iowa, 2013), 16.

8. Léon Ville, *La Lutte et les lutteurs, Traité pratique* (Paris: Rothschild, 1891), 31–32.

9. *La Liberté guidant le peuple* [Liberty Leading the People] was created by Eugène Delacroix in 1830 to commemorate the July Revolution that overthrew King Charles X.

10. Léon Ville, *La Lutte et les lutteurs*, 31.

11. A fuller account of the encounter between Arpin and Marseille can be found in *Kings of Wrestling*. Desbonnet quotes the entire article that appeared in *Le Figaro*, 18 June 1854. The story is also recounted more elaborately (and with more poetic license) in Léon Ville's *Lutteurs et Gladiateurs* (Paris: Tolra, 1895), 138–41.

12. Frédéric Loyer, *Histoire de la Lutte et du Catch en France* (Caen: Presse universitaires de Caen, 2009), 65.

13. The governing class of Paris seemed to have very conflicted views of wrestling, and this can be

confirmed by the many times that the activity was banned. Part of the reason for this was no doubt political since the capital was periodically wracked by violent disturbances and revolts, and the two most significant bans occurred in the early 1850s and the early 1870s, both times of civil unrest. Wrestling was thought to be a breeding ground of subversion and revolution. Part of this distrust was class based since wrestling was usually a working-class diversion.

14. The diaspora of French wrestlers at this time almost certainly helped spread the flat-hand, Greco-Roman style of wrestling farther than the borders of the French nation.

15. *Le Figaro* (25 June 1865), 6. Another paper, *Le Nain jaune* (22 July 1865), went even further by declaring that Paz's gymnasium "is an establishment so necessary to Paris that it astonishes me that it has not existed for such a long time. But the simplest ideas are always the last."

16. Although he tried to keep the matches honest, at least one wrestler says that the manager of the Paz Gymnasium tried to get him to take a fall, but he refused. See section on Lacaisse, p. 61.

17. Léon Ville, *Lutteurs et Gladiateurs*, 148–50.

18. "Côté des hommes," *La Vie Parisienne* (5 January 1867). See the appendix (pp. 197–99) for the entire article.

19. Léon Ville, *Lutteurs et Gladiateurs*, 150.

20. Gaston Escudier, *Les Saltimbanques, Leurs Vies leurs moeurs.* (Paris: Lévy, 1875), 240–41.

21. Rossignol-Rollin's original name was Claude-Eugène Rossignol, but an early theatrical manager, Nestor Roqueplan (1805–1870), got rid of the first names and since he did not care for "Rossignol" (in French this means nightingale), he called him simply "Rollin." See *The Kings of Strength*, pp. 142–44, for the complete story of the impresario's name changes.

22. Paul Pons, *La Lutte*, 9–10.

23. For two months in 1871 the people of Paris revolted against the national government and set up a revolutionary people's Commune. This was anti-aristocratic and anti-clerical and controlled by the working class. Eventually, the government gained control and put down the revolution with much bloodshed, but the anger of the proletariat simmered for decades afterward. See Robert Tombs, *The Paris Commune 1871* (London: Routledge, 2013).

24. Jean-Baptiste had seven children, but only two of them, Adrien and Ambroise Marseille, ran wrestling establishments. See https://cirque-cnac.bnf.fr

25. Jules Vallès, *Le Tableau de Paris*, 85.

26. Frédéric Loyer, *Histoire de la Lutte et du Catch en France*, 116.

27. The term "Apache" has little to do with actual Native American tribes; instead, it is used to describe hooligans or violent street criminals.

28. Edmond Renoir, "La Lutte et les Lutteurs" *L'Illustration* (17 May 1890), 440.

29. Eugène Paz, *La Gymnastique et le Moniteur official de la gymnastique, du tir et de l'escrime*, 5 May 1889, 135.

30. Georges Vigarello, *Une Histoire Culturelle du sport: Techniques d'hier et d'aujourd'hui* (Paris: Robert Laffont, 1988), 181.

31. When the matches were fought honestly, the combat of two equally large individuals often resulted in bouts that were long and dull and that often consisted "chiefly of wrestlers circling and pushing to little result." Lee Casebolt, *From Sidebets to Sideshow*, 16.

32. There had been a world championship in Brussels the previous year, but it was a smaller and less prestigious event. Thanks to the press coverage and the hefty purse, the Paris tournament was the one that counted.

33. The best coverage of the Paris championships is by wrestling historian Phil Lions. See wrestlingclassics.com/cgi-bin/.ubbcgi/ultimatebb.cgi?ubb=get_topic;f=10;t=005539;p=0

34. Marc Dubreuil, "Le scandale des luttes" *La Presse sportive* (25 June 1914). The original report was in *La Vie au Grand Air* and the reporter was Nortane.

35. Professional wrestling revived somewhat in the 1920s and 1930s, but never to the same extent as in the first decade and a half of the twentieth century. Understandably, European wrestling was killed off by global conflict once again in the 1940s. Catch (freestyle) wrestling once again became very popular in France in the 1960s by which time many European households had television sets and could watch the rowdy fights in their own homes. See Frédéric Loyer, *Histoire de la Lutte et du Catch en France*, 187.

36. In the Desbonnet archives at the French National Museum of Sport History in Nice, one can still peruse notebook after notebook filled with newspaper clippings reporting on wrestling matches that the historian had carefully kept throughout his life. Desbonnet's love of wrestling was clearly enthusiastic and long lasting.

Foreword

1. The ancient Greeks had rules to prevent injuries, but their form of wrestling was different from the so-called Greco-Roman wrestling of nineteenth-century France. In ancient wrestling, it took three points to win a match, and these might be scored by causing one's opponent to touch his back, hip, or shoulder to the ground, if a man conceded defeat due to a painful hold, or if he was pushed out of the wrestling area. See Michael B. Poliakoff, *Combat Sports in the Ancient World: Competition, Violence and Culture* (New Haven, CT: Yale University Press, 1987).

2. Pankration, which literally means "all force," is a combination of wrestling and boxing. It was a dangerous sport, in which everything was permitted except biting, gouging, and attacking the genitals.

The Kings of Ancient Wrestling

3. Georges Dubois (1865–1934) became fencing master at the Opéra Comique around 1905. *Iphigénie en Aulide* was produced in December of 1907.

The Kings of Ancient Wrestling

1. Desbonnet was born in Lille, France. Natives of Gascony ware familiarly known as being excessively braggadocious.

2. Most of the ancient stories in this section were adapted from Guillaume Depping, *Merveilles de la force et de l'adresse* (Paris: Hachette, 1869) 3–104.

3. A fuller biography of Milo of Crotona can be found in *The Kings of Strength*, pp. 61–62. Also see "Titormus of Aetolia and his Loneliness," in: B. Kratzmuller, M. Marschik, R. Mullner, H. D. Szemethy, E. Trinkl (eds.), *Sport and the Construction of Identities / Sport und Identitätskonstruktion: Proceedings of the XIth International CESH-Congress, Wien, 2007*, 222–29.

4. I have used the modern term "kayfabe" (first used 1988) since it seems the most accurate translation of the French term "la lutte chiqué" or fake wrestling. Kayfabe means acknowledging the staged, scripted nature of professional wrestling, as opposed to a competitive sport. See https://ewrestling.fandom.com/wiki/Kayfabe

5. Bertrand du Guesclin was a Breton knight and an important military commander on the French side during the Hundred Years' War. From 1370 to his death, he was Constable of France for King Charles V. It is now thought that he was born in 1320. Brittany is the home of *Gouren* or Breton folk wrestling.

The Kings of Wrestling: The Early Years

1. The man's robust health and supreme strength are confirmed by another early chronicler. "During the fifteen years of his wrestling career [the invincible Meissonnier of Avignon] had defeated all the men who had dared to put themselves in front of him. He was strong as a buffalo, impervious to pain and with an iron constitution. One could predict for him a life as long as one of the biblical patriarchs." Eugène Paz, *La Gymnastique et le Moniteur official de la gymnastique, du tir et de l'escrime*, 5 May 1889, 135. In the stories surrounding his life, Meissonnier is frequently linked with biblical references.

2. Aside from his wrestling career, Meissonnier is most famous as the subject of a magnificent portrait made in 1848 by the artist Paul Baudry, *Torse d'homme dit aussi Le lutteur Meissonnier, le Rempart d'Avignon* [Torso of a man also known as "The Wrestler Meissonnier, the Rampart of Avignon"]. It is currently in the collection of the Musée Calvet, Avignon. The wrestler's final statement recalls Jacob's fight with the angel in the book of Genesis.

3. The Salle Montesquieu was located at number 6 Rue Montesquieu in the 1st Arrondissement of Paris. It began life in 1830 as the Bazar Montesquieu, a vast hall filled with shops and businesses, but it was also used as a concert hall and a venue for all sorts of gatherings, including dances and sporting events. It was transformed into a restaurant in 1854.

4. The Terrible Savoyard is described similarly in another contemporary source as "a colossus with vigorous arms that are solidly attached to broad shoulders, with the torso of Hercules and the legs of an elephant." E.T. "Les lutteurs de la salle Montesquieu," *L'Illustration: Journal universel*, 20 March 1852, 192.

5. This account appeared in the Parisian newspaper *Le Figaro*, 18 June 1854.

6. Cette is now spelled *Sète*, and it is a seaside community in southern France. According to Léon Ville, *La Lutte et les lutteurs* (Paris: Rothschild, 1891), 32–33, after his defeat, Arpin continued to wrestle all over Europe and he toured North America in 1872, and if Desbonnet is correct, he then drank himself to death. As with many legendary wrestlers of this early period, there are alternate stories that attempt to improve on reality. For instance, according to one wildly inaccurate account in the *Journal du Loiret* newspaper, Arpin died dramatically at the age of 30 in 1858 when his spine was broken during a wrestling match in Nimes as ten to fifteen thousand horrified spectators looked on. See https://editionsarthema.fr/lutteur-arpin-le-terrible-savoyard/

7. Joseph Charlemont the elder (1839–1930) was most famous for establishing the rules of French boxing. He was also skilled in both English and French boxing styles.

8. French boxing is also known as *savate*. Flat-hand wrestling is the style practiced by most athletes at this time; it was later renamed Greco-Roman to give it a more elevated sound.

9. The "Coup d'Arpin" is a three-quarter facelock often called in English "the snaplock."

10. *Robert Macaire and Bertrand* was a knockabout farce about two inept confidence men. It was first performed in 1839 in Paris, but became very popular all over the world.

11. Louis-Armand Leboucher (1807–1866) was the author of several works on both French and English boxing. The Valentino Hall (Salle Valentino) was a very large ballroom and meeting hall located in the Rue Saint-Honoré.

12. In his book *La Boxe Française, Historique et biographique* (Paris: Académie de Boxe, 1899) Charlemont says that Dickson had been in France at least since 1852 and had been successful in boxing against French fighters. The battle with Vigneron was as much about nationalism as it was about sport. One anonymous poet felt the urge to translate his raptures into verse (p. 95):

The Englishman exhausted himself in vain before his opponent
Who, always smiling, controlled his anger,

And ended the fight with the most brilliant move
By placing a blow skillfully behind the neck.
Dickson staggered again, throwing back his head;
Generous Vigneron, as his rival fell, withdrew from the fight.
The satisfied audience proclaimed him the winner,
The unrivaled master of skill and heart.

13. Eugène Paz (1837–1901) operated one of the largest and most popular gymnasiums in Paris. He advocated hydrotherapy and gymnastics as a way to improve the French people both physically and morally. He opened his grand gymnasium in 1865 and published such important books as *La Santé de l'esprit et du corps par la gymnastique* (1868), *La Gymnastique obligatoire* (1868), and *La Gymnastique raisonée* (1893). See "Les Précurseurs de la Renaissance Physique: Eugène Paz" by Lehmann [pseud. of Edmond Desbonnet] in *La Culture Physique* 3/32 (15 April 1906), 463–64.

14. The wrestling costumes were described by one witness at the Paz Gymnasium. "[The wrestlers'] legs are encased in blue trunks, and over the trunks they wrap a red calico waist sash. Only the men's backs and chests remain bare." "A côté des hommes" *La Vie Parisienne*, 5 January 1867 (see the appendix for the full article). The athlete's attire was considered too brief and revealing for respectable women, and none were admitted to wrestling matches until later in the century. After women were allowed to witness wrestling matches, the participants were often forced to wear tights and long-sleeved tops as a gesture to modesty. Sending dirty athletes to the showers was also a new concept at a time when bathing was not considered a necessity. See Georges Vigarello, *Le propre et le sale: l'hygiène du corps depuis le Moyen Age* (Paris: Seuil, 1987).

15. The Jockey Club was originally organized in 1834 as the "Society for the Encouragement of the Improvement of Horse Breeding in France," to codify and regulate horse racing in France. It soon attracted rich and powerful members who were active in a much wider array of sports. They were thus a prestigious choice for the judges at the wrestling meets that Paz conducted.

16. See the chapter on Rossignol-Rollin.

17. Like many other large buildings that served as wrestling venues, the Casino on the Rue Cadet originally housed a large and popular dance hall. Dancers took over the Casino on Tuesday, Thursday, and Saturday, but on the other evenings there were alternate entertainments, including wrestling. The building was destroyed during the Franco-Prussian War of 1871. See https://www.terresdecrivains.com/Le-Casino-Cadet

18. According to Nizier du Puitspelu in *Les Vieilleries Lyonnaises* (Lyon: Bernoux et Cumin, 1891) 109–10, Richoux was described as "a superb colossus, but admirably proportioned and of an impetuosity that was no less admirable. He claimed to have been the personal orderly to Marshall de Castellane (1788–1862), and it was supposedly on the great soldier's advice that Richoux first took up wrestling."

19. The Le Peletier Arena was actually a flimsy wooden construction that only lasted a short while (possibly only 1867–70).

20. **Desbonnet's note**: Do not confuse this Creste, the true Bull of Provence, with the Crest who came along a generation later and whom we will discuss elsewhere. Besides, we often find similar homonyms: Fournier, Faouët, Apollon, Pietro [Dalmasso], Arpin, Achille, Sandow, Attila, Pons, Napoli, etc. Wrestlers indeed have a tendency—which for my part I think is deplorable—of appropriating to themselves a name to that was made famous by someone other than them. In the course of this work, we will therefore always take care when we speak of these usurpers of glorious names, to precede the said name with the epithet "the false" to avoid any possible confusion for our readers.

21. Mr. Falcet, described as "a political tout" and "unofficial defense attorney," is mentioned in the proceedings of the Commune in *Histoire de la Commune de 1871* (Paris: Mercure de France, 1912) vol. 2), 24, as appearing at a hearing. Themis is the Greek goddess of justice. The Chevalier de Carrières was the illegitimate son of the Duke de Berry, a royalist who was assassinated in 1820.

22. The "coup d'Arpin" See note 12.

23. L'homme masqué became so popular that soon there were many masked wrestlers, and their mysterious, slightly sinister appearance made them all the more successful. By coming to the arena in a fancy carriage, the masked wrestler was beginning to build a colorful persona that was easily identifiable; this technique for drawing attention and standing out from others has been used successfully by others in professional wrestling. The masked, heroic wrestler continues today, especially in Mexican lucha libre.

24. There is considerable mystery surrounding the masked wrestler (this was the whole point, of course), and many articles purported to expose the identity of this man. The newspaper *Le Nain Jaune* (29 August 1867) speculated that he was a photographer named Charvay (spelled differently from Desbonnet's Charvet). *Le Petit Parisien* (15 January 1889) says that there is no doubt that the masked wrestler was a well-known *boulevardier* (man about town) named Mr. Charavet. Journalist Jean de France in *La Petite Presse* (25 January 1889) declared that the masked wrestler was a physician living in Nice who "often wrestled with illness, and he often emerged victorious, but he never wore a mask." It was supposedly this Dr. Charavet who was the famous masked wrestler of 1867. Chances are good that they are all wrong. Many speculate that he was probably just Charavay whom Desbonnet says was the manager of the Arena.

25. The "collier de force" (collar of strength) is an illegal hold in Greco-Roman wrestling.

26. The closure of the Le Peletier Arena was probably brief, and by the autumn of 1870, it was all moot since the city was besieged by the Germans, and all normal life was suspended.

27. The Exposition Universelle of 1889 was held in Paris from May to October, and the most prominent building of this world's fair was the Eiffel Tower. The Arena was originally built for bullfights, but it also hosted sporting events. The Quai Debilly is now the Avenue New York on the banks of the Seine near the Place Trocadero.

28. Swiss wrestling or Schwingen is a traditional form of fighting in which men wear special trousers with large loops attached to the waist. These are used to bring down an opponent.

29. One of the earliest reports of women's boxing was a battle between Nell Saunders and Rose Harland in New York in 1876. It was also an exhibition sport at the 1904 St. Louis Olympics, but it was generally considered a freak show rather than a legitimate sport. I have not been able to identify Misses Nelly and Mary, but several female boxers came over from America (where it was more popular) to give exhibitions in London, so these two might have been Americans.

30. Although Apollon, Louis Uni was not a particularly great wrestler, for a long time he was almost certainly the strongest man in the world. He is the subject of a long chapter in the *Kings of Strength*, pp. 379–414. Desbonnet considered him to be a "super athlete."

31. Battaglia was born in Vira-Gambarogno, Switzerland, in 1852; he specialized in lifting feats, and his biography can be found in *Kings of Strength* on p. 197. Theodore Vienne (1864–1921) was the organizer of the first wrestling championship in France in 1898 at the Roubaix Velodrome near Lille.

32. **Desbonnet's note**: I had the pleasure of attending these two championships as a member of the judging panel.

33. The championship at the Casino de Paris was held in November 1899. In 1900 the *Journal des Sports* disappeared when it was absorbed into another magazine, *Le Vélo*.

34. The third Paris world championship was held in November and December of 1900 (not 1899). The overall winner was Laurent le Beaucairois, and this victory made him a star.

35. Desbonnet was clearly fascinated and delighted by Rossignol-Rollin, and he has a more complete biography in *Kings of Strength*, pp. 141–45.

36. In mid-nineteenth-century Paris, respectable women were not allowed to attend wrestling matches. This changed around the 1880s when fairground wrestling was more common and the wrestlers wore less revealing trunks.

37. Charles Emmanuel Marie Mangin (6 July 1866–12 May 1925) was a general and hero of the French wars of conquest in Africa. His nickname was "the Butcher."

38. Desbonnet gives Exbroyat very little credit for his role in the history of professional wrestling. Many historians believe that Exbroyat codified the rules of "flat-hand" wrestling and invented the system of fairground *baraques* or booths.

39. It is impossible to know if Rossignol-Rollin actually was the first to give his men ferocious or colorful names, but he was definitely the best one at it.

40. La Canebière is the main street of Marseille's old quarter. The original phrase used by Desbonnet to describe the young man is not happy as a lark, he is "gai comme un nègre" [happy as a Negro].

41. James, "the Terrible Negro of Jamaica" is listed as being in Exbroyat's troupe at one time.

42. This thought occurs in Book II of *The Republic*.

43. The Brotteaux neighborhood is in eastern Lyon, and is now a very prosperous district.

44. From the classic play *Le Cid* (II,2) by Pierre Corneille.

45. The gymnasium in the Rue des Martyrs is the one run by Eugène Paz.

46. **Desbonnet's note**: There is no doubt that this whimsical homonym was the attraction that guided Monselet to the arena.

47. **Desbonnet's note**: In *Quo Vadis* by Sienkiewicz, the Lygean Ursus crushes the wrestler Croton in an identical way.

48. **Desbonnet's note**: We had the good fortune to be able to consult Rossignol-Rollin's papers.

49. Jules Vallès, *Le Tableau de Paris* (Paris: Berg International, 2007) originally published in 1882 recorded wrestling booth finances as follows. Value of equipment: 6,000 francs; wages of a wrestler: 70 to 80 francs a week. No contract, verbal agreement; wages of a *comtois* (accomplice who wrestles as "an amateur"): 90 to 100 francs per week; Entry fee: 10 to 15 centimes; registration fees paid to the fairground: 3,000 francs. Eighteen years later, Frantz Reichel in "La Lutte: Un sport du music-hall" *Le Sport Universel Illustré* (15 September 1900) reports that an unnamed wrestler (probably Paul Pons) earned 17,000 francs annually, and "in the end he became quite wealthy thanks to a contract which guarantees him 1,500 francs per fight."

50. There is a bit more information available on Jean Exbroyat than Desbonnet claims, and had he dug a bit deeper, he could have uncovered more. His admiration of Rossignol-Rollin might have colored his scanty appreciation of Exbroyat. It is difficult to know with any certainty where fairground wrestling began, but it was probably in Bordeaux or Lyon. According to Cougnet, in 1848 (Fioravanti in *La Vie au Grand Air*, 17 November 1901, 678, says that the date was 1852) Exbroyat was apparently the first to organize a group of wrestlers who went from one carnival or fair to the next, and most historians give him the credit for devising the *baraque* system in which a stable of wrestlers travels around giving demonstrations and accepting challenges from local amateurs. He also seems to have codified the rules of wrestling, approving of some moves and forbidding others. He is given credit for introducing *la lutte à main plate* or "flat-hand wrestling." This outlawed

punching, gouging, and any holds below the waist. The Roman wrestler Basilo Bartoletti purportedly changed the name of this style to "Greco-Roman" wrestling to give it a more sophisticated and noble sound. See A.[lberto] Cougnet, *La Lotta Greco-Romana sul Tappeto* (Milan: Hoepli, 1912), 49–54, 124–27.

51. Desbonnet wisely doubts the veracity of this encounter. There are several accounts of the incident. There is one by Léon Ville who describes the fight between the black American and Broyasse in great and gory detail, but there is no date for the incident, and it is almost certainly apocryphal. I have found no mention of it in either American or French sporting newspapers. See Paul Pons's version of these events in the appendix. He claims that there is not a word of truth in the entire episode.

52. The Société des Sauveteurs du Rhône was headquartered in Lyon and established in 1859 to rescue those in peril on the river.

53. "Double muscles" is a very rare phenomenon now called "gross muscle hypertrophy" in which the hormone myostatin causes excessive muscularity. See https://www.nbcnews.com/id/wbna5278028

54. Garelli was 2 meters in height, and he could lift 1,000 pounds. He was from Genoa, Italy, and he was active in the mid-nineteenth century.

55. The newspaper *Le Sport* (7 May 1856) described Dumortier as a "young man of perhaps an inferior stature and strength ... but he is a wrestler with surprising grace and vigor."

56. Both men were famous nineteenth-century French politicians.

57. Not exactly a statue on a plinth, but Marseille is buried very respectfully in his home town of Lapalud. The marble plaque on the grave reads, "Here lies Henri Marseille the Miller of Lapalud, champion of Greco-Roman wrestling who by his strength and courage brought renown from afar to his village."

58. Louis-Napoleon, the Prince Imperial (1856–1879) was an active person, but the idea that this young heir to Napoleon III would wrestle in public is absurd.

59. Marseille was as tough as he was proud, and he seldom let injuries slow him down. "He could never resist a provocation. Thus it was that one day in Brest, he was challenged by a famous professional. Marseille accepted the gauntlet, and the day of the match was fixed. But in the intervening time, Marseille broke his arm. Despite everything, he wanted to honor his word, so he wrestled with his arm in a sling. And he beat his adversary." From *Gazette anecdotique, littéraire, artistique et bibliographique*, 1896, quoted in https://www.shcourbevoie.fr/marseille-lutteur-legendaire/

60. This refers to the card game *bataille* (battle), otherwise known as "war."

61. In fact, the article is not quoted "in its entirety" since Desbonnet quotes only a brief excerpt. The article is from the 20 March 1852 issue of the magazine, and it is signed with the initials "E.T."

62. Jean-Baptiste (1833–1914) had seven children, but only two of them, Adrien and Ambroise Marseille, ran wrestling establishments. See https://cirque-cnac.bnf.fr

63. It is not clear why Desbonnet doubts the wrestler's name, but it seems to be exactly as he presents it: André Christol. His nickname in France was "the Little Hunter," and he traveled all over the world wrestling with whoever would meet him. He was most active in the United States and Australia where he was known as "the French Demon." See https://www.prowrestlinghistoricalsociety.com/bio-0160.html

64. Critic Léo Rubbi in the Bordeaux newspaper, *La Lorgnette: journal consacré aux intérêts artistiques*. 25 May 1862, compares Rossignol-Rollin's bombastic and eloquent style with Coudol's simpler oratory. "Mr. Coudol displays less pretension: he does not believe in his eloquence and he is right; he sometimes appeases the turmoil just by looking like a Frenchman from Moissac [i.e., a thorough provincial] and speaking with the accent of that region. This results quite simply in a full or nearly full houses. The essential goal of the directors is attained, and nothing else matters very much to them."

65. Hyères is a town on the French Riviera, and the isles off the coast.

66. Paul Rigal "the Auvergnat" (native of the region of the Auvergne in southern France) and his brother were wrestlers and impresarios.

67. The Place Maubert is on the Boulevard Saint-Germain in the 5th Arrondissement of Paris.

68. The illegal stranglehold used in the match is the *collier de force* (collar of strength). It is described as follows: "Take the head of the adversary in the crook of the right elbow, the left hand on his right shoulder, the right hand leans on the left wrist to form a headlock. If this move is done correctly, is considered extremely dangerous, and it is almost impossible to extricate oneself from it when the head that has been seized in the crook of the elbow is securely held behind and under the armpit." François le Bordelais, *La Deuxième Leçon de Lutte* (Neuilly-sur-Seine, 1907), 14–15. Naturally, eye-gouging is also an illegal move, but when a wrestler is in danger of suffocation, no one could blame him for getting out of it in any possible way.

69. The Folies Bergère opened in 1896, but from the 1890s to World War I, it was most famous for its bare-breasted chorus girls. In addition, it served as an elegant music hall where variety acts were also presented. These included singers and circus-style acts with acrobats, snake charmers, acrobats, strongmen, and wrestlers. In the 1880s and early 1900s there were several important wrestling tournaments held there. See Charles Rearick, *Pleasures of the Belle Epoque: Entertainment and Festivity in Turn-of-the-century France* (New Haven, CT: Yale University Press, 1985), 81–97.

70. A position in the manual of arms in which a weapon, usually a rifle, is held vertically in front of the body.

71. A town in the Haute-Pyrénées Department near the Spanish border.

72. Architect Victor Louis designed the *Salle de Spectacle de Bordeaux* in the late eighteenth century.

73. Bordeaux's principal fairground near the city center.

74. Bernard offers to give the young sailor *Escarpins* or pumps which are more appropriate for athletic competition.

75. A town in the Haute-Pyrénées Department near the Spanish border. Apparently, the gate sculpture no longer exists.

76. The Gironde is the region around Bordeaux, so technically this term means anyone from that area, but it has another meaning. During the French Revolution, the Girondins was the name given to the more moderate faction in the National Assembly who disapproved of the radicals. They were all eventually executed in the Terror. Thus, Milhomme's message is a pun indicating that wrestlers from Bordeaux are coming to Paris to get revenge.

77. In his obituary in *Le Sport* (5 October 1854), it reports that Rabasson's real name was Antoine Serres. "He always played honestly and was sometimes defeated (who has not?), but he also acknowledged it by saying, 'I've been pinned.'"

78. According to *Le Sport* 12 October 1854, Rabasson was popular with audiences because of his lack of swagger and braggadocio. He was "gentle, sociable, a good comrade; he was above all modest, a quality that always kept him very popular with the public." His wrestling abilities were also admirable. "His small size combined with his unparalleled vigor made him elusive, and his surprising agility gave him an immense advantage over those against whom he fought."

79. Agen is on the Garonne River about 135 kilometers southeast of Bordeaux.

80. Bear baiting (*combat d'ours et chiens*) was particularly popular in northern Spain and in the Pyrenees of southern France.

81. Ambroise's nickname *Pépine*, is a variation of the word for little seed or pip. The expression "avoir un pépin" also means to hit a glitch or to have a bit of trouble.

82. Deligne and Mathieu were probably well matched. Both men had a reputation for brutality since Deligne had used illegal holds on Lacaisse in an attempt to strangle him.

83. Mathieu's story was common with wrestlers who had no education, few resources, and little in the way of life skills. To these he could also add the vices of alcoholism and excessive violence.

84. Although it does not seem to be the case in this instance, amateurs were often allowed to win wrestling challenges because it made the crowd happy to see a local boy defeat a professional. It also showed a solidarity against authority. As circus historian Henry Thétard has noted, when the public roots for the underdog, "there is a sort of very Parisian hatred for the one who represents the boss, the established order, the natural course of things." Quoted in Jacques Garnier, *Forains d'Hier et d'Aujourd'hui* (Orléans: Auteur, 1898), 90.

85. Traditional Swiss wrestlers wear sturdy belts with which they grab their opponents.

86. Langon is in southwestern France south of Bordeaux.

87. Fioravanti in *La Vie au Grand Air* (17 November 1901) says that Faouët died in 1879 of an abscess of the liver, but he also had a "maladie de poitrine" (a chest ailment). The article further states that Faouët and Dalmasso never wrestled together since he was dead just as the Italian was beginning to wrestle. It appears that Dalmasso began wrestling seriously in the mid-1880s, so this statement might be correct.

88. Desbonnet omits an interesting anecdote in Faouët's biography. He could be a very violent person, especially when he was in his cups. On 1 January 1869 he was involved in a particularly egregious brawl with a fellow wrestler, Thiebaud Bauer, "the Muscled Apollo" (1847–1902). He was hauled into court where he testified, "I do not know why we were fighting any more, nor does Bauer. We had been drinking together and we began to quarrel without knowing why. Bauer bit my thumb, and I bit his finger."

The court then allowed Rossignol-Rollin to speak. "Gentlemen," he said, "I know Bauer and I know Faouët; I knew Faouët and I knew Bauer. This latter, sirs, I would not insult him by comparing him to a sheep—that would be exaggerating the violence of his character; Bauer is gentler than a lamb, gentlemen, when he is in his normal state; unfortunately, when he has a glass of wine in his body, Bauer ceases to be a lamb and becomes a tiger, a veritable raging lion.

As for Faouët, gentlemen, I know him well too; I knew him when he was only a student. He is not in the habit of drinking, and, as with his comrade Bauer, I can say that a lamb in comparison with him has an irascible and hot temper. Faouët is a man with a lot of talent, but when he's been drinking, he's an idiot. As such, I recommend him to the court."

The court sentenced Faouët to a fine of 25 francs, but he was let off lightly since the damage he did to Bauer's finger must have been serious. Bauer was feeling too bad to attend the hearing, and it was judged that he had already suffered enough so he was not fined. A day later he was scheduled to wrestle Deligne despite his gravely wounded hand which was wrapped up "in a complicated system of bandages." After only a few seconds, it was obvious that Bauer was in too much pain and his face turned deathly pale, and he was about to pass out. Rossignol-Rollin stopped the fight.

"You have failed in your duties, Bauer. You have behaved badly and you deserve the punishment of being humiliated in front of all Lyon. Justice has now been done. Leave the arena." As he was going, the director called after him, "And if you ever bite anyone again, you will cease being *Muscled* Apollo, and you will henceforth be *Muzzled* Apollo!" Article in *La Petite presse*, 9 January 1869. Bauer was perhaps not the angelic lamb that Rossignol-Rollin described. He was actually a violent, dipsomaniacal bully and brothel owner who died in California. See www.wrestlingepicenter.com/RIP/ThieBauer.html

89. Although he was a mighty athlete, Faouët was clearly an intelligent man and had more facets to his character than the reporter on the society paper *Le siècle illustré* (30 July 1867) expected. The correspondent thought that the "Wild Beast of the Jungle" had the makings of a journalist after he encountered the wrestler at the salon of the well-known journalist Émile de Girardin (1802–1881). Faouët and de Girardin had a serious discussion about the unification of Germany, but the writer could not resist making a joke. "The opinion of M. de Girardin differed essentially from that of M. Faouët, so in a fit of anger the latter pinned his opponent, and naturally then became editor-in-chief of *la Liberté*" (de Girardin's newspaper). Of course, no such thing actually happened.

90. *Le Journal des sports* was first published in 1893 and appeared for the last time in August 1900.

91. *Acromegaly or giantism* is a rare condition where the body produces too much growth hormone, causing body tissues and bones to grow more quickly.

92. Professor Georges Dubois published *Comment on devient Champion de la Force* [How to Become a Strength Champion] (Paris: Berger-Levrault, 1908). After World War I, Dubois wrote about and championed sport for the blind. I have not been able to identify Dr. Mouls.

93. Acromegaly is a disorder in which the pituitary gland produces too much growth hormone. Symptoms include enlargement of the face, hands, and feet.

94. Henri Joigneret was a strongman and wrestler who operated an athletic cabaret in Paris around 1885. Pietro is Pietro Dalmasso.

95. Artist Gustave Doré created several images of giants, but the one with the most tragic expression is that of Goliath which is included in his engravings that illustrate the Bible from 1866.

96. **Desbonnet's note**: "This trick has since been repeated many times in the so-called mileage contests that amuse motorists, delight judges, and comfort automobile manufacturers. These are all phony contests, thus proving that fakery is not the exclusive prerogative of fairground wrestlers." Mileage or "consumption" contests were very popular in the first decade of the twentieth century; they measured the amount of fuel consumed by an auto with the least amount consumed winning. As Desbonnet explains, fakery was rampant. See *La Vie au Grand Air*, 21 April 1901.

97. Unlike in the United States, Negro wrestlers like Laperle were welcomed in the wrestling establishments of France. These fighters were often very popular with the audience, and they lent an air of exoticism to the activities. Caribbean or African wrestlers were more or less expected. "The Negro is the special object of attention; a booth of wrestlers lacking its 'Bamboula' loses all its flavor." Christiane Py and Cécile Ferenczi, *La Fête foraine d'autrefois: Les années 1900* (Lyon: la Manufacture, 1987), 79. Naturally, this attitude can be interpreted as racist and condescending, but at least it allowed black athletes to earn a living and to gain a measure of respect in the French entertainment industry.

98. The Battle of Reichshoffen was one of the first engagements of the Franco-Prussian War in August 1870. It was fought near the village of Wörth in eastern Alsace. It was a heroic although ultimately futile maneuver that cost many French lives but did not change the course of the war.

99. This street is in the 8th Arrondissement of Paris.

100. Rambaud's most enduring fame comes from his work for the artist Alexandre Falguière (1831–1900). In 1875 he and another wrestler, Blas, "the Proud Spaniard," posed for the two principal figures in *Les lutteurs* [The Wrestlers]. The painting was based on a photograph, and shows the two men engaged in a standing wrestling hold. Blas died of cholera in 1856.

101. Jeantien (along with his sometime partner Dumas) was a wrestling impresario in Bordeaux. He was described in the newspaper *La Soirée bordelaise* (1 January 1896) as "talkative and ironic." Dumas had rolling eyes, sentimental tattoos on his arm, a deep voice, and an ability to mix metaphors. Describing one wrestler as "courageous as a desert lion who knows how to jump between two seas."

102. Desbonnet earlier says that Lépi was from Normandy not Italy.

103. Dubois was enough of a fat, boastful character to be honored with a satirical poem in a humor magazine. It reads in part, "Here I am—I am Dubois. Dubois, the wrestler with no equals." He offers to help any woman "bake a few turnovers." He claims to have "something in my velvet suit that will forever fix up what is ailing you." He concludes by inviting his potential paramours to visit him. "Come and see me, it's not that hard, It only costs five sous at the fair!" Alfred le Petit, "Dubois the Hercules" in *La Cloche d'argent* (29 November 1884).

104. Alexandre de Lucenski organized through his magazine, *Journal des Sports* the World Wrestling Championships in Paris in 1898. The competition took place at the Casino de Paris, and Paul Pons emerged as the overall winner.

105. According to the reporter from *La Fronde* newspaper, Bainaize was impressive at the Grand Prix of Wrestling in Paris in 1899. "Bainaize made a great impression—his hair is completely gray, and he seemed very aged. Despite this he defended himelf and attacked with vigor. Using a superb rolling waist hold, he pinned his opponent." *Supplément quotidien du journal La Fronde* (12 January 1899).

106. The Salle Gangloff was a café-concert in the Paris neighborhood of Montparnasse. It was run by Horace Delattre (1865–1937), a songwriter and entrepreneur.

107. Achille Mouchon was born in Ghent and had a troupe of wrestlers that toured Belgium, the Netherlands, and France in the 1870–80s.

108. Jean-Baptiste Vuillod (1850–1917) was an extraordinary person. He appeared briefly as a "Cannon Man," and then he fought valiantly in the Franco-Prussian war, married the daughter of a senator, and afterward became a very successful wine wholesaler. He was elected to several offices in Saint-Claude in the Loire region until he was sent to the French Chamber of Deputies as a senator. As one journalist wrote, "Physically, his countenance is good-natured, his jovial and ruddy colored face outwardly indicates his pleasant character and harmonizes extremely well with his brawny build. Basically, his visit to the Folies Bergère seems to have been only the whim of a strongman, proud of an absolutely exceptional muscular vigor." De Nérolles, "Causerie," in *Journal du Dimanche*, 29 October 1893.

109. Prior to his death in 1926, the old strongman had gone completely blind and was reduced to begging in front of the gate to the park in Fontainebleau. See "Mort de l'athète Bainaize" *La Culture Physique* 30/438 (Oct. 1926), 610.

110. Unfortunately, Desbonnet (as usual) does not provides a date for the tragic fight between Abdullah and Nicolas Guitchen, but it must have been in the mid-1880s. In July 1884 there was a series of ads placed in the newspaper *Le Figaro* announcing that Marseille would present "Abdullah Jeffery, the strongest wrestler in the world" at his booth at the Neuilly Fair.

111. According to *The Pleasure Guide to Paris* (London: Nilsson, 1903), the Deux Canons dance hall was a "resort of thieves and low characters." The Alcazar d'Hiver was a café-concert, which had a marginally higher reputation; it was in operation from 1858 to 1902.

112. La Salle Chaine was a large assembly hall located in what is now called L'avenue Jean-Jaurès in the 19th Arrondissement.

113. *Le Club des bouchers* [Butchers' Club] in the northern suburb of Paris, La Villette, is well documented, and several athletic events were held there. See Edmond Desbonnet, "La révélation de Deriaz" in *La Culture Physique* 15 September 1910, 579–82.

114. Around 1890, Professor Arasse operated a gymnasium at 7 Rue de Ménilmontant in Paris. After the death of his friend Nicolas Guitchen, Arasse decided to found a new gym and manage it. It was used by all the great wrestlers and strongmen of the day. See Henry Thétard, "Au pays des hommes en caleçon, VII" *L'Auto-vélo*, 2 October 1937.

115. Gravier's book is actually titled *Mémoirs d'un Hercule (1859–1901)* (Paris: Molière, 1903).

116. The Théâtre Chateau d'Eau (currently Cabaret des Étoiles) was a music hall located in the Rue de Malte in the 11th Arrondissement of Paris; the Théâtre de l'Ambigu was in the Blvd. Saint-Martin.

117. The *Hôpital Lariboisière* is located in the 10th Arrondissement of Paris. It first opened its doors in 1854.

118. The *Cimitière de Pantin* is located in the suburb of Pantin. It opened in 1886 and is the largest cemetery in Paris.

119. The "understander" is the powerful man on the bottom of an acrobatic display who has to support those who are above him.

120. Desbonnet says that Mazin died in 1907 at the age of sixty-two (in which case he was born in 1865) due to cardiac problems. "In Mazin we lose one of the most knowledgeable men in the subject of wrestling." Obituary in *La Culture Physique* 1 April 1907 (4/54), 232.

121. L. Manaud in the sporting paper *L'Auto-vélo* (18 October 1900) praises Fournier for his preference for experience and strategy over brutality in wrestling. "Fournier is a member of that constellation that considers wrestling a sport where brute force should not take precedence over everything."

122. A lifting feat of such magnitude (well over 1,000 pounds) seems almost unbelievable, but Desbonnet was usually accurate in such matters. So, "Experto crede Roberto" (Trust one who knows).

123. Frank de Montmartre was renowned for "beating the most famous English wrestlers of the epoch." See "Le Championnat de lutte du monde," *La Vie au Grand Air* (1 January 1900), 227.

124. The Étaux brothers were a group that appeared in the 1880s–90s.

125. Le Palais de Cristal was opened in 1880 and was a rich and elegant music hall. It justified its name because it had an enormous stairway with crystal balusters. See www.musichall-marseille.fr/salles-spectacle.php?salles=5

126. Raoul le Bordelais was greatly respected in his native city, Bordeaux. On 20 December 1900 *La République nouvelle* of Bordeaux reported on the recent wrestling championship in Paris that was won by Laurent le Beaucairois, but it singled out Raoul for his skill and wisdom as a referee. His "unarguable competence" meant that he "judged well and judged quickly." Above all, he is an "enlightened, sincere, and honest sportsman, Raoul le Bordelais managed the matches with an authority that was undeniable; firm, unshakeable in his decisions, for us he was the most precious of collaborators."

127. Desbonnet collected plaster casts of arms molded from those of famous athletes and which he displayed in his headquarters.

128. See the longer biography of Pietro Dalmasso by Cougnet in the appendix of this book.

129. Other Italian sources list Dalmasso's birthdate as 1850. Chieri is a town near Turin. Dalmasso died "in Marseilles, youthful and strong right up to his final day in 1929, at the age of eighty-one years."

(Andre Geiger, "L'époque héroïque de la lutte, par un témoin," *Match, l'intran* 24 April 1934, 15). If the age is correct, it would mean that his birth year was 1848.

130. Apollon was the stage name of Louis Uni (1862–1928) whose biography is presented in *The Kings of Strength* pages 379–414.

131. The Pouyat porcelain company was begun in the early 1800s in Limoges. It ceased operation in 1932.

132. *Le Petit Centre* began publication in 1882 and ceased in 1904.

133. The Place de la République is the largest pedestrian square in Limoges.

134. Cirque Plège was formed in 1859, and it first visited Limoges in 1884. https://www.circus-parade.com/2017/03/26/cirque-plege-direction-antoine-plege/

135. Garemin was manager of the Alcazar Theater in Limoges in the late 1880s. Robin was probably the wrestler nicknamed *Badingué*; he was first mentioned fighting at the arena of the Quai Debilly in 1889.

136. Desbonnet uses the expression *à la béarnaise* to describe Felix Bernard's early life. This refers to the childhood of King Henri IV (1553–1610) who spent his youth in the countryside and among peasants rather than in some fancy royal court. It was believed that this made Henri a better ruler because he knew the life of the simple peasants. In Bernard's case, it sounds more like parental neglect since the boy hated his life.

137. The marshes of the Landes region were notoriously unhealthy places that were drained only with much heavy work. It is little wonder that Bernard yearned to escape.

138. A Bordeaux native, Paul Puy contributed to a number of sporting journals at the turn of the century, and he was particularly interested in cycling.

139. The Gymnase Piazza was located at 32 faubourg Saint-Martin in Paris. It specialized in teaching wrestling and acrobatics.

140. Czar Alexander III (1835–1894) was generally detested by most Russians, and in return he had a very low opinion of his people. Alexander slept with a revolver beneath his pillow, and it is said that he fatally shot an aide-de-camp who surprised him. One hopes it was not the father of General Semichoff. Gabriel Bonvalot (1853–1933) went on several expeditions to Central Asia in the late 1880s.

141. Lancashire-born wrestler, Bob Marshall entered several championships in the 1890s–early 1900s. He participated in the 1908 London Olympics.

142. Cotch Mehmet (1864–1939) was one of the Turkish wrestlers who amazed the French with their strength and skill.

143. Bernhard Leitner (1865–1959) performed as a strongman, and in his act he broke chains that had been tightly wrapped around his thorax or his biceps. Eugène Tailler "Big Eugène" or "Eugène of Paris," was a wrestler and an instructor. He even taught wrestling in Russia. As for the tour of England, it must have been a *succès d'estime* if the reporter from *The Sketch* (August 21, 1895) is to be believed. He found the men (Pierri, Pons, Bernard, etc.) to be rather stupid and unresponsive. This is possibly because the reporter did not speak much French and the wrestlers had only a rudimentary understanding of English.

144. By so carefully avoiding a name for the disease that killed Bernard, Desbonnet probably wants readers to assume that the malady was of a venereal nature.

145. Desbonnet's exact expression is, "le bon garçonnisme." It means literally "good-old-boyism."

146. George San Marin was a wealthy, titled Romanian aristocrat who liked to dabble in athletics. It is clear from Desbonnet's note and from his listing in *Kings of Strength* (pp. 297–99) that he admired the man's physique but had little respect for the Romanian's sporting abilities. The implication that he paid genuine athletes to take a fall only confirms this opinion. **Desbonnet's note**: This "it is reported" is doubtful. San Marin was always very mediocre as a wrestler and often paid for his victories to those who were members of the gymnasium."

147. Othematoma is known as cauliflower ear or "wrestler's ear," and it is a permanent deformity to the connective tissue and cartilage due of trauma.

148. Emile Michelet in his article, "Saltimbanques et Lutteurs" (*Paris illustré*, 27 October 1888) gives a few more biographical details about the athlete. "The negro wrestler Bamboula was born in Guadeloupe where he was originally a sailor and then a stevedore in Bordeaux. He found his vocation in the Marseille fair booth." The journalist betrays his racism by comparing Bamboula to an ape. Although he "is a wrestler of greatest strength, thanks to his flexibility and his simian agility. His twisting and turning delights the audience." He admits that Bamboula is a skilled and classic wrestler, and his physique is beautiful, "but as with all Negroes, his torso is less developed. His huge arms measure biceps of forty-five centimeters in circumference. He fights gently when he is not drunk and pins his opponent without hurting him. But if he meets an unfair opponent, his native savagery returns" and "the Negro is filled with an irresistible barbaric frenzy."

149. I have omitted the painting *Mars and Venus* which Desbonnet uses in this section. It appears in *Kings of Strength* on page 195. The descriptive caption is identical to the one in the present book.

150. Despite the not-so-subtle racism of the French public, Bamboula truly was a popular figure in the 1880s. An account in *La Vie Parisienne* (7 July 1883) confirms that he had little trouble charming female spectators. "Bamboula, the public's favorite Negro, abruptly caught the attention of a little lady who laughed while looking at him; at

these times, Bamboula speaks almost fluently. He knows the French of the salons only imperfectly, but he knows excellent French when he wants to tell someone off."

151. Like many other wrestlers, Bamboula's death must have been unheralded and unnoticed, so ascribing a final date is extremely difficult. The name "Bamboula" first appeared in the 1830s to describe an African or Caribbean dance, but it came to be used as a racist term for any Negro. It was also a name often given to black horses or domestic animals. Several newspapers in 1884 gave the gruesome details of Bamboula's "death." In this report, the wrestler got on a train in Paris, and during the trip, he stuck his head out the window of the train just as it was entering a tunnel, and he was instantly decapitated. Others later said that it was not Bamboula who got his head knocked off; it was another black wrestler, Laperle. There is a great probability that it was neither. See "Mort d'un lutteur nègre" *Le Lez, Journal théâtral* (10 July 1884). The point of the article seems to be to ridicule the stupidity of anyone who would do such a foolhardy act. There were, in fact, many Bamboulas, so most of the newspaper anecdotes are useless in trying to piece together the life of this extraordinary man.

152. The Boulevard Marguerite-de-Rochechouart is situated at the foot of Montmartre. Desbonnet mentions twice that Laurent of Paris is actually a provincial from the East, so he is a fraud on many levels.

The Kings of Wrestling: Contemporary Wrestlers

1. Stryi (as the city is spelled today) is in the oblast (region) of Liviv, western Ukraine. There is some confusion about Zbyszko's birthdate, but the most trustworthy seems to be 1881 since this is the one quoted on the wrestler's Social Security documents. Galicia was a multiethnic region in the Austro-Hungarian Empire, but Cyganiewicz always identified as Polish. Some sources say that he was born in Jodłowa near Krakow (now Poland), but I will use the birthplace that Zbyszko presumably supplied to Desbonnet himself.

2. The Windobona Club (named for the ancient Roman name for Vienna, Vindobona) was a prestigious athletic organization in Vienna. See Desbonnet's article "Le Club athlétique (Windobona) à Vienne Autriche" *La Culture physique* 2/14 (Apr. 1905), 31–33.

3. It is odd that Desbonnet concentrates on Zbyszko's measurements and weightlifting prowess rather than his wrestling career, to which he gives rather short shrift—one sentence. As the wrestler's most reliable historian, Graham Noble has noted, Zbyszko was active in wrestling for a long time, "from the turn-of-the-century days of strongmen and Greco-Roman tournaments held throughout Europe to the new world of professional wrestling which came into being in America in the 1920s and 1930s." He had participated in a number of championships and tournaments before 1910 when *Kings of Wrestling* was published, so Desbonnet should have been aware of these activities. For a more complete rundown on Zbyszko's career, see Graham Noble, "The Lion of Punjab: Part II Stanislaus Zbyszko," 2002. https://ejmas.com/jalt/jaltart_noble_0602.htm Ivan Maximovich Poddubny's biography is on pages 134–36.

4. Van Tol participated in the world championship of 1903, but he did not attract the attention of any sports writers. See "Le Championnat du monde" in *L'Auto*, 2 May 1903. Van Tol competed as a heavyweight at the 1908 London Olympics; see "Wrestling. Olympic Competitions. The Likely Champions," *Sporting Life* (London) 2 July 1908, but he did not place in any of the matches.

5. Perhaps Pierrard's lifting and wrestling prowess was equaled only by his marital record. According to an article in *Détective: Le grand hebdomadaire des faits-divers* (11 April 1929) the former Belgian wrestler had twenty-two wives and fourteen children. He confessed that he just liked redheads—apparently lots of them. The article says that he moved to California, and he has lived in Hollywood for the last fifteen years.

6. Lassartesse greatly impressed Desbonnet with his physique. "He was superb! Besides, I have to admit that personally, I had been immediately conquered by the physique of this young man, and I surmised that he must have a remarkable resilience and agility." Lassartesse was not only a great wrestler but he had other talents. He "has since made a big reputation as a wrestler, somewhat neglecting weightlifting. The fact remains that Gabriel Lassartesse can be considered quite an exceptional athlete, of truly exceptional muscular quality, perhaps unique." Edmond Desbonnet, "La révélation de Lassartesse" *La Culture Physique* 7/127 (15 April 1910), 251–52.

7. Lassartesse was also an aggressive and implacable wrestler. In a newspaper report in *La Charente*, 15 May 1903, it was reported that during a match at the Casino de Paris, Lassartesse roughly grabbed his adversary, "but he dodged the attack by jumping off to the side by the footlights. Lassartesse. jumped on him in turn and tackled him so roughly that the man was thrown from the stage onto the orchestra. A musician was bruised, but the wrestler was unharmed."

8. Essebona was almost certainly from Dagestan or Ossetia, Muslim regions in the Caucasus that have long celebrated wrestling, physical prowess, and toughness. Perhaps this is because of the harsh life in the mountains, battles with nearby groups. Influence from Turkish wrestling might also have influenced the popularity of this sport. See "A Wrestling Culture that Helps Keep Boys Away from Fighting" https://www.nytimes.com/2018/03/18/world/europe/russia-dagestan-wrestling.html

9. The first mention of Sossiko Essebona in *La*

Culture Physique was in 1907, so presumably that can date the man's age. It appears that Essebona never came to Paris.

10. In the early days of his career, Dumont was both a strongman and a wrestler. His hometown newspaper, *Le Réveil du Havre*, 2 December 1893, reported that at a wrestling match against Ganzoin, Dumont won, but because he had tired himself out doing strongman stunts earlier in the day, he had a great deal of difficulty pulling off a win. One of those feats was the "Roman Torture" feat in which he restrained two horses who were pulling in opposite directions. The reporter made it clear that M. Ganzoin, on the other hand, had done no such thing and was fresh and rested.

11. In a front-page article in Desbonnet's first magazine *L'Athlète*, 16 May 1897, the author states that Dumont has a very well-presented act, "his equipment is pretty, his costumes are superb, and what's more, Dumont is marvelously proportioned, his legs are especially admirable."

12. In the years before the First World War, Dumont and his partner Émile Vylé, another experienced manager, toured France and abroad with a group of wrestlers. Vylé later wrote a series of articles about this time in *Le Miroir des sports*, "Trente ans de la vie d'un Speaker" 1 March 1933.

13. Max Lebaudy (1873–1895) was a wealthy playboy who was interested in horse racing, whoring, yachts, and cycling. He was a notorious young jackanapes, and he undoubtedly needed a burly bodyguard like Crest.

14. Hector Berlioz wrote his great, sprawling opera *Les Troyens* (The Trojans), of which *La Prise de Troie* was the first part, three decades previously. The Opera of Paris mounted the first part of his great epic of Aeneas and the Trojan War in November 1899, and it is this version that the wrestler Crest was involved. The scene with the wrestlers occurs in the second act. See www.hberlioz.com/champions/operas6914e.htm

15. This is a clever pun because the printer substituted the homonym "luth" (lute) with "lutte" (wrestling).

16. Desbonnet implies that there were other issues besides the climate that contributed to the early death of this wrestler (perhaps alcoholism). No one seems to have had a very high opinion of Alix the Negro. There is a brief reference to him in the magazine *Paris illustré*, 27 October 1888, 683, describing him as "slender, fairly knowledgeable, but not having enough stamina."

17. Zaremba competed in many tournaments and championships often under the stage name "Schwarze Toni" (Black Tony). He began his professional career in 1881, and in addition to more conventional lifts, he did many teeth lifts. At the height of his strength, Zaremba lifted a 625-pound stone with his teeth. He also won first prize in a finger-wrestling tournament. See *Illustrierte Atletik-Sportzeitung*, 23 July 1904, 467.

18. The *Tournoi de la ceinture d'or* was a wrestling tournament that was held at the Folies Bergère between 1902 and 1904.

19. Maisons-Laffitte is a prosperous suburb northwest of Paris famous for its nearby racetrack.

20. The *Société de la Croix Verte* was dedicated to helping people in medical emergencies. In World War I they devoted themselves to victims of gas attacks.

21. In the obituary for Raoul, "La Mort d'un Prodige" *La Culture Physique* 4/52 (1 March 1907), 120–21, Dr. J.-E. Ruffier noted that the young athlete had wasted his athletic gifts foolishly "on love, on alcohol, and on food." An urban legend states that Raoul hired some assassins to kill his old rival Poddubny, but instead they killed le Boucher and his death was covered up as meningitis. There is no truth to this version.

22. Pons made at least one telling comment about Yusuf in his book *La Lutte* (Paris: Lafitte, 1912), 19. He says that Yusuf was "probably the strongest man of any who have ever had a career in wrestling."

23. It is highly unlikely that the events occurred as they are recounted by Desbonnet's "friend and pupil." It has all the markings of a long, rambling and ultimately pointless shaggy dog story. Cannon was in India in 1891, and he wrestled Pierri on 9 December in Bombay/Mumbai. According to a newspaper report found by wrestling historian Phil Lions, "Cannon and Pierri had issued an open challenge for 1,000 Indian rupees, but no one took up the challenge to wrestle them. Cannon then said they were willing to even wrestle in the local Punjabi style (kushti), provided a rule about the shoulders being pinned to the ground was included (there was no such rule in the local style). No one accepted that challenge either, so Cannon and Pierri wrestled each other." WrestlingClassics.com Message Board: Results: India and Sri Lanka (1891–1892)

24. Czaia wrestled at the Folies Bergère, but he was badly defeated in every match. His most dramatic loss came when he grappled with the Serbian giant Antonitch. According to the report in *L'Auto-vélo* (13 December 1907), "After having received a few blows with his forearm on the back of the neck, Antonitch, knocked Czaia down with the back of his arm and grabbed him by the shoulder. Antonitch crushed him, he even crushed him so much that Czaia was partially suffocated and collapsed on his own and remained stretched out on the mat." Apparently, he was not seriously injured, but he had the wind knocked out of him. He fought the next evening with similarly dismal results.

25. Almost all contemporary reports say that Belling was born in Berlin, but others put his birthplace at Mecklenburg or even Austria. *The Boxing World and Mirror of Life* of London (25 May 1895) described Belling as "a handsome and well-built Teuton" who is "a man of gigantic proportions and built from the ground upwards on the most approved pattern."

26. Belling took some of his wrestling profits

and opened a pub in London. He later ran afoul of the law, and a warrant was issued for his arrest for keeping a gaming house. See *Police Gazette* (London), 28 January 1898.

27. Reiber wrestled in the 1908 tournament at the Casino de Paris, but he did not do very well. See *Sporting Life*, London, 20 November 1908.

28. According to an article in *Münchner Neueste Nachrichten*, 3 November 1907, Hitzler was born in Oberbechingen (Bavaria) 1 August 1870. In 1899 he endured the marathon match with Gambier that Desbonnet mentions. The match lasted ten hours and forty-four minutes, and it ended with Gambier's defeat.

29. According to Fioravanti, in" La Lutte à Paris" in *La Vie au Grand Air*, 6 December 1902, 826, the "unforeseen obstacle" that Desbonnet mentions is that Koch fell ill and could not compete. He further describes Koch as "the perfect type of German athlete: big, corpulent (but not excessively) and very well-muscled."

30. Bahn may have been born in Germany, but he was always referred to as "German American" when he wrestled in the Fatherland. His nickname "Samson" is also used. See *Münchner Neueste Nachrichten* 3 June 1927. According to E.G. Drigny in "Encore une tentative de rénovation de la lutte Gréco-romaine professionnelle" *Le Miroir des sports*, 10 December 1929, 446, by the late 1920s Bahn was wrestling in France where he had become an "impopulaire" or bad guy whom audiences loved to hate.

31. The biography of Karl Abs (1851–1895), the great *Plattdeutsche Eiche* (Low-German Oak) is told in *Kings of Strength*, 202.

32. Emile Vervet continued to wrestle until the late 1920s, and when the writer Jean Delorme saw him in a fairground wrestling booth in 1926, the old athlete was rather pathetic since he had lost his former impressive physique as well as his hair and mustache; worst of all, he had lost his former cocky attitude. It made the writer sad to see Vervet in that condition. "He is one of the last representatives of a dying sport—or rather of a dying business." "Grandeur et decadence de la lutte" in *Le Plaisir de vivre*, 8 July 1926, 15–16.

33. Magnus Bech-Olsen (1866–1932) wrestled throughout Europe and in the United States, and everywhere he drew huge crowds. His most notable matches in the U.S. were a win over Ernest Roeber at Madison Square Garden in New York (21 March 1900) and a loss to Frank Gotch at Convention Hall in Kansas City, Missouri (15 June 1905). From the mid–1890s to around 1905 he was one of the most popular wrestlers in the world, but he is given only two sentences in this book; worse still, in the original text Desbonnet misspells his name as "Beck-Olsen."

34. In addition to having a beautiful physique, Schneider was a competent wrestler who traveled all over Europe and Russia. In 1909 he or his handlers got the idea of reusing the old "masked wrestler" trick from the early days of French wrestling, and this created a sensation. It was reported that Schneider was responsible for twenty-one sold-out shows in a row. Others were quick to jump on the masked bandwagon, and there were similar fighters almost everywhere before it all died down. See WrestlingClassics.com Message Board: The Russian giants of the early 20th century

35. Anderson's true love seems to have been weight lifting, but there was little money in that activity, so he switched to the much more remunerative field of grappling. After his wrestling career was over, Anderson returned to Sweden where he opened a restaurant. See *Starke Arvids minnen* [Memoirs of Arvid the Strong] (Stockholm: Bonnier, 1924).

36. Georg Strenge (1875–1953) born in Prenzlau, Germany.

37. Josef Šmejkal was actually born on 1 March 1879 in Prague's Vinohrady District, but his family soon moved to nearby Nusle. Like most wrestlers in the years before World War I, he traveled around from one tournament to another. In 1912 he fought Frank Gotch, but he not only lost the match, but his manager ran off with his two-thousand dollar fee. Šmejkal's other great opponent was fellow Czech athlete Gustav Frištenský whom he fought four times between 1904 and 1923; in 1913 their match was filmed, and it provides a rare record of both men. Šmejkal died on 8 April 1942. Unfortunately, the wrestler's prime came a bit later than Desbonnet's time, so he does not get the attention that he deserved. See the excellent biography at https://vysehradskej.cz/big-joe-z-nusli/

38. According to modern sources, Nikola Petroff (or Petrov) was born in Goma Oryahovitsa, Bulgaria, in 1873 and died in 1925. Throughout his career Petrov entered around 150 tournaments and won 17 of them. See Josef Švub, Retrospektiva Wrestlingu: Nikola Petrov https://www.musclefitness.cz/retrospektiva-wrestlingu-nikola-petrov/ Petroff also features prominently in the story of bringing the first Turks to France in the mid-1890s. See the excerpt from Pons *La Lutte* in the appendix.

39. Unlike Hackenschmidt, Raicevich was never a paragon of male beauty (at least not as he matured). He became obese in later life and wrestling trunks were never the right sartorial choice for someone with his body type. Journalist Geminello Alvi described him after a wrestling competition in Milan. Raicevich "proudly displayed his bare and pinkish chest measuring 128 centimeters, which seemed even more immense because of his short arms, his low buttocks and his shins adorned below the knee by sock garters.... His shaved head made him look like a convict, and it also worsened the brevity of his forehead which was already too short. Yet his meek eyes betrayed that inclination to worry and to be upset which boxers and wrestlers easily suffer from." "Il piccolo gigante e il lottatore nero:Giovanni Raicevich, l'uomo più forte del mondo," *La Repubblica*, 11 December 1906. In spite of his appearance, he was extremely popular

with the public, and his success as a movie star and matinee idol speak to his charisma and energy. See John D. Fair and David L Chapman, *Muscles in the Movies* (Columbia: University of Missouri, 2020), 155–60.

40. Although Giovanni was the star of the family, there were two other very powerful brothers, Massimo (1878–1915) and Emilio Ruggiero (1873–1924) who was also an uncommonly powerful wrestler. Massimo was killed fighting the Austrians in World War I and Emilio Ruggiero died of "pernicious phlebitis" after being injured in a wrestling match in Buenos Aires. Dino Cafagna, *L'uomo più forte del mondo: La Leggenda di Giovanni Raicevich da Trieste* (Trieste: Luglio, 2015), 138–39.

41. La Calmette is a small town in southern France near Nimes.

42. Some reporters would agree with Aimable's self-assessment. The *Vichy-journal* (10 August 1902) described him as "a wonderful wrestler having suppleness and agility, who does not seem to use his strength and slithers like an eel out of the hands of his powerful adversaries."

43. Aimable uses the expression "Pigne, pange et pougne!" meaning "I'll take them on one, two, three!"

44. *Le Populaire*, the newspaper of the French Socialist party (25 June 1919), described Aimable de la Calmette Jr., and his participation in the world championships of Greco-Roman wrestling as one of a number of promising new wrestlers who are "men who make us not want to miss the fiery fights in the finals."

45. A biographical article in the *Internationale illustrirte Athleten-Zeitung* (14 February 1897) gives some additional details on his life and travels. Charles Fengler emigrated to America in 1885. In 1891 he began wrestling and soon became an amateur champion. In 1892 Fengler got to know the famous wrestlers and teachers Ernst Roeber and William Muldoon, who trained him and engaged him with their troupe. In 1895 he left for Australia where he had great success. He returned to Germany and worked as a professional wrestler in the Rigoletto Troupe, a music-hall group, but he stated that he would go back to America as soon as his obligations were finished. In England he was advertised as "Fengler of New York" and he had a well-publicized match with Nikola Petroff at Sandow's School in St. Jameses Street. See *Mid Cumberland & North Westmorland Herald*, 11 December 1897 in which Fengler was defeated. As late as 1901, Fengler is still being described in the *Münchner Neueste Nachrichten* (1 March 1901) as the "Australian Champion."

46. The Zaporozhian Cossacks were a social and political group of people who inhabited central and eastern Ukraine. They were once a semi-nomadic group of freebooters but were folded into the Russian army in the late eighteenth century.

47. Judging the outcome of a wrestling match by points was an evolving process that was not settled until the first decades of the twentieth century. There are references to a vague point system to score these matches, but the only way to win in many early fights was for the wrestler to pin his opponent. Some prestigious matches featured a jury or a panel of judges who would make the final call in difficult or controversial decisions. The members of this body conferred with one another privately and did not have to justify their verdicts to the public. With the rise of Olympic wrestling, a more scientific method of scoring was required, and the points system was more or less settled by the rule-loving British at the 1908 London Olympic Games. See Martin Polley, *The British Olympics: Britain's Olympic heritage 1612–2012* (English Heritage, 2011), 110–11.

48. Ivan Maximovich Poddubny was born in Krasenivka (Zolotonosha county), a village in central Ukraine, in 1871. He died in the southern Russian town of Yeysk in 1949.

49. The French public got a good view of Antonitch at the 1903 Gold Belt Championship, and his gigantic stature immediately caught the attention of his audience. The reporter from *Le Radical de l'Allier* (15 March 1903) remarked that his extraordinary height makes Antonitch "look slender, and since he is only twenty-two years old his physique has not yet developed its full musculature. In two or three years, he will be a formidable example of the human race."

50. Antonitch was born in 1881 in Caribrod, a town in southeastern Serbia near the Bulgarian border. According to German historian Karl Jänecke, Antonitch's physique was not at all grotesque. "Despite his huge height, all parts of his body are in good proportions. He is perfectly healthy and meets all the conditions for a heavyweight wrestler. Owing to his tremendous strength, it was almost impossible to resist his head locks or the half- and full-nelson." Another historian, Adolph von Guretzki added that "Due to his phlegmatic nature and kind-heartedness typical of extremely strong people, he lost a number of high rankings in tournaments." Josef Švub, "Retrospektiva wrestlingu: SIMON ANTONIĆ" https://www.muscle-fitness.cz/retrospektiva-wrestlingu-simon-antonic/ It is not known when he died, but his last known appearance in the wrestling ring was in 1937 when he appeared at the Elysée-Montmartre Theater. "Since the Serb Antonitch last wrestled in Paris, wrestling fans have not had the opportunity to see the giant on the mat again." (*L'auto-vélo*, 23 May 1937). The Serbian grappler was almost 60 years old at this point, and I can find no later references to him in French papers.

51. Although he had an impressive physique, Kuschke's career was not as stellar as Desbonnet predicted. He wrestled around 1905–07.

52. Bordeaux loved its native son. Gambier's real name was Jean Dumec, and he was born in 1866. Even in the depths of the World War II his fellow citizens held a gala wrestling

tournament at the Alhambra Theater to help out the seventy-eight-year-old grappler. See *L'Athlète*, 6 November 1944.

53. Gambier was always a crowd favorite as proved by the reaction of the crowd in 1901 when he defeated Cotch Mehmet. The reporter for *L'Opinion des Charentes* newspaper (30 November 1901) reported that "It was a moment of delirium and everyone jumped up; women threw flowers, men threw hats, gloves, canes, newspapers into the air, anything that came to hand. Gambier had to return five times to acknowledge the applause."

54. The tournament in Brussels is generally considered to be the first major international competition of Greco-Roman wrestling ever.

55. There is an interesting and amusing anecdote that Desbonnet published later. It illustrates the problems that wrestling impresarios had to deal with. Here it is in its entirety.

Ch. Denis, "Peyrouse, the impresario loses his calling and attempts to commit suicide" *La Cutlure Physique* 15 March 1912 (9/172) 22–23.

A few years ago, Léon Dumont was passing through Lyon in the company of a troupe of wrestlers that he was touring with in the South of France. He thought it would be useful to refurbish the wardrobe of some of his companions. Among these was the famous Peyrouse, "the Lion of Valence," who was the first to benefit from the director's generosity.

Peyrouse was therefore taken to an honest local tailor who in a short time had made him a superb velvet suit in the finest taste. Then when the troupe was all assembled, Dumont decided to leave for St. Etienne where he had arranged for a series of shows. The group was to meet at the station, but just as they were to leave, they realized that "the Lion of Valence" did not answer the roll-call. Dumont grumbled somewhat, but he made the best of a bad situation, thinking that the tour of St. Etienne would compensate him for the price of the suit. And they left without otherwise worrying about Peyrouse.

In the meantime, the missing wrestler had quietly remained in Lyon, where he just happened to have encountered a local man. Enticed by the profits that Dumont was making, Peyrouse told himself that, after all, there was something good in the trade and it wouldn't be unpleasant to try it. He decided then and there to become an impresario; unfortunately, he lacked two essential things: a troupe and money. Peyrouse thus confided his plans to his associate as he dangled all the benefits that could be derived from such an affair, and the other, who was a skillful shoemaker but quite ignorant in matters of wrestling. He asked nothing better to form an association immediately, to which he contributed 150 francs; Peyrouse would contribute "his knowledge" of the trade, and as for a troupe, they would deal with that later.

Provided with this sum, Peyrouse decided to give his first session in a small community not far from Lyon. Shouldn't you first save on travel costs? Advertisements, no matter how well-crafted, brought in only about forty people when the wrestling began. Peyrouse had solicited two amateurs from the country, to whom he had generously distributed a five-franc coin to serve as "amateurs," but just the two were really not enough, and the cobbler was worried about it. The improvised impresario replied that there was nothing to be concerned about and that it was enough for the two of them to wrestle vigorously in order to fill out the program. The brave shoemaker certainly did not expect such a proposal since he knew nothing about this kind of sport. Nevertheless, on the assurances of Peyrousse who promised not to hurt him, he was forced to accept the plan.

And after the usual spiel introducing the "local man" as a fearsome athlete despite his relatively puny appearance, the wrestler and the cobbler marched into the arena and prepared to fight. Unfortunately, Peyrouse came on too strong and was quite rough, and in the heat of the moment he forgot the promises he had made to his partner. After a somewhat violent reverse waist hold, the apprentice wrestler was brutally slammed down on his shoulders so violently that he had to be carried home with great care.

Sometime later, Dumont once again passed through Lyon and inquired about his faithless companion; after multiple searches, he went to the famous shoemaker, the only one likely to inform him about his impresario for a day. He found him in his bed still suffering from his injuries and grumbling in welcome. "Ah, that rogue of yours! Can you believe that after borrowing 150 francs from me, fracturing two ribs, breaking three teeth, and taking off an ear, he still found a way to run off with my wife?"

Following this escapade, Peyrouse on the other hand, led a rather joyous but short-lived existence, and when he met up again with his ex-boss, Léon Dumont, the employer quickly forgot his grievances, and hastened to return the "Lion of Valence" back to his troupe. This suited Peyrouse just fine because his funds were very low.

An evening was specifically booked for Orleans. The travel arrangements had been made in Paris, and at the appointed hour everyone showed up—with the exception of Peyrouse of course. Dumont feared that the wrestler had flown the coop once again, and because he still cared about him, he sent someone in search of him. One of Peyrouse's friends was delegated. He did not find Peyrouse either at home or at the Pons Gymnasium; he then went to a restaurant located in the vicinity of La Cigale which Peyrouse sometimes frequented. At the door, as he was entering the establishment, he was blocked by a crowd of curious people noisily discussing the case of a customer who had attempted suicide.

All the same, the wrestler's friend went in, and his surprise was great when he saw Peyrouse, miserably slumped in a chair, his enormous head between his hands, lamenting his missed opportunity. By this time, he was drunk and no longer knew exactly what he was doing. Peyrouse had decided that the best thing to do was to take a revolver out of his pocket and coolly do himself in by aiming at his image in the mirror. This shattered, to the great displeasure of the restaurant owner who simply could not understand anyone who was disgusted with life, because he no longer had a wife or a shoemaker left to exploit and (under the pretext of ending his life) would take out his frustration on someone else's furniture.

And it was only after paying for the damage, that the friend of the "Lion of Valence" was able to convince him that life was worth living again. Afterward, the two left town, this time by the first train to Orléans where his friends, who had already arrived, reveled in the story of the failed "suicide."

56. Count Georgy Ivanovich Ribeaupierre (1854–1934) was a Russian sportsman who encouraged his countrymen to compete on the international stage. He later became a member of the International Olympic Committee.

57. According to an article in *La Joie de la maison* (19 January 1898), Pytlazinski "was trained as an electrician, and he practiced this profession in Paris at the time of the last World's Fair. He trains by wrestling, running, and by working out with three-pound dumbbells. He abstains completely from alcohol, does not smoke and drinks lots of milk."

58. Jess Ingeman Petersen was born in the Danish town of Odder (near Aarhus on Jutland), but he spent most of his life in France where he married a French woman and became a naturalized French citizen. Fortunately, his wife gave him both stability and a level financial head, so he did not end up in misery and poverty when his wrestling career was over. But even a good woman was not enough to shield him from all of life's vicissitudes.

He bought a pretty villa in the northern French town of St. Quentin, but it turned out to be right in the path of the advancing German troops in World War I and was totally destroyed. Consequently, Petersen and his wife were reduced to near penury. By the early 1920s he was desperate, and he appealed to both the French and Danish governments for compensation. One of his appeals was printed in the Danish newspaper the *Roskilde Dagblad*, 18 August 1922. "All my trophies, belts, medals, etc., are gone. These represented the pride of my youth from a time when I was an undefeated Danish athlete for twenty years. Of course, I can live without these things, but I cannot build a house again and create a home for myself unless I get a helping hand from home." Petersen made similar appeals in the French press, and it is not known if he was successful or not, but by 1923 he was forced out of retirement and back into the wrestling ring when he appeared in "a series of professional wrestling matches" in Denmark (*Midt-Jyllands Folketidene*, Silkeborg, 20 July 1923).

According to his obituary in the Paris newspaper *Le Franc-tireur*, 30 October 1946, he had become "holder of the French Navy rescue medal and public education officer. He was also a horse racing judge." Jess Petersen clearly had a long and adventurous (though not always pleasant) life.

59. It would appear that Sturm's greatest claim to popularity was his appearance. Munich's: *Allgemeine Zeitung*, of 10 April 1906 reported on a wrestling match in that city, but the journalist was soon distracted by the fighter's physical appeal. "Albert Sturm, nicknamed *der schöne Mensch* (the beautiful man), whose nude studies hang not only in every art shop but also in almost every artist's studio, is known to have an almost ideally beautiful physique and such pronounced muscle groups as are seldom found in any other athlete." The sporting paper *L'Auto-vélo* (6 December 1903) similarly described him at the Gold Belt Tournament as "that handsome German athlete who has caused everyone to admire him."

60. Before Sturm arrived in Paris, he went to England to try his luck there. *Sporting Life* (9 December 1902) reported that the young wrestler fought at the Royal Music Hall, Holborn. "The international troupe received an acquisition in the form of Albert Sturm, an athlete who was stated to have wrestled a draw with Hackenschmidt. The German's showing last evening stamped him as a clever as well as powerful wrestler, and being but twenty years of age, should render a good account of himself in his future engagements." The claim that he fought to a draw with Hackenschmidt is highly unlikely. In a later match with Hackenschmidt in Glasgow as reported in the *Daily Record*, 22 July 1905, Sturm showed "skill and alacrity," but in the end he was pretty effectively trounced by the great Estonian athlete.

61. Sturm survived the First World War and he resumed his wrestling career into the 1920s. *AZ am Morgen Allgemeine Zeitung* (1 January 1926) reports that he was appearing with a group of wrestlers at Munich's Circus Krone. He also survived the Second World War, but I have found no information about where he was living at the time of his death on Christmas Eve 1946.

62. Ibrahim Mahmut (1862–1917) was nicknamed *Hergeleci*, "trainer of unbroken horses," and he was an accomplished oil wrestler. He was judged overall Turkish champion in 1914.

63. Turkish wrestling has a long history, and Desbonnet seems to be right: there are very few rules, and fouls are rare. See Johnathan Seeley, "Now the Main Event: Greased Wrestling," *New York Times* (7 May 1972). https://www.nytimes.com/1972/05/07/archives/now-the-main-event-greased-wrestling.htm There was no mention of oiling the men's bodies, so perhaps this part of the tradition was foregone.

64. Journalist and impresario Léon Sée wrote a much fuller account of this violent wrestling match for *La Culture Physique* (15 October 1907), 585–56. Yusuf was described as "heavier, more massive, an incarnation of irresistible strength." Ibrahim

Mahmut was "muscled as Orientals rarely are, as large as his adversary and a hundred times more agile than he." Toward the end, the hour-long fight became very brutal and bloody, but both men had agreed to fight in the Turkish style, so it was allowed to continue. "All blows were authorized," until finally, "with one hand [Yusuf] gave his adversary an excruciating twist that I cannot describe, while with the other he literally tore Ibrahim's nostrils out. The latter, his face bleeding, and despite suffering that would have made a bull collapse, still resisted." But the French public and the panel of judges had had enough of this savagery. Tom Cannon tried to separate the men using his hands, but when this was unsuccessful, he started beating the men with a cane. The audience then rushed the stage and were intent on lynching Yusuf, but a company of policemen then arrived and grabbed the Turk (it took three men on each side of him to keep him in control) and marched the men off to the station followed by an angry crowd who chanted "Kill him!" at Yusuf. When the police chief had heard what happened, he asked Ibrahim Mahmut if he wanted to lodge a complaint. To which he replied, "Me? Never. We were just wrestling." He then added, "In Turkey, when men wrestle, women weep." The two men never completed their interrupted match, but Léon Sée remarked that it seemed that Yusuf had proven himself the stronger of the two. The match also showed that Western audiences were not ready for the violence and bloodshed that was apparently commonplace among the Turks.

65. Despite the racist and offensive statement, Mourzouk was famous and formidable enough for someone to impersonate him in the wrestling championship in Copenhagen (1903). The negro wrestler sent a letter to *Le Monde sportif* (15 January 1904) saying that someone used his name in the tournament. At the time of the contest in Denmark, Mourzouk was in Tunisia visiting his family.

66. L. Manaud in *L'Auto-vélo* (25 November 1901) said that he was looking forward to seeing Weber in action. Unfortunately, it was not a good performance for the German in his bout with Vervet. By the second round it was obvious that Weber was tired and eventually he took the defensive move of lying on the floor. "There he stayed as a prudent defense; he flattened himself out like a flounder." Eventually, he was pinned by his French rival.

67. Heinrich Weber was raised in Mülheim am Rhein, now a suburb of Cologne. As a teenager he was inspired by seeing Karl Abs wrestle, and began wrestling at a local athletic club. As an amateur, Heinrich Weber became German champion in Duisburg in 1899. Weber turned professional in 1900, and he participated in many tournaments for over twenty years. In 1903 he became the world's lightweight champion and in 1909 he was judged second in the heavyweight division behind the famous Russian wrestler Ivan Poddubny. He also worked as a coach, and one of his most famous students was Stanislaus Zbyszko. After the end of his wrestling career, Heinrich Weber acted as an organizer of professional wrestling tournaments, but died completely impoverished in Berlin in 1958. See https://de.wikipedia.org/wiki/Heinrich_Weber_(Ringer,_1875) and Adolf. von Guretzki, *Der moderne Ringkampf* (Leipzig: F. W. Gloeckner & Co.,1922), 119–21.

68. Ali Nurullah Hassan was born in either 1867 or 1870 and died in Constantinople in 1912. Desbonnet uses an alternate version of his name, "Nourlah," and he is better known in English-speaking countries as Ali Hassan but he is the same person.

69. The Turks must have realized that their style of wrestling was shocking to French audiences, and when Nurullah wrestled against Kara Ahmed, they had made several concessions. First, they would wrestle to a decision, second the Turks would not douse themselves with oil, and third they would wear French wrestling trunks. The wrestlers must have also decided to tone down the violence: "Although the fight was entirely freestyle, we did not have to regret any brutality on the part of one or the other of the antagonists." In this match, Nurullah defeated his opponent. *Le Sport picard* (17 February 1900).

70. Kara Osman was born in the city of Filibe (now Plovdiv, Bulgaria) in the Ottoman Empire. His name in Turkish was Filibeli Kara Osman after his birthplace. After touring in Europe, Osman came to the United States where he wrestled various comers, most notably in 1911, Frank Gotch (who won). In 1900 Kara Osman was set to wrestle the great boxer Jim Corbett, and one Wisconsin newspaper (probably quoting some news release) reported that the Turk measured over eight feet tall and "it is claimed is more powerful than the average strongman." *Watertown Republican* newspaper, 6 March 1900.

71. Winzer competed in a few wrestling tournaments, most notably in Dusseldorf in 1910, but he was eliminated in the first round.

72. Edouard Pontié was a sports journalist and writer who was the editor of various magazines, most prominently *La Vie sportive illustrée*. It would seem that his *History of Wrestling* was a series of articles in one of his magazines rather than a book.

73. The phrase "Seeing Negroes in the Night" probably refers to a work of art, *Combat de nègres pendant la nuit* [The fight of Negroes in the Night] by writer Paul Bilhaud from 1882 at the Exhibition of Incoherent Art. The work was intended to be an ironic statement since it consisted of a framed canvas that was painted totally black. See https://www.switchonpaper.com/portrait/artiste/redecouverte-des-arts-incoherents-quand-la-legende-devient-realite/

74. A massive eruption of *Mount Pelée* on May 8th, 1902, was responsible for the deaths of more than 29,000 people and considerable property destruction.

75. Negro-Roman wrestling is a racist version of

Greco-Roman wrestling implying that Anglio was not a worthy or educated opponent. It also mocks the generosity of deluded do-gooders. Pontié's entire article reeks of racism.

76. Anglio had a very successful wrestling career, and an article in *La Culture Physique* (15 December 1913) 10/215, 28, gives a few more biographical details. By this time Anglio had married an equally tall French woman who "despite the massive proportions of her lord and master, she completely measures up to him." Anglio made a big impression when he was out and about and was always treated with respect. Often crowds of boys would follow in his path and shout out "Johnson! Johnson," mistaking the massive West Indian for the famous American boxer.

77. This chapter is excerpted from an article in *La Culture Physique*, 1 October 1906 (3/42), 707–09, and it was lifted almost word-for-word from an article by Frantz Reichel in *Le Sport universel illustré* "Un Match à Sensation" (7 July 1900), 510. Another article on the great Indian wrestler appeared earlier in the issue of 15 August 1906 by Dr. Calixte Pagès (1857–1934). This one analyzed the historical, practical, and environmental reason for Gulam's massive size and great strength.

78. In 1900 there was a large and elaborate World's Fair in Paris, and since the date also coincided with the second Olympiad of the modern era, it was hoped that the Games could be held at this time. Unfortunately, the Games suffered from poor organization and abysmal marketing, and this caused many events to be cancelled or conducted over an extended period of five months in venues that often were inadequate. The wrestling championships never took place, but even if they had, it is unclear if Gulam would have been permitted to participate since he was a professional. See André Drevon, *Les Jeux olympiques oubliés, Paris 1900* (Paris: CNRS, 2000). There was a wrestling tournament in December of 1900 held at the Casino de Paris under the auspices of the sporting magazine *L'Auto-vélo* but Gulam did not participate in it.

79. In 1890, de Chambure had begun a press-clipping service, *L'Argus de la presse*, and it had become a great success. See Auguste de Chambure, *A travers la presse* (Th. Fert, Albouy, 1914).

80. The pehlwani (Indian wrestling) exercises have since been well documented, but this was apparently the first time that Desbonnet had learned of the specific workout routine. Lunges, dunds (Indian pushups) and light weightlifting produced a very strong physique. There is no mention of doing bethak (squats), so perhaps Desbonnet was not getting the entire picture nor is there any mention of club swinging, stone lifting or any other exercises that would have required special equipment. Even so, Gulam seems to have adapted to life in the West pretty well.

81. *Rustam-e-Hind* is usually translated "Champion of India." *Rustam* is derived from the name of a Hercules-like character in a Persian epic poem.

82. The kikkar tree is the acacia.

83. Pehelvan Kikkar Singh Sandhu (1857–1914) was indeed a famous wrestler, but he was not a broken-down wreck after his loss to Gulam. Kikkar Singh fought many other matches, and his last one was at the great Delhi Durbar held in 1911 to celebrate the coronation of King George V. Due to his advanced age, he lost that match. See https://www.thesikhencyclopedia.com/biographical/hindu-bhagats-and-poets-and-punjabi-officials/kikkar-singh-pahilvan/

84. Shri Sir Nripendra Narayan, Maharaja of Cooch Behar (1862–1911), was a handsome and popular man who spent a good deal of time in Europe. See https://henrypoole.com/individual/maharaja-cooch-behar/

85. The Ghurkas live primarily in Nepal and Northeast India. As soldiers they are known for their toughness, courage, and loyalty.

86. Sialkot is located in Pakistani Punjab. The wrestlers of this region are certainly not as wild and savage as Desbonnet makes them out to be—even in the early years of the twentieth century. They just were not European.

87. There was incredible press coverage leading up to the match; consequently, many sportsmen had put money on the fight. The "interests" that were not happy with the outcome included many wealthy, powerful people who had bet on the match and were not satisfied with anything less than an outright pin by one of the contestants. The wealthy Maharajah of Cooch-Behar might have wagered thousands, although his position as head of the panel of judges might have made this unlikely. Other rich sportsmen were willing to put up wagers. We know of one prominent man who bet on the outcome—the visiting Shah of Iran. Although it might have been meant in jest, the article by V'H Sanlait in *Le Littoral sportif* (18 August 1900) tells of an interview in which the Shah (speaking a few days before the match) asks how one could fail to trust a man like Gulam who eats so many chickens and rabbits, and he hints that he could not resist putting money on the match. "From Roubaix to the Great Ferris Wheel in Paris to Vienna, from all the corners of France, the thousand-franc notes have shown up. It is wonderful. It is the touchstone of success."

88. Accounts of the match written for Indian consumption were naturally more disposed to ascribe an unconditional victory to Gulam. The Anglo-Indian publication *India* (26 October 1900, 207) announced that Gulam had won the match outright. The results were even more surprising because the Punjabi fighter had "displaced his shoulder bone during the contest … and this makes his victory remarkable indeed."

89. Stanisław Julian Ignacy Ostroróg (also known as *Walery*) 1863–1929 was a Polish photographer active in Paris. He specialized in society and theatrical portraits.

90. Desbonnet might have been convinced of Gulam's superiority, but newspaper accounts told a different story. One of the most thorough

reports was in the English-language *New York Herald* (Paris) 13 August 1900. They told of thousands of infuriated fans who nearly started a riot because they believed that "the champions were not in earnest." Early on, Gulam managed to throw his adversary, Kurtdereli but that was all. He could not manage to turn over such a mass of muscle as the Turk and touch his shoulder blades to the ground. After the referee made the men get on their feet and start again, neither man was able to gain the upper hand. It was "a fruitless effort," that caused little more than heavy breathing and copious sweating. "A stony, purposeless lull" was the result with neither man making much attempt to grapple effectively. That is when the public began to lose patience. "There was hissing and hooting and loud cries to have their money back." Then they started throwing things: "pennies, crumpled paper, sticks and even a portion of the balustrade." The audience was in an ugly mood, and after fifteen equally inconclusive minutes, the match was stopped and the win was reluctantly awarded to the Indian who won four points to one over the Turk. It was, almost everyone agreed, a very unsatisfactory wrestling match.

The reporter from *Le Journal* of Paris (13 August 1900) was as disgusted as everyone else. "It is my opinion that there have been enough of these exhibitions that are wrestling matches in name only. We have to put an end to them or else the public, the good paying public, will end up getting angry. For a few months we have been shown only phony matches and parades. Only real sporting encounters can repair the harm done to wrestling by such useless spectacles."

The suspicion that the wrestling match had somehow been fixed makes no sense. If that were the case, there would have been a clear-cut winner. There can be little doubt that the men were fighting "on the level," but they were so equally matched in skill and/or strength that it proved to be extremely disappointing for the audience. It appears that Gulam simply did not have adequate experience in Greco-Roman wrestling to overcome (or overturn) the stubborn Turk. This discouraging turn of events probably affected Gulam's decision to return to his homeland. Unfortunately, he died there of cholera just one year after his trip to Europe.

91. Schmelling turned professional in 1908 so that he could participate in the tournament. He appears to have been well-educated and well-read, so he was perhaps independently wealthy. Schmelling spoke "only slightly hesitant French" as well as fluent German and English. He said that he was well read in French literature; Balzac, Daudet, Zola were all favorites. Since most wrestlers were poorly educated working-class men, Schmelling stood out all the more. He was asked what had drawn him to wrestling. He replied, "My natural strength. With no training, I cleaned and jerked a 240-pound barbell with two hands. While visiting the Athletic Society of St. Petersburg, I became friendly with Eugène de Paris [Poddubny's trainer], and this remarkable professor initiated me into the arcana of the fine sport of wrestling." Edmond Desbonnet, "La Lutte au Casino de Paris," *La Culture Physique* (1 December 1908) 5/94, 1531.

92. Schmelling seemed to be afflicted with illness at convenient times in his amateur wrestling career, and this might have reflected an egotism that others hinted at. Léon Sée wrote that in the match with Poddubny in which he was defeated, Schmelling "suffered psychologically much more than physically. He was painfully wounded in his pride and recognizing, moreover, that he had found someone better than he, Schmelling swore never to fight again. He kept his word." Léon Sée and Edmond Desbonnet, "Une Bourre fameuse," *La Culture Physique* 1 September 1910 (7/136), 547–549.

93. Cartanji participated in the tournament at the Folies Bergère in January 1899.

94. Tom Cannon (1852–?) was one of Britain's finest wrestlers, but he was no match for Sabès who fought him in 1892. After only twelve minutes, the Frenchman grabbed Cannon in a rear waistlock and brought him down. According to *Le Sud-Ouest* newspaper of Bordeaux (22 April 1892), "A few protests from the Anglo-American contingent were made, but the majority of the audience endorsed the judgment of the panel of judges."

95. According to one version of the story, it was Sabès who unwittingly began the "Turkish invasion" of wrestling in 1894. See the section on Yusuf for more information.

96. There were quite a few of these novelty races organized in France between 1893 and 1905.

97. Two well-known cyclists mostly active in the final years of the nineteenth century.

98. Chappe appears to have wrestled principally in the 1890s.

99. The wrestler's name is often written as "Court-Derelli," but his original name is Kurtdereli Mehmet. According to historian Phil Lions, the man's name actually refers to a place, and it can be translated as "Mehmet from the village of Kurtderi."

100. Balikesir is in a mountainous inland region of Turkish Asia Minor.

101. Some sources say that his birthdate is 1864. He was born in the Ludogorie area in what is today Bulgaria, and he died in 1939 near Balikesir, Turkey.

102. Daumas, "Pique-Planque," was an odd looking individual; he was massive in size and weight with broad shoulders, but his most unusual feature was that one of his eyes was missing. He was often nicknamed "Cyclops." See "La Lutte et les lutteurs" *L'Illustration* (18 February 1899), 107.

103. Doublier's first name is variously given as Jean or Joseph; it seems that it was actually Jean-Claude. According to many sources (see section on Yusuf), Doublier was encouraged to bring the Turks that he found wrestling in the Sublime Porte back to France in order to secure revenge on

Sabès, the vainglorious wrestler who several years earlier had given Doublier a sound drubbing in the arena. The truth seems to be much more complicated. According to Paul Pons in his book *La Lutte* (Paris: Pierre Lafitte, 1912), 316–22, Doublier was convinced that the powerful Turks would create a sensation in France. There is no mention of Sabès in this account, so it throws the whole story into doubt. See the account from the Pons book in the appendix.

104. Doublier had promoted Greco-Roman wrestling in Turkey for at least a decade before bringing his protégés to France. The French-language newspaper *Stamboul* (20 October 1883) mentions that "A large crowd of people exclusively of the stronger sex" attended a wrestling exhibition at the Verdi Theater in Constantinople. Several of his Turkish pupils as well as the man himself put on a stirring performance.

105. Munich-born Sauerer was trained by another well-known German grappler, Michael Hitzler. In 1901 the *Münchner neueste Nachrichten* (7 March 1901) reported that Saurerer fought another of Hitzler's pupils, Achner, and it was clear that the men wrestled with knowledge, sportsmanship, and skill. "All the holds and positions that a wrestling match can have were demonstrated by the two fighters. These showed that they were worthy students of their master Hitzler. Sauerer won over Achner in thirty-six minutes and thirty-nine seconds by means of a double nelson and the subsequent use of the bridge. It was a fine hard-won victory and an honorable defeat."

106. His nickname in French is *le Terrassier* which means both "road worker" or "navvy," and also "he who brings things down to earth," so it is an appropriate name for a wrestler.

107. François was not above less respectable fights. The newspaper *XIXe Siècle* (16 December 1905) reported that the former flour merchant would wrestle "Delphin the Dwarf" in a "sensational match." Delphin must have been a feisty fellow, for he made sure the newspaper knew that he was also issuing a challenge to all jiu-jitsu amateurs (the Japanese style of fighting was very fashionable at that time), and he claimed that he could drop the men within the space of only a few seconds.

108. According to the obituary in the *Illustrierte Athletik-Sportzeitung* (7 June 1902), 357, it was probably stress that killed the great man. After his initial tour of Europe, "the Turkish Bear" returned with a French wife and a great deal of money. He decided to take his winnings and run a small café in Constantinople. "In doing so, Kara may have become too prone to a stroke. It is not known whether he left the café because of bad business or for the love of his wrestling profession; he loved it enough so that he returned to France earlier this year, where he was sufficiently victorious in several competitions so that he was immediately offered numerous advantageous engagements." The page-long article concludes that Kara Ahmed "was a good man with a truly good heart, whom his colleagues were without exception fond of, and whom those who knew him will surely cherish in fond memory."

109. Kara Ahmed's contract for the world championship states that he was to be awarded the modest sum of twenty-five francs a day for the two months of the wrestling contest. He was also to be paid for his travel expenses for a trip from Constantinople to Paris, but this was for second-class accommodations. The contract is dated 7 November 1899, and the document is in the collection of Christian Gaildraud, Limoges, France.

110. Kara Ahmed won the world championship in 1899 when he defeated Laurent le Beaucairois, but he returned to Paris in 1902. Léon Manaud, reporter for *L'Auto-vélo* (24 January 1902) was at the station to greet him, and he found the Turk to be in fine condition. "The champion of 1900 still had the same physiognomy. The face was open, the eyes lively, and he crushed my fingers when he shook my hand energetically, while his good and broad face bloomed with a good and frank smile." But he noted that Kara Ahmed had grown much fatter since the last time he had seen him; he weighed 123 kilos according to the baggage scale at the train station. Later that year, the great Turkish wrestler died.

111. *L'Auto-vélo* (13 January 1935) says that the wrestler died "after a short illness" at his home in Tarascon and that he had been the manager of an athletic club. According to a report in the Paris newspaper *Excelsior* (13 January 1935), Laurent's real name was Jean Laurans, and he was "a transportation entrepreneur." *L'Express du Midi* of Toulouse (13 January 1935) reports that after he retired, the great wrestler spent his time "advising young sportsmen, especially in wrestling and physical education." Laurent had "always kept his legendary affability, which had given him his reputation as a fair and honest athlete."

112. Schackmann was one of French wrestling's best "bad guys." He was the German wrestler that French audiences loved to hate, and he was apparently a master at this role. Almost everyone was in on the game. Even the German paper *Münchner neueste Nachrichten* (11 January 1910) said that Schackmann, "displays a type of wrestling that earned him the title *L'etrangleur* (the strangler). After each of Schackmann's victories, Paris newspapers report "Schackmann est conspué" [Schackmann is booed].

Things turned ugly as soon as World War I began, and toward the end, poor Schackmann was no longer the beloved bad guy. He was the genuinely detested enemy. This is confirmed by an article in *La Liberté* Paris (9 July 1918) entitled "Schackmann, the Boche Wrestler." The anonymous author reminds his readers of the villainous German. "Schackmann was a dreadful red-headed colossus. In tournaments he portrayed brutality and savagery. With him, illegal holds became his common currency, and Greco-Roman wrestling very soon degenerated into a more or less genuine fistfight. The audience shouted, whistled, booed, and threw pennies, benches, and epithets—as you might imagine. Schackmann's well-known brutality and the antipathy that he inspired in the audience enlivened the programs at the championships; it animated and gave the performance some variety without which the show often lacked spirit and interest. We would see Schackmann administer illegal holds then we would applaud when nine times out of ten he was called to account by his adversaries." In a grim conclusion, the reporter asks his readers, "Where is Schackmann today?" He does not know, but offers some speculation. "One of our friends believes that he recognized his cadaver in a trench. I have also heard that quite simply he is in a concentration camp. Wherever he is, his wicked face is still a symbol of the Boche war."

Fortunately, the German wrestler survived the war, and things had cooled down by the mid-1920s as is verified by an article by Henry Decoin in *Paris-soir* (26 December 1925) ironically titled "Schackmann the Assassin." The author immediately clears the air. "To tell the truth, Schackmann was a nice guy, not cruel at all, gentlemanly to an exemplary degree, gentle as a lamb and wearing his heart on his sleeve. He wrestled to live; he earned thirty to forty francs a day and built a little hut in an area where he raised chickens and rabbits and lived with his family. As some people play valets in Molière, Schackmann played brutes in wrestling tournaments. He was paid to do it, and he did it magnificently." He then tells an anecdote to prove his point:

One day at the Folies Bergère, the fight between Raoul the Butcher and Schackmann attracted a big crowd. A few wrestlers conceived a way to play a joke on good old Schackmann. They went off to find him and said to him, "Schack, listen up: this evening Raoul is going to wrestle "for real." "With me?" "Yes! He boasted about it. Seems he's out to get you." But the gentle Schackmann, was thrown into a panic, and he replied, "But what did I do to him?" The jokesters left Schackmann to his sad thoughts and went to visit the admirable Raoul. They explained to him that the German wrestler had boasted of manhandling him and depriving him of all prestige. Raoul was maddened with anger, and decided to take revenge and right from the start to tackle poor Schackmann onto the mat. That evening in Raoul's dressing room, Schackmann entered. He was fearful, worried, upset, and agitated. He walked up to the great French wrestler, stammering, "Look, Raoul, you're crazy! You must have been hit in the head. Why do you want to wrestle 'for real' with me? I've done nothing to you—unless it was unintended, and in that case, I ask your pardon." And since Raoul did not laugh, Schackmann decided to do something silly. "Listen," he said, "if you go easy on me tomorrow, I will bring you two lovely hens." And Schackmann was not beaten after thirty-nine minutes of excellent wrestling.

113. The jousting tournament or *joutes à la lance* was a nautical battle in which two teams in boats rowed toward one another, and a jouster with an extremely long lance would attempt to knock his opponent off his perch at the back of the boat. It had always been an activity that was played on the water and was especially popular in Lyon and Cette. In 1904 some geniuses at the sporting newspaper *Le Vélo* had the idea of staging a river joust at the Casino de Paris music hall using a complicated system of tracks, wires, and pulleys. "If boats and jousters are essential, experience has shown that it is perfectly possible to do without the liquid element without the spectacle of the jousting tournament suffering in the slightest." (Fioravanti, "Les joutes à la lance au Casino de Paris," *La Vie au Grand Air* 17 March 1904), 206. Thanks to his heavy, squat physique, Bonnelli was perfect as the jouster, and he emerged victorious at the end of the competitions in April 1904.

114. Les Halles was the central fresh food market for Paris. It was closed in 1973 and is not a shopping mall.

115. Bonnelli might have been strong, but he was neither a paragon of male beauty nor a wrestler who inspired terror. *Le Petit Parisien* (21 December 1898) reported on a match between him and the great Paul Pons. There was little surprise at the outcome. Pons was around two meters tall, and Bonnelli "is smaller and very fat. He has a short neck, which Pons grabbed without being able to hold on to it. In the end, however, Bonnelli was pinned by a headlock. This outcome was expected, but the defense was honorable."

116. Halil Adali was born in 1870 and died in 1927. Adali came to America in the late nineteenth century, and he fascinated Yankee audiences just as much as he did Europeans. An extensive, illustrated article in *The San Francisco Call*, November 6, 1898, quoted Leo C. Teller, the Turk's American manager, with his colorful assessment of his man's abilities. "He is as quick as a cat, and for vast and comprehensive variety of tricks he is a wonder. I doubt if our American wrestlers know as many deft movements as he does. I have never witnessed such dexterity in a big man in my life, and if he ever gets an opponent's head below his waist, he will make it so uncomfortable for him that the unfortunate man finding himself in that position will do some active work trying to get out of it."

The article mentions that Adali was planning on a match with the American champion, Tom Jenkins. In an article in *The Times* of Washington, DC (6 November 1898), the match with the American champion was described as a fiasco. Jenkins literally ran away from Adali, and despite being chased around the mat, the Turk could never catch him. For forty-five minutes little wrestling took place. Eventually Jenkins was caught and quickly pinned. Jenkins later made up a ridiculous story about avoiding the fight because the Turk broke one of his ribs.

117. Desbonnet misspells the wrestler's name

as "Dickmann." He participated in the Gold Belt of 1903 and was praised for his technical knowledge and his good manners; he was said to be very courteous. See *L'Ouest-Éclair* of Rennes (1 December 1905).

118. Pons drowned in 1915 while he was fishing in the Garonne River near Agen in southwest France. According to the report in *Le Petit Parisien* (16 April 1915), the retired wrestler was in a boat casting a net, but while doing so, he lost his balance and fell into the river and was tangled in the weights and the rope attached to his wrist. He was pulled out of the water a few moments after the incident, but it was too late and all attempts to revive him were futile. Pons was an avid hunter and fisherman, and so his demise is sad and ironic.

119. Pons was intelligent, literary and articulate. He wrote an autobiography that was originally published in *La vie au Grand Air* in several installments (number 146 to 498, 1907–1908). These chapters were later made into his book, *Vingt ans de lutte suivi de ma leçon de lutte et de l'histoire de la lutte* (Corbeil: Crété, 1900). He next published *La Lutte* (Paris: Lafitte, 1912), which incorporates much of the earlier work but also includes instructions for wrestling. See the appendix for excerpts from this book.

120. According to Adolf von Guretzki, *Der moderne Ringkampf* (Leipzig: Gloeckner, 1921) Van Den Berg died "of a nervous condition" in 1913.

121. Most people were struck first by the Dutchman's tall, blond, handsome appearance. *The Referee* of London (22 June 1902) called him a "Hercules of beautiful make and shape (an athletic poem if such thing there be)." It was Van Den Berg's match on Christmas Eve 1900 with the great George Hackenschmidt that caused the greatest acclaim for the Dutch wrestler, even though he lost the bout. The fact that he could keep up with the massive Russian for over twenty-five minutes says a great deal about Van Den Berg's abilities. According to *L'Auto-vélo* (25 December 1900) "Hackenschmidt triumphed, but not without difficulty. He had to work hard and look for all possible and imaginable combinations to get the better of his opponent. Several times he even took a little risk; his shoulders were very close to the mat, and if Van den Berg had shown a little more presence of mind, it might have been possible for him to take advantage of the sometimes-exaggerated temerity of someone who is nicknamed the Russian Lion."

122. Although Cochard's feat was quite amazing, Desbonnet was not convinced that such exertion was good for a person's health. In the October 1902 issue of *L'Éducation Physique* (25–26) he wrote, "This physical overexertion [i.e., carrying the sack] killed him, for he came back from this race with a cardiac illness which has recently done him in."

123. Despite his great strength (particularly in the deadlift), Cochard was not in the top rung of wrestlers. *L'Auto-vélo* (28 November 1901) reports that he was rather outclassed in a match with a German wrestler and had to leave the ring after a severe fracture of the arm.

124. I have been unable to determine what incident is referred to here. Was it a fight in a demi-mondaine's parlor? A personal quarrel? Perhaps it merely alludes to the rivalry for a woman. Maybe it is just an inside joke that general readers are not expected to get. There is little doubt that Cochard would have no trouble attracting the affection of any woman. Desbonnet described him as, "A good-looking boy with blond, short-cropped hair, well proportioned and with superbly muscled arms; he is what one could call a superb young fellow." *La Culture Physique* (1 July 1906, 3/36), 571.

125. Wilhelm Stalling first appeared as a professional wrestler in 1904/05, but he had little success in his chosen field. He said that he was from Bremen and proclaimed himself "Champion of Holstein," but he never enjoyed more than very modest athletic success. As Hans Langenfeld has speculated, "It is questionable whether he was able to earn a living with his unsuccessful record and expensive trips to more distant venues for wrestling tournaments. He was probably dependent on a job outside of athletics where he could capitalize on his strength in other ways." See Hans Langenfeld, "Die zweite Welle der Sportbewegung" *Jahrbuch 2003*, Niedersächsisches Institut für Sportgeschichte (Göttingen: NISH, 2003) 141–42. Stalling attempted to revive interest in himself in 1909 by claiming that he had been victorious over at least two great stars of wrestling, but rebuttals from both men, Ernst Siegfied and Giovanni Raicevich, announced that Stalling had not, in fact, pinned them. They had each won over Stalling in less than ten minutes. See *Illustrierte Sportzeitung* (Munich, 15 October 1909), 980, and 11 December 1909, 1173.

126. The correspondent of *Le Radical* newspaper (11 December 1901) was clearly impressed by Constant le Boucher. "Physically, Constant is a handsome athlete, dark-haired, white-skinned, vivacious…. Healthy, well proportioned, the shape of this athlete is most aesthetic…. Unlike many of his colleagues, Constant is modest, I would almost say shy."

127. An article in *L'Auto-vélo* (22 November 1906) titled "Le Brasseur de Couvin" by Robert Coquelle says that Constant retired from wrestling to become a brewer in a village in the Belgian Ardennes. He had married and his wife's family were all brewers, so he took over the business.

128. According to A. v. Guretzki in *Der moderne Ringkampf* (Leipzig: Gloeckner, 1921), Constant was killed in an automobile accident, but this is incorrect. He reached the ripe age of eighty-four, and died in 1961.

129. In his obituary in *La Santé par les Sports* 1/6 (1 Oct. 1911), 281, Desbonnet speculates that the thirty-seven-year-old wrestler died of "overtraining caused by his hard profession, and especially the abuse of life's pleasures which wore Quéniart out prematurely."

130. The reporter for *L'Auto-vélo* (10 January 1902) at a wrestling tournament in Lyon agreed that Fénelon was a master tactician, calling him "decidedly one of the finest wrestlers that has ever been seen in Lyon." The second round brought out Fénelon's best qualities against his Belgian opponent Omer de Bouillon. "The two rivals took turns leading the dance, multiplying their attacks with prodigious speed. The public was thrilled and applauded with frenzy. Headlocks followed headlocks, but it was impossible for the Belgian wrestler, despite his weight advantage, to bring his rival to the mat. Unfortunately, all his tactics and headlocks were in vain, and Fénelon was pinned in the third round.

131. The four other brothers were Maurice, Adrien, Ulysse, and Octave. In all there were eight Deriaz brothers, but not all of them pursued athletic careers.

132. The American Artists' Association was located at 74 Rue Notre-dame-du-champs.

133. The "Borghese Achilles" is now identified as the war god Ares, and it is still in the Louvre.

134. Émile Deriaz defeated Ahmed Madrali on the third evening of the Gold Belt tournament at the Folies-Bergère on 26 November 1904. The reporter for *L'Auto-vélo* (27 November 1904) could hardly control his enthusiasm for the match and for Deriaz. He compared him to a panther. "He rushed at the Turk, and without the slightest effort he managed to take hold of him with a rear waist hold and throw him out of the ring directly on both shoulders! Madrali had been taken down, but because of his protests, the judges (in agreement with the referee) ordered the match to start over on the basis that the throw was irregular because Madrali had tripped on the ropes around the ring. I must admit that I did not understand this bizarre and unfair ruling, but very happily, Deriaz put things right by taking down his redoubtable adversary a second time with a waist hold."

The reactions of the very partisan crowd were understandable. "You had to be there yesterday evening to realize what happened after the victory of the popular Deriaz. In the boxes and the orchestra, elegantly dressed women stood on their chairs applauding the Swiss; hats and canes flew into the air, flowers were thrown on the stage, and Deriaz had to return to the stage ten times to receive the applause." Unfortunately, a few days later, Madrali fought Deriaz once more, and this time he was defeated by the great Turkish wrestler (*L'Auto-vélo*, 4 December 1904).

135. The World Championship of Strength took place at the Paris Hippodrome on 5 March 1909.

136. It is unfortunate that Desbonnet presents this absurd tarradiddle as being a factual account of how the three "Terrible Turks" came to western Europe and beyond. See the section by Paul Pons in the appendix to get a more accurate picture of how Yusuf and his compatriots came to France.

137. Roeber and Yusuf actually wrestled two times, but they failed to reach a clear-cut decision in either match. The first was at Madison Square on 26 March 1898, and this is the one where Roeber left the ring and refused to fight. The second—and more notorious—meeting was held on 31 April 1898 at the stately Metropolitan Opera House. Desbonnet seems to have conflated the two. The decision in the first match was explained later by one of the officials of that fight. Referee Hughy Leonard wrote about the match in *The Washington* (D.C.) *Herald*, May 3, 1908, 7, and he noted that Yusuf used a trick that the referee had never seen before. After the men had wrestled without much progress, Yusuf got increasingly angry and he "grabbed his own wrist and rushed at Roeber. Then with the forearm, he jolted Roeber in the ribs and the latter fell off the stage. It was a foul of the most pronounced kind, but a trick just the same. It was executed very cleverly, too, and had a layman been in the ring, the chances are that the Turk would have escaped detection. The thrust loosened all the ligaments of Roeber's ribs, and he was disabled for several days." The second wrestling match (if such it can be called) between Yusuf and Ernst Roeber was as memorable as it was violent. The account in the *New York Times* (1 May 1898, 4) is more evenhanded than most. "The affair started as a wrestling match, pure and simple, with the two contestants striving as best they knew for mastery, but at the end of twenty minutes it degenerated into a prize fight with Roeber and Yusuf as the principals, and with managers, prizefighters, and spectators as seconds." The Turk lacked wrestling finesse but had great size and strength, and when this failed to pin his opponent, he lost his temper and slammed Roeber against the ring posts with full force—twice. Then Roeber lost his temper, and "the little man threw his knowledge of wrestling to the winds, and urged on by the shouts of the incensed spectators, went at the Turk with bare knuckles." When the referee jumped between the men trying to separate them, that was the signal for everyone to climb up into the ring and participate in a general melee. Boxer Robert Fitzsimmons caused a great deal of commotion when he started swinging at anyone who did not agree with him, and when the police were called, their first job was to remove the boisterous boxer. When enough calm had been restored, the referee declared that the bout was no contest. That was when the audience became incensed at the farce, and a riot was soon a real possibility. Fortunately, members of the New York Police Department saved the day.

138. The French liner *SS La Bourgogne* sank off the coast of Nova Scotia early in the morning of 4 July 1898. In addition to Yusuf and his gold belt, 548 other passengers lost their lives. Yusuf's brutality and cowardice should be taken with a grain of salt. It is clear that Desbonnet did not much care for the man, so this animus might have colored the account.

139. Maupas (whose real name was Émile Maupain) came to Quebec around 1904 and eventually established a training center at "Camp

Maupas" in the Val-Morin region. Here he trained many athletes; his most famous pupil was wrestler Yvon Robert (1914–1971). Maupas was killed in 1948 when a charge of dynamite he was using to clear some debris exploded in his face. See biography by Gilles Janson in *Dictionnaire des grands oubliés du sport au Québec* (Québec City: Septentrion, 2013), 276–81.

140. Before turning to wrestling, Nollys and his "brother" had a music-hall act that displayed their talents as "strongmen-acrobats." The reporter from the magazine *L'Art lyrique et le Music-hall* (6 December 1896) described the bill at the Casino de Paris but singled out the two brothers. "I will say that the audience seemed most particularly to enjoy the work of the Nollys." The man posing as Nasque's brother was the strongman and acrobat Joseph Wattée. Joseph Wattée was an excellent athlete and acrobat. One day in winter he was rehearsing a new strength feat but did not warm up properly, and he ended up tearing his biceps. This accident greatly diminished his strength, and he could no longer earn a living as an acrobat, so poor Wattée fell into a fit of depression. On 15 November 1903 he committed suicide by throwing himself out of his third-floor room. He died instantly. See Edmond Desbonnet, "Un Larbin Costaud" *La Culture physique* (1 March 1911), 8/148.

141. Dr. Vladislav Krajewski (1841–1901) is considered the father of Russian weight lifting. He was the founder of the St. Petersburg Athletic and Cycling Club and invited many muscular young men to come and live with him in the Russian capital. His palatial home had excellent training facilities, and he could thus supervise and monitor the men he was training. According to strongman and wrestler George Hackenschmidt, "I owe practically all that I have and am to him." http://www.ironmanmagazine.com/index.cfm?page=article&go2=1275.

142. Perhaps because pale or light-complected people often flush red when they are excited.

143. Hackenschmidt's second victory over the amateur Schmelling in May 1899 meant that he was crowned Russian champion. The Russian Lion admitted that "Schmelling was one of my toughest opponents!" George Hackenschmidt, *The Way to Live: Health & Physical Fitness* (London: Health & Strength, 1908), 123.

144. According to a notice in the newspaper *L'Auto-vélo* (4 August 1902) Cayol later was the director of the Circus Alexandre in Marseilles.

145. The Germans preferred the Continental clean. This means that the barbell is brought to the lifter's belt or chest and rested there before completing the lift.

146. After his wrestling career was over, Zaïkine turned to aviation. He was an early barnstormer who would fly demonstration flights all over Russia. His reputation as an aviator was just as great as that of a wrestler and strongman. Zaïkine became quite wealthy and invested his profits in land. Unfortunately, all was lost in the Bolshevik Revolution of 1917, and he fled to the West. He is buried in Kishinev, capital of Moldova. See http://02varvara.wordpress.com/2008/07/13/ivan-zaikin-wrestler-and-aviator/

147. *L'Auto-vélo* (27 June 1908) reported, "In Germany and in Russia Romanoff is considered an unbeatable man. This handsome athlete reminds us a little of Paul Pons (some of his parts). He debuted in France when he was hardly twenty years old, and already that that time he wrestled Petersen, Pons, Laurent, and many others." His name is often transliterated to "Romanov."

148. The False Rabasson had taken the name of a more famous wrestler, Rabasson "the Little Peasant" who was active 1850–60. See his biography on page 69. The False Rabasson was active as a wrestler from 1901 to 1909.

149. Born in Liège 1885; died in Paris 1965. His birth name was Henri Herd, but he took the name "Constant" in honor of his boyhood idol, Constant the Butcher. See https://connaitrelawallonie.wallonie.be/fr/wallons-marquants/dictionnaire/herd-henri-dit-constant-le-marin#.Y-kF7MfMJD8

150. Constant le Marin was a much-loved wrestler, especially in his native country. As soon as the First World War was declared in 1914, Constant volunteered, and after his country was invaded by the Germans, he went to Russia to fight the Austrians. While operating his armored vehicle, he was wounded horribly in the shoulder and the leg, and he narrowly avoided having his leg amputated. Fortunately, he recovered from his injuries, and by the early 1920s he had even reentered the wrestling arena. See "Constant le Marin retour de Russie" *L'Auto-vélo* (23 February 1918). During the Second World War, Constant went to Paris in May 1940, and then to Bordeaux where he worked at a refugee camp before leaving for Argentina. He returned in 1946 and opened a gymnasium in the basement of a café that he operated. There he gave wrestling lessons to young would-be athletes. He died on 4 November 1965. https://connaitrelawallonie.wallonie.be/fr/wallons-marquants/dictionnaire/herd-henri-dit-constant-le-marin#.Y-kF7MfMJD8

Appendix and Metric Conversions

1. There is one good source for the history of Russian wrestling, and that is Louise McReynold, *Russia at Play: Leisure Activities at the End of the Tsarist Era* (Ithaca: Cornell University Press, 2003). The chapter on sporting life (76–112) contains the best account in English of Russian wrestling that I have found.

Appendix 1

1. Étienne Arnal (1794–1872) and Jacques Odry (1779–1853) were both well-known actors who specialized in comic roles.

2. Peter's Tavern in the Passage des Princes near the Opéra Garnier was a favorite haunt of

journalists and was known for its hearty fare, including British ales and porters. Alfred Delvau, *Les Plaisirs de Paris: Guide pratique* (Paris: Achille Faure, 1867), 74.

3. These ring weights were often used to measure out large quantities of goods (beans, potatoes, wheat). They were usually in the shape of cast-iron blocks or cones to which rings had been attached to the top.

4. Rabasson [1824?–1854] died of a strangulated hernia after a brutal wrestling match. It was anything but a "bourgeois" death. See his biography in the main text (pages 68–69).

5. Blas "the Proud Spaniard" posed for one of the two principal figures in Falguière's painting *Les lutteurs* [The Wrestlers]. He was perhaps not entirely ignorant of art.

6. A bouillon is a large restaurant selling simple fare, but specializing in bouillon (beef broth). The former Salle Montesquieu was the first of many Bouillon Duval restaurants. The Montesquieu Hall was converted into a restaurant in 1854. Léon Faucher (1803–1854) was a politician and economist, Adolphe Granier de Cassagnac (1806–1880) a journalist and conservative politician, and Count Émilien de Nieuwerkerque (1811–1892) a society figure and sculptor.

7. Pierre the Savoyard is almost certainly the same as Peter the Coachman in the first section of *Kings of Wrestling*.

8. The faithful coachman, *le cocher fidèle*, was a stock character in comedies and the name of a popular restaurant in Paris.

9. I have been unable to verify the statement about the banning of wrestling in Paris. According to Léon Ville, *La Lutte et les Lutteurs* (Paris: Rothschild, 1891), 31–33, the Montesquieu Hall presented wrestling matches for only three years, but they were the best in Paris. "After the close of the Montesquieu Arena [in 1854], wrestlers returned to the South of France and for fifteen years Parisians could see wrestling only at fairgrounds." This is untrue, but perhaps he meant that all the best wrestlers had drifted away. One modern author, Tim Corvin, *Pioneers of Professional Wrestling 1860–1899* (Bloomington, IN: Archway, 2014), 6, says that both wrestling and *savate* were banned in Paris in 1856 "due to a spate of crudely fixed matches." Unfortunately, he offers no source for this information. Since Dumortier is not mentioned as the cause for this interdiction, it is not clear what incidents are being referred to.

Appendix 2

1. By "honest" Vallès means that the match had not been predetermined and the moves were real. The *Foire du Trône* (Trone Fair), also called the *Foire aux pains d'épices* (Gingerbread Fair), is an annual carnival that is held every Easter near the former customs house on the eastern approaches to Paris. One of the traditional treats to be had there is the gingerbread, sold most often in the shape of a pig.

2. When an amateur accepted a challenge to fight with one of the professionals in a wrestling booth, the director gave him either a symbolic glove or a pair of wrestling trunks.

3. This might be Don Ramon whose biography is in *Kings of Wrestling*.

4. As Evander Holyfield discovered to his cost in 1997 during his boxing match with Mike Tyson, it is quite possible to bite off a part of the ear of an opponent.

5. According to an article in *Le Petit Journal* (Thursday, 31 May 1866), Blas died of cholera in 1866.

6. It appears that Leboeuf went to England (at least briefly). There is a report of a Monsieur Bonnet Leboeuf wrestling in Birmingham in 1870. He is described as "a grey-haired, thick-set, muscular man of forty-five years of age who stands 5 feet 11 inches and weighs 16 stone 11½ pounds." *Birmingham Daily Gazette*, 31 January 1870.

7. These were two clubs or debating societies that flourished during the French Revolution and were characterized by noisy arguments.

8. Dubois is mentioned as wrestling in 1870 in Birmingham along with his colleague Leboeuf (see note 6 above). The reporter says that the French wrestler is "of gigantic proportions, weighing 19 stone 6½ pounds." Dubois later that same year operated his own *baraque*, and there is a painting of it by Bussiliet in the collection of the Musée Carnavalet. https://www.parismuseescollections.paris.fr/fr/musee-carnavalet/oeuvres/la-baraque-du-lutteur-dubois-boulevard-de-la-villette#infos-principales

9. Dubois (1830–1880?) was a master of chicanery, and he had a devilishly clever way of keeping his carnival booth full. See *Kings of Strength* (177–79) for the very amusing story.

10. For a biography of Papillon, see *Kings of Strength*, 135–36.

11. The name for these "professional amateurs" is probably derived from the comtois draft horse, a strong but unglamorous breed.

12. All three of these men had well-known schools of wrestling and/or boxing (both French and English style). By advising fighters to take off their gloves, the author implies that one can only confront savage bullies like the ones described in this section is by fighting dirty.

Appendix 4

1. Details of the Cannon vs. Bernard match (11 November 1889) can be found in the main text of *Kings of Wrestling*.

2. According to the *Guide du professeur de gymnastique* by O. Cruciani (1888), the gymnase et salle d'armes de la Sorbonne was at 12 Rue Victor-Cousin.

3. Ernest Molier founded the first amateur

circus in Paris, in 1880. It eventually featured sensational shows, and (more importantly) personalities from high society who performed as strongmen, equestriennes, and acrobats. See Vincent Ducrey, Raphaël Turcat, Pascal Jacob *Le rendez-vous mondain de la belle epoque, Le Cirque Molier* (Paris: Beaux Arts Editions, 2019).

4. Georges San Marin was a prominent figure in the sporting life of Belle Epoque Paris. The Romanian aristocrat made his athletic debut in 1888 where he wrestled Pietro Dalmasso wearing black silk tights and a black mask. He next appeared at the Hippodrome in the same costume. He was a frequent performer at the Circus Molier. His full biography can be found in *Kings of Strength*, 297–99.

5. San Marino's assistant was a man named Laforêt. According to Desbonnet, he was muscular and was equal to Sandow in performing the bent press. *Kings of Strength*, 299.

6. Joseph Charlemont (1839–1918) was a great champion of *savate* (French boxing); he had an important school and he wrote several books on the subject. I assume that Renoir's "Cercle Mollier" is a misspelling, and he meant to say "Cirque Molier." By saying "Pietro is Pietro" he means to say that San Marin did not have a chance against the great Franco-Italian wrestler.

7. There are more extensive biographies of Pascault, Magisson, Laporte, and Van Huyssen in *Kings of Strength*, 297–97.

8. From the poem "Namounah" by Alfred de Musset.

9. *Tirer la bourre* (serious fights) and *partie à la colle* (prearranged outcome). The latter expression is not used very often, and it probably refers to being stuck with an unpleasant task. The more common expression is *une partie chiquée* (a phony match).

Appendix 6

1. "It is characteristic for Parisians to sit for hours over dinner. The Café de Madrid at night resembles closely a garden party given at the château of some private estate." Also: "During the season, between five and seven, all of smart Paris may be seen at the Pavillon d'Armenonville. At this hour the tables in the garden are filled with pretty women in chic toilettes, accompanied by faultlessly dressed gentlemen whose bank accounts have managed thus far to survive." F. Berkeley Smith, *How Paris Amuses Itself* (New York: Funk & Wagnalls, 1903) Chapter two, "How Paris Dines."

2. "La Tsarine" is a work by Russian composer Nikolai Tcherepnin.

3. In Brittany "Feasts of Atonement" (or indulgence) are elaborate religious processions to a local church after which there is a fair, and it is here that wrestling is often held.

4. In Gouren or Breton wrestling, participants are required to fight barefoot and wearing a special white shirt or vest with a belt and black trousers. They try to throw each other to the ground by gripping the shirt or vest.

5. *Pelote* is a traditional Basque game similar to handball played with a long, narrow basket attached to the player's hand. The ball is hit against a wall.

6. The Boulevard Barbès was a rough working-class neighborhood not far from the Gare du Nord. The *Fortifs* were the old fortifications that ringed Paris but were by this time merely an open space just outside the city limits.

7. I have found no mention of Docquerroy in any newspapers, so the name might be misspelled or he might have been a uniquely Parisian favorite. The expression *tête de Turc* (Turk's head) means scapegoat or whipping boy.

8. Robin is most likely the wrestler who appeared in 1889 at the arena at the Quai Debilly. His nickname was *Badingué* (foolish or halfwit); this was also one of the satiric names attached to Emperor Napoleon III, so perhaps Robin was an avid Bonapartist.

9. French playwright Henri Meilhac (1830–1897) had just died; hence he is referred to as "poor."

10. French wrestling—Greco-Roman or "flat-hand" style.

11. Henri Marseille the elder died in 1897 and he was succeeded by his brother Jean-Baptiste, so the writer must have been confused about the dates and the family relationships.

12. A louis was worth twenty francs. At the turn of the century in France, a common workman earned four to five francs a day, and a skilled carpenter could expect eight francs per day. Thirty louis was therefore a sizeable sum.

13. In the 1880s–90s Paul Robin (1837–1912) was the director of the Prévost Orphanage who instituted experimental libertarian education. It caused suspicion because it was the first institution of its kind to have both boys and girls together in the same orphanage.

14. François le Bordelais (pseud. of Paul Levacher) had a wrestling school in Paris and was the author of two books on wrestling techniques.

15. Courteline, pseud. of Georges Moinaux (1858–1929) French dramatist known for his satiric comedies.

16. The Fête de Paris had been held in the lawn between Les Invalides and the Pont Alexandre III at least since the 1880s. The festival later became a trade fair and moved to roomier locations.

Appendix 7

1. The lull was caused principally by political upheaval in France. In 1848, the July Monarchy of King Louis-Philippe was overthrown, and the Second Republic was established. That ended after Louis-Napoleon Bonaparte staged a coup d'état and proclaimed himself Emperor Napoleon III in 1852 and thus began the Second French Empire.

Wrestlers found it much more convenient to avoid the capital at this time, since most assemblies were banned for fear of revolutionary activity. For a variety of reasons, wrestling matches attracted a crowd that was suspicious to the authorities, so they were among the first to be banned. See the introduction for details.

2. The Second Empire ended in 1870 when the emperor's forces were routed by the Prussians in the Franco-Prussian War. Germany invaded France and chaos ensued when Paris declared itself a self-governing commune (the first Communist state). More killing, disruption, and retribution followed, and it was not until the mid–1870s before anything like stability returned to the nation. Again, wrestlers and other entertainers avoided Paris, and normal life was suspended for several years.

3. This debacle occurred in November 1889. See the text of *Kings of Wrestling* for a more accurate description of the event. According to Paul Pons ("Vingt ans de lutte" *La vie au grand air*, 11 March 1908, 176), "No other wrestler has ever had the soul of a businessman equal to that of Cannon." This was his way of saying that Cannon would do anything for money.

4. Kurtdereli and Kara Ahmed often shouted out the traditional Ottoman war cry, "Hoah! Hoah! Aïde!" See chapter on Kurtdereli in the main text of *Kings of Wrestling*.

5. See *The Kings of Strength* (pages 156–57) for a biography of Noël le Gaulois (pp. 259–60).

6. The Salle Gangloff was located at 6 Rue de la Gaité in the Montparnasse quarter of Paris. According to journalist L. Manaud in *La Vie au Grand Air* (24 December 1899), Gangloff Hall was "the true cradle of the renaissance of wrestling."

7. The Bal Bullier was a dance hall located at 31 Avenue de l'Observatoire. It was a popular place for students to dance, drink, and generally have a good time. Sajous was the manager, but he left Montparnasse in 1897 for the "wide open spaces" (la grande campagne). His successor was Horace Delattre. See Jean Emile-Bayard, "Montparnasse théâtral dans le passé et le present," *Le Quotidien* (26 August 1928).

8. "Mario" was Delattre's nom-de-théâtre. "En revenant de Sursenes" was first published in 1890. Delattre later moved on and is listed as a stage manager and director at the Gaité-Montparnasse Theater in 1911.

9. Bébé was a midget wrestler (his name means "baby"). "Full of affability, endowed with a rare agility, squirmy as a marmoset, he unites the most diverse aptitudes." *Le Buffon* (18 August 1867). Charles "Bibi" Poiré (1866–1935) was a renowned wrestler and strongman who had a fine chest, but he was famous for having the most beautiful arm in France. Desbonnet said that his biceps looked like "a coconut has been inserted under the skin." See *Kings of Strength* 231–32.

10. Favouët (real name, Denoix) wrestled under the nickname of "The Terrible Coachman." He was described as "a man of tall stature and of Herculean strength. Added to that he has stamina a that is equal to any test." "Le Championnat de lutte du monde," *La vie au Grand Air* (1 January 1899), 226.

11. This is a slender but beautifully illustrated book showing a number of wrestling holds. Illustrations by A. Lefort Ylouses. First published by Madrid in 1899, but it went through many editions. The next year it was joined by volume two of the same series, but this volume was also reprinted several times.

12. Pytlazinski's book is *Tajniki Walki Zapaśniczej (Francuskiej)*/The Secrets of Wrestling (French Style), but the only edition that I could find was published in Warsaw in 1929, so this might be a later revised edition of an earlier work. It is in Polish, not Russian.

13. This is, of course, complete nonsense (as Desbonnet would have been quick to note). By repeating this old canard about "muscle binding," the author shows his lack of knowledge.

14. The Cooperative society of coachmen and drivers *La Syndicale Levallois* was a group of drivers that banded together in the late nineteenth and early twentieth centuries.

15. The Académie de Billard was in the Café Gibelin, 18 Rue de la Sorbonne, Paris.

16. General George Ernest Boulanger (1837–1891) was a demagogue and politician who was extremely popular in the working-class districts of Paris. He was an ultranationalist who nearly became dictator of France.

Appendix 8

1. This is almost certainly Paul Pons.

Appendix 9

1. The Croix Rousse district is atop a hill in Lyon. It was once a working-class neighborhood where many of the city's silk workers lived.

2. Desbonnet says that Rossignol-Rollin was a former actor, not a former lawyer. He was almost certainly both. See *Kings of Strength*, 143–44.

3. It is virtually impossible to prove the claim that Wolff invented fake weights, but such is the story that was passed down. See Georges Le Roy, *Strength Athletics and Swedish Gymnastics* in *Iron Game History*, 5/2, 30, for a fuller explanation of Wolff and his act.

4. A low hill now overlooking the Left Bank and the Quartier Mouffetard in Paris.

5. In modern American pro wrestling, "kayfabe" is a term referring to the practice of maintaining the illusion that everything performed in the ring is real.

6. Strongmen, weight lifters, and bodybuilders have long been drawn to wrestling because it pays better than other athletic professions. Apollon, Poiré, Maurice Deriaz, and many others from

the earliest days of French wrestling have done so. There are many examples in modern wrestling.

7. In the original version of the story published in the issue of 21 March 1908 in *La Vie au Grand Air*, Pons tells a slightly different form of the story. In this, the pretty acrobat is not Doublier's wife; she is "his lady-friend" (*son compagnon*). Perhaps the story was later "cleaned up" so as not to offend those with tender sensibilities. Desbonnet says that Mrs. Doublier had a strength act that was "well mounted, but of course it was made up of deceptive tricks which the ignorant audience believed to be real feats of strength." *Kings of Strength*, 314–15.

8. I have been unable to identify Chofa. It is either very small or the spelling has been garbled by Pons. Historian Phil Lions suggests that it might be an old and now forgotten name for a town; he says that it would probably be spelled Çofa, and this means "shepherd," but no town exists by that name. (email to author, 16 April 2023). If it existed at all, it was probably in the Balkan provinces of the Ottoman Empire.

9. Mamouchi (sometimes mamamouchi) is a fictional pompous title, supposedly Turkish; it corresponds to muckamuck or muckety-muck.

10. Pons implies that the Doubliers were performing in something akin to a brothel.

11. It is unclear when Doublier and his wife first came to Constantinople, but it must have been sometime around the early 1880s. The first notice of him in the Turkish press is in April 1883 announcing that he would give strongman shows and also do some wrestling at a theater. The 1 May 1883 issue of *Stamboul* states that he and a Greek opponent wrestled before the sultan himself, and after winning, Doublier received a purse of 100 Turkish pounds. In the issue of 22 September 1883, it states that two palace wrestlers were given permission to leave for Europe under the management of Doublier, "the well-known Hercules," in order to give exhibitions of Turkish wrestling. It is not known if this tour was ever completed. Doublier had returned by October since he began a series of wrestling matches and athletic exhibitions that were all reviewed very favorably. It was reported on 19 January 1884 that the wrestler was in the Georgian capital of Tiblisi where he gave a wrestling exhibition with an Armenian opponent. This is the last reference to Doublier in any Turkish newspaper that I found, and it is unclear why he no longer gave performances in the Turkish capital. There are no further articles in *Stamboul* at any time about him or his wrestlers who created such a stir in Europe and America. Perhaps he toured the provinces for a while and when he returned, his public had lost interest in him. It might have been sometime during the decade of 1884 and 1895 when his lack of money caused him to work on the docks.

12. It is unclear who "Mehmet" actually is. The name is one of the most common in Turkey, so his given name is little help. He might have been Cotch Mehmet, but this is unclear. Neither does Mehmet appear in the famous photo of Doublier and the other three Turks, so he might have gone off on his own or returned to his homeland. I am grateful for Phil Lions's help in an attempt to solve this matter, but even he is unsure of Mehmet's identity.

13. In French the hold is called "la tirade à la nuque" and it became Yusuf's signature move since few opponents were able to resist it.

14. Wrestler Kara Ibo was described by Pons as "Strange and mysterious" because he would disappear for weeks at a time, and he refused to tell anyone where he went. He also had an unknown source of income since he never seemed to do any work except to wrestle occasionally. See *La Lutte*, 307–10.

15. In Turkish wrestling, an adversary need only be thrown to on his back with "his navel to the sky" to claim a victory. Touching both shoulders is not necessary to win.

16. The Gymnase Piazza was located at 32 Rue faubourg Saint-Martin in the 10th Arrondissement. It was a favorite of wrestlers and gymnasts.

17. The chronology and location of these matches are unclear from the account given by Pons, but they were probably held at the Folies Bergère in 1895. According to wrestling historian Phil Lions, "In late December 1894 Doublier signed a contract with the popular Paris music hall Casino de Paris for the three Turks to wrestle there for a month in March 1895. For that month's worth of matches the Turks were to be paid 3,500 French francs each plus 500 francs for travel expenses. That was big money back then. However, in late February 1895 there was a fire at Casino de Paris and the venue had to be shut down for a while. As compensation, the Casino paid the Turks 25 francs for every day they missed out on working (their contact was March 1 through March 31) and they also gave them an additional sum of 1,000 francs. The plan was for the Turks to wrestle still at the Casino, as soon as the venue reopened. However, in the meantime Doublier struck a deal with a different Paris music hall (Folies Bergère) and the Turks ended up wrestling there instead. The reason why we know all of this is because in January 1896 the Casino sued Doublier for breach of contract, which is where all this information came out. The Casino won the suit and Doublier had to pay the Casino 3,000 francs." wrestlingclassics.com/cgi-bin/.ubbcgi/ultimatebb.cgi?ubb=get_topic;f=10;t=005061;p=0

18. In the version of Pons's story that appeared in *La Vie au Grand Air* (4 April 1908), after speaking with Fournier on the sly, Doublier made doubly sure that Yusuf would win by slipping the avaricious Turk two gold louis and saying, "If you can pin that one, victory is ours."

19. The upright posts were part of a theatrical set. The term that Pons uses is "portant du décor" or set brace.

20. [**Pons's note**: The only defeats that Yusuf and Nurullah suffered were inflicted on them by Paul Pons who, two years later, was to win the World Championship at the Casino de Paris.] Pons

won the World's Championship in December of 1898, but there is no mention of his having defeated the Turks. His principal opponent was Pytlazinski. The Turks wrestled in Paris at the Cirque d'Hiver in 1895, and there is evidence that Pons might have fought Yusuf, but no results were published.

21. The word should be *çabuk* (hurry up).

22. Pons seems to be saying that it was novelty as much as wrestling skill that contributed to the Turks' success. They, like black wrestlers, were esteemed for their exotic appeal as much as their athletic abilities. Later, no wrestling tournament or fairground establishment was complete without a few racial "oddities" to give their audience a thrill. This was the age of "human zoos" or ethnographic displays where imperialism, racism, and objectification combined to create a sort of freak show out of unfamiliar cultures. It should be remembered that at this time (1850–1950) no World's Fair was complete without its village of curious "natives." See Gilles Boetsch, Pascal Blanchard, and others, *Human Zoos: The Invention of the Savage* (Paris: Musée du quai Branly/Actes Sud, 2011). The Turks were a little different because they were actually much stronger and more adept than most of their European opponents, and this must have added a frisson of uncertainty and perhaps racial or national fear when they were witnessed by white audiences. Perhaps it is also what partially motivated Doublier to play the cruel trick of serving pork to his unsuspecting charges. It might also have been revenge for Yusuf's theft of 1,200 francs from his manager.

23. According to most Koranic scholars, unintentionally eating pork is not a sin. "And there is no sin on you concerning that in which you made a mistake, except in regard to what your hearts deliberately intend. And Allah is Ever Oft-Forgiving, Most Merciful." [al-Ahzab 33:5]

Appendix 10

1. *Pallone col bracciale* is a game in which the teams bat a ball against a wall (like handball), but they wear large, heavy wooden wrist guards to hit the ball; the *tamburello* is a racket-like instrument used in a variation of the same game.

2. *Broetto*, *sburrita*, and *caciucchi* are all fish stews that are similar to the more famous Provençal dish, bouillabaisse. As a gourmand, the author was acutely aware of the many variations in these stews.

3. The wealthy Rothschild family had many holdings in Marseilles and the Côte d'Azure. Perhaps the most famous of these is the Villa Ephrussi near Nice. Cougnet was born in Nice when it was part of Italy, so his knowledge of the region and the language are put to use in this work.

4. Pietro had many stage names throughout his career, and more than one seems to have been bone-themed. In the mid-1889s he was marketed under the name of *Mangeur d'os* (Bone Eater). *Gil Blas* 4 July 1885.

5. The Fiera Ambrosiana della Porta Genova is a celebration held in Milan and the Fiera di San Agostino is held in Senigallia near Ancona on the Adriatic coast.

6. The unnamed *baraque* was almost certainly that of Mangematin. This entrepreneur with the bizarre name (it means "Morning Eater") worked a number of schemes to keep him and his troupe in the public's eye. Dalmasso and Mangematin devised a clever plan by which Pietro won every match until he encountered a red-masked opponent who defeated him. Although the mysterious opponent was supposed to be a member of the diplomatic corps or a British nobleman, it was actually Mangematin. *Gil Blas* 4 July 1885.

7. "Tirer la bourre" literally means to tear the hair. The expression probably originates from the world of hunting and refers to the fact that dogs were allowed to rip apart pieces of their prey, fighting vigorously for a tuft of its hair. In the world of wrestling, it means to fight in earnest (as opposed to having a predetermined outcome).

8. I have been unable to find evidence of Pietro's troupe of women wrestlers, but the Belgian wrestler and strongman Victor Salvator had a troupe of female wrestlers who appeared at the Folies-Bergère in February 1883. (*Kings of Strength*, 271). There is no specific mention of Dalmasso's lady wrestlers in any of America's major newspapers, but a troupe of "female wrestlers from the Cirque Imperial, Paris" toured the Midwest in 1883 (*Indianapolis Journal*, 8 August 1883). Were they Dalmasso's, Salvator's or some other group? Female wrestlers had been popular in France for a long time, but they were mostly confined to less prestigious venues (brothels, low hotels, fairground booths etc.). In some American cities, such entertainments would have been banned entirely.

9. Cuarenta Onzas (his name refers to a purse of 40 gold ounces that he won in an early wrestling match) was a vicious Argentine-Italian wrestler named Pablo Raffetto (1841–1914), who was famous for his disdain of rules and sportsmanship. He often "positioned himself in the middle of the circus ring, as if he were a nandubay tree, and no one could bring him down even with ropes and lassos if he did not want to. Then when he was tired of letting himself be tampered with by his adversary, he took the assailant by whatever part he happened to grab—by the neck, the belt, the feet, the arms, the nose, and in an instant, he was tumbling into the impervious sand. He then exclaimed in a ringing voice, "Bring me another one," as he crossed his arms looking like a Roman athlete, or as if he were simply ordering up a plate of polenta. Meanwhile the crowd shouted enthusiastically, '¡Viva Cuarenta Onzas! ¡Viva Raffetto!'" Rafael Bareda, "Los atletas de mis tiempos" (Buenos Aires: *Caras y Caretas* Dec. 19, 1910).

10. There is no evidence to support the idea that Dalmasso was any more honest or "sincere" than other professional wrestlers of the time. Since he managed several troupes of athletes, he was

probably just as willing to play the game as any others. By insisting otherwise, Cougnet is merely continuing the myth of the purity of the sport.

11. Perhaps this means that Dalmasso taught swimming in the Seine near La Samaritaine department store near the Pont Neuf in Paris. There is also a Samaritaine swimming pool near Bouzancy in eastern France.

12. This hard-fought match occurred at the Championship at the Casino de Paris on 24 December 1898. *Gil Blas*, 26 December 1898. The newspaper account says only that Wetasa was "seriously injured" in the match. Another report in *La Presse* (26 December 1898) assured readers that despite the ferocity of the action, the match was "courteous and scientific."

13. This brief autobiography was published on the twenty-fifth anniversary of Bartoletti's wrestling career (25 May 1891 *La Stampa*). "I was born in Rome on February 20, 1846, in 1860 I emigrated from my native land and enlisted in the Italian army taking part in the campaigns of 1860–61, 1866 and in 1867, I was with Garibaldi in Mentana. Adherent to my duties as a patriot, having no possessions or fortune, I was obliged to avail myself of the physical strength and dexterity with which nature had granted me to earn my living. On March 21, 1866, still in the military, I fought against two expert wrestlers here in Turin and was victorious; later I fought all over Italy, Austria, France, Africa, Egypt, and in America, taking down the strongest champions of all kinds, and I still depend on wrestling." Despite his glorious career, the old wrestler died on 5 October 1910 in poverty and solitude, forgotten by the crowds that had once adored him. His last days were spent in a dreary apartment in Milan. "He was the first wrestler of Italy. He practiced his art with great enthusiasm, supported by the greatest popularity." Obituary in *La Corriere della sera*, Milan (6 October 1910).

14. By 1872 Bartoletti was a seasoned performer and company manager. *La Stampa* (Turin) 5 June 1872, reported on his opening performance in that city. "The varied and pleasant entertainment was a real success; the gymnastic exercises, the tricks, the wonderful jumps and the wrestling were applauded, and throughout it all the director of the company Signor Bartoletti displayed all his wonderful agility and strength."

15. **Note by Dr. A. Cougnet**: "This is confirmed by the previously noted Professor A. Zucca, then a member of the Andrea Doria Gym of Genoa."

16. In many references Bartoletti is given credit for inventing the term "Greco-Roman wrestling" rather than continuing to call it flat-hand or French wrestling. There is no evidence that he devised this name, and the many sources who give this information do not cite any evidence for it. It may just be a common myth that has been passed from one scholar to another.

17. **Note by Dr. A. Cougnet**: "'Forbidden arms' because in earlier times, those who had demonstrated extraordinary arm strength and were able to administer fatal blows in cases of hand-to-hand fights, it was thus tantamount to using their arms as prohibited weapons."

18. **Note by Dr. A. Cougnet**: "In fact he is still living in Genoa. I was told that he is selling postcards with his portrait and the following words: 'BASILIO BARTOLETTI First wrestler of Italy, who in the period of 40 years in his career as a wrestler has accepted 12,272 wrestling challenges. A fire at his theater, which happened in La Spezia, brought him into poverty since he was unable to work due to age and a weakening of his legs. He was thus forced to sell his photograph for a living.'" The fire in the theater happened in December 1903.

19. *Il Caffaro* newspaper was published in Genoa from 1875–1943.

20. The old Teatro Manzoni was in the via Urbana. It opened in 1876 and was shut down in 1960.

21. *La Stampa* of Turin (23 May 1889) reported this debacle a little less melodramatically. "Yesterday evening at the Manzoni theater there was an immense crowd of people. The greatest attraction was the fight between the famous Bartoletti and the German wrestler Rayos. The expectation was extraordinary, indescribable. The spectators seemed pointlessly tumultuous, and many bets were made. At the first powerful assault the two champions both fell to the ground on their bellies. Then they got up and the attacks increasingly followed one after another. The spectators, were electrified as they screamed and stormed. Even the wrestlers were dripping with sweat. Bartoletti's wrists were seen to bleed. Finally, after twelve minutes, both wrestlers happened to land on their backs, but in a skillful move Rayos extended himself over the body of his opponent and slammed his shoulders on the floor. A burst of applause and boos welcomed the outcome of the match for either the winner or the loser. After arising, Bartoletti, begged the public to come back the next evening for the rematch. Meanwhile the German wrestler left the ring amid cheers."

The rematch took place as promised, and once again there was a large crowd. "The fight between Bartoletti and Rayos was fierce, almost ferocious. At last, Bartoletti managed to take down his adversary but his opponent touched the ground with only one shoulder. Meanwhile Bartoletti who was worn out, exhausted and bleeding from his mouth withdrew. The audience screamed and stormed; some even protested formally. The victory was doubtful since Rayos only touched the floor with one shoulder. There will be a new challenge tomorrow. These are distressing spectacles that are unworthy of a civilized people." *La Stampa* (24 May 1889). In fact, there was no other rematch.

22. See *Kings of Strength*, 136–38 for a biography of Felice Napoli.

23. Eugen Sandow (1867–1925) was a great athlete but never a very reliable source, and in G. Mercer Adam, *Sandow on Physical Training* (New York: Selwin Tait, 1894), 37–9, he mentions fighting Sali

and his pupil Milo. Sandow's match with Sali was in July 1889, and Sandow was declared the winner (*Corriere della sera*, Milan, 21 June 1889). Sali demanded a rematch, and that happened the next evening, but after half an hour of wrestling, the Italian claimed to suffer from a sprained arm and was unable to continue. Also see section on the athlete Sali, in *Kings of Strength*, 185. Sandow does not mention his loss three months later to the Roman wrestler Collodi (*La Stampa* 12 October 1889) nor does he recall his match with Bartoletti which ended unsatisfactorily when the older man claimed to be too tired to continue (*Corriere della sera*, 14 October 1889).

24. The Rasso Trio formed and reformed many times over the years, but the principal strongman of the group was Georg Stangelmeier (1868–1932). The Rasso Trio debuted their strength and wrestling act at the Eden Theater in Milan in 1892. (*Corriere della sera*, Milan, 7 June 1892).

25. See Borra's brief biography in *Kings of Strength*, 323. Borra was born in Milan and thanks to his short stature, his father wanted him to become a jockey, but the strongman had other ideas. His strength act was very flashy, and in the course of it he balanced quite a few heavy objects on his chin. The lady whom he lifted was his wife (who was herself very strong). He was known as Milo Borra or sometimes Milo Brinn. See Biagio Filizola, "Luigi Borra: Milo" *Health and Strength*, October 2006 #4, 9.

26. See *Kings of Strength*, 319–20.

27. According to Hermann Waldemar Otto, *Artisten-lexikon: biographische notizen über kunstreiter* (Düsseldorf: Lintz, 1895), 149, Orontes's birth name was L'Anquilla, and he was born in Milan in 1850; he died at the age of ninety-one in the same city (*Corriere della sera*, 11 January 1941). In addition to wrestling, he also performed as a strongman and a gymnast.

28. It is highly doubtful that any such contest with Sandow took place. I could find no announcement in any American paper that mentioned a lifting contest with Sandow or, indeed, any mention of Cereseto at all.

Appendix 11

1. Zirkus Salomonsky operated regularly from December 1873 to 1878, so either Guretzki was mistaken in the date or the wrestling exhibitions were outside the regular circus season.

2. See the biography of Abs in *Kings of Strength*, p. 202.

3. Exbroyat never toured in America. This is just more of the "Broyasse" nonsense.

4. See the biography of Dupuis in *Kings of Strength*, p. 92.

5. Taro Miyake (*Miyake Taruji*) (c. 1881–1935) operated a school of jiu jitsu in London from 1904 to around 1914. Akitao Ono was in London between 1907–1908.

6. Heinrich Stark (also known as Heinrich Schwartz) was a professional wrestler who was active from 1899 to around 1916.

7. Breslau is now Wrocław and it is in Poland. Saft was nicknamed "The Bull of Breslau," and journalist André Corbel "Silhouettes de Lutteurs" in *La Culture Physique* (11/21, 1 January 1914, 11) was very enthusiastic about Saft. "At the Saint-Honoré Circus, we recognize only one god, one sun, one man, and that man is Saft. Ah! Rossignol-Rollin, why do I not have your eloquence to sing of Saft and his broad shoulders, his … musculature and above all his terrible strength that even he may not be aware of.… Despite being German and having a rather gruff personality, he is very popular."

8. Although Guretzki reverses the name (Schmidt-Westergaard), the wrestler is more often identified as Paul Westergaard-Schmidt, and he was actually born in 1886 and died in 1963. See https://billiongraves.com/grave/Paul-Westergaard-Schmidt/35114845.

9. He died in 1960. Spandau is a *Bezirke* or borough of Berlin. Schwarz was the son of a Munich innkeeper, and in 1900 he was sent to be apprenticed to a butcher in Vienna. There he encountered wrestling, and against his parents' will he started training in this field. His first great successes as a professional were in Russia starting in 1907. Many other championship victories followed. These ended in 1914 when he was drafted into the army and sent to fight in Serbia and Italy. He was wounded several times and was released in 1917. Despite his injuries he had improved by 1920 and became the European heavyweight champion in Berlin. He retired from wrestling in 1930. His son Hans Jr., was also a wrestler and later a film actor who appeared in many movies. In his prime Schwarz had a very fine physique, and there are several nude photographs of him that were produced in Russia. https://de.wikipedia.org/wiki/Hans_Schwarz_(Ringer)

10. Ernst Reiter was actually born in Klenau in what is now Poland. He died in March 1945 on his estate near Königsberg. He was killed during the Russian invasion of East Prussia near the end of World War II. Reiter seems to be one of the few upper-class men who took up wrestling. In the First World War he saw action in Romania where he was injured in his knee, and during the Second he was stationed in Norway for a while and served as first lieutenant. Later he made his way back to East Prussia, and there he met his death when the Red Army marched through the region. https://www.peoplesboard.de/pboard/index.php?thread/23634-others-steckbrief-ernst-siegfried/

11. Alphonse Steurs was more likely born in 1875 on his parents' farm in Oud-Turnhout and died on 7 December 1955 in Morkhoven, a village near Antwerp. He lived in or near Antwerp almost all his life. After his military service, he went to work on the port mainly transporting coal to the ships. He later became a professional

wrestler and went on several world tours. https://www.kleinantwerpen.be/museum/verdraagzaamheidsplein/fons-steurs/

12. This probably means that the Americans wanted him to agree to prearranged matches. The author does not give a source for this information, but Weber toured the United States in 1909–10.

13. Strenge won the first prize at the contest for the Kraft und Artisten Klub in 1903. *llustrierte Athletiksportzeitung* 12/2 10 January 1903, 20.

14. André Corbel in "Silhouettes de Lutteurs," *La Culture Physique* (10/215, 15 December 1913, 15) says that Urbach was very unpopular with the French. "One only has to announce his name, and it arouses a volley of boos, for Urbach is not exactly the fair-haired boy of theater audiences." He had a stammer and was said to be brutal with his opponents, and because of this he was one of the most hated heels (bad guys) in catch-as-catch-can wrestling.

15. Urbach was not particularly subtle with his wrestling skills, but he was definitely persistent. This is proved in a match he had in the Bavarian capital. "In the decisive meeting Warjak (Finland) against European champion Willi Urbach (Cologne) there was little technology, but more strength. Both fought a fairly stubborn fight until midnight, in the course of which Urbach delivered three full-nelsons to the Finnish giant to great applause. Due to the time limit, the game had to be stopped after 2 hours and 11 minutes." (*Allgemeine Zeitung*, Munich, 28 November 1924)

Bibliography

Books and Monographs

Andersson, Arvid. *Starke Arvids minnen* (Stockholm: Bonnier, 1924).

Anonymous. *The Pleasure Guide to Paris* (London: Nilsson, 1903).

Boetsch, Gilles, Pascal Blanchard, and others. *Human Zoos: The Invention of the Savage* (Paris: Musée du quai Branly/Actes Sud, 2011).

Cafagna, Dino. *L'uomo più forte del mondo: La Leggenda di Giovanni Raicevich da Trieste* (Trieste: Luglio, 2015).

Caillois, Roger. *Les Jeux et les hommes: le masque et le vertige* (Paris: Gallimard, 1967).

Casebolt, Lee. "From Sidebets to Sideshow: The Influence of Gambling on the Development of Professional Wrestling in America, 1870–1911" (master's thesis, University of Northern Iowa, 2013).

Chapman, David L. *Sandow the Magnificent: Eugen Sandow and the Beginnings of Bodybuilding* (Champaign: University of Illinois Press, 1994).

Charlemont, Joseph. *La Boxe Française, Historique et biographique* (Paris: Académie de Boxe, 1899).

Corvin, Tim. *Pioneers of Professional Wrestling 1860-1899* (Bloomington, IN: Archway Publishing, 2014).

Cougnet, Alberto. *La Lotta Greco-Romana sul Tappeto* (Milan: Hoepli, 1912).

Depping, Guillaume. *Merveilles de la force et de l'adresse* (Paris: Hachette).

Desbonnet, Edmond. *The Kings of Strength* (Jefferson, NC: McFarland, 2023).

Drevon, André. *Les Jeux olympiques oubliés, Paris 1900* (Paris: CNRS, 2000).

Dubois, Georges. *Comment on devient Champion de la Force* (Paris: Berger-Levrault, 1908).

Escudier, Gaston. *Les Saltimbanques, Leurs Vies leurs moeurs.* (Paris: Lévy, 1875).

Fair, John D., and David L Chapman. *Muscles in the Movies* (Columbia: University of Missouri Press, 2020).

Garnier, Jacques. *Forains d'Hier et d'Aujourd'hui* (Orléans: Auteur, 1898).

Grasso, John. *Historical Dictionary of Wrestling* (Lanham, MD: Scarecrow Press, 2014).

Guretzki, A. v. *Der moderne Ringkampf* (Leipzig: Gloeckner, 1921).

Hackenschmidt, George. *The Way to Live: Health & Physical Fitness* (London: Health & Strength, 1908).

Horton, Aaron D., ed. *Identity in Professional Wrestling: Essays on Nationality, Race, and Gender* (Jefferson, NC: McFarland, 2018).

Hough-Snee, Dexter Zavala. "Wrestling" in John Nauright (ed), *Routledge Handbook of Global Sport* (New York: Routledge, 2020).

Janson, Gilles. *Dictionnaire des grands oubliés du sport au Québec* (Québec City: Septentrion, 2013).

Kent, Graeme. *A Pictorial History of Wrestling* (London: Spring Books, 1968).

Lamoureux, Christophe, *La Grande parade du catch* (Université de Toulose-Le Mirail, 1993).

Langenfeld, Hans, "Die zweite Welle der Sportbewegung." *Jahrbuch 2003*, Niedersächsisches Institut für Sportgeschichte (Göttingen: NISH, 2003).

Laprade, Pat, and Bertrand Hébert. *Mad Dogs, Midgets and Screw Jobs: The Untold Story of How Montreal Shaped the World of Wrestling* (Toronto: BCW Press, 2013).

Lavigne, Jean-G. *Lexique de la Lutte* (Montreal: Bibliothèque national du Québec, 1976).

le Bordelais, François. *La Leçon de Lutte* (Neuilly-sur-Seine, 1899), in two volumes. The second volume appeared in 1907.

Loyer, Frédéric. *Histoire de la Lutte et du Catch en France* (Caen: Presses universitaires de Caen, 2009).

Lynch, Matthew P. (translator). *Boxing & Baton, Cane & Chausson, The Julien Delauney Method* (Monee, IL: Independently published, 2023).

Lynch, Matthew P. (translator). *French Wrestling by Leon Ville* (Columbia, SC: Independently published, 2023).

Lynch, Matthew P. (translator). *Hooks, Trips, Throws, & Takedowns: Standup Grappling: The Cherpillod Method* (Columbia, SC: Independently published, 2023).

Lynch, Matthew P. (translator). *Wrestling's Renaissance: Leon Ville's 1891 Grappling Manual* (Monee, IL: Independently published, 2023).

Martell, William. *Greco-Roman Wrestling* (Champaign, IL: Human Kinetics, 1993).

Morton, Gerald W., and George M. O'Brien. *Wres-

tling to Rasslin': Ancient Sport to American Spectacle* (Bowling Green, OH: Bowling Green State University Popular Press, 1985).
Nizier du Puitspelu. *Les Vieilleries Lyonnaises* (Lyon: Bernoux et Cumin, 1891).
Poliakoff, Michael B. *Combat Sports in the Ancient World: Competition, Violence and Culture* (New Haven, CT: Yale University Press, 1987).
Pons, Paul. *La Lutte* (Paris: Pierre Lafitte, 1912).
Pons, Paul. *Vingt ans de lutte suivi de ma leçon de lutte et de l'histoire de la lutte* (Corbeil: Crété, 1900).
Py, Christiane, and Cécile Ferenczi. *La Fête foraine d'autrefois: Les années 1900* (Lyon: la Manufacture, 1987).
Rearick, Charles. *Pleasures of the Belle Epoque: Entertainment and Festivity in Turn-of-the-century France* (New Haven, CT: Yale University Press, 1985).
Vallès, Jules. *La Rue* (Paris: Achille Faure, 1866).
Vallès, Jules. *Le Tableau de Paris* (Paris: Berg International, 2007 [1882]).
Vigarello, Georges. *Le propre et le sale: l'hygiène du corps depuis le Moyen Age* (Paris: Seuil, 1987).
Vigarello, Georges. *Une Histoire Culturelle du sport: Techniquies d'hier et d'aujourd'hui* (Paris: Robert Laffont, 1988).
Ville, Léon. *La Lutte et les lutteurs, Traité pratique* (Paris: Rothschild, 1891).
Ville, Léon. *Lutteurs et Gladiateurs* (Paris: Tolra, 1895).
Waldemar Otto, Hermann. *Artisten-lexikon: biographische notizen über kunstreiter* (Düsseldorf: Lintz, 1895).
Zucca, Alberto. *Acrobatica e atletica* (Milan: Hoepli, 1902).

Newspaper and Journals

Allgemeine Zeitung (Munich)
L'Athlète
L'Auto-vélo
La Corriere della sera (Milan)
La Culture Physique
Gil Blas
La Gymnastique et le Moniteur official de la gymnastique, du tir et de l'escrime
L'Illustration
llustrierte Athletiksportzeitung
Illustrierte Atletik-Sportzeitung
Illustrierte Sportzeitung (Munich)
Internationale illustrirte Athleten-Zeitung
Le Journal des Sports
Le Miroir des sports
Münchner Neueste Nachrichten
Le Nain Jaune
Paris illustré
Le Petit Parisien
The Referee (London)
La Repubblica (Milan)
La Santé par les Sports
Le Siècle illustré
Le Sport
Le Sport Universel Illustré
Sporting Life
La Stampa (Turin)
Le Vélo
La Vie au Grand Air
La Vie Parisienne
La Vie sportive illustrée

Index

Numbers in **bold** indicate the primary entry

Abdullah, Jeffrey 66, 74, **93–95**, 96–97, 103, 283
Aberg, Alexander 284, 288
Abs, Carl 101, 104, 283, 290–91
Achilles (of Mont Ventoux) 80, **86–87**
Ahlgren 285
Aimable of La Calmette 101, **133–34**, 140, 163, 228–29, 284, 292
Alcazar Theater 44–45, 67, 96, 107–8
Alfred (Chest of Steel) 97
Alfred (Parisian Model) 35, 37, 39, 42, 48, 50, 67, 189
Alfred de Paris 213, 215
Alix the Negro 39, **120**
Alliot 42
Ambroise (Little Pip) 70, 74, 89
Ambroise (the Savoyard) 28, 42, 44–45, 49, 53
Amédé 42
Ancelin 37
Anderson, Arvid **130–31**
Anglio Anastase **146–48**
Anthèlme 29–30, 50, 188, 191
Antonitch, Simon 18, **136**, 140, 180, 248, 276, 285–86, 291
Apollon (Louis Uni) 39–40, 76, 105, 111, 116, 127, 159, 167, 225
Arasse, Prof. 978
Arpin (False) 70
Arpin, Charles 9–11, 15, **29–33**, 35, 38, 50, 56, 59, 60, 68, 83, 85, 91, 188, 191, 195, 225, 229, 232, 241–42, 284
Auguste (the Sailor) 42, 49, 241–42

Baby (the Cavalryman) **82–83**, 91
Bacquet 29–30
Bahn, Paul **127–28**
Bainaize 42, 73–74, **90–93**, 225, 231–32
Balandrin 191, 195
Bamboula 29–30, **112–113**, 202, 284
Baraque 12–13, 15, 200, 203, 212, 219, 225
Baraud (Sand Seller) 42
Bäre of Finland 285

Bartoletti, Basilio **277–79**
Battia 50
Bazin (the Artilleryman) **114**
Bébé 226
Bech-Olsen, Magnus **129–30**
Belarbe 50
Belling, Paul **125–26**
Béranger 28, 35, **51–53**, 71, 91, 189–90, 225, 231
Berger 55
Bergez **70**
Bernard, Félix (old) 42, 54, **64–67**, 69–70, 83, 89, 96, 101, 247, 274
Bernard, Félix (young) 39–40, 59, 64, 74, 85, 95, 101, 103–4, **109–12**, 154, 167, 170–71, 202, 204, 225–27, 230, 244, 246–47, 259, 276, 284
Bernard, Paul 226, 230
Bibby, Edwin 284
Blanc 31
Blanchard 50
Blas (the Spaniard) 29–30, 35, 68, 85, 148, 188, 191–93, 206
Blasse 50
Blondin 355
Bonnelli, Joseph 159, **164–65**
Bonnes, Pierre 173, 179
Bonnet (the Ox) 37, 45, 50, 59–63, 71, 101, 181, 195, 225
Bordeaux, France 11, 18, 33, 37, 42, 44, 50, 52–53, 60, 63–68, 70–74, 76–77, 80–83, 85–86, 89, 95–97, 100–1, 103, 190–11, 117, 120, 137–38, 144, 154–55, 160, 166–67, 171, 173, 191, 220–21, 225, 229–30, 239, 243–44, 247, 258–59, 273, 284
Borra, Milo 280–81
Bouillon, Omer de **159**, 284, 286, 291–92
Bouyard 28, 30
boxing (English) 33, 40, 65
boxing (French) 31–33, 65, 85
Boyer of Marseilles 39, 103, 176
Boyer of Nimes 39
Brémont 42
Bronzina 44
Butchers' Athletic Club 97

Cadet of Moissac 192
Cannon, Tom 61, 94, 101, 104, 110–11, 117, 123–25, 138, 142, 154–55, 163, 167, 174, 201, 225–26, 229, 274, 284
Carcassonne 191–92
Cartanji 155, 228
Cartere 50
Casino de Paris 16–17, 40, 48, 111, 118, 144, 167, 225, 227–28, 230, 234
Casino rue Cadet 36
Catin **63**
Cayol, Alexander 179
Cazeau, Raymond 18
Cereseto 281–82
Chalzet **160**
Chappe, Louis **155–56**, 226
Charlemont, Joseph 31, 33, 84, 204
Charles (the Arab) 42
Charpentier 35, 189
Christol (Coral Fisher) 42, 53
Christol, André **58**, 103
Citerne, Clovis **112**
Clément Lauvaux (the Navvy) **160–61**, 164
Cochard, Julius 169
Coeur-de-roi 71, 84
Commodus (Roman emperor) 25
Comtois (wrestling accomplices) 195
Constant le Boucher 40, 111, 121, 129, 140, 155, 159–60, 164, **169–70**, 228–29, 244, 276, 284
Constant the Sailor **180–81**
Conver (Fafon) 39, 50
Cooch-Behar, Prince of 152
Coudol 59, 62, 68
Crest 39–40, 61, 111, **119–20**, 202
Creste (Bull of Provence) 19–30, 35, 37, 42, 46, 48, 50, 56, 63, 188, 197, 199, 242
Czaia, Janos 125

Dalmasso, Pietro 26, 39, 58, 62, 74–76, 80, 95–96, 103, **104–5**, 138, 159, 204, 221 225, 244, 246–47, 259, **271–76**, 284
Daumas, Victor (Pique-Planque) 157, 228–29

327

328 Index

Delacroix, Eugène 9
Deligne of Dijon 35, 50, 61, 72, 101
Deligne of Norway 42
Deriaz, Adrien 172
Deriaz, Émile **172-73**, 178
Deriaz, Maurice 18, 172
Desbonnet, Edmond 3-7, 14, 18-19, 183
Desbordes, Pierre **105-7**
Dickson 33
Dieckmann **166**
Docqueroy 221
Don Ramon **98**, 243-44, 192
Döppel, Karl 285
Doré, Gustave *frontispiece*, 79-80
Dornier, Antoine 31, 191, 195
Doublier, Joseph 16, 76, 131, 136, **157-58**, 173-74, 183, 249-251, 259-270, 283-84
Dubois (the wrestler) 37, 42, 50, **87-89**, 195
Dubois, Georges 21, 78, 172
DuGeusclin, Bertrand 27
Dumas of Bordeaux 42, 86
Dumont, Léon **118-19**, 146, 148, 280
Dumortier (the Agile Lyonnais) 28, 27, 42, 48, 50, 53, **54-55**, 59, 70, 101, 189
Dupalamut 50
Dupuis, Jean 284

Eberle, Heinrich 18, 284-85
Edouard (Bear of the Jura) 45-47
Egeberg, Hans 18
Erlenkamp, Ernst 284
Étaux Brothers 103, 120
Étienne (the Shepherd) 28, 37, 42, 48, 50, 53, 55-56, 59, 64, 101, 189, 242
Eugène of Paris 39
Évillard (the Tonkinese) 39
Exbroyat, Jean 7, 10, 12, 41-42, **49-51**, 238-41, 243, 284

Fakery in wrestling 2, 17, 43, 61, 64, 67-68, 78, 81, 226, 233-34, **245-46**, 261-62, 274-75
Faouët (Beast of the Jungle) 35-39, 42-46, 54, 64, 67, 70, **75-76**, 81, 87, 101, 124, 176, 225, 241-42, 244, 247, 273, 284
Favouët (Denoix) 226-27, 230
Felice Napoli 279-80
Fénelon 101, 164, **171**, 230, 245, 247, 258, 276
flat-hand wrestling 8-9, 31, 40, 46, 189, 195, 253; *see also* Greco-Roman Wrestling
Folies Bergère 16, 48, 61, 93-94, 96, 110-11, 118, 122, 124, 146, 167, 173, 201, 211, 223, 225, 228-29, 247-58, 270, 274-75, 284
Forty Ounces 274-75
Fournier, Paul **101-2**, 104, 122, 202, 204, 259, 283

Franco-Prussian War 14, 41, 203, 225
François (le Breton) 173
François (Miller of Darnétal) 101, 242
François (the Bordelais) 93-94, **103**, 221, 224-25, 227-28, 230, 284
François (the Flour miller/seller) **160-61**, 164, 226, 230
François of Martinique 164, 179, 202
Frank of Montmartre 103
Freysinet 101
Friman of Finland 285
Fristensky, Gustav 18
Fruchinet 42

Gambetta, Léon 56
Gambier, Maurice 101, 104, 127-28, **137-38**, 140, 143, 155, 163, 221, 225, 227-28, 230, 244, 247, 276, 284
Gangloff Hall 91, 226-27, 231-32
Garaô 52-53
Garelli 50, 52, 59-60
Garibaldi (wrestler) 70
Garnier, Étienne **73**
Gaspard 70
Gaulois, Noël le 153, 226
Gérardy (Marquis of Pisa) 163
Gingerbread Fair 191, 273; *see also* Trône Fair
Glatigny, Joseph 57-58
Gold Belt Tournament 121-22, 127, 129, 136, 140, 144, 146, 148, 180
Gorgeous George 2
Grand Prix of Paris 16, 140, 155, 157, 177, 228-29
Grangé 35
Great National Arena 31-32, 35
Greco-Roman wrestling 1-2, 8, 15-16, 26, 39, 110, 118, 132, 157, 161, 183, 237, 271-73, 276, 280; *see also* flat-hand wrestling
Grün, John 283-84
Guitchen, Auguste **95-97**
Guitchen, Nicolas 94, **95-97**
Gulam 123-25, **148-53**, 157, 175

Hackenschmidt, George 48, 132-33, 154, **177-79**, 276, 284
Halil Adali **165-66**, 286, 292
Hansen-Esch, Josef **285**
Hein, Albert **285-86**
Henri (Ocean) 29-30
Henry, Alphonse 161, 226, 230
Hervas 101
Hippodrome (Paris) 29, 31, 121, 123, 152, 201, 204
Hitzler, Michael **126-27**, 129, 158, 292
Huhtannen, Otto 285

Industrial Revolution 7
International Athletic Arena 39-40

Internationalization of wrestling 1, 7-8, 183, 246-47

Jaberjon 50
Jacquet 50
Jägendorfer, Georg 171
James the Negro 12, 29, 35, 37, 43, 50, 103, 199
Jankowski, (Ursus) **175-76**
Jeannot (Bear of Tornay) 95
Jeantien 67, 83, 86, 89
Jenkins, Tom 18, 290
Jockey Club 11, 34
Johannson of Sweden 285
Joigneret, Henri 80, 84, 95
Journal des Sports 16, 40, 77, 220, 227-28
Juge (Sunshine of Lyon) **58**

Kampf 283-84
Kara Ahmed 123, 142, 151, 157, **161-62**, 163, 249, 276, 286
Kara Ibo 256
Kara Osman 101, **145**, 157-58, 169, 173-74, 226, 229, 255, 257-58, 260, 262-63, 270
Kayfabe [fake wrestling] 25, 245
Kikar Singh **151**
Koch, Jacobus **127-28**, 165, 284, 290, 292
Kornatz, Karl **286**
Krajewski, Dr. Vladislav 153, 177
Kuhlo **123-25**, 148
Kurtdereli Mehmed 149, 152-53, **156-57**, 228
Kuschke, Emile (the Saxon) **136-37**

Lacaisse 35, 40, 42, **60-61**, 67, 110, 230
Lacroix 29, 42, 48, 50-52, 59, 91, 189, 231
Lagneau 42, 49
Lagrange, Dr. Ferdinand 105
Lagriffe 70, 81
Lamberti 280-81
Lancilotti 279
Laperle the Negro 75, **80-82**, 283
Lassartesse, Gabriel **117**
Laurent of Beaucaire 101, 121, **162-64**, 176
Laurent of Paris **113**
Le Peletier Arena 37, 39, 56
Leboeuf, Bonnet 191, 194-95
Leboucher, Louis Armand 33, 85, 196
Lecomte, Charles 97
LeFram 42
Lefrein 55
Leitner, Bernhard 111
Lenoir, P. 159
Lépi the Giant **79-80**, 86
Lepp 283-84
Lille, France 5, 112-13, 162
Limousin (Émile Bruyère) 39, **138**, 146, 160, 247
Lindors of Finland 285
Little Pierre 95

Loubet 50
Louis of Lyon 202
Louis of Tarare 42
Louis (the Boatman) 243
Loyer, Frédéric 15
Lubin (Gallant Mastodon) 45–47
Lucenski, Alexandre de 40, 91, 227
Lucien (Cri-cri Hoarse-Voice) 242–43
Lundin, Hjalmar 18
Lurich, Georg 284
Lyon, France 7–8, 13, 29, 35–36, 39, 42–45, 48–54, 58–59, 63, 72, 91–92, 101, 114, 148, 162, 171, 173–74, 188–91, 195, 202, 238–41, 243

Madrali, Achmed 119, 173, 178
Mahmut, Ibrahim **142**, 162
Mangematin 66, 274
Marcellin (mime) 67
Maritemp 50
Marseille, Henri (the elder) 10–11, 15, 29–31, 35–37, 39, 49–50, 55–58, 82, 85, 91, 101, 188, 191, 195, 225, 229, 231, 241–44
Marseille, Jean-Baptiste (the younger) 29, 42, 48, 57, 95, 113, 187, 189–90, 201–4, 219, 221–23, 225, 229, 247
Marseilles, France 32, 42–43, 63, 72, 103, 176, 179, 229, 252, 272, 275
Marshall, Bob 111
masked wrestlers 16, 37–39, 56, 189, 204–5, 230, 283
Masnada 282
Maspoli, Alexandre 179
Masson brothers 37, 50, 195, 284
Mathieu of the Loire 50, **71–73**
Maupas, Émile **175–76**
Maximin (Roman emperor) 25
Mazard of Uzès 28–29
Mazin, Louis 95, **100–1**, 164, 226, 230–31
Mehmet, Cotch 101, 111, 117, 138, 159–60, 255, 257–58, 260–63, 265–66, 269–70, 276
Meisinger, Simon 284
Meissonnier **28**, 50
Memich 101
Milhomme (Pitiless) 37, 42, 45, 48, 50, **67–68**, 70–71, 89, 101
Milo of Crotona 2, 25, 189, 278, 282
Molier Circus 203
Monselet, Charles 45
Montal 42
Montastruc, Jean-Pierre **76–80**, 102
Montesquieu Hall 9–11, **28–31**, 56, 68, 85, 188, 191, 199, 225, 283
Montey, Jules 95
Mordon **75**
Mordunt 42
Moret, Célestin 160, 226, 230, 232
Mouchon, Achille 92

Mourzouk **143**, 146
Muldoon, William 104, 134, 284

Napoléon I 9–10
Napoléon, Louis 9, 14
Napoléon, Louis (Prince Imperial) 56
Naucke, Emile 284
Neuilly Fair 15, 57, 102, 218
Nicolas (le Boucher) 284
Nigoux 95
Nino, Francesco 280–281
Nollys, Ignace 159, **176–77**
Nurullah 101, **144–45**, 155, 157–58, 167, 173–74, 226, 229, 252–55, 257–58, 260–61, 263, 265–66, 269–70

Odin of the Loire 29
Olivier 50
Olympic Games 2, 9, 62, 69, 108, 220, 225, 233
Oronte, Terenzi 280–281
Osvaldo 280–81

Pamongki-Osman 256
Paris Commune 14
Paul (Hole Puncher) 42
Paul "le Mastoc" (the Hulk) 95–96, 176, 230
Paul (the Miller) 66, 95
Paul the Negro 37
Paz, Eugène 11–12, 33–35, 60–61, 197–98, 225
Péchon, Henri **104**
Peillon 50
Périer 37
Pernet 42
perpendicular "Olympic" wrestling 26, 69, 187
Peter (the Coachman) 37, **38**, 189, 191
Petersen, Jess 48, 121–22, 125, 129, **140**, 180
Petroff, Nicolas 101, 111, **131–32**, 138, 140, 154, 157, 161, 169, 171, 250–55, 284–85, 288, 291
Peyrousse **139**, 229, 243
Piazza Gymnasium 111–12, 221, 226, 258
Picard (the Agile Bordelais **89–90**, 101, 103
Pichat 50
Pierrard, Jean-Pierre **116–17**
Pierri, Antonio (the Greek) 101, 124–25, 140, 174
Pilota of Genoa 278
Plantevin 29–30, 50
Plège Circus 108–9
Poddubny, Ivan 48, 116, 121, 126, 129, **134–36**, 154, 179–80, 181, 284–85, 291
Pohl, John **128–29**, 134, 154, 284, 286, 292
Poiré, Charles (Bibi) 226
Polydamas of Thessaly 25
Pons Gymnasium 121, 170, 247–48

Pons, Paul 3, 16, 40, 48, 84, 101–2, 104, 111, 118, 121–22, 124, 127, 136, 138–40, 154, 163, **166–67**, 174–75, 179–80, 183, 221, 225–30, 237, 273–74, 276–77, 279, 284, 286
Pujol 28, 35, 42, 59, **61–63**, 71, 101, 199
Pytlazinski, Wladislaw 39, 101, 104, 111, 128, 133, 138, **139–40**, 161–62, 227–28, 230

Quéniart, Jules **170–71**
Quinconces, Places des 64–65, 67
Quintois 50
Quiquine 28, 50, 242

Rabah the Negro 242
Rabasson 29–30, 35, 50, 60, **68–69**, 83, 108, 188, 191, 241
Rabasson (False) **180–81**
Radvany of Hungary 285
Raicevich, Giovanni **132–33**, 284
Raicevich, Massimo (Roberto) 276
Raicevich, Ruggiero (Emilio) **132–33**, 284
Rambaud (Resistance) 19, 31, 43, **84–85**
Rambeau (Serpent of Ariège) 101
Raoul of Cahors 230
Raoul (the Bordelais) **103–4**
Raoul (the Butcher) **121–23**, 135–36, 140, 180, 248
Raphael of Porte Neuve 50
Rasso brothers 280
Raulin (Toothless) 42, **98–100**, 242
Rayos 279
Régnier Dynamometer 116–17, 167, 175, 285
Reiber, Leonhard **126**
Reitmeier, Franz 285
Rémond 42
Renaud, Jules 95–96
Ribeaupierre, Count 139, 153
Richoux, Félix 28, **35–37**, 39, 42, 56, 59, 75, 225
Rigal Brothers 60, 283
Rivoire 29–30, 35, 50, 56, 68–69, 188, 191
Rivollon 42, **75**, 226
Robin, Paul (Badingué) 39, 108, 206, 221, 223–24
Robinet, Auguste 39, 131, 138, 140, 167, 227, 229, 284
Roeber, Ernest 174–75
Rogers, Joe 289
Romanoff the Russian **180**, 285, 291–92
Rossignol-Rollin 13–15, 35–36, **40–49**, 51–54, 58–59, 62–64, 68, 70–72, 75–76, 78, 81–83, 91–92, 98, 103, 106, 184, 186–90, 225, 231, 241–43, 283
Rouge (Matthieu's) 72–73
Rouget, François le 67
Roumageon, Jacques 160
Rousset 42, 50

Index

Sabès 101–2, 104, 1178, 126, 140, 143–44, **154–55**, 163, 173–74, 176, 221, 227–28, 230, 244, 247, 259–60
Sabin 42
Saft, Karl **285**
Salamonsky Circus 283
Sali, Giulio 279
San Marin, George 112, 204–5, 225
Sandow, Eugen 279, 282
Saurer **159–60**
Savate (French boxing) 31–33, 65, 85
Schackmann **164–65**, 226, 232
Schilling, Joseph 94
Schmelling, Alexander 101, 136, **153–54**, 179
Schneider, Oskar **130**
Schwarz, Hans **288–89**
Siegfried, Ernst 119, 284–85, **289–90**
Šmejkal, Josef **131**, 289, 292
Sorakichi 284
Sorbonne Gymnasium 111, 203, 209
Sossiko Essebona **117–18**
Stalling, Wilhelm **169**
Steedman 111
Steurs, Alfons 18, 286, 289, **290**
Stockmann 37
Strenge, George **130**, 284, **292**
Sturm, Albert **141–42**, 284
Swiss wrestling (Schwingen) 40, 75, 205, 247, 280–81

Tamiot 42, 50
tattoos 230–31
Theagenes 25
Thiers, Adolphe 56
Titormus 25
Tivallon 242
Toby **58–59**, 95
Tosoni of Brescia 280
Treuvé (Bibus) 42, 49, **53–54**
Triat, Hippolyte 5
Triat (the Millstone Man) 243
Trillat (Savoyard) 95, **102**
Trône Fair 57, 67, 192–93; *see also* Gingerbread Fair
Tuomisto of Finland 290
Turck 194

Urbach, Willi 290, **292**

Va-bon-Train (Well Underway) 242
Valentino Hall *frontispiece*, 33
Van Den Berg, Dirk 195, **167–68**, 284
Van Tol, J.E. **116**
Le Vélo 149, 157, 228
Vervet, Émile **128–29**, 248, 288
Vie au Grand Air, La 18, 237
Vigarello, Georges 16
Vigneron, Louis 29, 31–33, 35, 85, 196
Vignon 42
Ville, Léon 9, 12, 212
Villier, François 87
Vimard 42
Vincent (Iron Man) 29, 36–37, 42, 48, 50, 54, 59, 76, 189–90, 243
Vuillod, Jean-Baptiste 92

Waléry, photographer 6, 153
Weber, Heinrich 129, **144**, 154, 284, **290–91**
Westergaard-Schmidt, Paul **288**
Westergreen of Sweden 285
Wetasa, Cyrill 130, 227–28, 230, 276
Winter Circus 267
Winzer, Heinrich **145**
Wolff of Luxemburg 50, 195, 243–44
women's wrestling 223–24, 274
wrestling tournaments 1, 16–18, 60, 63–64, 68, 95, 97, 121–22, 127, 129, 136, 138, 140, 144, 146, 148, 155, 157, 159, 162, 164, 179–80, 183, 203, 221, 234–35, 245, 261, 263, 275–76

Yusuf Ismaelo 61, 71, 76, 98, 101, 124, 142–44, 155, 157–58, 161, **173–75**, 221, 226, 229, 253–63, 265–70

Zaïkine, Ivan 136, **179–80**
Zaremba, Anton **120–21**
Zbyszko (Stanislaus Cyganiewicz) 48, **115–16**, 135, 285
Zucca, Alberto 277, 281

www.ingramcontent.com/pod-product-compliance
Ingram Content Group UK Ltd.
Pitfield, Milton Keynes, MK11 3LW, UK
UKHW051850210426
5322IPUK00025B/651